CLASSICAL TRAGEDY
GREEK AND ROMAN:
8 Plays

in Authoritative Modern Translations
Accompanied by Critical Essays

❧

Edited by

Robert W. Corrigan

❧APPLAUSE❧
THEATRE BOOK PUBLISHERS

An Applause Original

CLASSICAL TRAGEDY: Greek and Roman
edited by Robert W. Corrigan

Library of Congress Cataloging-in-Publication Data

Classical Tragedy: Greek and Roman / edited by Robert W. Corrigan.
    p.   cm.
    Contents: Prometheus Bound / by Aeschylus — Oresteia / by Aeschylus — Antigone / by Sophocles — Oedipus the King / by Sophocles — Medea / by Euripides — The Bakkhai / by Euripides — Oedipus / by Seneca — Medea / by Seneca.
   ISBN 1-55783-046-0 : $10.95
   1. Classical drama (Tragedy) — Translations into English.
   2. English drama (Tragedy) — Translations from classical languages.
   3. Mythology. Greek — Drama. I. Corrigan, Robert Willoughby, 1927 -   .
PA3626.A2C67   1990
882'.0108 — dc20   90--30152
                                       CIP

APPLAUSE THEATRE BOOK PUBLISHERS
211 W. 71st Street
New York, New York 10023
212/595-4735

First Applause Printing, 1990

Classical Tragedy
Greek and Roman

CONTENTS

Aeschylus
ORESTEIA

Translated by
Tony Harrison

ONE: AGAMEMNON

Characters   *Watchman*

Chorus

Herald

Agamemnon

Clytemnestra

Cassandra

Aegisthus

NOTE: This text is written to be performed, a rhythmic libretto for masks, music, and an all male company.

Watchman

No end to it all, though all year I've muttered
my pleas to the gods for a long groped for end.
Wish it were over, this waiting, this watching,
twelve weary months, night in and night out,
crouching and peering, head down like a bloodhound,
paws propping muzzle, up here on the palace,
the palace belonging the bloodclan of Atreus —
Agamemnon, Menelaus, bloodkin, our clanchiefs.

I've been so long staring I know the stars backwards,
the chiefs of the star-clans, king-stars, controllers,
those that dispense us the coldsnaps and dogdays.
I've had a whole year's worth so I ought to know.
A whole year of it! Still no sign of the signal
I'm supposed to catch sight of, the beacons,
the torch-blaze that means Troy's finally taken . . .

The woman says watch, so here I am watching.
That woman's not one who's all wan and woeful.
That woman's a man the way she gets moving.

Put down your palliasse. Dew-drenched by daybreak.
Not the soft bed you'd dream anything good in —
Fear stays all night. Sleep gives me short time.

Daren't drop off though. Might miss it. The beacon.
And if I missed it . . . life's not worth the living!
Sometimes, to stop nodding, I sing or try singing
but songs stick in my gullet. I feel more like weeping
when I think of the change that's come over this household,
good once and well ordered . . . but all that seems over . . .

Maybe tonight it'll finish, this watching, this waiting,
an end to the torment we've yearned for ten years.

Come on, blasted beacon, blaze out of the blackness!

[*Sees beacon.*]

It's there! An oasis like daylight in deserts of dark!
It's there! No mistaking!
                              Agamemnon's woman —
best let her know the beacon's been sighted.
Time all the women were wailing their welcome!

Troy's taken! Troy's down and Troy's flattened.
There'll be dancing in Argos and I'll lead the dance.
My master's struck lucky. So've I, I reckon.
Sighting the beacon's a dice-throw all sixes.

Soon I'll be grasping his hand, Agamemnon's . . .
Let him come home to us, whole and unharmed!

As for the rest . . . I'm not saying. Better not said.
Say that an ox ground my gob into silence.

They'd tell such a story, these walls, if they could.

Those who know what I know, know what I'm saying.
Those who don't know, won't know. Not from me.

[*Exit* WATCHMAN.]

[*Enter* CHORUS.]
Chorus
Ten years since clanchief Menelaus
and his bloodkin Agamemnon
(the twin-yoked rule from clanchief Atreus —
double thronestones, double chief-staves)
pursued the war-suit against Priam,
launched the 1000 ship armada
off from Argos to smash Troy.

Mewing warcries   preybirds   shrilling
nest-theft   childloss   wild frustration
nestlings snaffled   preybirds soaring
wildly sculling   swirling airstreams
using broad birdwings like oars
birthpangs   nothing   nestcare   nothing
nothing   fostered nestlings   nothing

crying   mewing   preybirds   shrilling

But one of the god powers up above them —
Apollo   Pan   or Zeus high he-god
hearing the birds' shrill desolation,
birds, guest-strangers in god-spaces
sends down the slow but certain Fury
to appease the grudge the greived birds feel

So Zeus protector of man's guestright
sends the avenging sons of Atreus
down on Paris son of Priam
because of Helen, lust-lode, man-hive,
Helen the she manned by too many hes.

Bedbond   no   not bedbond   spearclash
swordhafts shattered   hacked bones smashed
sparring   skirmish   dustclouds   bloodstorm
Trojans   Greeks   not bedbond   bloodbath

The war in Troy's still in a stalemate
marking time at where it's got to
till the fulfilment that's been fated.
Once the Fury's after victims
no sacrifices   no libations
stop the headlong grudge's onrush.

But as for us   recruiter's refuse,
too old to join the expedition,
shrivelled leafage left to wither,
we go doddering about on sticks.
Neither the nurseling nor the senile
have juice enough to serve the Wargod.
Wargod-fodder's prime manhood.

Argos geezers, back to bairnhood,
ghosts still walking after cockcrow,
old men, dreams abroad in daylight.

She-child of Tyndareos, Clytemnestra,
what news have you had, what fresh reports?

You've given orders for sacrifice. Why?

All the godstones of this bloodclan
earthgods   skygods   threshold   market
look   they're all alight   all blazing

Look here   and there   the flaring firebrands
coaxed into flame by smooth-tongued torch-oils
brought out of store for great occasions

If you can tell us give us some comfort
soothe all that grief that's chewed into our guts.
Hope glimmers a little in these lit godstones,
blunts the sharp chops of gnashing despair.

Gab's the last god-gift of the flabby and feeble —
singing the omens that mobilized Argos:

Two preybirds came as prophecy
blackwing and silverhue
came for our twin kings to see
out of the blue   the blue

The right side was the side they flew
spear side   luck side   War
one blackwing   one silverhue
and everybody saw

and everybody saw them tear
with talon and with claw
the belly of a pregnant hare
and everybody saw

and everybody saw the brood
from their mauled mother torn
wallowing in warm lifeblood
and dead as soon as born

blackwing and silverhue
prophesying War
the twin preybirds that cry and mew
hungering for more . . .

Batter, batter the doom-drum, but believe there'll be better!

Calchas the clanseer cunning in seercraft
when he saw before him the armed sons of Atreus
knew what menfolk were meant by the preybirds —
Agamemnon   Menelaus   battle-hungry hare-devourers . . .

"Hosts commanded by twin birds
soldiers who leave these shores
first Fate will waste Troy's crops and herds
then make the inner city yours

The moment when the iron bit
's between the jaws of Troy
may no skycurse glower down on it
and no godgrudge destroy

Artemis   pure she-god   stung
with pity for the hare
all mothers and their unborn young
come under her kind care

her father's hounds with silent wings
swoop down on that scared beast
Artemis   she loves wee things
and loathes the preybirds' feast."

blackwing and silverhue
prophesying War
the twin preybirds that cry and mew
hungering for more . . .

Batter, batter the doom-drum, but believe there'll be better!

Artemis pure she-god   stung
with pity for the hare
all mothers and their unborn young
come under her kind care

kind even to the lion-pup
you're the one we cry to, you!
Kind to wild beasts at the pap

stop bad signs coming true.

Apollo   he-god   healer   your she-kin
Artemis   intervene   prevent her
sending winds on the fleet from the wrong direction
keeping the armada too long at anchor,

making a blood-debt sacrifice certain,
a sacrifice no-one wants to eat meat from,
a sacrifice no-one wants to sing songs to,
whetting the grudge in the clanchief's household,
weakening the bond between woman and manlord,
a grudge wanting blood for the spilling of childblood,
a grudge brooding only on seizing its blood-dues.

These omens both fair and foreboding
Calchas the clanseer saw in the birdsigns —

Batter, batter the doom-drum, but believe there'll be better!

So Agamemnon first clanchief of Argos
found no fault in the clanseer's foretelling
and went where the winds of his life-lot were listing,
the Achaian armada still anchored off Aulis.

Wind-force and wave-swell   keep the ships shorebound
men sapped of spirit   supplies running short
foodpots and grain jars   crapping their contents
ship planks gape open   frayed cables and rigging
time dragging   each day seeming two days
the flower of Argos   bedraggled and drooping

Calchas the clanseer   saw into the storm-cause —
Artemis   she-god   goaded to godgrudge

The clans and the clanchiefs   clamour for sea-calm
The god-sop that gets it   makes their guts sicken
The cure for the stormblast   makes strong men craven

The clanchiefs of Argos   drummed their staves on the earth
and wept and wept   and couldn't stop weeping

Then the first he-child of Atreus   Agamemnon
choked back his crying   and finally spoke:
hard   hard for a general   not to obey
hard   hard for a father   to kill his girl
his jewel   his joy   kill his own she-child
virgin-blood   father-guilt   griming the godstone

Can I choose either   without doing evil
leave the fleet in the lurch   shirker   deserter
let down the Allies   we've all sworn allegiance

They're asking for blood   it's right what they're asking

a virgin's blood only will calm the wind's bluster

So be it then   daughter!   there's no other way

Necessity   he kneels to it   neck into the yokestrap
the General   harnessed to what he can't change
and once into harness his whole life-lot lurches
towards the unspeakable horror   the crime

so men get gulled   get hauled into evil
recklessness starts it   then there's no stopping

so a Father can take his own she-child   take her
and kill her   his she-child   his own flesh and blood

The war-effort wants it   the war-effort gets it
the war for one woman   the whore-war   the whore-war

a virgin's blood launches the ships off to Troy

Her shrillings   beseechings   her cries   Papa   Papa
Iphigeneia   a virgin   a virgin

what's a virgin to hawks and to war-lords?

He says a god-plea   her father   her *father*   then orders
attendants to hoist her   up   on to the godstone

she bends herself double   beseeching Papa   Papa
wraps her clothes round her   making it harder
up   up   she gets hoisted   like a goat to the godstone

a gag in her mouth   her lovely mouth   curbed like a horse's
so that this bloodclan's not blasted by curses

her garments stream groundwards   the looseflow of saffron
clothing drifting   clothing trailing   she darts them all glances
that go through their hearts   deep into them   wounding

a painting   a sculpture   that seems to be speaking
seeking to say things   but locked in its stone

they know what her eyes say   that gang round the godstone

often they'd seen her   at meals with her father
in the place beside his   when they sat at his table
the welcoming table of King Agamemnon

she sat beside him   his innocent she-child
singing the lyresong after libations
the melodious gracethanks   to Zeus   the Preserver

What came next   didn't see   so can't tell you

What Calchas foretold all came to fulfilment

Suffering comes first   then after awareness

The future's the future   you'll know when it's here
forseeing the future's to weep in advance

The present's enough   and what's going to happen
let it be what we've hoped for   us   the poor remnants
so long the sole bulwark of monarchless Argos

[*Enter* CLYTEMNESTRA.]

Clytemnestra, we come to you as we would to our clanchief
for it's right that we honour the wife of the clanchief
when the manlord himself's not here on the thronestone.
Is it good news and firm news or mere wishful thinking
that makes you sacrifice now on the godstones?

Clytemnestra

Like mother, like daughter . . . May last night's good news
give birth this dawnlight to a day like her mother.

What I've got to tell you's beyond all you've hoped for.
The Greek armies have taken the city of Priam.

1. **Ch:**   Taken Troy? Did my ears hear you right?
    Clyt: Wasn't I clear? Troy was taken last night.

2. **Ch:**   My eyes fill with tears, tears of sheer joy.
    Clyt: Then your eyes know it's true our taking of Troy.

3. **Ch:**   Can you be certain with no news that's concrete?
    Clyt: Yes, unless the whole thing's some he-god's deceit.

4. **Ch:**   Or some dream of Troy taken which *seems* to you true.
    Clyt: I put trust in seeming no more than you.

5. **Ch:**   Some rumor has reached you the war's at an end?
    Clyt: I'm no simple childwit! Don't condescend!

6. **Ch:**   So Troy has been taken *when* did you say?
    Clyt: Last night, she who just gave birth to today.
    Ch: The news came so fast over such a long way!

Clytemnestra
Firegod Hephaistos flashed out from Mount Ida
flame after flame bore the beacon's despatches,
jaded flame to fresh flame bearing the firenews.
Ida to Crag Hermes on the island of Lemnos.
From there its third stretch to the top of Mount Athos,
the peak that Zeus favors, then further upwards
and over the ocean dazzling and flaring
luring up fish-shoals to see what the flash is,
a fire-tailed comet transmitting its message
to the watchtowers scanning the sky on Macistos.
They weren't caught napping. They flung the flame onwards
and it hurtled over Euripus and watchmen
marked it from their Messapion outpost.
They kindle heaped brushwood and speed the flame further
It gathers momentum. It doesn't diminish.
It streaks like a meteor over Asopus
And lands on Cithaeron and sparks off the next one.
Again not neglected. So eager the watchmen

they get up a blaze that doubles the last one.
From the bog of Gorgopis to Mount Aegiplanctus
the bright chain of firelinks remaining unbroken.
They spare no effort and heap on the kindling,
the flamehair streaming out over the headland
that faces gulf Saron and then dropping southwards
to the crag of Arachne that borders on Argos
and straight to the roof of the palace of Atreus,
the flame that was fathered in Troy's conflagration.

My torchbearers bore all the batons of blazes

That's the sign, the proof you've been wanting
all the way from Troy, from my manlord to me.

Chorus

The gods will get all our thanks for their bounty.
But your tale's such a marvel we'd like it repeated.
We'd like all the details. You said first that Hephaistos . . .

Clytemnestra

Troy's held by the Greeks is the truth you're not grasping.
Pour oil on to vinegar in the same foodpot
they'll never blend in brotherly bloodbond.
So life-lots in conflict cause cries that conflict:
the Trojans all tearful, their arms round their fallen
embracing cold corpses, the widows, the orphans,
knowing their own lives mean only bond-chains,
keen for their bloodkin, their nearest, their dearest;
the Greeks, their whole night spent in harsh skirmish,
famished for breakfast swoop down onto Troy,
no billets allotted, all discipline broken,
each man for himself, the luck of the straw-lot,
they bed themselves down in the houses they've captured,
free of the nightfrost, rough beds in the open,
sleep, for once without sentries, and wake up refreshed.
So provided they don't give Troy's gods provocation
and leave unmolested their sacrosanct seats
there's a chance that the victors will never be victims.
I hope our platoons aren't driven by lootlust

to bring what's tabooed back home here as booty.
They still need some safety on the last lap back home.
And even if the Greeks give grudge to no godheads
the dead that they've slaughtered can't sleep for ever.
Let disaster stop at the place it's reached so far,
the cycle be broken, and hope start to happen.
Let a lift-lot that's lucky get crowned with the laurels.

You've heard all my feelings, those of a woman.

[*Exit* CLYTEMNESTRA.]
Chorus
You feel like a woman but talk like a man talks
Now I've heard all your proofs now I can offer
the gratitude due to the gods who guard Argos.
The joy we feel now seems worth all we've suffered.

Zeus the high he-god with Night as his helper
cast a vast trammel over Troy's towers —
men get meshed in it   women   children
all dragged ashore and beached in harsh bondage.
Zeus cast it   Zeus   protector of guestright.
Zeus got the bullseye when he shot Paris
an arrow that took ten years to its target.

The Zeus-shot they call it   no doubting it either.

Zeus says it   it happens   his plans get accomplished.

So if somebody tells you gods take no notice
when the sacrosanct's trampled on   trod underfoot
point to what's happened   and call him a cretin
point to what's happened   ruin for recklessness
men over-ambitious   treasure-stuffed mansions
measureless riches that can't buy the best things

sufficiency's ample   real wealth is awareness

surfeit   satiety   gold tons are no bulwark
if the godstone of justice gets booted to blackness
true bloodright shattered to atoms of nothing.

Wordpower   temptations   techniques of inducement
soften the wretch up for their master   Destruction

Guilt can't be curtained   it glows through the nightdark

Base battle-bronze battered gets blackened and mottled
so a man's baseness gets clotted with bloodguilt.

The chased culprit's got as much chance of escaping
as a boy has of catching a blackbird bare-handed.

Time spatters the guilty   the blood a man sheds
smears his whole people his touch clarts his clan.

Now he starts praying   the gods make their ears stone
the deaf gods trample him mid-supplication.

It was like that with Paris   guest-stranger and welcome
at the hospitable table of the bloodclan of Atreus —

his gratitude   guest-thanks   grabbing of Helen

and what did Helen bequeath to her people
spearclash and shieldclang   the massive armada

the dowry she went with to Troy was   destruction.

"A bad day for this house   a bad day for the master
look at the bedclothes   still rumpled with passion"

Menelaus apart   he's brooding his loveloss
stunned into silence   a shadow   a ghostman

statues mean nothing   stone's eyeless and lifeless

his sleep's full of dreamwives   Helen-shaped shadows
that bring ease a moment then vanish away

he tries to grasp her   she slips through his fingers
shadowing off down the flyways of sleep . . .

This is the anguish of the country's chief household

It doesn't stop there though   grief goes all over
each house in Argos sent someone to battle

and gets back for menfolk   jars full of cinders
a plectrum of sorrows plucks women's griefstrings:

"Geldshark Ares god of War
broker of men's bodies
usurer of living flesh
corpse-trafficker that god is —

give to WAR your men's fleshgold
and what are your returns?
kilos of cold clinker packed
in army-issue urns

wives   mothers   sisters   each one scans
the dogtags on the amphorae
which grey ashes are my man's?
they sift the jumbled names and cry:

my husband sacrificed his life

my brother's a battle-martyr

aye, for someone else's wife —

Helen, whore of Sparta!

whisper   mutter   belly-aching
the people's beef and bile: *this war's
been Agamemnon's our clanchief's making,
the sons of Atreus and their 'cause.'*

Where's my father   husband   boy?
where do all our loved ones lie?
six feet under near the Troy
they died to occupy."

The people's rancor's a terrible burden
a whole clan can curse with one venomous voice.

Night's got something under its dark cloth

listen   dangers hum under its cover

gods see carnage   get the massacre marked —

Furies   the trackers   fulfilling the bloodgrudge
trip the transgressor   tread him into the ground
blown up and bloated   rubbed out into nothing
no-one can save you among blurs and shadows.

Rising too high's a danger   it's risky
the pinnacles get the thunder's first flameclap
the cragpeaks feel the first storm-flash

Enough is enough when unmarred by mean mangrudge
Conqueror   captive   don't want to be either
I want to wear neither laurels nor bondchains.

1. Those fires make the rumors fly through the street.
    Is it all true, or some he-god's deceit?

2. Who's such a childwit to believe the flame first
    then feel despondent when the bubble's been burst

3. Women! Women are always ready to act.
    before they know if a rumor's true fact.

4. Women are gullible. Minds like dry straw —
    one whoosh of belief and then nothing more.

We'll know soon enough what that blaze was about,
those beacons and bonfires, the new-fangled flamegraphs,
whether there's anything in it or whether
it's just the wishful thinking women indulge in.

Look, there's a herald coming up from the seashore,
the mud of the trenches caked dry on his tunic.
He's wearing the olive-wreath, and there, look, behind him,
look at that dustcloud. That means that it's real news
not feminine flame-a-phores kindled on mountains,
but words spoken, man to man, and spoken directly.
He'll say rejoice or . . . that mustn't happen . . .
So far, so good. And let it continue . . .
and if there's anyone wants anything else for this bloodclan
I hope that he gets what his malice deserves.

[*Enter* HERALD.]

Herald
    Homesoil! Argos ground! Clanland! Home!
    A ten year absence ends in this bright dawn.
    Most hopes were shipwrecked. One scraped back safe,
    the hope that I'd make it back home here to die,
    die, and find rest in the earth I most cherish.
    Earth Earth Sun Sun!
    Zeus godchief highest of he-gods
    Apollo godseer Pythian prophet
    those arrowshafts shot at us, hold back the volleys,
    god-aggro enough on the banks of Scamander.
    Now be the cure-all, the soul-salve Apollo.
    Hermes, he-god, and herald the godclans,
    guardian of heralds to men down below,
    and heroes under whose gaze we were drafted,
    welcome us back, those few spared the spearthrust.
    House of our clanchiefs, homes of my bloodkin,
    thronestones and godstones facing the sun's glare,
    if ever you once did, welcome your king back,
    look on him with kind eyes after his absence.
    Like a bright firebrand blazing through darkness
    to stop us all stumbling, King Agamemnon.
    Welcome him warmly. He's earned your warm welcome.
    He swung the god-axe, Zeus the Avenger's,
    tore Troy's roots up, dug her earth over,
    her god-shrine shattered, her altars all gutted,
    fruitful earth scorched into futureless dustbowls,
    an empire gone putrid and tossed on time's midden.
    Troy's neck got his yoke on, your clanchief's,
    first he-child of Atreus, most lucky of life-lot,
    worthier than any of the honours he's taken.
    I doubt raper Paris thought it was worth it.
    The town he brought doom on won't boast of his bridesnatch.
    Branded for wife-theft he lost what he'd plundered,
    his ancestral bloodclan razed root and branch.
    Priam's sons paid for it. An eye for an eye,
    or more like ten thousand eyes for each one.

1. **Ch:** Welcome Herald! You're home. The war's far behind.
   He: I kept alive for this. Now death I don't mind.

2. **Ch:** Did you long for your home here back at the war?
   He: What else do you think my weeping is for?

3. **Ch:** You could say it was sweet, in a way, your disease.
   He: Sweet? A disease! What riddles are these?

4. **Ch:** That longing you had. We caught it here too.
   He: You longed for us as we longed for you.

5. **Ch:** So much that our gloom made us groan with despair.
   He: What made you so gloomy? Our being out there?

6. **Ch:** It's best for our safety if no more is said.
   He: With the clanchiefs away what caused you this dread?
   Ch: Like you we too wouldn't mind being dead.

Herald

Suffering. Suffering only the gods escape it entirely.
If you'd known firsthand our louse-ridden billets,
cramped berths on board, claustrophobic, foul bedding,
what didn't we have to complain of you tell me.
Ashore was no better. Worse. We bivouaced
under the walls with the enemy firing.
Drenched either by drizzle or dew from the ground.
Clothes moldy with mildew. Locks crawling with lice.

First unbearable cold, snow blowing off Ida,
blizzards killing birdflocks frozen in flight.
Then heat! and even the ocean seemed stifled,
slumped, zephryless, in unruffled siestas,
slack billows lolling in the deadest of doldrums.

But why go on? What's the point? The pain's over,
and for the dead so over and done with,
they'll never lust after a life-lot again,
The dead are dead. Who wants a head-count?
Why should the living scratch open old scabs.
We've left it behind us. Goodbye to all that!

We're what's left. There's some good for the living.
The pain and the losses don't quite overbalance.
We can shout out to the universe proudly:
The bloodclans of Argos in battle alliance
having mashed into ashes Asia's town Troy
now nail up these god-spoils to Hellas's he-gods.

For all that we'll get the credit and praises
and Zeus the god's whale's share. He made it happen.

That's all. That's all there is for the telling.

Chorus

Your news shows me that I was mistaken.
But you're never too old to learn a new lesson.
Clytemnestra, she should be first to hear the whole story.
The leftovers and scraps of it satisfy me.

[*Enter* CLYTEMNESTRA.]

Clytemnestra

I started my truimph cry some time ago
when the first flame-messenger arrived in the darkness
proclaiming the capture and downfall of Troy.
And what did the men say? "Just like a woman!
One beacon, that's all, and she thinks Troy's been captured"
Mutterings like that made me feel stupid.
I went on with the sacrifice in spite of their moaning,
then the whole city began "behaving like women"
raising the triumph cry "shouting and bawling"
feeding the thankfires almost to bursting.
And why should you tell me anything further?
I'll have the whole tale from the mouth of my manlord.
And it's his welcome now that must be fully prepared.
No day in the life of woman's sweeter than that one
when she flings the door open to welcome her manlord,
her manlord brought safely back from the war.
Go. Tell him come quickly. He's loved by his people.
Tell him he'll find his wife faithful and bond-true
as when he first left her, and, like a good bloodhound,
his loyal servant, and his enemies' foe.

He'll find all his treasures still with his seal on.
Tell him I've accepted no man's attentions.
I'm no more a breaker of bedbond,
than, as a woman, I wield a man's weapon.

[*Exit* CLYTEMNESTRA.]
Chorus

All the words of the woman are clear enough
if those who are listening give all their ears.

[To HERALD.]
Herald, what about Menelaus our other clanchief?
You haven't said he's home safe as well.

1. **He:** Falsehood is something fair lies never hide.
      The mask of glad messenger just wasn't mine.
    Ch: Skins can be fair and the fruit bad inside.
      Can't good news and truth ever share the same vine?

2. **He:** Menelaus, he's missing that clanchief of yours.
      He's gone, his ship's gone. And *this* is all true.
    Ch: He set sail with you though when the force left Troy's
      shore:
      Did a sudden storm blow up and snatch him from view?

3. **He:** Storm! Yes, you've hit the bull's eye!
      "Storm's" a small word that encompasses hell.
    Ch: Is he still living, or did the chief die?
      Is there anyone there in the fleet who can tell?

4. **He:** No-one knows anything, at least not us men,
      only the sun that looks down from the sky.
    Ch: How did the storm start? Why did it? When?
      Was it godgrudge, and if a grudge, why?

Herald

A godgrudge! A godgrudge! Don't drag in *those* she-gods!
Some gods preside over pleasures, some pain.
Those she-gods go with the most galling godgrudge.
This day's a homecoming meant to be happy.
When a clan messenger's arrived shedding tears
to announce to his bloodclan what they've been dreading,

the rout of their armies, a mountainous death-toll,
with anguish for all in the rolls of the fallen,
the best lads in their tonloads tangled and landed
and gashed by the flesh-hook, the fish-gaff of Ares,
gaff-flukes and grapnel barbs gory with fleshbits —
if he comes so overbalanced with trouble
then that's the time to start hymning the Furies.
But if the news is good that he's bringing
and the city's wild with relief and success
who wants to be first to get the good curdled
and blurt it all out: "Shipwreck. Shrewgrudge!
the grudges of she-gods shattered the Greek ships."

Flame and saltwater are scarcely a bloodbond.
This time they were though, elements merging,
and their bond-proof — smashing our ships into splinters.

Blackness. Waveforce. Sea heaving and swelling.
Fierce thrashing galesqualls whistling from Thrace,
hurricanes blasting, rain lashing and pelting,
ship-prow smashing ship-prow, horned beast goring beast,
beasts with their horns locked butting each other.
You know when a collie not used to its charges
scatters the daft sheep every direction,
colliding, collapsing, that kind of chaos . . .
well that's how the waves were. Next morning
the Aegean had mushroomed with corpses and shipwreck.
Our ship though, amazing, still whole and undamaged.
Some god interceded, got our ship a pardon.
Our helm had been guided by the hand of some he-god.
Our ship was one that didn't get shattered.
Couldn't believe it escaping that wave-grave,
couldn't believe our life-lot so lucky.
We were shocked in the clear light of morning,
chewing the cud of the nightmare we'd lived through.
Our ship-throng had suffered a terrible thrashing.
If any of the others survived they'll be thinking
we're finished, finished, as we still do of them.

May everything still turn out for the better.
Menelaus, let's suppose that he's made it,

let's hope he's still somewhere under the sunlight.
Zeus can't want the whole bloodclan blasted.
That's the truth you wanted.   You've got it all now.

Chorus

HELEN wrecker HELEN Hell
the one who first named her knew what was fated —
HEL- a god guided his tongue right -EN
HEL- spear-bride gore-bride war-whore -EN
HEL- ship-wrecker man-breaker Troy-knacker -EN

From silken bowers scented and flowing with curtains
to seas that are breathed on and ruffled by zephyrs,
and after her warhosts bristling with metal,
trail-hounds snuffling the vanishing oar-spoor,
tracking the beached ships up leafy Simois,
trail-hounds scenting the seatracks and bloodslicks.

Godgrudge and mangrudge ganging together
Shepherded the blood-bride surely to Troy,
delayed counterblow to the sullied table,
the wrong done to Zeus protector of guestright.
They paid the blood-price, the bridegroom's bloodkin
chanting the bride-hymn, hymning the bedbond.
The new hymn they've learnt in the city of Priam's
not about bedbond but a loud bawl at death
calling Paris the doomgroom, the doomgroom.
War-whore Helen brought suffering, slaughter,
bloodgrudge, futility, childloss and bloodflow.

Story: Man & Lion. This is it —

Lion-cub brought in from the wild
still whimpering for the tit
Man treats it like a child

They dandle it they fondle   stroke
they sit it in their laps

delight of children and old folk
sits up and begs for scraps

Time passes and the man's cub grows
no more a wean to rock to sleep
suddenly its nature shows
cub savages your sheep

its thankyou for its bed and board
its gratitude for care
your whole flock torn   clawed   gnawed
and bloodflow everywhere

Blood everywhere   blood everywhere
the whole house smirched   defiled
anguish   carnage   and despair
for fostering that child

That harmless orphaned furry beast
greeting for its nurse
was nothing but a fury-priest
a grudge-sent slaughter curse.

Helen to Troy   first windless calm   windless
a priceless treasure   yielding with soft feel
delicate eyeglints   rare orchid with heart-thorns
then abracadabra the nuptials turn nasty,
jinxwoman Helen   wormwood   lovegall
bringing the children of Priam disaster
spurred on by Zeus as protector of guestright,
blood-price   spoil-spouse   connubial Fury.

Wealth-pride never dies childless   never
but always breeds children that go to the bad —
that's half of the story but what I say's this:

Wealth coupled with Hubris   that's the dark pedigree
that sends its black seeds from infant to infant

When bloodright gives birth the children are blotless —

Hubris I breeds Hubris II

O dark ancestral tree
Old arrogance will soon breed new
gory genealogy

Wealth-pride is the furious son
of a fiendish blood-dark mother
Violence is the other one
and dead spit of his brother

Justice shines through hovel smoke
she loves the man who's straight
Justice eats off plates of oak
scorns dainties off gold plate

Hands bespattered with shed blood
raise gilded rafters to the skies
Justice searching for the good
leaves with averted eyes

Justice doesn't kneel to fame
kiss affluence's feet
isn't dazzled by a name
gold-coined but counterfeit

Justice isn't put out of her stride
Justice can't be turned aside

[*Enter* AGAMEMNON *with* CASSANDRA *and Trojan spoils.*]
Chorus

Bloodshoot of Atreus, destroyer of Troy
what's the best title to give you   what honor
that isn't too high for you or too hackneyed?
What name does you justice   gives you your due?

The world's mostly mummery   sham and not gut-truth.
Someone's wretched and people start sighing
the griefshow stops a lot short of the heart.
Someone's happy, they act the same hollowly
glum visages forced into grins that are joyless.
But a good judge of livestock knows his own cattle —
their eyes say one thing   he knows the other

their cow eyes may water   he knows it's not love.

I can hide nothing   now I can tell you
when you first marshalled the armies for Helen
your image was evil   I thought you misguided
to wage a long war for one lustful woman
so many cold grave urns for one gadding girl . . .

now though my heart's full   and I greet you
your victory makes everything worth it
the omens I loathed then seem justified now.

And while you were fighting   those who remained here
some have been faithful   and others . . .
but you'll soon sort out the sheepmen and goatmen.

Agamemnon

First I greet Argos and the gods of this bloodclan.
They give me safe passage and helped me smash Priam.
They stopped their ears to Troy's pleas and entreaties.
They cast their votes and pitched all the pebbles
into the bloodpot. Nothing went into the pot for aquittal
Hope hovered round it but hope's got no franchise.
Troy! you can almost see it smoking from Argos!
The rubble and debris still breathe out destruction,
the ashes of surfeited Asia still sighing,
the sickly cachou breath of soft living and riches.
The thanks owed our gods for their bounty's boundless.
Remember them, everyone, now in our triumph,
now that we've got Troy caught in our sweepnet.
They raped one woman. We razed the whole city.
Ground it to powder. Made mincemeat of Troy.
The monster of Argos, the horse-monster did it,
chock full of shock-troops, clearing Troy's bulwarks
just when the Pleiades were starting to wane,
leaping the battlements the ravening lion
glutted its bloodlust on Troy's royal children.

What you said about praising and joy I agree with.
Not many can look on success without mangrudge.

Grudge gangrenes the gut. The suffering's twofold:
one's own lack of luck, another's good life-lot.
I know what I'm saying, knew only too well
how men can dissemble, make friendship a sham.
Most of my comrades were shadow men, shadows.
Only Odyseus, first reluctant and cussèd,
once into harness pulled his weight beside me.
And whether he's dead or alive isn't certain . . .

As for the matters of bloodclan, clan-rite and clan gods
we'll call the clan council to meet in full conclave.

Emergencies needing immediate attention —
drastic surgery. Cauterize. Cut out the canker . . .

Now into the palace, my household hearthstone,
to give the thanks due to all my great godkin.
They sent me out. They brought me back safely.
I've won this once but I have to keep winning.

[*Enter* CLYTEMNESTRA.]
Clytemnestra
Kinsmen, old men of Argos gathered before us
I'm not ashamed to confess in your presence
my love for my manlord. Time removes shyness.

I don't need to hear stories, I suffered firsthand.
I suffered greatly with my man at the warfront.
For a woman to sit alone at home waiting
with her man at the war's a terrible burden.
There's no end to the rumors she has to keep hearing.
News-runners arriving in rapid succession
bawling the worsening news to the bloodclan.
If my manlord received the wounds rumor gave him
he'd gape open now like a sea-fisher's grabnet.
I was driven distracted . . . rope round the rafters . . .
neck in the noose . . . getting tighter . . . half-throttled . . .

[*To* AGAMEMNON.]
That's why our child isn't here now in Argos,

our child, our bed-bond's first bloodshoot,
our *he*-child, Orestes.   No need for suspicion.
He's in Phocis with Strophius, our ally and friend.
Strophius warned me of possible troubles,
the threat to your life in the perils of warfare,
the likelihood here of popular rising.
When people are down they get trampled further.
My words have no wiles, and no guile to gull you.
Now my eyes are pumped dry. No more tears to squeeze out.
Eyes bleary with weeping and sleepless night-vigils
hoping the beacons from you would get kindled.
If I slept, *if,* a mere gnat-whine would wake me,
loud as a bugle bray, wake me from dreaming
And what did I dream of? Your danger. Your deathwounds.
Ten years of tight corners crammed into a catnap!
All that I suffered but no longer feel fettered,
I'm free to say welcome, my lord, to your house,
welcome as the watchdog is in the sheepfold,
mainmast of our vessel, chief central rooftree.
Like an only child to its father you're welcome,
welcome as land is to those on the ocean,
welcome as dawn is after long nightsqualls,
as a spring is to travellers thirsting for water.

The release! Yanking necessity's yokestrap off!

Now, my great manlord, come down from your warcar.
But don't let those feet that have trampled Troy under
step on mere earth.

[*To* SLAVES.]

Why are you waiting?
Carry out my commands for strewing the pavestones,
drag the dark dye-flow right down from the doorway
Let bloodright, true bloodright be the king's escort.
No sleeping for me till the gods get their pleasure.
The she-gods of life-lot, I'll be their she-kin,
the female enforcer of all they have fated.

Agamemnon
>She-child of Leda, my household's best bloodhound,
>your words, like my absence, lasted too long.
>Our praise-singers spout out such paeans for payment.
>We are a warhawk, no woman wanting such welcomes.
>Such prostrations, such purples suit pashas from Persia.
>Don't come the Khan's courtiers, kowtow or cosset.
>Don't grovel, suck up, salaam, and stop gawping!
>Such gaudy displays goad gods into godgrudge.
>Give honors to humans more meant for mankind
>than such stuffs even skygods won't scorn to be swathed in.
>The mortal who blackens such silks with his bootsoles
>best beware of bad trouble, best look to his life-lot.
>My fame's managed so far without fancy footmats.
>The greatest of godgifts is canniness, caution.
>Luck has to last the whole length of a lifetime.
>If happiness fails in the last lap it's futile.
>Fortune can only be first. All after it's failure.
>Good luck gets the champion's laurels or nothing.
>Runners up in the race are degrees of disaster.
>My stride's strong and steady till disaster's left standing.

1. **Clyt:**   Then stride "strong and steady" on what we have strewn.
   Ag: No, it smells baleful. No blessing or boon!

2. **Clyt:**   Is "great" Agamemnon godstruck, afraid?
   Ag: No, but I stand by the statement I made.

3. **Clyt:**   And potentate Priam? Would *he* tread it or not?
   Ag: That Trojan satrap? Traipse over the lot!

4. **Clyt:**   Are you afraid of what the people might say?
   Ag: The voice of the people exerts its own sway.

5. **Clyt:**   Mangrudge is proof that a man's reached great heights.
   Ag: And only he-women go looking for fights.

6. **Clyt:**   Give way from the grace of your great victory.
   Ag: Would that give you joy, that gesture from me?
   Clyt: Let me win a little, great manlord. Agree!

Agamemnon
> If it means so much . . .
> [*To* SLAVES.]
> > here, help get these boots off.
> Campaign comrades, loyal old leathers.
>
> Keep godgrudge off me as I tread on this sea-red.
> I'll feel that I'm walking the women who wove it.
> Mounds of rich silver went into its making.
> So much for me . . .
> [*Indicates* CASSANDRA.]
> > This stranger needs looking after.
> The gods like some kindness from those who have triumphed.
> Be kind. Nobody wants to end up in bondage.
> Pick of the booty, the Trojan spoil loot-pearl,
> this girl's the men's gift to grace their commander.
> Well, since I've yielded, I'll do what you ask me,
> and tread on your red path into my palace.

[AGAMEMNON *begins walking on the cloth towards the palace doors.*]

Clytemnestra
> The sea's there for ever. No-one can drain it.
> And it oozes for ever the dyes of dark sea-red
> to stain all the garments this house has a wealth of.
> The gods have made sure that we've never been lacking.
> And if gods had prescribed it as a rite for his safety
> I would have trampled each inch of rich raiment.
> If the treeroot's living the house gets new leafage
> spreading cool shade at the time of the dogstar.
> Your return's like a rare spell of sunshine in winter,
> like Zeus when he ripens the sour grapes for the vintage.
> A master's presence then 's the finishing stroke.
>
> O Zeus, Zeus who brings all things to fulfilment
> my fulfilment lies in serving your purpose.

[*Exit* CLYTEMNESTRA.]

Chorus

> Fear whirrs its wings round my heart
> my soul flies into the future
> the songnotes darken with prophecy.
>
> Certainty's thronestone's deserted
> nothing says go to my panic
> Can't spit out the gobbets of nightmare
>
> Sand's silted over the marks of the hawsers
> Time's covered up the chainchafe of anchors
> where the dogships strained at their leashes for Troy
> and they've returned   my own eyes can see them
> and still I'm uneasy   terrified   why?
>
> Listen   a dirgesong nobody's strumming
> Listen   the Furies monotonous humming
> Listen   strings tuned to the terror that's coming.

[*Enter* CLYTEMNESTRA.]

Clytemnestra

> You too, Cassandra. Cassandra, come in!
> Zeus can't be angry. He wants you to join us
> to share in the household's ritual washing
> taking your place among all the slave-girls
> at the godstone to one who keeps this house wealthy.
>
> Come down from the warcar. Why be so haughty?
>
> If it has to happen, enslavement,
> they're lucky to fall to hereditary masters.
> The ones who suddenly come into a fortune,
> get rich by a windfall, they're brutal to slaves.
> We'll treat you kindly according to custom.

Chorus

> It's you she's addressing, Cassandra, no savvy?
> You're fast in the fate-net, the shackles of life-lot.
> You can't scramble out. Best do as you're bidden.

Clytemnestra

> Sparrowbrain! What does she jabber in, ba-ba gibberish?

I'll try her again. Go inside! Go inside!
Chorus
Go. It's best. And you haven't much choice.
Do as you're bidden. Come down from the car.
Clytemnestra
I don't have time to stand about waiting.
The sacrifice. It's standing now at the godstone.
The victim's prepared. My dreams reach fulfilment.

If you want to partake in our worship, then come.

[*To* CHORUS.]
Nothing gets through. Try her in dumbshow.
Chorus
An interpreter's needed. Somebody clever.
She's like a wild animal caught in a net.
Clytemnestra
Maniac, more like, listening to voices.
Her father's city's caught fast in the net.
She'll go champing her chops on the chainbit
until her mettle and madness froth off as blood.
I'm not staying here to be sneered at by slavegirls.

[*Exit* CLYTEMNESTRA.]
Chorus
I pity the creature. She needs understanding.
Come down, poor woman, down from the warcar.
Necessity. Neck into the yokestrap!
Cassandra
otototoi popoi da!
Apollo   Apollo
Chorus
Apollo? Then that *otototoi*'s all wrong!
Apollo hates death-notes and dark sorts of song.
Cassandra
otototoi popoi da!
Apollo   Apollo
Chorus
Listen! Again. Apollo hates the sort of note

that comes strangled and anguished out of her throat.
Cassandra
   Apollo Apollo   waygod   destroyer
   Again you're Cassandra's appalling destroyer!
Chorus
   She's in a trance, about to prophesy.
   Even in bondage her gift doesn't die.
Cassandra
   Apollo Apollo   waygod   destroyer
   where have you brought me   what house is this?
Chorus
   The house of Atreus. That much *I* know.
   It's a poor prophetess asks me questions though!
Cassandra
   ah ah ah
   god-shunners   kin-killers
   child-charnel   man-shambles
   babe-spattered abattoir
Chorus
   She's like a bloodhound nose to the ground
   tracking the kill that's got to be found.
Cassandra
   I track down the witnesses
   children   babes   shrieking butcher
   barbecued childflesh wolfed down by the father
Chorus
   Your prophetic powers none of us doubt.
   But that kind of vision we can well do without.
Cassandra
   I see   somebody   evil   something
   agony   agony   more   more   more
   no-one can bear it   no-one can stop it
   help's far away over the ocean
Chorus
   Now I'm lost, though till now the tale was clear.
   We breathe *that* story in our atmosphere.

Cassandra
> husband   bed-mate
> body washed in your bath-trough
>
> hand over hand   hauling the catch in

Chorus
> Now it's got worse. I can make no sense
> of these dense riddles that grow more dense.

Cassandra
> net   hell-net
> she-snare   bed-mate   blood-mate
>
> the deathpack howls over its victim
> the fiendswarm surrounds it for stoning

Chorus
> Don't rouse the Furies. Don't start them humming
> you make me feel hopeless. Don't drag them in.
>
> The heart loses blood as cloths lose dyestuff
> and the sun oozes light at its setting.
>
> Death moves in fast. I can feel his shadow.

Cassandra
> Look there   there   look
> bull   cow   bull cow   don't let them grapple
> he's caught in the robe-net   she gores him and gores him
> butting and butting   with blood-crusted horn
> slumps into bathblood   bloodsplash

Chorus
> I'm no good at oracles telling the future
> but I recognize evil in what she keeps saying.
> Evil's all   men get out of oracles.
> Her words spell out terror, and smell of the truth.

Cassandra
> him   me   him   me   him   me
> woecups   mine slops over the brim
> what have you brought me here for?
> to die beside you   what else?

Chorus
> Sing your own deathdirge, nightingale.
> You're like the brown bird shrilling your grieftrills
> warbling insatiably Itys O Itys!

Cassandra
> Wings   wings   no weeping   no wailing
> Cassandra   bloodblade and hackblock

Chorus
> This nightmare, this maelstrom, where does it come from?
> Strange cries, shrill shriekings! Where will they end?

Cassandra
> Paris   blood bridals   kin-doom
> Scamander   Scamander   Cassandra's Scamander
> I was a youngster on your riverside once
>
> Griefstreams of Acheron   I'll sing beside you.

Chorus
> That's clear enough. A child couldn't miss it.
> Your death songs pang me and pain me like snakefangs
> Your anguish tears me in two just to listen.

Cassandra
> Troytowers tottering   Troytowers destroyed
> sacrifice   sacrifice   beast after beast
> all father's cattle   utterly useless
> the Troy of my father   ashes   all ash
>
> I'm on fire too   come crashing to earth.

Chorus
> What is it wringing these cries from your body?
> These painpangs and griefsongs? Don't understand.

Cassandra
> Off with the brideveil then. Look into truth's pupils
> The truthgust. It's rising. Blowing fresh headwinds
> sweeping sea-ripples into dawn's molten cauldron,
> then building a woe-wave as big as a mountain.
> Riddles are over. Keep close on my track now
> as I scent out the spoor of ancient transgression.
> Listen. The rooftops. Monotonous humming

that drones on forever and means only terror.
The blood-bolstered fiend-swarm holds its debauches,
cacophonous squatters that can't be evicted,
chant over and over the crime where it started
cursing a bedbond a bloodkin defiled
trampling all over the flowing bed-linen.

Have I shot wide or am I on target.
Swear I know all the curse of this bloodclan.

Chorus
And if I did swear, what good would it do,
what would it alter? But it's a wonder
a stranger like you knows the truth of our story.
It's as if you'd witnessed all you're describing.

1. **Cass:** Apollo the seergod put this power in my head.
     Ch: A god, and so lovesick he'd bribe you to bed?

2. **Cass:** I've always thought it too shameful to tell.
     Ch: Shame's a luxury for when life goes well.

3. **Cass:** He got me flat on my back. I felt his breath. Hot.
     Ch: And did the he-god get what he wanted, or not?

4. **Cass:** I told him he could then later said no.
     Ch: You've already been given the god-vision though?

5. **Cass:** I foretold Troy's downfall, the Trojans' defeat.
     Ch: And didn't Apollo make you pay for your cheat?

6. **Cass:** Yes, no-one ever believed me, not one single word.
     Ch: But we have believed all we have heard.

Cassandra
ah ah ah ah

truthpangs truthpain tornado and maelstrom
doomfever doom-ague shakes my body again

look on the rooftops dream-shadows children
killed by their bloodkin, their hands full of *ugh*
offal and giblets their very own innards
held out to their father as succulent morsels.

The lion plots vengeance   the lion that's gutless,
the lion that lolls in my master's own chamber
waiting to welcome my homecoming master
(master, that's what as his slave I must call him)
Commander of triremes, crusher of Priam,
but blind to cabal, the insatiable hell-bitch,
licking his hand   ears pricked in welcome.
furry and cur-like concealing a Fury
red-blooded, intrepid, the man-slaying woman
what name of monster's best to describe her?
Blood-sucker   basilisk   two-headed shark-hag,
rock-trog skulking for sailors to wreck them,
hell-dam fire-breathing war   war   at her husband,
boundless in brazenness, hear her hosannas
like battle-cries raised when the victory seems certain.
But how well she dissembles that so wifely welcome.

Whether I'm believed or not doesn't matter
Whatever you do the future will happen.
Through pity and tears you'll know the true prophet.

Chorus

Thyestes eating his children, that I got, yes.
I sicken and tremble at truths so unfeigning.
The rest I can't fathom. I'm lost I'm afraid.

1. **Cass:**   Agamemnon. He's the one you'll see dead!
   Ch: Ssshh! Such things shouldn't even be said.

2. **Cass:**   Even unspoken this sore won't heal.
   Ch: It will if the he-gods hear our appeal.

3. **Cass:**   And while you're appealing his throat's being slit.
   Ch: I don't know the man who would dare to do it.

4. **Cass:**   If you say *man* then you don't understand.
   Ch: I don't know the man, nor how it's been planned.

5. **Cass:**   And yet it's your language you're hearing me speak.
   Ch: No oracle's clear, though they all speak in Greek.

Cassandra

ah   ah   fire in me   Apollo's

Two-legged lioness tupped by the wolfman
when the great lion's gone she'll kill Cassandra

brewing the witchbane   her bubbling grudge-broth
into the cauldron   death-dose for Cassandra

She sharpens the swordblade to hack down her husband
a hacking he earned by bringing me with him.

Why do I wear these garments that mock me,
the trappings of prophetess, rod, garb and raiment.

[CASSANDRA *tears off the regalia of prophetess.*]
I'm going to die but you'll go before me.
It's some satisfaction to trample these trappings.
Go and bestow these "gifts" on another.

ah   Apollo   Apollo   clawing my clothes off.
He grabs the prophetess garb off my body.
He mocked me, Apollo, though dressed as his prophet.
He wanted me scorned and derided by bloodkin,
called vagabond, mountebank, gypsy and starveling.
The god-seer casts his prophetess to disaster.
My father's own priestess now mere beast oblation
lifeblood flowing hot off the hackblock.

We won't die forgotten. Gods always notice.

He'll come our avenger, our bloodgrudge-fulfiller,
he'll come motherkiller, wanderer, exile,
setting the copestone on this bloodclan's corruption,
the father's corpse drawing the son back to Argos.

Why these tears? These eyes saw Troy levelled.
And those who destroyed her doomed also to die.
Now it's for me to die . . .
[CASSANDRA *approaches the palace.*]
                            the doorway to death
I pray for a clean blow, no painful convulsions,

my blood ebbing gently, closing my eyes.
Chorus
Such suffering, child, such pain in your wisdom.
If you can foresee death then why do you go to it
so meekly like a god-destined goat to the godstone?

1. **Cass:**   There's no escape now. No more delay.
   Ch: "While there's life there's . . ." you know what they say.

2. **Cass:**   No hope for me though. It's pointless all flight.
   Ch: How bravely you seem to face up to your plight.

3. **Cass:**   Yes only the doomed are ever called brave.
   Ch: But isn't it noble to face up to the grave?

4. **Cass:**   You mean like my father and brothers all died.
[CASSANDRA *moves towards the palace and recoils.*]
   Ch: What is it? Fear? Was that why you shied?
Cassandra
Ugh!   Ugh!

5.   **Ch:**   What was that cry for? What sickens your brain?
   Cass: The palace! It stinks like an abattoir drain!

6.   **Ch:**   It's the sacrifice made for our clanchief's return.
   Cass: It stinks like the gas from a burial urn.
   Ch: It's only the incense the priests always burn.
Cassandra
I'll go inside, wailing our deaths, mine, Agamemnon's.
Enough of life! Friends, I'm no frightened fledgling
flinching with fear when the bushes get shaken.
From you what I beg 's the bearing of witness,
when woman for woman my killer's killed also
and the man mated to doom gets killed for your clanchief.
I beg this favor as a stranger going to die now.
Chorus
I pity you, so open-eyed about dying.
Cassandra
A few last words, a requiem dirgesong
I ask the sun whose last rays I'm addressing

that when the avengers cut down the assassins
one stroke's for the slavegirl butchered defenseless.
Man's life! Luck's blotted out by the slenderest shadow.
Trouble — a wet sponge wipes the slate empty.
That pain's also nothing makes life a heartbreak.

[CASSANDRA *enters palace.*]
Chorus
> Human beings in their pride
> restless and dissatisfied
>
> No palace dweller bars his door
> to opulence and cries: *No more!*
>
> the gods let our great king destroy
> the topless towers of Priam's Troy
>
> vanquisher conquistador
> crowned with all the spoils of war
>
> now the blood that Atreus shed
> falls on Agamemnon's head
>
> he's to die but what's the good
> his death too cries out for blood

Agamemnon [*Within.*]
> ah!

Chorus
> Whose was that voice screaming in terror?

Agamemnon [*Within.*]
> ah

Chorus
> That was the king unless I'm in error.
> Now we should take council and every man
> should say what he thinks is the safest plan.

1. In my opinion we ought to bring
   the whole city here to help the king.

2. And I say rush in, break down the door
   catch them with swords still dripping with gore.

3. I'm also for action. I'll second that.
   Any action at all 's better than chat.

4. It's quite clear, I mean quite clear to me
   their action 's a prelude to tyranny!

5. They don't discuss, they do, and while we prate
   they stamp their boots on all debate.

6. But I haven't a plan and no-one can
   go into action without a plan.

7. Agreed! Hear, hear! There's no way talk
   can make a dead man get up and walk.

8. Just to save our skins shall we stand by
   let murderers rule us, our clanchief die?

9. No. Never! As for me I'd sooner die
   than live two seconds under tyranny.

10. But can we, from the cries we heard,
    infer that murder *has* occurred?

11. We should have proof before we act.
    Guesswork's not the same as fact.

12. I think the meeting as a whole's agreed —
    conclusive evidence is what we need.

[*The palace doors swing open and reveal* CLYTEMNESTRA *standing over the bodies of* AGAMEMNON *and* CASSANDRA.]

Clytemnestra

I've spoken many words to serve the moment
which I've no compunction now to contradict.
How else but by lying and seeming so loving
could I have plotted my enemy's downfall?
How rig the net so it can't be leapt out of?
This is the bloodgrudge, the grudge's fruition
something I've brooded on quite a long time.
I've done what I meant to. I wouldn't deny it.
Over his head I cast a vast trammel

the sort that hauls in whole shoals at each casting.
He couldn't get out of his rich, flowing doom-robe.
Twice I struck him. He screamed twice, then crumpled.
Once he'd fallen I struck him a third blow,
one struck for Zeus in his role as corpse-keeper.
He lay there gasping and splurting his blood out
spraying me with dark blood-dew, dew I delight in
as much as the graincrop in the fresh gloss of rainfall
when the wheatbud's in labor and swells into birthpang.

So that's how it is, old men of Argos.
Cheer if you want to. I revel in glory.
He's had his libation, spurts from his bloodvein.
He poured woe and bitterness into our winebowl.
He's got the last goblet and laps up the leas!

Chorus

Your words revolt me. How can you trumpet,
so unlike a woman, over your manlord?

Clytemnestra

Still you can treat me like a woman who's witless?
My heart's made of steel, and as I have stated
whether you like it or not there's Agamemnon.
This is the swordhand that brought him to bloodright.
I hacked down my husband. That's how it is.

Chorus

Woman! Some earthbane's driving you crazy.
To brave the damning voice of the people!
You've sown and you'll reap. Banishment. Exile.
Driven out of the country. Cursed at and spat at.

Clytemnestra

O *now* you're ready with banishment, exile,
the people's hatred and public damnation.
And how did you punish this murderer here?
Meant as little to him as slaughtering cattle.
His sheepfolds were bursting, he butchered his she-child,
the she-child I labored to launch on her life-lot,
as some specious god-sop to settle the stormsquall.
You should have banished *him* for pollution,

but it's now that you start to play at stern judges.
Banishment! *If* you can make me. *If* you enforce it.
If I prove the stronger I'll teach you some wisdom.
You'll go back to school and learn some hard lessons.

Chorus

You're maddened by powerlust, raving.
Your brain's beweeviled with blood-deeds.
Your eyes have red bloodflecks for pupils.
Your doom's to be honorless, friendless, defenseless
and stabwound for stabwound you'll reap retribution.

Clytemnestra

Then listen to this, the oath that I'll swear by.
By bloodright exacted on behalf of my she-child,
by Iphigeneia whose bloodgrudge has roosted,
by the Fury for whom Agamemnon's the booty,
I swear I'll never let fear to my fireside
as long as the hearth's kept alight by Aegisthus,
loyal friend always, my shield, my protector.

Look at him, Shaggermemnon, shameless, shaft-happy,
ogler and grinder of Troy's golden girlhood.
Look at her, spearprize, prophetess, princess,
whore of his wartent, his bash back on shipboard.
They've got their deserts the two of them now.
There he lies. She's sung her swansong and lies
as she should do stretched out alongside him,
his "dear's" death a side-dish to the banquet of his.

Chorus

Please send me my end now, but not too painful,
let me lurch gently out of my life-lot
now that our king's been dragged under the death-yoke.

Two women made him suffer then die.

Wild Helen causing the death-throes of thousands
now you've won your garland of glory,
a blood-wreath whose redness can't be rubbed off.

Clytemnestra

Don't call on death or surrender to torment.

Don't turn your hatred on Helen my she-kin.
Don't think she alone brought the Greeks to their ruin
as though only she were the cause of their anguish.

Chorus

As far back as Tantalus the grudge-demon started,
harried this bloodclan from those days to these days,
harries it now in the shapes of these she-kin,
Clytemnestra Helen those carrion crows
cawing discordantly over our gables
maws crammed with corpseflesh and carrion gobbets

Clytemnestra

Better to blame the blood-guzzling grudge-hound
battening on us for three gorgings of gore.

He kindles the gore-lust in the guts of our bloodkin.
As one sore scars over new pus starts spurting.

Chorus

Insatiable bloodgrudge, gore-ogre, flesh-glutton
goes on and on plagueing and galling
but what isn't godsent? Zeus is behind it.
Nothing occurs but the gods make it happen.

King Agamemnon, how can we mourn you,
how give a voice to bereavement and loveloss,
there in the spider's web spewing your life out
the impious weapon swung by the spousefiend?

Clytemnestra

Spouse? No! Wife? No! What swung the swordblade's
the semblance, the shape of this corpse's spouse only.
Wielding the weapon was no wife and no woman
but his family's phantom, Atreus the flesh-chef
offering flayed these fully fledged victims
one for each butchered and barbecued babe.

Chorus

You guiltless? You guiltless? And who'll be your witness
though some god must have helped you fulfill the
    bloodgrudge.
Black Ares amok, wading deep in the blood-bog —
the bloodgrudge that goads him the cold joints of children.

King Agamemnon, how can we mourn you,
how give a voice to bereavement and loveloss,
there in the spider's web spewing your life out,
the impious weapon swung by the spousefiend?

Clytemnestra

His death's no worse than the one he inflicted
when he forged his own link in this house's doom-chain.
He suffered the fate he made others suffer —
Iphigeneia still wept for, sweet flower, his she-child.

Don't go boasting in Hades, steel-slinger, sword-brute,
you got back your stabwounds, all you inflicted.

Chorus

My mind's off its moorings. Its foundations are shaking.
No longer a drizzle, a hammering bloodstorm,
Fate strops its blade for more and more blood-bouts.
Earth   Earth   Earth   why didn't you take me
rather than let me live to see the king humbled
sprawled out in his blood in a bathtub of silver.
Who'll bury the body? Who'll sing the gravedirge?

[*To* CLYTEMNESTRA.]
You wouldn't surely, first kill our clanchief
then pour specious tributes over his tombcairn?

Who'll mourn him with real grief and not a mask only?

Clytemnestra

That's not your business. I hacked him down and the sword
     hand
strong enough to strike him can dig him a ditch.
No mourning. From no-one. All that's forbidden.
Iphigeneia   she'll greet him by the waters of sorrow
flinging her arms round her father to kiss him.

Chorus

Choler for choler, bloodgrudge for bloodgrudge.
while Zeus the high he-god is still the gods' clanchief
the law for the living is killers get killed.
Blight's in the bloodstream, curse in the corpuscles,
the feet of this clan bogged down in the bloodquag.

Clytemnestra
>The future, the truth, you're beginning to see them.
>I'll make a bond with this palace's bloodfiend.
>What's happened so far I'll accept and fall in with,
>hard though that is, I'll do it, provided
>the fiend leaves this house and finds other quarters
>to ravage the people and goad them to murder.
>Riches mean nothing. A little suffices
>if only this frenzy of kin-killing ceases.

[*Enter* AEGISTHUS *from a side entrance with a silent bodyguard, and "anti-chorus," the same number as the chorus.*]

Aegisthus
>A great day when bloodright comes into its own.
>This proves there are gods who see crimes and punish.
>I'm happy, so happy to see this man tangled
>in robes of dark red the Furies have woven,
>fulfilling the bloodgrudge caused by his father.
>This man's father, Atreus, once king of Argos.
>there being some dispute as to who should be clanchief.
>drove my father (his brother) Thyestes away.
>Thyestes came back as a suppliant begging
>at least his life sparing, the minimum mercy,
>no son's blood staining his father's own threshold.
>But this man's father, Atreus, Atreus the godless,
>whose mask of warm welcome kept hatred hidden
>threw a great banquet as if for Thyestes
>and dished up his children as the daintiest titbits.
>The fingers and toes he chopped off to disguise it
>and my father alone of the guests got this childstew.
>Not being aware what it was he was eating
>he bolted the banquet that blasted this bloodclan.
>When he knew what he chewed, he choked on the childstew,
>shrieked, reeled backwards, spewed out the offal,
>turned over the tables and cursed the whole bloodclan
>grinding the meat into mush with his boot-heel.
>
>And that's why your clanchief's lying there murdered.
>And I wove the net we got him ensnared in.
>Third son of Thyestes, I plotted for bloodright.

Driven out with my father while only a baby
as a man I've returned escorted by bloodright.
In exile I had all the threads twisted ready
biding my time for the trap to be fashioned.
Now I'd die happy, happy now bloodright's
got Agememnon caught fast in fate's trammel.

Chorus

Aegisthus, gloating on carnage. Revolting!
You did it, you plotted it, *you*, single-handed?
The people will stone you. You don't stand a chance.

Aegisthus

Pretty grand talk to come out of the galleys!
We've got the tiller. Get on with the rowing.
Old as you are, you still can learn lessons
though you'll find wisdom a tough course to take in.
Prison. Starvation. They motivate scholars,
make even dodderers like you get good totals.
Don't push on the horse-goad. You'll get yourselves hurt.

Chorus

Woman! Waiting at home for the menfolk
wallowing in, befouling a warrior's bedbond!
How could you bring down a great soldier?

Aegisthus

Whinny like that again and you'll rue it.
The songs of Orpheus may have tamed creatures,
yours work on me in the other direction
A dose of the strongarm will soon get you docile.

Chorus

You, rule Argos? You, who let a mere woman
murder the king when you hadn't courage.

Aegisthus

Deception, that was the work for the woman.
I, with my bloodgrudge, was under suspicion.
Agamemnon's gold will buy off his people.
And those who won't be bought will be broken.
No colts without collars. Hunger and darkness
they teach the mettlesome quieter manners.

Chorus
> Couldn't kill the king with your own hands could you?
> Let a woman get her clan and her clangods corrupted,
> the gods of Argos. But I tell you . . . Orestes . . .
> if he's alive (and luck guide his life-lot)
> he'll kill this couple, our bloodgrudge-fulfiller.

1. **Ae:** You want your first lessons already, I see.
   Ch: Comrades, you're needed. Stand firm with me.

2. **Ae:** Draw your swords out. Ready. Stand by.
   Ch: Stand by. Not one of us here's afraid to die.
   Ae: I'm glad that you told me So go ahead, die!

Clytemnestra
> [*Interrupting.*] No No, my dear, no more blood-letting.
> There's been enough. Enough. Old men of Argos,
> go home now quietly before you regret it.
> We did what we had to. Let it rest there.
> The fiend's hooves have galloped over our spirits.
> Let it rest there. Take advice from a woman.

Aegisthus
> But they, they gibe at me, mock me.
> You're pushing your luck you old foulmouths.
> I'm your new ruler. Don't you forget it.

1. **Ch:** Argives don't grovel to your evil sort.
   Aeg: Then Argives like you will have to be taught.

2. **Ch:** Not if Orestes comes back to his own.
   Aeg: Exiles eat hope, all gristle and bone.

3. **Ch:** Grow fat on injustice. Shit on the state!
   Aeg: I'm warning you, old fool, before it's too late . . .

4. **Ch:** Cock-a-doodle-doo, the dungheap lord,
   crow a bit louder, your hen will applaud!

Clytemnestra
> Let the terriers yap, all bark and no bite!
> You and I, we'll rule this house, and set it right.

[*Exit* CLYTEMNESTRA *with* AEGISTHUS, *into the house of Atreus.*
CHORUS *disperses silently.*]

END OF PART ONE

TWO: CHOEPHORI

Characters   *Orestes*

Chorus

Electra

Pylades

Clytemnestra

Nurse

Aegisthus

Servant

[ORESTES *and* PYLADES *at the grave of Agamemnon.*]
Orestes
>Hermes, he-god, who can go in and out of the ground,
>he-god still wary to keep power with the fathers,
>now I have need of you, back home from long exile.
>This is the gravemound of Agamemnon, my father.
>Help my cries through the ground to his ghost.

[*Cuts off two locks of hair.*]
>I lop off one lock and so move into manhood.

>And this one for your mound as a mark of my mourning.

>Your son and heir wasn't here to salute you
>no final farewell as the earth was flung over.

>Look! There! What's that? That procession of women,
>wending this way, all dressed in drab dirge-clothes.
>What's it in aid of? More doom? More disaster?
>They're carrying jars, jars full of libations.
>I suppose that they're sops for my father's sore spirit.
>It must be! There, among all the mourners
>is my she-kin Electra, wasted by weeping.

>Zeus! High he-god! Help it to happen,
>the vengeance I want to take for my father.

[*To* PYLADES.]
>Pylades, you and I stand aside, keep out of eye shot
>till we're sure of the meaning of the rites we're to witness.
Chorus
>Coerced into keening by Queen Clytemnestra
>for King Agamemnon as if for our bloodkin
>we carry these ghost-sops out to his gravemound.
>Lashed out to lament the lost lord of Argos
>we Trojans trench flesh ruts into our faces.
>There's no need to coerce us, we cry anyway.

>Our lives have been one long meal of mourning,
>one life-long banquet, one blow-out of bale.

We claw our clothes open, mad in our mourning.
Our ripped pap-wraps shriek as we shred them.

This bloodclan's doom-demon disguised as a dream
crashed through into Clytemnestra's calm midnight
and squeezed from the queen's throat a throttling shriek,
a cry that re-echoed through each recess and corner
and pounded for entry to the coops that we're penned in.
The whole household heard it. Our hair stood on end.
Then spoke a clanseer whose knowledge was nightmares.

"The bitter dead below bellow for blood-dues"

So godsops she sends, empty gifts and libations
meant to ward off what gnaws her at night-time,
sends me out here as soon as the dawn breaks
that woman hated and loathed by the he-gods.
The grave-charms she wants get choked in my gullet.
What godsop or bribe makes spilt blood unspilt?
Shed blood's shed for ever. The dead stay dead.
This bloodclan, this house, what hasn't it suffered?
Murk, man-shunned and sunless smothers the bloodclan
when the clanchief, its light, is stifled by death,
death-doused, mouldering under his gravemound . . .
He counted for something, the king of this bloodclan,
battle-proof power, both strife-proof and plot-proof.
The lips of his people respected that power,
their hearts honored their hero and helmsman.
Now all honor's usurped by terror the tyrant.
Success gets sucked up to. The god is good life-lot
All grovel to that as to godhead or greater.
But to those who loll in the luck of their life-lot
the justice of bloodright's the bolt from the black —
some netted at noontide, others are night-time,
daylight or darkness, both nourish their doom.
When the earth's gullet's choked on the gore it has gulped
the bloodgut clots rock-like and can't reach earth's gut.
Guilt in the guilty likewise stays clotted
the cankers of guilt craze the culprit and kill him.

The blood of the killed, the bed blood of virgins
(both dooms we endured in the downfall of Troy)
is worn by the guilty like gauntlets of gore.
All the world's waters forced through one funnel
and sprayed at the bloodspot as much good as spittle!
Necessity! That brought us to where we are now,
hauled from our homeland, dragged here as drudges,
lugged into a life-lot, unloving and loathly,
brought into bondage, doom's dragnet round Troy,
we bite hard on the horsebit, gulp down our gall,
and go through these griefshows as she commanded.
But our grief is no shamming, the tears shed are true,
mourning our helplessness under harsh masters,
our massacred menfolk, the mass-graves of Troy.

Electra

Women, Troy's warspoils, now palace work-slaves
whose work gives the palace its appearance of order,
since you've been sent to attend me, give me advice.
What graveside grace goes best with these griefcups?
What address would my father find even decent?
"To the man from the woman, to the loved from the loving"!
Call Clytemnestra, my mother, a woman who loves!
I don't have the nerve, the effrontery for that.
What to say as I pour honey, then milk, wine and then water? —
What's usually intoned here 's useless, insulting.
"To those who send grave-gifts, send the good they deserve."
The good they deserve 's the same fate as my father's.
No words, but a silence the way he was slaughtered
pouring the griefcups as if they were slop-pails.
Friends! Serfwomen, freeborn, both fettered to fate,
shackled to shame we share the same hatreds.
Between us there need be no sort of secret.

Chorus

I swear by the cairn that keeps the king's dust
I speak all my secrets, and you have my trust. . . .

1. El: Speak then. I swear the same oath you all swore.
    Ch: For those you can trust pray as you pour.

2. **El:** Those I can trust. Who near me 's still true?
   Ch: Yourself! Those who hate Aegisthus are too.

3. **El:** Then myself! And you? Do you count on my side?
   Ch: Judge only my words, then you can decide.

4. **El:** Who else can be counted? Consider and say . . .
   Ch: Orestes! *Orestes!* Though still far away.

5. **El:** Orestes! Orestes! The best thing to say!
   Ch: For those you can't trust, the killers, pray . . .

6. **El:** Pray what? Tell me, I'm eager to learn . . .
   Ch: Pray that a man or a god will return.

7. **El:** Return to reckon the guilt of those two?
   Ch: No! Kill them. That's all. *Blood for blood.* That will do.

8. **El:** Demand gods to deal death! It that right or good?
   Ch: Right and good! Right and good! Blood demands blood.

Electra
  God-guide and ground-god, god-go-between, herald.
  linking upper and nether, the dead and the living,
  Hermes, he-god, help me and get them to hear me,
  the spirits I pray to, that prosper this palace,
  and get her to hear me, the greatest of she-gods,
  EARTH who pushes all beings out of her belly,
  suckles her creatures, and swells with their corpses.
  Get her to listen. I pour the libation
  and pray to my father:
                  'Pity! For me! For Orestes!
  This bloodclan's benighted and he's its bright beacon.
  We're both dispossessed, deprived of our bloodright.
  She bartered her bairns and bought as her bed-mate
  Aegisthus who shares in the guilt of your killing.
  Electra's a bondslave, and Orestes an exile.
  Clytemnestra and Aegisthus, basking and idle,
  loll in the luxury made by your labors.
  I pray Orestes returns with luck in his life-lot
  and my life-lot unsullied, not marred like my mother's,

heart and hands blameless, unblemished by blood.

These prayers on our part. And for them we oppose
I pray the bloodgrudge-fulfiller will soon be appearing,
the butchers be butchered, and pay blood for blood.

Agamemnon, come up at the head of the ground-gods.
Agamemnon, come up with Earth the great she-god,
bring blessings and bloodright blazoned with laurels.
These are my prayers, and I pour your libations.

[*To* CHORUS.]
You water the seed of my prayer with your wailing.
As I pour deliver the dead a due grave-dirge.

Chorus
Tears drop on your dark head
drop by drop the way you bled

Your grave holds both bad and good
what we beg is "blood for blood."

Agamemnon, mind in murk,
hear our words, make them work —

Bloodgrudge-fulfiller
come   kill the killer

big bow bent back
sword in slash hack.

Electra
Gulped by Gaia the drinks have got through
through to my father . . .

[*Sees lock of hair.*]
                              . . . but here's something new!

1. **Ch:** Fear makes my heart jig. What have you found?
    El: A lock of hair has been laid on the mound.

2. **Ch:** A man's or a woman's? Who put it there?
    El: It looks like a bloodkin's, this lock of fine hair.

3. **Ch:** A bloodkin's? I don't understand. Don't leave me to guess.

El: It's mine or it's no-one's this mystery tress.

4. Ch: Your mother, the murderer, she wouldn't dare . . .
   El: Yet I've a feeling I know it, this hair.

5. Ch: Whose is it then, if you say it seems known?
   El: Whose I don't know, but it's so like my own.

6. Ch: Orestes! Orestes has sent us this secret sign.
   El: It can only be his hair, if it's not mine.

7. Ch: Orestes in Argos? Too risky if that's what you meant.
   El: No, for the sake of his father he had the lock sent.

   Ch: Only *sent*! The more cause to weep for him then.
   Orestes will never see Argos again . . .

Electra

A surge of choler and grudge sweeps over my spirit,
Spitted on pain like a stabwound or spearthrust.
Drops like the spindrift spat off a seaswell
break from my eyes at the sight of this curl.
Who else from Argos would this lock belong to?
Never hers, the murderess, my mother. My *mother*!
She's stifled and smothered all motherly feelings.
How can I know it's Orestes for certain.
Only hope makes us so foolish and stupid.

If this hair had a voice and was sent as a herald
then I wouldn't waver or be so distracted
and I'd know by its clear spoken message
that either it came from a head I detested
or was the bloodkin's I longed to believe it,
a grace to my grief, a grace to this gravemound.

The gods I've invoked are wise to what seaswells
we're whirled on, like sailors in shipwreck.
If we were meant to, then scrape home we will.
A great oak can sprout from the tiniest acorn.

I call on these gods for my prayers to be answered.

[*Enter* ORESTES *and* PYLADES.]

Orestes
>They're answered, those prayers. The gods favor you.
>Now pray that our future is fortunate too.

1. El: *Our* future? Prayers answered? What do you mean?
    Or: You prayed to see something. Now you have seen.

2. El: How do you know what it was that I prayed?
    Or: For your much-loved Orestes to come to your aid.

3. El: Then how can you say that the gods favor me?
    Or: You've got what you prayed for. Look! I am he!

4. El: Stranger you're weaving some net or some snare.
    Or: If you are entangled, I'm also trapped there.

5. El: You mock my misfortune, make it a game.
    Or: I mock my own then, my misfortune's the same.
    El: Orestes! Orestes! Is that really your name?

Orestes
>You look at me and still can't recognize
>your bloodkin, your brother before your eyes.
>Yet when you looked at the lock I had laid
>you gasped as if gazing straight into my face.

[*Indicates lock of hair.*]
>Look that's where I lopped it from. Match it with mine.
>Look how alike, how akin the two locks are

[*Produces a piece of weaving.*]
>Look at this weaving your fingers once fashioned,
>the stroke of your batten, the patterns of beasts.

[ELECTRA *excited.*]
>Easy! Still! Keep all emotion masked within.
>Our "nearest and dearest" would like us destroyed.

Electra
>Beloved, beacon of this blacked-out bloodclan,
>the seed of deliverance watered by weeping.
>The love of four bloodkin belongs to you only —
>loathed mother, lost father, sacrificed sister

and brother, the bloodkin I truly believe in.

Brute force and bloodright and Zeus the high-he-god
be your protectors in pursuing our bloodgrudge.

Orestes

ZEUS, high he-god, steel us to the struggle,
fledglings left fatherless when the great eagle
got snarled in the shuffling coils of the she-snake,
fatherless fledglings, famished orphans too feeble
to carry the quarry off back to the eyrie,
fledglings and fatherless, Orestes, Electra,
both outcasts alike and blocked from their bloodright.
Eagle Agamemnon gave the he-gods a gift glut.
The godstones of Argos bubbled with bloodflow.
Cut down his egrets, your guts will go goatless.
With the bole of the bloodclan blasted no bull's gore
will gurgle down godstones on sacrifice days.
So nourish the nestlings, build up the bloodclan
though now it looks much too low to be lifted.

Chorus

Quiet, if you want your bloodclan rebuilding.
The whole space of Argos whispers with spies.
It only needs one to report to our rulers,
One day very soon I hope we'll be watching
their flesh spit through flames and bubbling pitch.

Orestes

Apollo stays close till all gets accomplished.
His oracle told me to push through our bloodgrudge.
And if I flinched from fulfilling the bloodgrudge
by killing those guilty of killing our father
he warned me my heart's blood would harden and freeze.
By not taking their lives my own would be taken
but not before tasting great torture and torments.
He detailed diseases, malignant malaises
the unappeased dead demand as appeasement —
skin-canker, skin-scabs, flaying the flesh raw,
crusted with fungus sprouting white bristles,
the perpetual prowling of the black pack of Furies

whose dark nightly saltlick 's the blood of my father,
darts from deep darkness, shafts shot from below
for the killing of bloodkin who bay for their bloodgrudge.
Frenzy and mania, phantoms at midnight,
venomous shadows that slink into his sleeptime.
He blinks, rubs his eyes. They're still at his bedside.

Harried and hounded out of his homeland,
a palsied pariah, scarred over by scourges,
flayed by brass flail-rods, a leprosied carcase.
Such scapegoats share in no wine-bowl libations.
No-one spares him bed, bread, or broth-bowl.
All godstones are barred him, and, gobbled alive
by bubos and fleshblight, he perishes friendless.

When that god says *do it* no-one says no.

Without any god-goad I've still got my grudges,
Still got my grief for Agamemnon, my father.
Dispossessed, I need no spurs to my spirit.
And these men of Argos, whose glory is greatest
who braved long war boldly and battered down Troy,
now sheepish and slave-like to a woman and she-man
who queens it beside the real clanchief, his consort.
This weapon I wield will unmask the woman.

Chorus

She-gods of life-lot
ZEUS high he-god

only gods can stop the rot
drag good up out of bad

Bloodflow for bloodflow
deathblow for deathblow

blood-debt for blood-debt
keeping the blades wet

bloodshed for bloodshed
keeping the blades red

What you do gets done back
you/him   him/you

hack slash   slash hack
three generations through

She-gods of life-lot
ZEUS high he-god

Orestes
Father, father doused in doom
kept immoveable by death
what can grope through your grave-gloom
unbreachable by light or breath?

What words can worm their way
through the sour soil of sorrow
what beacon of bright day
burrow your dark barrow?

From all the bloodclan's grave-rites
they barred and blocked your bones,
never-budging, held by night's
death-heavy anchorstones.

Chorus
The gnashing jaws of fire gnaw
only the corpse's rotten flesh.
His bloodgrudge goes on craving gore
and doesn't crumble into ash.

When bloodkin keen the killer feels
their dirges haunt him like halloos.
The hounds of grief bay at his heels,
the dead demanding their blood-dues.

A bloodkin's dirge is a keening net
its trammels trawl for guilt
mourning spreads its mesh to get
guilt netted   gaffed   and killed.

Electra
Now it's Electra your she-child

who mourns and beats her breast.
The wailing comes out rushed and wild
long cooped up and repressed.

Now listen to your she-child's dirge
he-child, she-child both in turn,
both exiles, outcasts urge
your spirit from its urn.

bout one bout two we lost to fate
the same fate that threw you
unless your spirit lends its weight
bout three will be lost too.

Chorus

Gods can make a gravedirge glad
dragging good up from the bad.

Instead of dirges we might sing

Welcome home, new clanchief, King!

Orestes

I wish that you had lost your life
to a Trojan in the War
not netted by a treacherous wife
your bathtrough grimed with gore.

Then hero's honor you'd bequeath.
We could have borne it if your bones
were still in Asia and beneath
a tomb of towering stones.

Chorus

A hero in a hero's grave!
A tombcairn like a tower!
The comfort of the clanchief's stave
Still wielding its old power!

A monument, a glorious mound
Dignity no shame
Agamemnon underground
with still unblemished name!

Electra

No hero's cairn, not killed, not dead!
No mass-grave by Scamander.
I want fate standing on its head
the goose hacked by the gander!

As your killers hacked you, hack,
hack down your killers first.
I want time to be turned back
my father's fate reversed.

Chorus

North of the North Wind lives a clan
spared the mortal lot of man

but this is South, a man cannot
turn back the tide of his life-lot.

Gold comes cheaper than new blood
but you are young and dream of good.

When you two drum your palms together
the pulse gets passed down to your father.

If those with bloodguilt beat the ground
their gloves of blood will dull the sound

but the dead respond to you
the guitless tone of your tattoo

underground the dead decide
Agamemnon's on your side.

Orestes

The bloodgrudge! ZEUS! It's been asleep.
Drag it up from its earthen bed.
The bloodgrudge bond that I've to keep
's to strike my mother dead.

Chorus

Aegisthus, Clytemnestra killed
I'll shout a joyful shout.
My heart's been bursting ages, filled
with all the hate I now let out.

Electra
> ZEUS your great steel fists one two
> crunch their skulls with all your might.
> Our country needs new trust in you
> bloodwrong to yield a new bloodright.

Chorus
> The law's the law: when blood gets spilled
> there's no rest till the killer's killed.

> Bloodflow for bloodflow the doomsong goes —
> blood shrieks for the Fury as it flows

> The Fury forges the long bloodchain —
> the slain that link the slain that link the slain . . .

Orestes
> Grudges of the dead below
> look we're the dregs of a royal race,
> the bloodclan of Atreus brought so low.

> ZEUS! Which way leads us from disgrace?

Chorus
> My heart-strings snap, my heart goes black
> it darkens if you weaken,
> but when I see your strength come back
> hope blazes like a beacon.

Electra
> *Our* strength's that we've survived the trials
> the one who bore us brought us.
> I'll bare my wolf-fangs when she smiles
> Wolf mothers breed wolf daughters.

Chorus
> As in Persia both fists pound
> a dervish-like delirium,
> till the skull's blood-pulses sound
> like a battered battle-drum.

Electra
> Wolf mother murdering your man!
> Agamemnon got no graveside
> lamentation from his clan,

dumped in a ditch you dug dry-eyed.

Orestes

A ditch! The wolf-bitch dug his shame
I'll hack my mother down to save
Agamemnon's blood-grimed name
then gladly go to my own grave.

Chorus

To stop his bloodgrudge in its tracks
she hacked off his cock, his hands, his feet,
cleavered the king with her man-axe
and jointed him like butcher's meat.

Electra

And I imprisoned in a poky pen,
cooped and kennelled like a rabid cur.
Let all the grief I poured out then
become the rage you pour on her.

Chorus

Yes, let it fire the rage you feel.
Two bouts are lost. The bout to be
depends upon your fire and steel,
hot heart, cool head to win bout three.

[*All addressing Agamemnon's tomb.*]

Orestes

Be in my corner, help me win.

Electra

Father all my tears say fight!

Chorus

All as one cry: back your bloodkin,
come up, come up into the light.

Orestes

Bloodright versus bloodright! Ours or theirs?

Electra

Gods, make it ours the juster cause.

Orestes

It scalds my skull to know your prayers
unlock doom's long-barred doors.

Chorus

> This clan's got ruin in its veins,
> its blood-strung lyre's cacophonous.
> The chords it strums are death-black strains.
> Its wounds don't scab. They spurt out pus.
>
> The only way such sores get better
> 's keep the cure within the clan.
> The clan's its own leach, own blood-letter,
> It's medicament's: man murder man.
>
> Groundgods down below it's you
> all our prayers are going to.
> Back Agamemnon's child-bloodkin
> and will with god-wills that they win.

Orestes

> You, the great clanchief, were killed like a cur.
> I pray for your help to be lord of your bloodclan.

Electra

> I pray for escape from the bondage I've suffered
> but not before shedding the blood of Aegisthus.

Orestes

> Then only then, in accord with clan custom,
> can a fitting funeral be offered with feasting,
> or, when fate and gore on the sacrifice crackle
> Agamemnon alone gets no goat to his glory.

Electra

> And, from what you bequeath me, your burial barrow
> will be overflowing with bridal libations.
> On the day that I marry your mound will mean most.

Orestes

> Earth, she-god, let my father back me.

Electra

> Persephassa, she-ground-god, grant victory.

Orestes

> Remember the bathtrough where you were struck dead!

Electra

> Remember the net-thing cast over your head.

Orestes
> In silk stuff not steelware you spewed out your blood.

Electra
> Humbled and hacked down under a hood.

Orestes
> Don't taunts such as these torment you down there?

Electra
> Shove your head through the earth to show us you care!

Orestes [*To Agamemnon's grave.*]
> Bloodright! I want it to back me in the bout   that's to be.
> I want the headlock on them that they got on you,
> flatten them to the floor as they flattened you.
> They outwrestled you, but I'll best then this bout.

Electra
> This last, then no more. Eagle Agamemnon
> your egrets call you from your grave-eyrie,
> fledglings and fatherless, he-child and she-child.

Orestes
> Don't let the seed of Pelops perish for ever.
> Death's no death when the blood-kinder flourish,
> blood-kinder, cork-floats that keep the net bouyant,
> when the flax-strings get sodden they keep it from sinking.
> For the sake of your spirit we've spent this time pleading
> Grant us your grace and your ghost's the first gainer.

Chorus
> Since his grave has been given no clan lamentation
> the length of your mourning was right and becoming.
> Now you've gorged on your grave-dirge, go into action,
> and find out where fate and your life-lot will lead you.

Orestes
> So I will but before I do battle I want to be told
> why she sent out this crowd of you carrying cups,
> libations so late for a crime past all curing.
> Neither the honey, the milk, the wine nor the water
> have savor or solace for skulls without senses.
> What you pour may be precious but paltry as godsops.
> The grave-gifts so meager, the crime so immense.

A man can daub tombs with all his hives' honey,
swill all his winestores over the stones,
empty his flocks' and herds' udders daily,
waste all his water, and still smell of murder,
so what do they mean Clytemnestra's libations?

Chorus

I know what they mean. Clytemnestra had nightmares.
Shaken by shadows that slunk into her sleeptime.
Now, though she's godless, she sends gifts to his gravestone.

1. **Or:** Is there more to the dream you can tell me about?
    Ch: She opened her legs and a serpent crawled out.

2. **Or:** Tell me the rest if you know how it goes.
    Ch: She swathed her snake-baby in swaddling clothes.

3. **Or:** This baby, this snake-thing how did she feed it?
    Ch: She says that it sucked at her very own tit.

4. **Or:** And did it not pain her to give a snake suck?
    Ch: Bloodclots came out with each mouthful it took.
    Or: No dream, mother, here's your snake-baby. Look!

Chorus

She shrieked out in her sleep and woke with a start.
All the doused torchlights made eyeless for night-time
blazed out of their blindness to comfort the queen.
At dawn she despatched us with the dead man's libations
to lance the pus-bloated source of her sorrows.

Orestes

Then by the earth and the grave of my father
I pray I'm this vision's fleshly fulfiller.
The snake came out of the same womb as I did
swathed in the same swaddling clothes as myself,
sucked at the same breast I sucked as a baby,
got bloodclots mixed in, as it sucked the sweet milk out,
so that she who gave suck screamed out in a panic.
Same womb, same swaddling clothes, same breast to suck on,
blood and milk, all point to me, and to murder!
the son in the snake-scales sent as her slayer.

Chorus

My reason tells me that you read the dream rightly.

Now give your instructions to those on your side,
who should work with you, who should be watchers.

Orestes

Simple.   My sister must stay in the palace
keeping the bond struck between us a secret.
By cunning they killed.   By cunning they'll die
caught in the same net they caught Agamemnon.
Apollo commands it and Apollo's a prophet
whose habit has never been falsehood before.

I, like a stranger with backpack and bundles,
will come in this guise to the gates of the courtyard,
with Pylades here, son of Strophius of Phocis
bound to our bloodclan by handclasp and spearbond.
We'll both of us speak like they do on Parnassus
assuming the accent of the folk back in Phocis.
If the gateman's ungracious and treats us with gruffness
on the grounds that this house is afflicted by fate
we'll stay so that passers-by stop and start saying:
"Aegisthus goes against all god-ordained guestright
by keeping these wanderers waiting unwelcomed."
But once past the gatelodge and into the palace
if I find that creature on the throne of my father
before he gets chance for looking me over
and asking "Where does the stranger hail from" I'll strike.
My answer to him will be straight to the point,
straight to the swordpoint, guts on my skewer.
The Fury that squats in this clan's never famished,
never gone short of its gore-shots to guzzle.
This third and last cup's to quaff undiluted.

Orestes

Electra, keep watch on what happens within
so that the details all dovetail in neatly.

[*To* CHORUS.]

Keep quiet where you can, to take care when talking.

[*To* PYLADES.]
> And Pylades, my companion, keep close to me.
> See I wield my sword well in the fight that's to follow.

[*Exeunt* ORESTES, PYLADES, ELECTRA.]
Chorus
> What Earth breeds is appalling.
> Monsters rock in the arms of the sea.
> Fearful sky-flames flare and fall
> through terrible void territory.

> Monsters, metors, sea, soil, space,
> things that fly, creep, crawl,
> of all these horrors the human race
> is the terror that tops them all.

> Male boasting, pride in being HE
> only one thing's got that beat
> bursting the bedbond bestially
> the female bitch on heat!

1. When Althaia was brought to bed
   with Meleager, fate
   prophesied he'd soon be dead
   if a log burnt in the grate.

   Plucked from flames under lock and key
   the half-burnt brand's the boy's life-charm.
   Safe with his mother, except that she
   will be the one who does him harm.

   Her son killed two of her bloodkin
   and murderous mother Althaia
   flung the half-burnt log back in
   the life-devouring fire.

2. King of Megara, Nisos,
   his life-charm was on his head,
   one strangely purple lock whose loss
   would mean he would be dead.

She knew this, she-child Skylla,
another bitch on heat,
she lopped the lock, foul father-killer
for the sake of the king of Crete.

The king of Crete had dangled gold
before her greedy eye.
For a paltry chain she sold
Megara and watched her father die.

Megara burnt, her people slain,
Minos keel-hauled her by her feet,
dragged her from his anchor chain
the whole way back to Crete.

This bloodclan too. A bedbond void
of love by which a man's destroyed.
The plot against your manlord's life,
you the cunning killer wife.

Against a man his enemies revered
and all his spear-foes justly feared.

You prized a fireless hearth instead
a spearless she-man in your bed.

3.   LEMNOS! Its very name is vile
Clytemnestra should have been
of that murderous and manless isle
the killer queen.

Queen of women who wield knives
or slaughtered husband's sword.
The Lemnos husband-killing wives.
LEMNOS — name to be abhorred.

The swordpoint pricks against the skin
ready to be driven in.

Bloodright pushes at the hilt
to broach the gory springs of guilt.

The transgressors, those who trod
down the laws of ZEUS, high he-god.

Bloodright's the whetstone where fate whets
the blades demanding old blood-debts.

Bloodgrudge leads the son at last
to purge the bloodspill of the past.

[*Enter* ORESTES *and* PYLADES *as Phocians.*]

Orestes

Gateman! Gateman! Can't you hear all this knocking?
Anyone there? Gateman! Gateman! Is there no-one on duty?
This is the third time of knocking. Is nobody there?
Are the good laws of guestright ignored by Aegisthus?

Gateman

I hear you. I hear you. Where you from, stranger?

Orestes

Go tell your masters there's someone with tidings.
And quick. The warcar of night drives on the darkness.
Time travellers were thinking about dropping anchor
in a place that makes all wayfarers welcome.
Fetch someone out in authority here.
Fetch the mistress. No, maybe the man would be fitter.
With women words have to be guarded and careful.
But man to man I can say what I mean and no hedging.

[*Enter* CLYTEMNESTRA.]

Clytemnestra

Stranger, all you've to do is declare what your need is.
Such a house can supply every kindness and comfort —
warm baths, beds that are balm to limbs worn by travel,
honest eyes that watch over your wishes and wants.
But if what you've come for is weightier counsel
that's work for the menfolk, and I'll see that you meet.

Orestes

I'm not from these parts but from Daulis in Phocis.
I was trekking to Argos, my gear in this backpack
when I meet with a stranger who asks where I'm off to.

I tell him Argos, and, when he hears that, this stranger,
Strophius a Phocian (that's who the man turned out to be)
says to me: "Since you're, in any case, going to Argos
you could save me a journey and take me a message,
a message concerning a man called Orestes.
Announce to the parents in Argos the death of Orestes.
Then ask if they want him fetched home, his ashes,
or if he's to lie here in Phocis for ever an exile.
A good bronze urn guards his ashes at present.
His ashes got tears shed. The man got some mourning."

I pass on his words as he spoke them, not knowing
if whom I'm addressing 's directly related.
It seems proper to speak to a parent in person.

Clytemnestra

Your news brings the whole house down on our heads.
Ungrappleable bloodgrudge that bullies this bloodclan,
possessing the piercing sharp eye of the preybird
takes aim from safe ambush to send its sharp shafts home.
You strip me of near ones, leaving me naked.
And now Orestes . . . who seemed to tread surely,
who kept clear of the clay this bloodclan gets stuck in.
He was the one hope we still held for this household,
the balm we all banked on for the bloodgrudge's orgies.
Orestes, our hope, must be crossed off the rollcall.

Orestes

With hosts such as you here so favored by fortune
I'd more gladly be a guest whose tidings were good ones.
Between host and guest there's no goodwill greater.
But the bonds that I've given both bind me to truth,
my bond to Strophius, my guest-bond as stranger.

Clytemnestra

Your words won't make you the less warmly welcomed.
If you hadn't brought them someone was bound to.
It's time now that travellers who've spent the day trekking
should cease feeling footsore and seek out their comforts.

[*To attendants.*]

Take them to where the man-guests get quartered,
him and the man who's his travelling companion.
Supply them with comforts this palace is famed for.
Serve them in all things or answer to me.
Meanwhile I'll convey your news to the clanchief
and along with all our true loyal supporters
we'll hold a clan council and consider the case.

[*Exeunt* CLYTEMNESTRA, ORESTES, PYLADES.]

Chorus

Loyal supporters of the true bloodkin
when can we let our pent feelings out,
when snatch out the galling gag of grief
and give Orestes the victory shout?

Earth she-god, high gravemound
dumped on the lord of the seas
send help up from underground
prosper these prayers and pleas.

Word-guile, word-guile gets things done
and ground-god Hermes who can throw
dust in the eyes of everyone
pushes the blade in from below.

It seems our fake Phocian is working already.
I see the old nurse of Orestes walking here weeping.
Cilissa! Where are you going to through the gateyard
with woe the unwanted one walking beside you.

Nurse

Queen Clytemnestra says "Quick fetch Aegisthus!"
to meet man to man with some strangers who've come,
confront them in person and hear the new tidings . . .
In front of the serfs she faked grief on her features
but her eyes through the mask wore nothing like mourning.
Nay they blazed like joy beacons at what had befallen.
The news that's been brought's a great bane for this bloodclan
but for Aegisthus a just cause for rejoicing.
This household's caused me perpetual heartache.

No bane to his bloodclan ever beat this one.
Death shook the house and I shrugged — but now it's Orestes,
my little Orestes, who I wore out my life for.
Came straight off his mother and got clapped to my paps.
Got these very breasts as a baby, Orestes!
Trouble! That lad gave me trouble in tonloads!
Led me a dance he did, demanding, demanding,
getting me up from my couch with his crying,
and when I was with him there was nothing he wanted.
They're like puppies, aren't they though, babies?
Still in their nappies what can they do? Nothing!
While they lack language they just keep you guessing —
is it hunger or thirst pangs or wanting to piddle.
their little bellies just do it regardless.
You have to read minds, keep one jump ahead
or else you get caught with their crap to clean out.
Wet nurse and washerwoman I was to Orestes.
Had him entrusted by King Agamemnon.
Now I hear that he's dead, my dear little baby.
I'm off to Aegisthus, the bane of this bloodclan.
When he hears of the death, he'll be glad and delighted.

1. **Ch:** How is he to come? Does she say how, the queen?
   Nu: How? Don't get you. Don't know what you mean.

2. **Ch:** I mean does she tell him to come armed or not?
   Nu: O armed and attended! His spearmen! The lot!

Chorus
Then tell him there's no need of his combatant gear.
Tell Aegisthus there's joy in what he's to hear.
Tell him come quickly the man we all hate.
"The messenger's mouth sets a twisted tale straight."

3. **Nu:** Are you trying to tell me this news makes you glad?
   Ch: Why not? If ZEUS will make good out of bad.

4. **Nu:** But Orestes, our one hope, he's gone as you know.
   Ch: Only a blind seer would say that was so.

5. **Nu:** What are you saying? Is there more to be known?

Ch: The gods will do their work. You do your own.

Nurse

I will. I'm off with my message. I've no doubt
the gods in their wisdom will sort it all out.

Chorus

Chief of the godclans, ZEUS, now send
this house a balanced end.

Let the lovers of good law
get the bloodright they've longed for.

Let the man who's gone within
meet with his enemies and win.

If you help him your godstone
will get more goats than it's ever known.

The colt of one dear to your heart.
's coupled to disaster's cart.

Now that he's nearly won his race
see he keeps up his winning pace.

Don't let him slacken off so late
and falter half-way down the straight.

Gods of this clan's rich stores
the feelings that we have are yours.

Let fresh bloodflow now wash clean
all the bloodflow that has been.

Dry old murder's loins make barren
the teeming womb of this blood-warren.

APOLLO, healer, whose light even
makes the deep dark cave a haven.

Let this bloodclan's latest one
lift his eyes up to the sun.

Let the beacon of bright freedom blaze
through the veils of murk and haze.

HERMES, guile-god, if you choose,
those you champion can't lose.

You blind their opponents so
they can't see the coming blow.

Those you help see through the dark
and shoot their weapons at the mark.

Their targets can't see. All they feel
's their hearts pierced suddenly by steel.

Then sing this bloodclan brought to land
out of the wild sea, beached on sand.

Like the women of fishermen who wail
until they glimpse the first white sail.

The wind drops, the dark sky clears
the women's wailing turns to cheers.

Cheers as the laden ships reach shore
and loved one suffer storm no more.

And when the deed is to be done
courage when she calls you SON

Shout back MY FATHER'S, call his name
do the blood-deed with no blame.

Be like Perseus, one who slew
a monster woman as will you.

Those below the earth and those above
want their bloodgrudge not son's love.

Plunge your sword up to the hilt
in the cause of this bloodguilt.

[*Enter* AEGISTHUS.]
Aegisthus
Here I am as the messenger summoned.
I'm told certain strangers have brought baleful tidings,
news most unwelcome, the death of Orestes.

The beast's back's already rubbed raw by its burdens
and now it gets plagued by another sore pack-gall.
Am I to take this as fact and as proven
or is it mere women's talk starting a panic,
words flying and burning themselves out for nothing?
Who knows anymore to make it all plainer?

Chorus

We heard the same story as you, but we're only women!
You don't need to listen to second-hand hearsay,
go inside straightaway and question the strangers.

Aegisthus

Yes, I want to have the messenger questioned
if he himself witnessed the death of Orestes
or whether he's simply passing on rumors.
I'm too open-eyed to be gulled or outsmarted.

[*Exit* AEGISTHUS.]

Chorus

Both bloodblades are now drawn out
for the final killing bout.

Either Clytemnestra's cleaver
finishes the clan for ever

or Agamemnon's son can light
the beacon, freedom, in black night.

In the blood-bout two to one,
back up Agamemnon's son.

[*A cry from the palace. Should be identical to cry of Agamemnon.*]

Aegisthus

Aaaaggghhh!

Chorus

Listen! Whose was that cry? The clan's in the balance.
But better we women withdraw till it's settled.
Whatever the outcome we must seem to be blameless.
One way or another the battle's decided.

[*Enter* SERVANT.]
Servant

> He's killed. The master! He's killed. The master. Aegisthus.
> Open the door to the women's apartments . . .
> A strong arm's needed, though he's past help, Aegisthus.
>
> Help! Help! Everyone's deaf there's no point in shouting.
> Deaf or asleep. But where's Clytemnestra?
> Her head's the next one due for the hackblock.
> The axeshaft's poised in the clenched fist of bloodright.

[*Enter* CLYTEMNESTRA.]
Clytemnestra

> Who's that shouting for help in the palace?

Servant

> The dead, the dead are hacking the living down.

Clytemnestra

> Ah, your riddle's by no means baffling to me.
> We're to be killed by the same guile we killed by.
> Get me my man-axe, my king-cleaver. Quick!

[*Exit* SERVANT.]

> We'll put to the test who's victor, who's vanquished.

[*Enter* ORESTES *and* PYLADES.]
Orestes

> It's you I'm after. He's had enough the one inside.

Clytemnestra

> Ah, dead, dead! My shield, dear Aegisthus.

Orestes

> Your *dear* Aegisthus? Then into his grave-bed.
> Continue your coupling as cold stiffened corpses,
> carry on tupping under your tombcairn.

Clytemnestra

> Orestes! Have pity! These breasts you nestled on
> and nuzzled the nipples for their nourishing milk.

Orestes

> [*To* PYLADES.] Pylades! What shall I do? Shame, pity, awe,
> all make me shrink from killing my mother

Pylades

    Remember Apollo and all that you swore
    Give grudge to mankind but not to the godclan

Orestes

    I remember. You were right to remind me

[*To* CLYTEMNESTRA.]

    Inside! I want to kill you on top of his body.
    Since you preferred him (when alive!) to my father.
    Aegisthus greater than King Agamemnon!
    The one you should have showered love on not hatred.

    Sleep beside your dear one even in death.

1. **Clyt:** I want to grow old with the son these breasts fed!
   Or: My father's murderess eating my bread!

2. **Clyt:** The she-god of Fate, son, she played her part.
   Or: The same she-god then drives my sword through your heart.

3. **Clyt:** Your mother's bloodgrudges, don't they make you scared?
   Or: Would a mother throw her son out if she had cared?

4. **Clyt:** Not thrown out, sent to an ally when Argos got hot.
   Or: *Sold!* A chief's son, a free man, and sold for what?

5. **Clyt:** Yes, if I sold you, what was my pay?
   Or: Too shameful to think of, let alone say.

6. **Clyt:** What of your father? What of his shame?
   Or: He suffered. You sat here. Spare him your blame.

7. **Clyt:** A woman suffers with her man at the wars.
   Or: But his toil supports her while she sits indoors.

8. **Clyt:** So you'll condemn me, your mother, to die.
   Or: Your own actions condemn you, mother, not I.

9. **Clyt:** Your mother's bloodgrudges llike dogs will hunt you.
   Or: I'm hunted by my father's so what can I do?

10. **Clyt:** Deaf as the gravehole my son pays no heed.
    Or: When my father was murdered *you* started to bleed.

11. **Clyt:** You! You were the snake crawled out of my womb.
    Or: Your nightmare was true. It showed you your tomb.
    You killed my father. I kill my mother.
    One blood-wrong gives birth to another.

[ORESTES *and* PYLADES *take* CLYTEMNESTRA *off.*]
Chorus
> I can spare some pity for this fallen couple,
> but better Orestes surfs over this bloodcrest
> than the eye of the bloodclan is shuttered for ever.

> Time brings bloodright to blast Troy.
> Agamemnon's house next call.
> Two lions enter and destroy
> the house, and now the lions fall.

> Orestes, guided by Apollo
> comes home and hacks them dead.
> The distant exile has to follow
> the god-goad in his head.

> At last this house is freed,
> restored to its old health.
> Dead the ones who let it bleed
> away its wealth.

> The killer had to be concealed.
> He counterfeited then attacked.
> Bloodright, Zeus's she-child, steeled
> his right hand as he hacked.

> At last this house is freed
> restored to its old health
> dead the ones who let it bleed
> away its wealth.

> APOLLO cries from deep cleftshrine
> *guile crushes guile, deceit deceit!*

We've got to trust whatever divine
power helps us to our feet.

The beacon's relit
light's in the halls

harsh chain and bit
cause no more galls

House of Atreus stand
get up off the ground.

Time brings it all about,
scrubs the blood off the bricks,
drives the bloodgrudge squatters out.
Now all three dice say six!

The beacon's relit
light's in the halls
harsh chain and bit
cause no more galls

House of Atreus stand
get up off the ground.

[*Palace doors open.* ORESTES *with bodies of* CLYTEMNESTRA *and*
AEGISTHUS. *The tableau repeats the stance of* CLYTEMNESTRA
over AGAMEMNON *and* CASSANDRA.]

Orestes

Here they are, the two tyrants who crushed you.
They killed my father and blasted the bloodclan.
Puffed up with pride they were, up on their thronestools,
and still in love, look, still clinging so closely,
carrying their bedbond into the grave-hole.
The pledges they gave have both been accomplished —
kill my father together, together to fall.

[*Shows robe.*]

Now look again, you who are here to bear witness.
The contrivance they fangled to fetter my father
both his hands and feet held fast and hobbled.

Spread the thing out. Gather round in a circle,
display the great cloak-shroud so that the father (not mine
but the sun who sees all things I mean by the father)
can see the crime of my mother in all its true grimness,
so when I stand trial the Sun will bear witness
that Orestes was right to go through with this killing.
Right to kill his mother. As for Aegisthus —
he got the just death all adulterers deserve.
What of her who hatched this horror up for her husband,
whose children she carried under her girdle,
a burden apparently loved but really abhorrent,
what about her? If she'd been shark-hag or viper
just the mere feel of her, without any fang-marks
would turn her poor victim purple with poison,
make him all stiff and all swollen with blood.
Her spirit alone spurts out putrefaction.

[*Shows robe again.*]

What shall I call It? What name gives it status?
Net to snare animals, shroud for a corpse,
drape for a bath-trough. No, net's the best name.
Call it a hunting net, trip-rope, a trap-robe,
an ideal device for roadside desperadoes
who lurk by the highway waylaying wayfarers.
With one of these they'd snare them in thousands.

Rather than end up with a wife like my mother
I'd rather die without heir, without he-child.

Chorus

In that net you bled to death
a butchered carcase bathed in blood.
For the one who still draws breath
suffering bursts into bud.

Orestes

Did she do the deed or not? This is my witness,
the cloth all becrimsoned by the sword of Aegisthus.
The embroidery rotted by time and by bloodstains.
Wailing over this web gives my father this gravedirge.

My dirge is for all the deeds done by this bloodclan.
I've won this bout but the laurels are blood-smirched

Chorus

no man's life-lot ever goes
painless till the post is passed
Man gets preyed on by his woes
from his first day to his last.

Orestes

I've got to tell you. The whole thing's unending.
My chariot races. I rein my team in as they're charging.
The uncontrolled horses crash into the trackrails.
They gallop my mind off, dragging behind them.
Fear squats in my mind, plays music for scaring.
But while I still have some grip I say to the Argives,
I was right to kill Clytemnestra: my mother,
daubed in my father's blood, hated by he-gods.
Apollo's voice was my chief provocation:
Do what you have to, and go away guiltless.
Don't do it and . . . The pains that he promised
were out of all range of man's usual troubles.
I go as a suppliant to Apollo's great godstone
where purifying fires are forever kept burning,
exiled for shedding the blood of my bloodkin.
Apollo said I should only seek help from this godstone.
I beg men of Argos now and in future
to bear witness as to how these horrors happened
I go as a wanderer, exiled from my bloodright.
Living or dead, I leave you my memory.

Chorus

The memory will be of a man who did well.
Don't burden your mouth with any bad-omens.
You've brought freedom back to the city of Argos
by lopping the heads off two serpents at once.

1. **Or:** Ah! Look! Coming! Gorgons. Garb black, entwined
    with snakes for hair. I've got to run.
    Ch: It's nothing, Orestes. It's all in your mind.
    Fear nothing. Your father's pleased with his loyal son.

2. **Or:**   These aren't in the mind. They're real and they're near.
           My mother's grudge-dogs close at my heels.
    Ch: Orestes, it's fresh blood on your hands makes you fear.
           It's only blood-frenzy your spirit feels.

3. **Or:**   Apollo! Look at them. More! More! More.
           Through black blood-ooze their eyes stare straight at me.
    Ch: Apollo's the one god to cleanse you of gore.
           The touch of Apollo will set you free.

Orestes
  You can't see them. I can though.
  They're baying for my blood. I've got to go.

[*Exit* ORESTES *pursued by* FURIES.]
Chorus
  Then let the god you go to, give
  you sustenance and help you live.

  This, the third stormblast to buffet this bloodclan.

  One: the banquet of babes, the bane of Thyestes.

  Two: the Achaean warlord hacked down in his bath-trough.

  Three: the deliverer . . .
                    or new doom in disguise?

  When will the blood-grudge be weaned
  off blood,
            when will it sleep,
                          the fiend?

END OF PART TWO

THREE: EUMENIDES

Characters   *Priestess*

Apollo

Orestes

Clytemnestra

Chorus of Furies

Athena

Procession of Women

[*Temple of Apollo at Delphi.*]
Priestess
> First in my prayers, Earth, Gaia, great she-god,
> primeval prophetess and eldest diviner.
> Then after her mother came Earth's she-child Themis
> who handed it on to the Titaness Phoebe,
> who bestowed it in turn on Apollo as birthgift.
> Leaving rocks and bog on the island of Delos
> Apollo made landfall on Attica's shoreline
> where Pallas has harbors bristling with ships' masts
> and then pushed on upwards as far as Parnassus
> escorted by offspring of Hephaistos the smithgod
> who laid roads for Apollo to lead him to Delphi.
> Those Athenians made the whole wilderness docile.
> When Apollo arrived, the people and Delphos,
> Delphos of Delphi, state-pilot and steersman
> greeted the young god with all welcome and worship.
> Zeus gave Apollo divine inspiration,
> make him fourth prophet here, and here he still is.
> Apollo's the mouth of Zeus, the high he-god.
>
> These prophet gods take first place in my prelude.
>
> Next Pallas Athene who stands before god-shrines.
> I honor the nymphs in the Corycian caverns
> hollow, where birds swoop, patrol place of spirits.
> Dionysus too has a presence in Delphi
> since the god headed his horde of Bacchantes
> and got Pentheus hunted and trapped like a hare.
> The spring of Pleistos, the power of Poseidon
> and Zeus the Fulfiller, the highest of he-gods!
>
> Now on the shrinestool, inspired and prophetic
> I hope that my powers are as strong or are stronger.
> Any Greeks here, come forward. Draw lots and enter.
> I'll give you the answers the god sends in trances. . . .

[PRIESTESS *enters the shrine. Silence. Then a scream. Then* PRIESTESS *comes out again on all fours like a dog.*]

Priestess

Terrible things to clap mortal eyes on
have made me bolt out of the house of Apollo.
Sapped of all strength my feet can't support me.
I scrabble on all fours. My legs have gone liquid.
A scared old woman crawling, worse than a baby.

Entering the innermost shrine with its garlands
I set eyes on a man at the shrine's central stone,
an abomination to gods in the suppliant's seat.
His hands dripped blood. He had his drawn sword out.
He held an olive-branch tipped with white wool tufts.
In front of this person, a strange group of she-hags
sighing and snorting, asleep on the thronestools.
Not women really, but more like the Gorgons.
I call them Gorgons but they weren't that exactly.
I once saw a picture of Harpiae, Graspers.
unflaggingly swooping on Phineus the Thracian,
keeping the blind king in perpetual tension,
filched his food off him or left it beshitten,
splattered their bat-bowels over his platters
and kept him terror-stricken and starving.
These were black like Harpiae but they were wingless.
The snorts from their nostrils would keep you a mile off.
Their eye-sockets glued with sickening ooze-clots.
Their grave-garb's all wrong for the statues of godheads
nor would it seem right in the houses of mortals.
Don't know what brute-clan this brood belongs to,
what region would want to boast that it bred them
and didn't wish now that their birth had aborted.
What happens now depends on the master of Delphi,
Doxias Apollo, sign reader, all powerful, healer.

He purifies other's homes, let him cleanse his.

[*Exit* PRIESTESS .]

[*The inner shrine revealed.* ORESTES *and* APOLLO.]
Apollo

No, I'll never desert you. I'll guard you for ever,
either close by you, or if not, at a distance.
Towards all your enemies, like those pursuers,
I'll never show mildness, nor ever mellow.
I've put them to sleep, these creatures men spit on,
blood-battening bat hags, shrivelled but virgin,
crone-kinder no kind caresses, covers or couples.
Who'd tup these terrors? No god, man nor brute beast!
They're born to brew bale. They're evil for ever.
Their abode's the bottomless void black abyss,
abominations both to men and Olympian he-gods.

But still you must run. Don't flag and don't slacken.
They'll hound you through the whole length of the landmass,
tracking you over the well-beaten foot routes
then across seas, through cities lapped by the ocean.
Don't surrender. Don't let your step falter
by brooding on all the pain that you'll suffer.
When you come to the city of Pallas Athene
sit down in safety, embracing her image.
There we'll find judges and words of appeasement
and means to release you from this burden for ever.

I moved you, I, to murder your mother!
Orestes

Lord Apollo, you know about justice none better,
and since you know don't forget how to use it.
Apollo's potency goes without question.
Apollo

Remember that then! Don't give way to panic.

[Invokes HERMES.]

And Hermes, my brother, kin through one father
(and what bloodkin exists any closer than that?)
watch over Orestes, be Hermes Escorter.
Shepherd my suppliant. Guide him to Athens.
Zeus ever respects the rights of the outlawed.

[*Exeunt* APOLLO, ORESTES. *Enter* GHOST OF CLYTEMNESTRA *who
speaks to the still unseen* CHORUS OF FURIES *within.*]
Clytemnestra
You're supposed to be Furies and I find you sleeping!
When Furies need naps they're no longer Furies.
Dishonored, defamed by the dead that I dwell with,
I walk underground through a gauntlet of ghost-cries,
catcalls that brand my phantom with blood-guilt.
Slaughtered though I was by the hand of my he-child
not one spirit's incensed at the sore fate I've suffered.
Look here at my heart with hackmarks all over.
Remember too all those midnight libations,
not winebowls, but liquor much redder and thicker,
poured at the hour when there's only you stirring
while mortals are sleeping, gods in god-spaces.
But you trample and spurn all my spendthrift libations.
He's given you the slip the quarry you're hunting
like a nimble deer clearing the spread of your net-mesh
belling his beast-taunts as he bounds off for freedom.
Listen! It's for my after-life that I'm pleading.
Wake up, she-gods of underneath spaces.
The Clytemnestra you're dreaming calls you from sleep.

[FURIES *are heard within moaning in their sleep.*]
Clytemnestra
O make your cow noises! Your quarry's escaped.
he's lucky in *his* friends. At least they aren't Furies.

[FURIES *are heard again moaning.*]
Snoring and sleeping! Does my pain stir no pity?
Mother-killer Orestes got out of your clutches.

[*More* FURY *noises.*]
Sleeping and whining! Whining and sleeping! Wake up!
Aren't Furies supposed to make people suffer?

[*More* FURY *noises from within.*]
Fagged out by fatigue it sleeps off its labors
the she-snake, whose fangs have been syphoned of venom.

[FURIES *whine louder and higher.*]
Chorus of Furies
> Get him! Get him! Get him! There he goes!

Clytemnestra
> Dreaming of hunting, like dogs, but not *doing*!
> Baying like bloodhounds that track in their slumbers.
> Dreaming not *doing*! Get up and get going.
> Sleep only blunts your rage at my bloodwrong.
> My bloodgrudge should boost you back into action.
> Bloodgrudge is a goad to upholders of bloodright.
> Let your breath billow round him its gore-reeking gases.
> Shrivel his flesh with hot blasts from your bowels,
> fart fire through your flues till he flops like a fruitrind.
> Hound him and hunt him till he sags like a skin-bag.

[*Exit* GHOST OF CLYTEMNESTRA. *Enter* CHORUS OF FURIES *one by one.*]
Chorus
> Wake up! Wake up! Wake up your she-kin as I woke you.
> Still asleep? Then shake off your stupor.
> Make certain the chase here wasn't for nothing.

[CHORUS *searches for* ORESTES.]
> All for nothing! Pointless, pointless pursuit!
> Running till we dropped. A little nap.
> All for nothing. The blood-guilty brute
> still wide-awake leaps out of our trap.

[*Calling into* APOLLO's *sanctum.*]
> Apollo, Apollo, thief of a he-god!
> we she-gods have the ancientest rights,
> that you, a young he-god ride over roughshod.
> Strutting young upstart! We spit on such slights.

> You pamper this suppliant you hide,
> and he's a mother-killing son.
> a god condoning matricide!
> who'd see right in what you've done?

> grudge gored my gut like a goad in a racehorse.

Felt on my flesh like the flail of a flogger
sharp, vicious, whistling like pliable ice.
They do things like that the new era he-gods,
get their way only by forcing the feeble.

Look at his thronestool sticky with bloodspill.
His navelstone's only a blood-sodden hackblock.
Prophet Apollo pollutes his own godstone.

Of his own accord gets his stone caked with bloodclots.
He's breached all the godbonds to bolster up mortals,
poaching the preserves of she-fate and life-lot.
That abomination Apollo's protecting Orestes!

Has he crawled into the ground? Let him.
Wherever he is the FURIES will get him.

He brings his blood-guilt. Next in the chain's
the bloodgrudge-fulfiller who beats in *his* brains.

[*Enter* APOLLO.]
Apollo
Get out! Get out! Out you go! Out you go!
Leave the prophet's earthcleft free of pollution
or a serpent with wings on and venomous fangbane
shot from gold bowstrings will go through your gutbag!
You'll spew up black slavver of gobbled up goreswill,
gore-clots your crones' gobs sucked out of corpses.
Not a finger of yours should befoul my own hearth-fane.
You belong where heads go splat off the hackblock,
eyes get gouged out and lugged from their sockets,
where bloodright's castrations, boys' ballocks battered,
men spitted on stakespikes screaming for mercy.
Your bat-snouts go snorting in society's bloodtroughs.
It's the food you get fat on makes you hated by he-gods.
all your appearance says blood food and filth baths.
You hags should live in the beast dens in jungles,
dark lairs all larded with shit and chewed gristle,
not here, contagious to all you come close to.
Get out! Out you go! You goats with no goatherd!

Chorus
>Thank you, Apollo! Now may we reply?
>Apollo, how can you pose as a simple abettor
>when you and you only bear all the bloodguilt?

1. **Ap:** How? At least explain that charge. But then you must go.
   Ch: He killed his mother, because you said so.

2. **Ap:** To avenge his dead father as any son should.
   Ch: You harbored him here with his hands red with blood.

3. **Ap:** I told him to come here to be purged of bloodstains.
   Ch: And we drove him here, but get abuse for our pains.

4. **Ap:** You're not fit to set foot here, such hags as you.
   Ch: We did only the work that we're destined to do.

5. **Ap:** And what "special mission" have you ever had?
   Ch: The mission of driving matricides mad!

6. **Ap:** And if it's her manlord a woman has killed?
   Ch: That wouldn't be bloodkin's blood that has been spilled!

Apollo
>So you'd scorn bondright, the man/woman bedbond?
>Hera, high she-god and Zeus, the high he-god,
>they even swore vows and were coupled in bondright.
>So you'd dishonor and cast on the midden
>the she-god of love, Aphrodite of Cyprus,
>she with whose help men form bonds of the closest?
>That bedbond's sanctified by the she-gods of life-lot
>and needs no other oath if the guardian's justice.
>So if one murders her mate in the bedbond
>and you slacken your rigid rule against slaughter
>then it's unjust your pursuit of Orestes.
>One crime you come down on, the other pass over.

>Athena must judge between bloodright and bondright.

7. **Ch:** He'll never escape, I'll go on pursuing.
   Ap: Do, by all means, it's your own bale you'll be brewing.

8. **Ch:** You can't belittle our rights for all your abuse.

Ap: I wouldn't take them, for nothing, even from Zeus!

9. Ch: Yes, we've heard you're well in with the throne!
But with shed mother-blood blazing the trail
I'll keep on pursuing till the end of the hunt.

10. Ap: You do your "duties." I'll do my own —
which is protecting my suppliant. If I fail
his rage will cause men and gods great affront.

[*Exit* APOLLO. *Exeunt* CHORUS *sniffing for the trail. Scene changes to Athens. Before the image of* ATHENA, ORESTES *clasps the image.*]

Orestes

Athena, high she-god, I was sent by Apollo.
Look on me kindly, I'm cursed and an outcast.
Though still a cursed outcast there's no need of more cleansing.
My bloodguilt's been blunted enough by my contact
with places and peoples who helped my purgation.
All this was decreed by Apollo at Delphi.
I've crossed land and sea to your house and your statue.
Until the issue's decided I stay beside you.

[*Enter* CHORUS, *one by one, still sniffing the blood-trail.*]

Chorus

Here! He's left a very clear track behind him.
We don't need his cries but only these bloodclues.
Like hounds tracking down a deer that's been bleeding
we bound between blood-drips till our quarry's cornered.
This manhunt's a killer. I pant with exhaustion.
We've combed the whole land, the coastline, the ocean,
swift flotilla of Furies, wingless sea-eagles.
My nostrils say here he's cornered and cowering.
The glad smell of gore smiles its warm welcome.

seek seek scour the ground
the mother-killer's got to be found

Sniff at the trail. The blood's still wet.
Don't let him flee from paying his debt.

He's there! And once again, look, begging protection,
this time his arms are wound round a she-god.
He won't pay his blood-dues. He wants to "stand trial."
What rubbish *trials* are when the blood shed's a mother's!

A mother's blood has run away
into the earth it goes to stay

The blood that trickles on the ground
's not balls of thread to be rewound.

Trial! This is the trial your trackers intend:
first suck red libations from limbs while they're living,
browse on your blood, all over your body,
broach you all bloodless, haul your husk off below,
a morsel of torment for your own mother's murder.
Down there you'll see all those who've offended
a god or a guest or the parents who got them,
get the blood-doom their deeds have duly deserved.

Hades, death-god holds assize
on a man's deeds when he dies

death-god Hades won't forget
the deed of blood and the blood-debt.

Orestes

I've been through them all, the forms of purgation,
rites which used speech, rites which used silence.
Here my wise mentor says words are in order.
The blood on my hands has already grown drowsy;
it lowers its eyelids. The stains have stopped staring.
It was washed off with pig's blood by Phoebus Apollo.
My hosts came to no harm by giving me housing.
So the mouth's unpolluted that pleads with Athena,
god-queen of the country, to come to my rescue.
She won't need her spear to make long-lasting allies
of me and my country, and the people of Argos.
Whether she's now in the Libyan deserts,
or by Lake Tritonis, her Libyan birthplace,
seated and skirted to receive men's obeisance,

or booted for battle, as brave as a he-god,
siding with her friends on the Phlegrean flatlands —

As a she-god she'll hear me over great spaces.
Come, Athena, come now to my rescue!

Chorus
Neither the power of Apollo, nor the power of Athena
can save you from perishing spurned and abandoned,
even forgetting that joy had a meaning,
broached of blood, banquetted on, flesh pod, shadow,
a shrivelled up fruitrind squeezed dry of its juices.
Won't answer! Spits what we say back in our faces.
Our little sacrifice all ready for slicing!
No need of godstones, we'll eat you still living.
It will swaddle you helpless, our "lullaby" listen —

She-kin, show our force. Join hands!
Dance the doom-dance steps, display
through our grim music that our band's
a power over men that gets its way:

Our mission's bloodright, we're not sent
ever to harm the innocent

Show us your hands. If they're not red
you'll sleep soundly in your bed.

Show us your hands. Left. Right.
You'll live unhunted if they're white.

Show us *your* hands. There's one we know
whose hands are red and daren't show.

With men like him whose hands are red
we are the bloodgrudge of the dead.

Our band of witnesses pursues
the bloodkin-killer for blood-dues.

NIGHT, Night, Mother Night
who bore us to uphold bloodright,
Leto's he-child takes away

the rights you gave us to our prey,
this cringing beast, this cowering whelp
evades us with that he-god's help.
Apollo's foiled us of the hide
of our allotted matricide.

Victim! Victim!
Listen! Our song!

The Furies' lyreless lullaby's
music maddening men's mind

Victim! Victim!
Listen! Our song!

it binds man's brain and dries
man's fruity flesh to rind.

The she-god of life-lot gave us these powers,
ours, ours, for ever ours.

Those who kill their kin I hound
until I've got them underground.

Even dead they don't go free,
I torment them endlessly . . .

Victim! Victim!
Listen! Our song!

The Furies' lyreless lullaby's
music maddening men's mind

Victim! Victim!
Listen! Our song!

it binds man's brain and dries
man's fruity flesh to rind.

When we came into being, they were marked out, the confines.
We and the Olympians have no intimate contacts.
Food's offered to either but not both together.
We don't wear white robes, they don't wear black ones.

Family strife, domestic pet
born in the wild and won't forget

When bloodkin kills bloodkin
that lets the Furies in

into the household keen-scented hound
blasting the building back into the ground

After the victim; hot on his trail
tracker Furies that never fail

He tries running. O let him try
a bloodkin's blood will never dry

He tries running. Fresh wet gore
keeps the Furies hot on his spoor.

We'll snatch back our prey from this she-god's protection.
There should be no question of such gods interfering
or muddying issues by setting up "sessions."
Zeus, the high he-god finds murderers hateful,
he bars that blood-dripping breed from his precincts.

Family strife, domestic pet
born in the wild and won't forget

When bloodkin kills bloodkin
that lets the Furies in

into the household keen-scented hound
blasting the building back into the ground

After the victim, hot on his trail
tracker Furies that never fail

He tries running. O let hin try
a bloodkin's blood is never dry

He tries running. Fresh wet gore
keeps the Furies hot on his spoor.

The pomp and proud carriage a man's puffed up with above
moulders to nothing when he's dragged off below.

He ses the drab black we're draped with to dance in,
hears the feet pounding the pulse of the bloodgrudge.

Down, Down, down I dive from a great height
and fall on him with all my weight

Down, Down, down I dive, my leaden tread
cracks the bloodkin-killer's head

Down, Down, down he goes with sickening thud
slipping in his bloodkin's blood.

Down he falls, and falling knows nothing, nothing.
A smother of madness clouds round the victim.
The groans of old murders thicken the bloodsmog
that billows all round and blacks out his household.

Down, down, down I dive from a great height
and fall on him with all my weight

Down, down, down, I dive, my leaden tread
cracks the bloodkin killer's head

Down, down, down he goes with sickening thud
slipping in his bloodkin's blood.

That's how it is, and that's how it's staying.
We've got all the skills. We get things accomplished.
We memorize murders. Were never forgetful.

We terrify mortals. We spit on their pleadings.
We relish our office, though spurned by the he-gods.

We're despised, we're rejected. The light we work by
is nothing like sunshine. Sharp and sheer-sided
our tracks are a peril to blind and to sighted.

So show us the man who can stop himself shaking
when he hears me lay claim to my rights and my titles
ratified by fate, and never, *never* rescinded.
My honors are ancient and in no way diminished
though I work underground, in the earth where it's sunless.

[*Enter* ATHENA.]
Athena

I heard far away someone crying: ATHENA!
I was on the banks of the Trojan Scamander
taking possession of my portion of spearspoil,
land won by the Achaeans, then awarded to me
and offered by me to the children of Theseus.

And summoned I sped here, the scales of my aegis
whipped by the winds as my feet raced me onwards.

[*Sees* CHORUS.]

I see a strange breed here, new to my country.
This breed doesn't scare me but causes me wonder.

[*To* CHORUS *and* OBSERVERS.]

Who are you? You and you, all here assembled?
the stranger prostrated before my own image.
and you, like nothing engendered by means that are normal,

neither like the she-gods that consort with the he-gods
nor like the humans in shape and appearance.

But since we've been made to share the same earthspace
it's wrong to abuse you as monstrous and shapeless.

Chorus

She-child of Zeus, we'll tell you all briefly.
We are the children of Night, and we're ageless.
Below ground where we live we're known as the Grudges.

1. **Ath:** So now I know your mother and what to call you.
   Ch: And soon you'll know also the work that we do.

2. **Ath:** I will, provided it's clear what you say.
   Ch: Kin-killers, we hunt them. They are our prey.

3. **Ath:** Where do you land him when you've netted your fish?
   Ch: Where all words for joy sound like gibberish

4. **Ath:** Are *his* deeds the reason that you're in full cry?
   Ch: He murdered his mother in cold blood, that's why!

5. **Ath:** Was he goaded or forced to against his own will?
   Ch: Forced! It was his *mother* this man dared to kill!

6. **Ath:** There are two parties present. I must hear them both.
   Ch: He won't let us swear ours, nor swear his own oath.

7. **Ath:** It's not justice you want but the mere outward show.
   Ch: How? You're the she-god of wisdom, say why that is so.

8. **Ath:** Sworn oaths would unfairly favor your cause.
   Ch: You question him then. The decision is yours.

9. **Ath:** The decision is mine. You'll give me your trust?
   Ch: Knowing your father it seems that we must.

Athena [*Addressing* ORESTES.]

Stranger, now it's your turn to speak and make answer.
Tell my your country, your bloodkin, what's happened
then make reply to the charges they've leveled.
Belief in your case brought you here to my godstone
clasping my image like the suppliant Ixion,
first man to kill, first cleansed of his killing.
Answer my questions and answer them clearly.

Orestes

She-chief Athena, let me remove the misgivings
implied in the last words you addressed me.
Unlike Ixion, *I* need *no* blood-absolution.
My undefiled hands cause no smirch to your image.
And this is the proof I can give of my cleansing:
The law is that one who's been guilty of bloodshed's
debarred from all speech until sprinkled with pig's blood
by one who's empowered to perform the purgation.
Long since and elsewhere I was purged in that manner
by sucklings with throats slit, streams with their currents.
So dismiss your alarm at likely pollution.
As for my bloodkin that's also told quickly —
I'm Argive, and when you ask me who is my father
I'm proud to reply that he *was* Agamemnon,
commander of all Achaia's great ship-force
with whose help you crushed Troy into nothing,

one of those clanchiefs who won you your spearspoil.
After Troy he returned to a death most unworthy.
My black-hearted mother, she killed my father.
She swaddled him first in a devious dragnet —
its red eyes still stare at the blood in the bath-trough.
Coming home after exile I killed my mother.
I killed her because she killed my dear father.
In all this Apollo was my god-accomplice.
Apollo jabbed sharp spurs into my spirit
and promised great pains if their guilt went unpunished.
Just or unjust? You must give judgement.
Whatever your verdict I'll take it as binding.

Athena

A hard matter, this, to judge for a mortal,
and even for me it's too hard to pass judgement
when retribution runs so close behind bloodguilt.
It's made all the harder since you've come to my godstone
a suppliant cleansed by all rites and procedures.
Still blood-stained I'd have you barred from my city.

[*Indicating* CHORUS.]

But these too have a cause which must be considered.
They have certain duties it's pointless dismissing
and if the verdict frustrates them of victory
they'll disgorge their grudge-venom into the ground.
and blight all the land with eternal diseases.
I let them stay or I drive them away —
That's the dilemma, my desperate decision.

I'll swear in a tribunal to be judges of murder
a tribunal for this case and all such for ever.

[*To* ORESTES *and* CHORUS.]

Gather your witnesses, gather your evidence,
your sworn support in the cause of true justice,
I'll pick and bring back the best men of Athens
to judge the facts fairly without any falsehood.

[*Exit* ATHENA. ORESTES *and* CHORUS *remain. Scene changes to Acropolis.*]

Chorus

All right's destroyed by this new dispensation
if the wrong cause of this killer's allowed to succeed.
One murderer's freedom gives license to all,
makes murder the norm not merely the nightmare
that gnaws at the sleeptime of fathers and mothers.
They'll be wide awake now when the wounds get inflicted.

We Furies were once mankind's sleepless watchdogs
inflicting transgressors with vehement madness.
Our anger and grudge have been put out to grass now
and all forms of death have the run of the world.
When he sees trouble looming over his neighbor
a man starts to wonder when his own turn will come
and asks someone else how to stop the contagion
and he offers philtres for safety. All futile!
And don't let someone smitten cry out the old cry
on bloodright or bloodgrudge or us, the *deaf* Furies.
Some father, some mother, their pain new upon them
might weep and might wail with such piteous appeals.
Bloodright! Like Troy it's all rubble and ashes.

Fear's a good gateman to stand guard of the passions.
Often men suffer to win some small wisdom.
Those men and those cities where fear has no franchise
will never show justice the slightest respect.
A life with no rules, a life of repression
anarchy, tyranny, you must respect neither.
Somewhere between's where the god plants his banner.
Out of two forces he makes a new fusion.
Going beyond bounds, overstepping the limits
that comes about where the gods get degraded.
The mind that is balanced, and keeps within confines
gets the happiness men struggle and pray for.
Above all respect the godstone of Bloodright.
Don't besmirch or befoul it with impious bootsoles
just because loot looms in front of your goldlust.
Blemishing bloodright makes catastrophe certain.

Honor mother and father, and welcome guest-strangers.
And the man who does right without fear's compulsion
he's the one who won't find his life-lot unlucky
or himself and his bloodkin blasted entirely.
But the man who scorns all and does what he wants to
and caring for no-one heaps up his wealth-spoil
and believes his snatched freight's assured a safe voyage,
will be forced to strike sail when the stormwaves start swelling,
his prow and his spars all pulped into splinters.
He shouts as he feels himself tugged by the tide-race.
He shouts to deaf ears. The gods' laughter mocks him,
the hothead who boasted that this couldn't happen,
helpless, aghast, as he's hurled at the headland,
and leaves on Right's reef the wreck of his life-lot,
and is lost, and unwept for, wiped out, forgotten.

[*Enter* ATHENA, JURY *of* 12 ATHENIANS, *and a* HERALD.]
Athena
Sound the trumpet, keep the people in order.
Let the shrill battle-horn the Etruscans invented
change mortal breath into blares from its metal.

[*Sound of trumpets.*]
This is a court now, and crowded with people.
We must have strict silence and closest attention
so the laws I lay down can be learnt by the city
and these hear their case decided on merit.

[*Sound of trumpets.*]
Now hear the laws I lay down, my Athenian people,
brought together to try the first case of bloodshed.
For the children of Aegeus, father of Theseus,
this council of judges will sit here for ever,
on this hill of Ares, the Amazons' camp-site
when they came to make war through their grudge against
Theseus.
They erected great turrets to overlook Athens
and sacrificed cattle to Ares the War God,
hence the name: Areopagus, rock-hill of Ares.

The people's reverence and the fear that they're born with
will restrain them day and night from acts of injustice
as long as they don't foul their own laws with defilement.
No-one should piss in the well they draw drink from.
Anarchy! Tyranny! Let both be avoided
nor banish fear from your city entirely.
A man without fear abides by no law-forms.
If you justly cherish this new institution
you'll have a bulwark known to no other humans
from Scythia down to the Peloponnesus.
This established tribunal will be totally bribe-proof.
The watchdog stays wakeful to let you sleep soundly.
This long address I intend for you and the future.

[*Enter* APOLLO.]

Athena

Lord Apollo, you are out of your precincts.
Explain your presence here at this meeting.

Apollo

I come as a witness. The man they're accusing
came as a suppliant and I gave him shelter.
I also purged him of the blood he had shed.
I'm his advocate too as well as a witness.
I share the blame for the death of his mother.

Begin the proceedings, that you preside over.
And make use of your wisdom to help us to judgement.

Athena [*To* CHORUS.]

The trial is now open. First, prosecution.
Speak, and put before us complete information.

Chorus

We may be many, but in this we're united.

[*To* ORESTES.]

Answer the question each one of us asks you . . .

1. **Ch:** You killed your mother. Say yes or no.
    Or: Yes, I can't deny it was so.

2. **Ch:** First fall to us! We win with two more.

Or: Don't crow too soon. I'm not on the floor.

3. **Ch:** Now how did you kill her? (Judges take note!)
   Or: I drew my sword and gashed open her throat.

4. **Ch:** Who was it drove you to dare such an act?
   Or: Apollo, and Apollo will witness that fact.

5. **Ch:** You killed your mother at Apollo's behest?
   Or: I did, and still think it done for the best.

6. **Ch:** I doubt if you'll think so once pinned by your doom.
   Or: I have faith in my father's help from the tomb.

7. **Ch:** Your mother's among them so don't trust the dead.
   Or: My mother, she had two guilts on her head.

8. **Ch:** Explain to the judges how you make two.
   Or: Her husband, my father, that's two men she slew.

9. **Ch:** She paid by her death. You still have to pay.
   Or: When she was alive did you make her your prey?

10. **Ch:** He wasn't her bloodkin, the man that she killed.
    Or: And you say that it's bloodkin's blood that I've spilled?

Chorus
How could it not be? How else could the mother
you murdered have fed you inside her body?
Dare you disown the bloodbond that's closest?

Orestes [*To* APOLLO.]
Now be my witness. Explain to the judges
whether I killed my mother with justice.
That I did the deed there's no point denying
but done rightly or wrongly, Apollo decide
and help me to state my case with the judges.

Apollo
To you the high tribunal sworn in by Athena,
I, Apollo, the prophet, who can't utter falsehood
say that Orestes here acted with justice.
Whenever I speak to man, woman or city
from the oracle shrine-throne I sit on at Delphi

it's always as mouthpiece of Zeus, the high he-god,
so if I plea for justice, I speak for the Father,
Zeus, the high he-god, whose will you must bend to.
No oath has more power than the oath of the Father.

Chorus

So Zeus, you say, was behind your instruction
that Orestes avenge the death of his father?
Does Zeus disregard the rights of his mother?

Apollo

It's not the same thing the death of a man, though,
a man also honored with Zeus-given chief-stave,
a *man*, moreover, killed by a *woman*
and not by war weapons, an Amazon's arrows,
but in a manner you'll hear, you, Pallas Athena,
and you sitting here to vote on this issue —
The man came home after ten years' campaigning
(and a fair judge would say that he'd gained himself glory)
came home from the wars to a "womanly welcome"!
And as he was stepping up out of his bathtrough
she pitched her dark doom-tent over his body,
she hacked down her husband while he was helpless,
fastened and feeble in the maze of its meshes.
A fine death for a man, clanchief, commander!
I show you the woman just as she was
to goad you to just grudge when weighing this issue.

Chorus

So Zeus thinks a father's death more important?
Yet Zeus was the one bound Kronos, *his* father!
Doesn't this act show a slight contradiction?

[*To* JUDGES.]

Consider this fact when reaching your verdict!

Apollo

Animals! Beast-hags hated by he-gods!
Chains, fetters, locks can all be unloosened,
there are many means to burst bonds and shackles,
but once a man's dead and earth's lapped his blood up,
the blood drains away and never returns.

Though Zeus can reverse all other conditions
he's never come op with a charm against dying.
Chorus

So then supposing this man *is* acquitted,
will the man who has shed the blood of his mother
live in the house of his father at Argos?
Who will want *his* hands griming the godstones?
What clans will want *him* at their ritual cleansing?
Apollo

I'll answer that, and this answer's decisive! . . .

The mother of what's called her offspring's no parent
but only the nurse to the seed that's implanted.
The mounter, the male's the only true parent.
She harbors the bloodshoot, unless some god blasts it.
The womb of the woman's a convenient transit.
I've got proof here at hand to back up my statement

that the male can father with no help from the female
here is the she-child of Zeus, the high he-god,
who was nurtured in no womb's watery shadows.
Such an offspring no she-god could bear on her own.

[*To* ATHENA.]

And I, Pallas, will do all that Apollo is able
to make them both great, your city, your people.
I sent him a suppliant here to your godstone
so that you'd have him as a true friend for ever,
a spear-friend and ally, his people, your people,
loyally bound in a bond that is lasting.
Athena

So, as both sides have spoken, I order
the judges to come to the justest decision.

1. **Ch:** All the shafts in our quiver, they're all of them shot.
    We need only your vote to make our word law.
    Ap: You've heard what you've heard. Let each cast his lot.
    Remember the god-bond that each of you swore.

2. **Ch:** Beware that in no way you dishonor our band.

       If we're dishonored we'll poison your grass.

Ap: Fear the oracles, that's my command.

       My oracles, *Zeus*'s, they must come to pass.

3. **Ch**: Your oracles will never be free of the blot

       from dabbling in blood-deeds more than you should.

    Ap: So you say Zeus the father was wrong or was not

       to purge Ixion first man to shed blood?

4. **Ch**: Words! Words! But if I don't get the bloodright that's due

       I'll come down on this country with all of my force.

    Ap: What young god or old god cares about you?

       The case will be mine as a matter of course.

5. **Ch**: You cheated old she-gods, the Fates, once before

       when you saved Admetus from a funeral pyre.

    Ap: We have to help suppliants, and all the more

       when he comes at a time when his need is most dire.

6. **Ch**: You befuddled the ancient she-gods with wine!

       You made the old dispensation mere jest.

    Ap: And that's all you'll be when the victory's mine.

       You can spew all your venom. We won't be impressed.

Chorus

You new he-gods trample the she-gods of old.

When I hear the verdict then I'll decide

whether or not this country gets blasted.

Athena

It's my duty to come to a final pronouncement.

I add my own vote to those for Orestes!

I myself was given birth by no mother.

I put the male first, although I'm unmarried,

and I am the wholehearted child of my father,

so I can't count the death of a woman

of greater importance than that of her manlord.

If your votes turn out equal Orestes still wins

Now turn the urns over and reckon the ballots,

those of the judges assigned to this duty.

1. **Or**: O Phoebus Apollo, what will it be?
    Ch: O Night, our dark Mother, are you here to see?

2. **Or**: Now for the end, a noose or new day.
    Ch: Either honor, or ruin, if he gets away.

Athena

Count the pebbles you've shaken out of the vote-pots.
Make sure there are no mistakes in your tally.
The slightest error could lead to disaster.
One vote could renew the strength of a bloodclan.

[*The votes are counted.*]

This man stands acquitted of the charges of murder.
The votes on each side turn out to be equal.

Orestes

Pallas Athena, you give my clan back its lifeblood!
You've given me back the fatherland barred me.
Once more Greece can say: Orestes of *Argos*,
restored to his bloodright by Pallas Athena,
by Apollo and by Zeus the Preserver.
Zeus saw my father's death in all its true grimness.
Zeus saw clearly that I needed preserving
from these terrible grudges who champion my mother.

Before I go to my country, I give you this god-bond —
this land and its people, now and for ever,
no clanchief of Argos will ever attack you,
or I'll come as a ghost if they've broken my god-bond,
and mar all their marches, make journeys joyless,
until they repent their rash expeditions.
But so long as they honor this city of Pallas,
stay loyal in peace, and in war keep their spear-bond,
then I'll come as a ghost more gracious and kindly.

Farewell Athena, and people of Athens.
Get a good headlock on whoever you wrestle.
Come from all bouts with the victory laurels.

[*Exit* ORESTES.]
Chorus

> You upstart gods
> you've ridden down
> the ancient laws
> snatched my honors
> out of my hands.
> My rancor's roused,
> my heart will ooze
> black venom out
> over the land
> until it's waste.
>
> Bloodright! Bloodright!
>
> Womb-blight, crop-blight,
> the earth all scorched,
> the people starving.
>
> The people mock me,
> my wrongs are too much!
> Daughters of Night
> degraded and crushed.

Athena

> Listen to reason. Don't take things so badly.
> You're not defeated. The votes came out equal.
> There was no dishonor to you in the verdict.
> Luminous proof came from Zeus the high he-god
> and he who had spoken the oracle witnessed
> that Orestes should not be condemned for his action.
> So why do you ravage the land with your rancor?
> Don't let your rage scorch all our fields cropless,
> your dewfalls of acid shrivel the seedpods,
> and I will make you the solemnest promise
> that you shall be given a cavern for refuge
> with glittering thronestools next to your godstones
> held in great honor by all here assembled.

Chorus

> You upstart gods

you've ridden down
the ancient laws
snatched my honors
out of my hands.

My rancor's roused,
my heart will ooze
black venom out
over the land
until it's waste.

Bloodright! Bloodright!

Womb-blight, crop-blight,
the earth all scorched,
the people starving.

The people mock me.
My wrongs are too much.

Daughters of Night
degraded and crushed.

Athena

You're *not* dishonored, so don't use your godhead
to blast this country of mortals with earthblight.
That would abuse your position as she-gods.
I have access to Zeus, and what's more have access
alone of all gods, to Zeus's munitions,
the mighty high he-god's missiles of thunder!
But this isn't a case for desperate deterrents.
I'd rather you yielded to gentler persuasion.
Take back your threats, don't spit spiteful poisons
over the fruitcrops, so that harvests don't happen.
Lull the black swell of your billowing bloodgrudge
and have half of my honors here, half of my worship.
The land's a broad land. It has people in plenty.
As the Furies you'll be favored with sacrificed firstfruits,
propitiations preceding childbirth or bedbond.
You'll only have praise then for my persuasions.

Chorus
> The ancient conscience
> pushed underground.
> The ancient conscience
> dishonored, despised!
>
> My nostrils snort
> with rage at my shame.
> Terrible anguish
> bores under my ribs.
>
> Night   Mother
> listen   my cry!
>
> The new he-gods
> with their fouls in the ring
> have robbed me of honor
> making me nothing.

Athena
> I'll allow you your anger since you are older.
> Your years in the world have given you wisdom
> and though yours may be greater, Zeus gave me insights.
> If you leave this land for an alien bloodclan's
> I tell you that you will learn to love this one.
> Time in its passage will honor my people,
> and you, enthroned by the shrine of Erechtheus,
> will get more in the way of rites and processions
> from my men and women than from the rest of mankind.
> On this land, my land, goad no-one to bloodshed,
> or let them strop their grudge on your whetstones,
> our youth up in arms and drunk with aggression
> battling like bantams in the strife between bloodkin.
> Let them battle abroad if they need to gain glory.
> I want no cocks fighting in my country's farmyard,
> birds of a feather I forbid to do battle.
>
> Such, if you'll have them, are the honors I offer.
> For the good *you* do, good returns and good god-gifts,
> a share in this country the gods above cherish.

Chorus

> The ancient conscience
> pushed underground.
> The ancient conscience
> dishonored, despised.
>
> My nostrils snort
> with rage at my shame
> Terrible anguish
> bores under my ribs.
>
> Night! Mother!
> Listen! My cry!
>
> The new he-gods
> with their fouls in the ring
> have robbed me of honors
> making me nothing.

Athena

> I'm making you offers which I'll go on repeating
> so that you'll never have any grounds for complaining
> that you, an old she-god, were spurned and dishonored
> by me a young she-god, nor cast out by my people.
> But if you have any respect for Persuasion
> and feel its soothing charm as I'm speaking,
> and the linctus of language can placate you and lull you,
> you'll decide to remain. But if you don't want to
> it wouldn't be right to bring down on this city
> your grudge or your anger, or harm to the people,
> when you've been offered a share in the land here
> with a full portion of honor now and for ever.

1. **Ch:** What kind of shrine did you say I'd possess?
   Ath: One free from suffering. Will you say yes?

2. **Ch:** And if I say yes what powers will I wield?
   Ath: *You'll* make them flourish, flock, family and field.

3. **Ch:** Would you entrust such powers to *me*?
   Ath: Yes, and prosper the fortunes of each devotee.

4. **Ch:** These powers, will you pledge they'll endure?
    Ath: I'd make no offers if I weren't sure.

5. **Ch:** You're beginning to charm me. My anger subsides.
    Ath: Live in this land and win more friends besides.

6. **Ch:** What charm for this land would you like me to chant?
    Ath: Nothing where darkness is dominant.

Athena
　　Bring blessings from earth, sea-billows and sky.
　　Let the wind warm the land as sun-filled sou'westers,
　　let farm-fields and flocks always be fruitful
　　and never fail folk who will farm them in future,
　　and as the land prospers so will the people,
　　especially those who give gifts to your godstones.
　　Like a green-fingered gardener tending his garden
　　I let the good grow, and nip the bad as it's budding.
　　I see that the good's wants get well enough watered,
　　protect their green life-lot from all blight and croprot.

　　Your part's to prosper my people in peace-time,
　　and mine, when the time comes for war-cries and weapons,
　　is to make certain my city's triumphant.

Chorus
　　I'll share in the homeland of Pallas Athena
　　and not degrade a city
　　that all powerful Zeus and Ares the War God
　　make guardians of godstones,
　　Greece's great glory.
　　I pray the golden sun
　　make the earth burst open,
　　the ground gush with good life-gifts
　　harvest after harvest.

Athena
　　I act on behalf of a people I cherish
　　and install among them these implacable spirits
　　whose province has been and is to manage mankind.
　　A man feels their onslaught but not where it comes from.
　　Crimes from the past get him hauled up before them.

And though he bursts his lungs with loud shouting
their silent grudge grinds him down into nothing.
Chorus
And no searing winds strip bare the orchards,
no scorching heat burn the new buds dry.
May Pan prosper the sheepfolds
doubling the increase at lambing
and Hermes of windfalls and godsends
disclose the rich streaks of silver
Athena
Listen to what the Furies, the *Furies* are pledging.
The Fury's a force both with the high he-gods
and with the powers beneath the earth's crust.
Anyone can see how they work among mortals —
one man's life-lot's as bright as a ballad,
another's life is one blinded with tears.
Chorus
I ban the death that descends too early
and cuts down a man who's barely reaches manhood.

Grant good bed-bonds to girls that are graceful,
you she-gods of life-lot, sisters and she-kin,
both being the offspring of one mother, Night.
You are present in every household,
at the family's feast-rites for death and delivery,
at the birth, and the death and the bedbond.
You are the most rightfully honored of she-gods.
Athena
These she-gods of all gods willing such good things!

How grateful I am that Persuasion was guiding
my tongue and my lips when they were resistant.
The Zeus of debates and assemblies presided
turning a battle to a debate about blessings,
the rivalry now only vying to bless best.
Chorus
May faction, sedition
for ever flesh-hungry,

civil disturbance,
cycles of slaying,
never bray in this city,
its dust never gulp
the blood of its people,
the state get ripped open
by the rages of bloodgrudge,
a chainlink of murder.
Let the linking be love-bonds,
common likes, common hatreds,
a group bond against
the troubles men suffer.

Ahtena

Listen!   They're learning to bless, groping for goodness.
I foresee great future good in these fearful faces.
If you show them the kindness they show you,
your city's set fair on the straight road of justice.

Chorus

Fare well, fare well, grow wealthy, grow great,
fare well, citizens so close to Zeus,
favorites of his favorite she-child.
Under the wings of Athena grow wise
with her father looking on you with favor.

Athena

Fare well you too.   Now I'll lead the way
to show you the chambers in the deep cavern
by the light of the torches of those who'll escort you.
Now, sped on your way by the savor of godsops
go to your underground shrines in the rock hill
and there keep what will harm Athens imprisoned
and set free only what will help her to victory.
Children of Cranaus, who reside on the rock-hill
escort on their way these welcome guest-strangers,
and give them the good will that they'll give to you.

Chorus

Fare well, fare well, mortals, immortals,
all of you here in the city of Pallas.

Only give grace to your new guest-strangers
and you'll never lack any luck in your life-lot.

Athena

I endorse all you pray for on behalf of my city.
And now by the light of the blazing torch-beacons,
I'll escort you to your underground chambers
along with those who tend to my godstone,
the flowers of Athens, once land of Theseus,
the women of Athens, girls, mothers, old women,
will come as a glorious group in procession.
Drape our honored guest-strangers in robes of deep sea-red
and lead then with torchlight held up before you,
so that these Furies, who turned out so kindly,
will reside and show love, and bless Athens for ever.

Procession of Women

Go to your home, children of Night,
honored with music and torchlight.

Silence while the Kind Ones pass.

Go to your home, underground and primeval
honored by sacrifice and libation.

Silence while the Kind Ones pass.

Grave powers, gracious and kindly,
attended by torches, follow us home.

Now echo our chorus, raise your own cry!

Peace between the Kind Ones and Athens!
ZEUS/FATE, high he-god and she-god
together helped all this to happen.

Now echo our chorus, raise your own cry!

END OF PART THREE

Form and Persecution in the *Oresteia*
by Kenneth Burke

This essay is a rewritten version of a longer section from a book now in progress. The original is mainly a step-by-step analysis of Aeschylus' *Orestes* trilogy. It was undertaken as an inquiry into the problem of poetic "catharsis," a term which Aristotle evidently considered of special significance for the analysis of the tragic pleasure, yet which happens to be left unexplained in his extant text. (In the discussion of "catharsis" in the *Politics*, the reader is referred to the *Poetics* for the major treatment of the subject.)

The matters considered in these pages were immediately preceded by: (a) a section designed to show that the meaning of "imitation" in drama has become "scientistically" obscured, by failure to approach Artistotle's concept of *mimesis* through his concept of the *entelechy*, with its peculiar stress upon "fulfillment"; (b) a section on "allusion" in Greek tragedy, the gaining of dramatic forcefulness and stylistic dignity by allusion to contemporary situations and to religious rites; (c) a section on "civic tensions," for the *ad interim* resolving of which by poetic means Greek tragedy was "cathartically" designed.

I

Aristotle's famous formula refers to "pity, fear, and like emotions." For obvious reasons, we chose "pride" as the third major motive involved in tragic catharsis. But instead of treating pity, fear, and pride as simple motives, we tried to show how, as regards their bearing upon "civic" matters, each of them has notable complications. For instance, we cited Kierkegaard, on pity as a form of contempt. (Such complicated pity, whatever it was on its face, might be a kind of elevation bordering even on superiority, in offering the lowly man a chance to feel sorrow for the simulated sufferings of the great.) We cited Aristotle's *Ethics* to the effect that there is a *nobility* of fear, as a citizen can prove himself worthy by fearing the right things. And as for the "tragic flaw" (which Aristotle generally calls the *hamartia*, while the playwrights usually prefer the more specific term, *hubris*, though they also often use *hamartia*): particularly by examining the uses of the term, *hubris*, in Aristotle's *Rhetoric*, we sought to emphasize its strongly civic and even legalistic nature as a word for *social insult* (in contrast with the more purely theological or "universal" tinge now generally given to the notion of "pride" as a motive in tragedy).

All told: We were here generally concerned with stylistic resources whereby the important social relations involving superiority and inferiority could be translated into a set of "mythic" equivalents. Disorders within the *polis* could automatically attain tragic scope and dignity by translation into a corresponding "supernatural" terminology of motives. Hence, any civic issue could be reflected in the mythic idiom that transcended the political or social order, even if it did have reference to the political or social order (and to the corresponding disorders).

At this point in our inquiry, a kind of calamity occurred. Since "catharsis" also has analogues with bodily processes, we asked how "pity," "fear," and "pride" might figure, when translated into bodily terms. That is: Considered in the personal order, the terms may be taken at face value (as anyone who has felt pity or asked for pity is equipped to "understand" the term). Socially, there may be complications involving invidious relationships, matters of social or moral inferiority and superiority. And as regards "the thinking of the body," the purging of the emotions might reveal analogies with the three privy functions of the "Demonic trinity." Primarily, pity might involve the erotic, since pity is in essence a form of love. A study of the imagery in Wagner's *Ring* helped here, because of the maternal, nursing connotations by which he identifies the incipiently erotic. Fear would be diuretic, as with Coleridge's line, "Urine, the soft flowing Daughter of Fright." And "pride" would be anal, as with the proverb, "The higher the ape climbs, the more he shows his tail." But, inasmuch as the three functions are morally confused (in accordance with what Freud calls the "cloacal" ambiguities), there would be many interchangeabilities among the three.

In any case, to our great dismay, at this point a section of the book began writing itself, a systematic concern with "the thinking of the body." But since editors are still, on the whole, uneasy as regards matters to do with the Beauty Clinic, no one has as yet inquired with much avidity after this Monster of a chapter, dealing with stylistic subterfuges whereby poetry mimics the body's purgative ways of giving-off, when unburdening itself of impurities.

Suffice it to say that we had proceeded thus: Our study of Poetics had been concerned with the problem of carving-out a poetics. We were thus trying to arrive at a poetics by a process of purification in our own essay, while at the same time we were working on the subject of purification in tragedy. And these two orders of motives so converged that we now found ourselves purgatively using body-imagery in our own critical essay by talking about the use of it in poetry. (We analyzed "the thinking of the body" in various writings, not only Aeschylean tragedy and Wagnerian opera, but *Alice in Wonderland*, Flaubert's *Temptation of St. Anthony*, and other works.) Then, after so radical a purge, we had purified our subject to the degree where we could consider tragedy in its most dignified aspect; namely: in terms of tragic form.

Years ago, in *Counter-Statement*, we had analyzed form as the arousing and fulfilling of expectations. We now found ourselves again covering some of this same ground, but with a notable difference. Originally, we had meant by "form" all those devices whereby an audience is led to acquiesce in the destiny, good or bad, of the various characters in a tragedy. Now, we saw that such a network of expectancies and fulfilments can be summed up *dramatically* in such terms as Law, Right, Fate, Justice, Necessity. Accordingly, if tragic favorites like *Dike, Themis, Moira, Nemesis, Ananke* were dramatic equivalents for the principle of expectancy we had called "form," then there would be a "persecutional" element in formal propriety or "inevitability." So we were to be concerned with the Great Persecutional Words, and to watch the developments accordingly, in the *Oresteia*.

Whatever the social origins of such motives may be, once they are converted into the fullness of tragedy they have become *cosmologized*. Whereupon an almost terrifying *thoroughness* of human honesty is demanded of us, as audience. For we now are in our very essence *persecuted*, and there can be no comfort until we have disclosed and appropriately transfigured every important motive still unresolved within us. That is, once the irresolutions of the body, of personal relations, and of social relations have been heroically transmogrified by identification with the Great Persecutional Words, which are in turn identified with the vastness of Nature and the mystery of Super-Nature, no pleasantly pluralistic dissipation of outlook is any longer tolerable. Whatever the diversity of the world (a diversity which one would be a fool to deny or not to appreciate) one must become pious in doing homage to some underlying principle of oneness. One cannot deny the persecution; one must admit it: for by nature of the cosmologizing, it is integral, and everywhere.

We recall the man who had been working steadily on the Orestes trilogy, throughout the morning, afternoon, and evening of one day. He told how, awaking in the night, he lay in the dark, with somewhat the sense of looking down upon the world as though it were a kind of relief map, stretched out beneath him. He could "see" or "feel" its curving, from the coast off to the Great Lakes, then down towards the Gulf, and on across the Plains and the Rockies to the Pacific. The reasons for this fantasy were obvious. The half-awakened, half-dreaming sleeper was responding to what Henry Sams has called "the illusion of great physical space and magnitude" in Aeschylus and Job.

But there was another step here. To the man lying there in the dark, this notion of the great curved world stretching out through the night was somehow frightful, even monstrous. He felt as though he had awakened from a nightmare, and had not yet shaken himself free of it. And this further step seems to have resulted thus:

In using the ultimate vastness of scene to dignify the tragedy, which was likewise infused with the spirit of the Great Persecutional Words, Aeschylus had contrived to infuse nature itself with the terrors of tragedy (hence also with the civic virtues that gain much in authority if backed by such terrors). All the magic of dominion was operating here, in all its dimensions. By thus making fear universal Aeschylus had made the universe fearsome. Hence, there was fear in the mere thought of all those places lying just where they were (though the sleeper, or semi-sleeper, had no sense of any specific danger threatening him). And when fear is thus made radical, an equally radical pity can be the only antidote.

But now we have (at least "in principle") a sufficient range of terms to consider the Poetic tactics of the Oresteia generally, and thus at least to get a glimpse into the kind of *thoroughness* to which the tragic playwright is necessarily vowed, once he sets out to cosmologize his fable in the spirit of the Great Persecutional Words.

II

First, to recall briefly the curve of the plot, in the trilogy as a whole, an aspect of form which Aristotle may have been led in part to slight because it is so "dialectical" (in its progress from one landing-place to another), and Aristotle was reacting against Plato's dialectic emphasis:

The Orestes Trilogy

In the introductory play, the *Agamemnon*, Clytemnaestra, plotting with her paramour, kills her husband Agamemnon and Cassandra, the prophetess whom he had brought home as booty from the sack of Troy. Clytemnaestra justifies the murder on the grounds that, to obtain the victory for his armies, Agamemnon had slain their daughter, Iphigenia, on the sacrificial altar. The play ends with the Chorus praying for the son, Orestes, to appear and avenge his father's murder.

The second play, the *Libation-Bearers* (*Choephoroe*), begins with Orestes' arrival. He kills both the paramour (Aegisthus) and the mother. But though he has murdered his mother in righteous retaliation, as the play ends he is beginning to be tortured by remorse. (Dramatically, this torture was objectified by his seeing of the Furies, ancient goddesses that punish blood-guilt.) And he is told that, to be cured, he must journey to the oracle at Delphi, called the "navel" of the world.

The third play, the *Eumenides*, deals with his final absolution. It begins at Delphi, where the Furies are still pursuing him, but have fallen asleep. It ends at Athens, where Orestes is finally absolved. And in the course of this absolution, the Furies themselves change their nature, becoming much milder (or, as we expressed it in a brief account of the Oresteia reprinted in *The Philosophy of Literary Form*, they change their emphasis from the punishment of evil to the rewarding of good). Athena says that we are here witnessing the "first" trial for murder as contrasted with the earlier feudal practice whereby the victim was avenged by kinsmen. And the development also allusively solemnizes a treaty of alliance recently made between Athens and Argos (the land of Orestes, who has been freed by an Athenian court).

In these plays, the equivalent of "original sin" (dynastically or tribally motivated guilt "feudally" inherited, as distinguished from personal transgressions) is located in the crime of Atreus, who slew the children of his brother, Thyestes, and served them to Thyestes at a banquet which was supposedly to celebrate the brothers' reconciliation. Within the conditions of the tragedy as treated by Aeschylus, this is the mythic origin of the blood-guilt that curses the House of Atreus. And the guilt calls forth violence that in turn calls forth violence, until the playwright contrives in his third play to change the rules of vindication by changing the very nature of Justice and Conscience.

Since the "original" offense is in the category of eating, a corresponding strand of imagery is maintained throughout: biting (with its variants, devouring, blood-sucking, disgorging, and the like). The Furies themselves represent the image in the extreme. For their basic role (they call themselves "Curses") is to objectify the vicious bite of conscience ("remorse").

Secondarily, the dog image fits here. Hence, not only are the Furies "dogs," in their desire to hound the guilty. But also, there are treacherous dogs, loyal dogs, subservient dogs, alert dogs (at the very opening of the play, the Watchman is expectant "like a dog"). The dog-image is excellent for such purposes because, besides its close relation to the terms for biting, the dog serves so well "Aesop-wise" to sum up characteristic human relationships. For, above all, note how neatly this image represents a basic ambiguity of social relations: the wavering line between loyalty and subservience (an essential concern, if drama is to be *civically* motivated in the fullest sense).

We experience a special flurry when Clytemnaestra likens herself to a dog watching over the house. She is a woman, she is to kill, she is to be killed; and women (the Furies, the bloodthirsty hounds of conscience) are to preside over her avenging (as indeed, finally, a woman, Athena, presides over a deal whereby the matricide is pardoned and the Furies are given a new abode underground, in what we might call "the Unconscious of the State").

Whatever the ultimate guilt may be, there must also be the guilt towards women as a *class*. Women, socially submerged, assigned to the innermost compartment of the house (the penetralia, or *muchos*), in an order where romantic love was best expressed homosexually, may thus come to stand for nearly all submerged motives. Their generic role as underprivileged would serve Euripides well, in fitting them to be dramatic personalizations for any aspect of the socially problematical. And in this trilogy, problems of social conscience, as reflected in the individual conscience, are finally resolved by an astounding intellectual (or even intellectualistic) feat whereby women's *biological* function of child-bearing is in effect denied, through being interpreted in purely social terms.

We refer to the dramatized legalism of the third play, with its ingenious hagglings designed to prove (in proof attended by much pageantry) that men are not really descended from women. The woman is but a nurse for the foetus which descends through the male line only, as with patrilineal descent of property. Hence, Orestes' guilt of matricide is absolved because, strictly speaking, he had no mother. Similarly, when presiding over the trial that frees Orestes, Athena points out that she was born without a mother, from the head of Zeus. The "Justice" of the Parliamentary Zeus is thus essentially discriminatory with regard to women.

Hence, as a rule of thumb we assume: (a) that in the Athenian *polis* there was an unresolved civic guilt with regard to women; (b) and that they could accordingly serve well as dramatic vehicles (however roundabout) for the expression of social or political tensions in general. (For instance, recalling *Prometheus Bound*, consider what it may mean that, after the rebel deity has been so terrifyingly confined and tortured before our very eyes, the Chorus of Women enters, announcing that the reverberations had penetrated to the innermost recesses of their cave. For here again is the word *muchos*, that names the penetralia, the women's compartments, of a house. It also is the equivalent of the Latin word for an inner bay, *sinus*. And in our chapter on "the thinking of the body" we have offered reasons for believing that the motives of internality are here carried to the point where, in the course of the plot, as imaginally defined in the text, the terror is not merely felt by the audience as witnesses; rather, it is ingrained in the very behavior of the drama, which at this point, after its fashion, *micturates*. That is, the drama does not merely make us afraid; rather, it itself *is* afraid. And inchoately it calls forth appropriate movements from the innermost recesses of the frightened mind, as reflected in a correspondingly frightened body.)

So much for the general view of the plays, and the place of our analysis in our concern with Poetics as a whole. Let us now list some of the major considerations that arose in the course of our making an index designed to follow the course of the plays step by step.

III

(1) Two kinds of accountancy. Evil in first play (slaying of Agamemnon) leads to evil in second (Orestes' slaying of the slayers, the usual feudal pattern). But evil in second play leads to good in third, after the "conscientious" legalistic manipulations whereby

tribal justice is replaced by parliamentary justice (which equals male supremacy). There are the great words for law and order (the *Dike* set). There are the corresponding words for threat, retaliation, vengeance, vindication, ruin (the *Ate* set). And there are the bridging terms, like those for pollution (*miasma*), pride, folly, venom, piety (*sebas*), with their correctives in rites of purification (rites that, since they involve blood-sacrifices, are forever circling back into the feudal genealogy whereby conflict begets conflict).

(2) We could make use of the distinction between a mathematics of continuity ("wave theories") and a mathematics of the discrete ("corpuscular theories"). See Eric Bell: *Mathematics; Handmaiden of the Sciences*. To "tick off" these plays step by step is to be astounded at the way in which the over-all curve of the development proceeds through a succession of discrete points. The plot is like the ticks of a clock progressing through time.

Presumably the dance-movements that underlie the logic of the choric utterances contributed much to this order. The lyrics of the chorus proceed by set stages (strophe, anti-strophe, etc.). A sensitivity to this kind of form encourages a plot to proceed like a row of falling dominoes, each knocking down the next.

The allusion to religious forms helped to this end. For instance, if the stichomythia was felt not merely as *dialogue*, but as rather an adaptation of the catechistic, then it would figure not merely as a brisk kind of conversation, but also as the *announcing of a disclosure* in the development of the plot. Thus the progress of the story could with maximum pointedness sharpen our perception of the relationship between the characters, as viewed successively in various pairings, with a corresponding disclosure (or "doctrinal" moment) to sum up each such relationship. Thus the road goes from station to station. And you might say that each step can be *given a formalistic title*, as though the dramatist (within the resources of his medium) were saying, "This is an introduction," "This is a foreshadowing," "This is a transition," "This is a summing-up," etc.

The method points *beyond* purely esthetic form, as usually conceived, to the view of the plot as being, in essence, not just this story or that, but a viaticum that carries us through the process of ritual initiation or cleansing proper to *any* such specific plot. . . .

Incidentally, we also suspect that, since stichomythia stood traditionally for disclosure, and since nurses traditionally recognized the child returning incognito as adult, Aeschylus could solemnly spoof in the stichomythia in which Orestes' nurse fails to discover his identity. (We have another reason to believe that there was spoofing here. For note how the nurse uses the great terminology of tragic cleansing, but in terms to do with her particular vocation, which involved the laundering of soiled diapers.)

(3) Besides the influence of the Choric patterns in sharpening the perception of stages, there would be the tradition of the "oracular" in general. Insofar as the culture took "Sibylline" ambiguities as the norm, it would be on the look-out for "prophetic" utterances. And such a quality of attention greatly assists the kind of formalistic pointing we have in mind. Thus, the play will not just somehow begin. In the choice of this particular beginning there will be an *announcement*. And so as regards all three plays. Similarly, the endings will be notable as such.

Or one must ask pointedly: Why the Chorus of *old men* in the first play, why of *slave women* in the second, why of the *Furies* in the third—why precisely these, at precisely these points? What formal "secret" underlies that progression? (Cryptology is all.) And, similarly, we will watch for the slogan-like lines that, in summing things up, use tricks of sound observable even across the gulf of our insensitiveness to the Greek, once we know what to look for. Or they may purposely use tricks of grammar that make them vague as to head and tail, like the design of a snake with its own tail in its mouth.

The problem of appreciation here is complicated by the accidents of survival. For instance, prophesying after the event, we find it beautifully appropriate that the second play should begin with an invocation to Hermes. Yet, had it not happened that Aristophanes, when looking for asylum from the risks of political criticism, chose Euripides as his victim, and in victimizing contrast quoted Aeschylus, the beginning of the second play would be unknown. And as regards endings, there are problems which, competent scholars tell us, still are not settled.

Meanwhile, "in principle" at least, we offer our suggestions. And even if our answers are not wholly satisfactory, since they are not complete, they may at least let us see in flashes down long corridors ... and piously, since fearsomely ... and fearsomely, since the logic of symbol-using becomes a logic of persecution, with entanglement in the labyrinthine nets of Agamemnon's killing, until or unless there is emergence into the stage of Peace, exulting as with the end of the *Oresteia* itself in the public celebration of a Great Pact. "Without the shedding of blood, there is no remission of sins," wrote Saint Paul. Forget it never, when meditating on the tragi-comedy of vindication.

(4) To consider a few of the strategic moments briefly: The first play begins: "Gods" (in the accusative case, thus grammatically pushing us forward); the second: "Hermes." The third: "First." So, for a beginning, a Watchman. What is he doing? He is watching and waiting. What will his first word be, to be appropriate? "Gods." Gods what? "Gods, I beseech." (This is a play by the civic-minded author of *The Suppliants*. And he well knew all the variants, complexities, refusals, and unwieldinesses, of supplication.) From the expectancy there will emerge, *gradatim et paulatim*, the annunciation looking towards Agamemnon's return—and the plot is on.

As for the second, "*Herme chthonie*" (Hermes, of the netherworld): This being the transitional play, and Orestes' murder of his mother being the transitional act, it is fittingly introduced by Orestes praying to Hermes, who is the tutelary deity of those on journeys (in transition), and is the power communicant between the living and the dead. (Maybe, in view of the parliamentary enlightenment which the third play is to celebrate, we should also note that Hermes was the patron of the Athenian businessmen; and later, during factional disputes, one conspiratorial night a gang of hoodlums in sympathy with the old aristocracy were to symbolize their political sympathies by mutilating all the statues of Hermes. But Aeschylus was writing at an earlier date, when the future of Athens, for all its factionalism, looked brighter.)

As for the final oracular beginning, "First" (*proton*): Surely, coming where it does, it is the most fitting of all. At the end of the second play, Orestes has been told that he must travel to the temple of Apollo at Delphi. In accordance with ancient Greek tradition, and the best modern psychology, the text refers to the centre-stone of this temple as the "navel" (*omphalos*) of the world. So, after the murder of his mother, to be cured Orestes must be thorough. He must go back to beginnings. (For reasons of space, we shall omit our accountancy of the steps whereby the opening passage moves from maternal firsts to the male Apollo. But, look at the text, and you'll find it there, clearly enough.) All told, after the *Agamemnon* and the *Libation-Bearers* have put us through the preparatory discipline of the father-murder and the son's avenging of it by a mother-murder, we are ready in the *Eumenides* to consider "beginnings" (whereat we move by degrees from the opening "First" to the final New Conscience as defined in the pageantry of the "First" legalistic trial, the turn from tribal "vengeance" to political "justice").

(5) As for the endings: Textual difficulties plague us here. But the general logic would seem to be this: Last play ends in the spirit of a final "allusive" shout* (in contrast with a prior moment of ritual silence, while a kind of Recessional is being completed). The second play ends on a question: When will this fury cease (more specifically, when will it be *lulled to rest*)? We'd like to think that the incompleteness in the closing lines of the first play were not due merely to a defect in the codex but were intentional. For variants of the word for completion, fulfilment, run through this trilogy like an *idée fixe*. It is the word that Aristotle makes equally important in his philosophic stress upon the *teleological*, the word that, in the Septuagint, translates Christ's dying formula, "It is finished." And to trail it through its many variations in these three plays, watching the imaginal associates with which it becomes successively identified as it proceeds, is almost like glimpsing the very essence of a culture. So we'd like to think that, when the stress upon the oracular is combined with such sensitiveness to fulfilment, the boastful lines at the end of the

---

*That is, the word was traditionally used to name a ritual shout made by women celebrating the Bacchic rites of the god's rebirth.

first play were deliberately left broken, as a device of stylistic prophecy, while the operatic nature of the medium might allow "naturally" for such an effect, since the words might at this point become submerged beneath a sudden swell of the music.

(6) As for the propriety of the Choruses: For the first play, the Chorus of Elders provides a good variant of the fulfilment theme (as Orestes' brusque action and intense suffering will depict fulfilments of a different order, in the category of full manly vigor). Dialectically, we began to note how, in the three biological stages that had their corresponding social status (childhood, manhood, and age), childhood and age were "alike" as contrasted with manhood. But we did not need to argue for the point, since Aeschylus explicitly has his Chorus of Elders liken themselves to children, with the oracular addition that age is like a dream dreamed by day. So they are well suited to such speculations on motives as are best possible when the full range of life from infancy to late death sets the perspective. (Was not the dramatist near ninety when he wrote these plays, in which old age is called the evil of evils?)

Why the Chorus of Slave Women, for figuring the motives of the second play? It suits well the themes of sufferance, lamentation, supplication, that go with any Aeschylean tragedy. (See the *Suppliants* for the several lines wherein the mimetics of beseechment are explicitly discussed, as a kind of pious diplomacy when dealing with Powers of any sort.) And this second play concerns, above all, a kind of Babylonian captivity, a waiting for the moment of liberation, to be got ambiguously through sacrifices.

The propriety of the Furies as Chorus for the third play is obvious. In these female hounds of conscience, the dog image comes to fruition. (George Thomson, among others, has made clear their role as the personification of matriarchal-tribal motives, in contrast with the Olympian-patrilineal kind of motives that will be affirmed in the pageantry depicting the "first" trial in accordance with political justice.) And if there is still a problem of conscience to be settled, what better way to settle it dramatically than by putting the very principle of conscience itself, as traditionally symbolized by the Furies, in a position where its transformation could be celebrated as pageantry?

Whereas the lyric function threatens the dramatic function in lesser dramatists, Aeschylus here finds a way of making it as dramatic as possible, since the Furies change their nature—and the great civic accomplishment in this enterprise comes from the skill by which the transformation of conscience is interwoven with political motives. The result is that the duplication of the State in the gods is dramatically presented as a derivation of the State from the gods.

And the transformations of conscience are, with astounding accuracy, related to emergent political institutions. As we have seen the primal curse previously translated into terms of personal relationship (specifically, relations between parents and offspring), it is now to be treated explicitly in terms of civic relationship. We could state this in another way by saying that, after the many stages of unfolding or uncovering, Aeschylus' search for the motivational origins of the plays has progressed to a point where the underlying civic motives can be explicitly (even systematically) disclosed. And the dramatic situation is such that, having passed beyond the stage of violence, the plot can treat of civic discord in a mixture of legalism and mythology that, by its conciliatory temper, gives us the happy sense of civic faction being transcended by civic unity.

(7) Since the trilogy leads up to and away from the matricide, we are particularly careful to ask what themes gravitate about this act. And so, above all, we focus upon that word "amphisbaena," uttered by Cassandra (who, as prophetess is sure to state the motivational essence) when she is trying to decide what the murderous Clytemnaestra should be called. For if Orestes is to slay not just a mother, but an "amphisbaena" (naturally, for the best of reasons) we must meditate upon that term, since by the rules of the myth Cassandra *cannot* be wrong.

Amphisbaena: from *amphis*, both ways; and *bainein*, to go. It is a serpent, in ancient mythology, beginning or ending at both head and tail alike. Meditating upon it, we may also recall that Clytemnaestra is called a serpent, as is Orestes (in her dream). Confining ourselves here to the statement of a position that must slight the arguments for it, offered elsewhere, we sum up thus:

We take this "prelogical" monster to be the mythic representation of the ultimate dreaming worm, the sheerly vegetating digestive tract, that underlies all human rationality, and out of which somehow emerge the labyrinths of human reason. The purely social kind of "justice" which is finally celebrated in the third play's pageantry, having to do with the mythic founding of the Acropolis, is in the last analysis a dialectical "transcending" of the basic biological worm (even in its "secondary" form, the design of the foetus placentally feeding, as figured "tertiarily" in the design of the child at the maternal breast).

To arrive eventually (and by a dramatically "radical" course) at such a scheme of motives as sprang like Athena, fully-grown, from the head of Zeus, the playwright must somewhere depict the *ultimate* slaying (if the rules are such that the sacrificial rite requires an ultimate slaying, to be complete). Here even the slain *mother* must *stand for* something beyond herself. And Cassandra tells us what; namely: the amphisbaena, which we take to be the mythic representation of the ultimate, vegetatively, non-verbally dreaming worm, circling back upon itself in enwrapt self-engrossment (somewhat as with the self-love of Aristotle's God, and likewise of many later theologians' Gods).

When in the second play we have heard the cry of Aegisthus, slain by Orestes off stage, and when Clytemnaestra has rushed in, asking what has happened, the traditional messenger (here a servant) answers enigmatically: "The dead are killing the living, I say." But Clytemnaestra immediately calls the remark a riddle. She is pointing up its "oracular" nature. For the expression so utilizes the resources of Greek grammar that it can also be interpreted in reverse: "The living kills the dead." The formula is deliberately designed by the dramatist to have this, shall we say, "amphisbaenal" nature. She goes on to interpret her statement in accordance with the *lex talionis:* "We are killed by treachery, even as we killed."

The feudal nature of vindication (by victimage) gives us many variants of this design: "Meet hate with hate . . . repay murder with murder . . . as he does, be it done to him," etc. Even in the seven extant plays of Aeschylus, we could probably trace literally hundreds of variations on the formula.

Here is the labyrinthine puzzle at the ultimate verbally attainable depths of the trilogy. For there is a notable respect in which the logic of symbols would transcend the very material body by which symbols are made usable (and in the tragic idiom, this moment of transcendence is figured in terms of victimage, of an ultimate slaying).

Do we, then, imply, that these tragedies are, in their motivation, reducible to terms so biologically absolute that, in the last analysis, they are concerned but with the unresolved conflicts between the verbal and the non-verbal out of which it arises and in which it is necessarily grounded?

Decidedly, not at all. The confusions of anal and oral, the kissing of carrion, the uniting of efficient and final cause in one locus, the joining of potency and actuality (matter and spirit), the combining of "father" and "mother" in a term such as "parent," (or, technically, the fact that a "thesis" and an "antithesis" cannot join battle except insofar as they have a "synthesizing" ground in common)—such bepuzzlements are all about us. Yet, the perception of their ubiquity and universality should not be allowed to obscure from us an ambiguity of this sort, which has exercised the author in many ways (as his *Rhetoric of Motives* attests) but which gained especial clarity for him when, recently, he was reading of *ziggurats* (towerlike temples, "zoned" into a series of steps that, pyramidally receding, would seem hieratically to figure the principle of the social pyramid). The "top" of each stage, he dialectically mused, is the "bottom" of the stage immediately above it. *Telescope* that design, as you necessarily do when you reduce it to a matter of *principle*, and an "amphisbaenal" relationship seems to result. "Mouth" and "tail" are brought together.

So, beginning over again, hence again recalling that the great Greek tragedies were devices for treating of civic tensions (read: class conflicts), and for contributing to social amity by ritual devices for resolving such tensions: We would note how the "amphisbaena" belonged, here too, as the figuring of a pattern.

Unfortunately, our remarks here look "Swiftian." So, to mitigate such suspicions, let us ask exactly what the difference may be. And, to that end, let us apply our perspective to the analysis of a passage in Swift's own works. We have in mind in Chapter VI of the *Voyage to Brodingnag*, where tiny Gulliver makes a seat-bottom out of combings from her gigantic Majesty's hair. He goes on to say: "The Queen would have had me sit upon one of these chairs, but I absolutely refused to obey her, protesting I would rather die a thousand deaths than place a dishonorable part of my body on those precious hairs that once adorned her Majesty's head." He continues: "Of these hairs (as I had always been a mechanical genius) . . ." and at this point, as regards our kind of lurking, we would forthwith adjourn to consider that astounding, Swiftly tortured adumbration of psychoanalysis, his tract *On the Mechanical Operation of the Spirit*. For satire is best understood, as a variant of tragedy, quite as tragedy is best understood, not just "universally," but by remembering always that it is designed to resolve *temporal* tensions.

Incidentally, we have elsewhere in our text observed how well the use of the traditional "myth" in tragedy contributed to simplicity of design. For whatever the complexities of a unique situation may be, the myth reduces these to a few basic relationships. In this sense, the tragic playwright's use of myth enabled him to get, in his medium, the kind of functional simplification that we have learned to associate with Greek sculpture at its best.

And, for the general picture, perhaps we should add one further consideration, to take account of the fact that traditionally a tragic trilogy was in turn *completed* by a satyr-play. For it would seem that all this astoundingly thorough concern with *completion* itself in turn was felt to require a completion. In our references to satire we have already hit upon a variant of such concerns but not wholly.

The satyr-play that rounded out this particular trilogy is missing. From our point of view, the loss to those who would systematically lurk, and would piously spy on great texts, is perhaps the greatest in all human history. For though we do know that the satyr-plays were *burlesques* of the very characters who were treated solemnly in the tragedies, we would like to think that, in the great days, the *same* characters were *finally* burlesqued who had been treated heroically in the tragic trilogy. Such an arrangement would be so very civilized. It would complete the completing.

Aeschylus
PROMETHEUS BOUND

Translated by
David Grene

Characters   *Might*

Violence (muta persona)

Hephaestus

Prometheus

Oceanos

Io

Hermes

Chorus of Daughters of Oceanos

SCENE: *A bare and desolate crag in the Caucasus. Enter* MIGHT *and* VIOLENCE, *demons, servants of Zeus, and* HEPHAESTUS, *the smith.*

Might

This is the world's limit that we have come to; this is the Scythian country, an untrodden desolation. Hephaestus, it is you that must heed the commands the Father laid upon you to nail this malefactor to the high craggy rocks in fetters unbreakable of adamantine chain. For it was your flower, the brightness of fire that devises all, that he stole and gave to mortal men; this is the sin for which he must pay the Gods the penalty—that he may learn to endure and like the sovereignty of Zeus and quit his man-loving disposition.

Hephaestus

Might and Violence, in you the command of Zeus has its perfect fulfilment: in you there is nothing to stand in its way. But, for myself, I have not the heart to bind violently a God who is my kin here on this wintry cliff. Yet there is constraint upon me to have the heart for just that, for it is a dangerous thing to treat the Father's words lightly.

High-contriving Son of Themis of Straight Counsel: this is not of your will nor of mine; yet I shall nail you in bonds of indissoluble bronze on this crag far from men. Here you shall hear no voice of mortal; here you shall see no form of mortal. You shall be grilled by the sun's bright fire and change the fair bloom of your skin. You shall be glad when Night comes with her mantle of stars and hides and sun's light; but the sun shall scatter the hoarfrost again at dawn. Always the grievous burden of your torture will be there to wear you down; for he that shall cause it to cease has yet to be born.

Such is the reward you reap of your man-loving disposition. For you, a God, feared not the anger of the Gods, but gave honors to mortals beyond what was just. Wherefore you shall mount guard on this unlovely rock, upright, sleepless, not bending the knee. Many a groan and many a lamentation you shall utter, but they shall not serve you. For the mind of Zeus is hard to soften with prayer, and every ruler is harsh whose rule is new.

Might

Come, why are you holding back? Why are you pitying in vain? Why is it that you do not hate a God whom the Gods hate most of all? Why did you not hate him, since it was your honor that he betrayed to men?

Hephaestus

Our kinship has strange power; that, and our life together.

Might

Yes. But to turn a deaf ear to the Father's words—how can that be? Do you not fear that more?

Hephaestus

You are always pitiless, always full of ruthlessness.

Might

There is no good singing dirges over him. Do not labor uselessly at what helps not at all.

Hephaestus

O handicraft of mine — that I deeply hate!

Might

Why do you hate it? To speak simply, your craft is in no way the author of his present troubles.

Hephaestus

Yet would another had had this craft allotted to him.

Might

There is nothing without discomfort except the overlordship of the Gods. For only Zeus is free.

Hephaestus

I know. I have no answer to this.

Might

Hurry now. Throw the chain around him that the Father may not look upon your tarrying.

Hephaestus

There are the fetters, there: you can see them.

Might

Put them on his hands: strong, now with the hammer: strike.

Nail him to the rock.

Hephaestus
It is being done now. I am not idling at my work.

Might
Hammer it more; put in the wedge; leave it loose nowhere. He's a cunning fellow at finding a way even out of hopeless difficulties.

Hephaestus
Look now, his arm is fixed immovably!

Might
Nail the other safe, that he may learn, for all his cleverness, that he is duller witted than Zeus.

Hephaestus
No one, save Prometheus, can justly blame me.

Might
Drive the obstinate jaw of the adamantine wedge right through his breast; drive it hard.

Hephaestus
Alas, Prometheus, I groan for your sufferings.

Might
Are you pitying again? Are you groaning for the enemies of Zeus? Have a care, lest some day you may be pitying yourself.

Hephaestus
You see a sight that hurts the eye.

Might
I see this rascal getting his deserts. Throw the girth around his sides.

Hephaestus
I am forced to do this; do not keep urging me.

Might
Yes, I will urge you, and hound you on as well. Get below now, and hoop his legs in strongly.

Hephaestus
There now, the task is done. It has not taken long.

Might
Hammer the piercing fetters with all your power, for the Overseer of our work is severe.

Hephaestus
Your looks and the refrain of your tongue are alike.

Might
You can be softhearted. But do not blame my stubbornness
and harshness of temper.

Hephaestus
Let us go. He has the harness on his limbs.

Might [*To* PROMETHEUS.]
Now, play the insolent; now, plunder the Gods' privileges and
give them to creatures of a day. What drop of your sufferings
can mortals spare you? The Gods named you wrongly when
they called you Forethought; you yourself *need* Forethought
to extricate yourself from this contrivance.

[PROMETHEUS *is left alone on the rock.*]

Prometheus
Bright light, swift-winged winds, springs of the rivers, num-
    berless
laughter of the sea's waves, earth, mother of all, and the all-
    seeing
circle of the sun: I call upon you to see what I, a God, suffer
at the hands of Gods—
see with what kind of torture
worn down I shall wrestle ten thousand
years of time—
such is the despiteful bond that the Prince
has devised against me, the new Prince
of the Blessed Ones. Oh woe is me!
I groan for the present sorrow,
I groan for the sorrow to come, I groan
questioning when there shall come a time
when He shall ordain a limit to my sufferings.
What am I saying? I have known all before,
all that shall be, and clearly known; to me,
nothing that hurts shall come with a new face.
So must I bear, as lightly as I can,
the destiny that fate has given me;
for I know well against necessity,

against its strength, no one can fight and win.

I cannot speak about my fortune, cannot
hold my tongue either. It was mortal man
to whom I gave great privileges and
for that was yoked in this unyielding harness.
I hunted out the secret spring of fire,
that filled the narthex stem, which when revealed
became the teacher of each craft to men,
a great resource. This is the sin committed
for which I stand accountant, and I pay
nailed in my chains under the open sky.

Ah! Ah!
What sound, what sightless smell approaches me,
God sent, or mortal, or mingled?
Has it come to earth's end
to look on my sufferings,
or what does it wish?
You see me a wretched God in chains,
the enemy of Zeus, hated of all
the Gods that enter Zeus's palace hall,
because of my excessive love for Man.
What is that? The rustle
of birds' wings near? The air whispers
with the gentle strokes of wings.
Everything that somes toward me is occasion for fear.
[*The* CHORUS, *composed of the daughters of* OCEANOS, *enters, the
members wearing some formalized representation of wings,
so that their general appearance is birdlike.*]

Chorus

Fear not: this is a company of friends
that comes to your mountain with swift
rivalry of wings.
Hardly have we persuaded our Father's
mind, and the quick-bearing winds
speeded us hither. The sound
of stroke of bronze range through our cavern

in its depths and it shook from us
shamefaced modesty; unsandaled
we have hastened on our chariot of wings.

Prometheus

Alas, children of teeming Tethys and of him
who encircles all the world with stream unsleeping,
Father Ocean,
look, see with what chains
I am nailed on the craggy heights
of this gully to keep a watch
that none would envy me.

Chorus

I see, Prometheus: and a mist of fear and tears
besets my eyes as I see your form
wasting away on these cliffs
in adamantine bonds of bitter shame.
For new are the steersmen that rule Olympus:
and new are the customs by which Zeus rules,
customs that have no law to them,
but what was great before he brings to nothingness.

Prometheus

Would that he had hurled me
underneath the earth and underneath
the House of Hades, host to the dead—
yes, down to limitless Tartarus,
yes, though he bound me cruelly
in chains unbreakable,
so neither God nor any other being
might have found joy in gloating over me.
Now as I hang, the plaything of the winds,
my enemies can laugh at what I suffer.

Chorus

Who of the Gods is so hard of heart
that he find joy in this?
Who is that that does not feel
sorrow answering your pain—
save only Zeus? For he malignantly,

always cherishing a mind
that bends not, has subdued the breed
of Uranos, nor shall he cease
until he satisfies his heart,
or someone take the rule from him — that hard-to-capture
    rule —
by some device of subtlety.

Prometheus

Yes, there shall come a day for me
when he shall need me, me that now am tortured
in bonds and fetters — he shall need me then,
this president of the Blessed —
to show the new plot whereby he may be spoiled
of his throne and his power.
Then not with honeyed tongues
of persuasion shall he enchant me;
he shall not cow me with his threats
to tell him what I know,
until he free me from my cruel chains
and pay me recompense for what I suffer.

Chorus

You are stout of heart, unyielding
to the bitterness of pain.
You are free of tongue, too free.
It is my mind that piercing fear has fluttered;
your misfortunes frighten me.
Where and when is it fated
to see you reach the term, to see you reach
the harbor free of trouble at the last?
A disposition none can win, a heart
that no persuasions soften — these are his,
the Son of Kronos.

Prometheus

I know that he is savage: and his justice
a thing he keeps by his own standard: still
that will of his shall melt to softness yet
when he is broken in the way I know,

and though his temper now is oaken hard
it shall be softened: hastily he'll come
to meet my haste, to join in amity
and union with me — one day he shall come.

Chorus

Reveal it all to us: tell us the story of what the charge was on which Zeus caught you and punished you so cruelly with such dishonor. Tell us, if the telling will not injure you in any way.

Prometheus

To speak of this is bitterness. To keep silent
bitter no less; and every way is misery.

When first the Gods began their angry quarrel,
and God matched God in rising faction, some
eager to drive old Kronos from his throne
that Zeus might rule — the fools! — others again
earnest that Zeus might never be their king —
I then with the best counsel tried to win
the Titans, sons of Uranos and Earth,
but failed. They would have none of crafty schemes
and in their savage arrogance of spirit
thought they would lord it easily by force.
But she that was my mother, Themis, Earth —
she is but one although her names are many —
had prophesied to me how it should be,
even how the fates decreed it: and she said
that "not by strength nor overmastering force
the fates allowed the conquerors to conquer
but by guile only": This is what I told them,
but they would not vouchsafe a glance at me.
Then with those things before me it seemed best
to take my mother and join Zeus's side:
he was as willing as we were:
thanks to my plans the dark receptacle
of Tartarus conceals the ancient Kronos,
him and his allies. These were the services
I rendered to this tyrant and these pains

the payment he has given me in requital.
This is a sickness rooted and inherent
in the nature of a tyranny:
that he that hold it does not trust his friends.

But you have asked on what particular
charge he now tortures me: this I will tell you.
As soon as he ascended to the throne
that was his father's, straightaway he assigned
to the several Gods their several privileges
and portioned out the power, but to the unhappy
breed of mankind he gave no heed, intending
to blot the race out and create a new.
Against these plans none stood save I: I dared.
I rescued men from shattering destruction
that would have carried them to Hades' house;
and therefore I am tortured on this rock,
a bitterness to suffer, and a pain
to pitiful eyes. I gave to mortal man
a precedence over myself in pity: I
can win no pity: pitiless is he
that thus chastises me, a spectacle
bringing dishonor on the name of Zeus.

Chorus

He would be iron-minded and made of stone, indeed, Prometheus, who did not sympathize with your sufferings. I would not have chosen to see them, and now that I see, my heart is pained.

Prometheus

Yes, to my friends I am pitiable to see.

Chorus

Did you perhaps go further than you have told us?

Prometheus

I caused mortals to cease foreseeing doom.

Chorus

What cure did you provide them with against that sickness?

Prometheus

I placed in them blind hopes.

Chorus

That was a great gift you gave to men.

Prometheus

Besides this, I gave them fire.

Chorus

And do creatures of a day now possess bright-faced fire?

Prometheus

Yes, and from it they shall learn many crafts.

Chorus

Then these are the charges on which—

Prometheus

Zeus tortures me and gives me no respite.

Chorus

Is there no limit set for your pain?

Prometheus

None save when it shall seem good to Zeus.

Chorus

How will it ever seem good to him? What hope is there? Do
you not see how you have erred? It is not pleasure for me to
say that you have erred, and for you it is a pain to hear. But let
us speak no more of all this and do you seek some means of
deliverance from your trials.

Prometheus

It is an easy thing for one whose foot
is on the outside of calamity
to give advice and to rebuke the sufferer.
I have known all that you have said: I knew,
I knew when I transgressed nor will deny it.
In helping man I brought my troubles on me;
but yet I did not think that with such tortures
I should be wasted on these airy cliffs,
this lonely mountain top, with no one near.
But do not sorrow for my present suffering;
alight on earth and hear what is to come
that you may know the whole complete: I beg you
alight and join your sorrow with mine: misfortune
wandering the same track lights now upon one
and now upon another.

Chorus

Willing our ears,
that hear you cry to them, Prometheus,
now with light foot I leave the rushing car
and sky, the holy path of birds, and light
upon this jutting rock: I long
to hear your story to the end.

[*Enter* OCEANOS, *riding on a hippocamp, or sea-monster*])

Oceanos

I come,
on a long journey, speeding past the boundaries,
to visit you, Prometheus: with the mind
alone, no bridle needed, I direct
my swift-winged bird; my heart is sore
for your misfortunes; you know that. I think
that it is kinship makes me feel them so.
Besides, apart from kinship, there is no one
I hold in higher estimation: that
you soon shall know and know beside that in me
there is no mere word-kindness: tell me
how I can help you, and you will never say
that you have any friend more loyal to you
than Oceanos.

Prometheus

What do I see? Have you, too, come to gape
in wonder at this great display, my torture?
How did you have the courage to come here
to this land, Iron-Mother, leaving the stream
called after you and the rock-roofed, self-established
caverns? Was it to feast your eyes upon
the spectacle of my suffering and join
in pity for my pain? Now look and see
the sight, this friend of Zeus, that helped set up
his tyranny and see what agonies
twist me, by his instructions!

Oceanos

Yes, I see,

Prometheus, and I want, indeed I do,
to advise you for the best, for all your cleverness.
Know yourself and reform your ways to new ways,
for new is he that rules among the Gods.
But if you throw about such angry words,
words that are whetted swords, soon Zeus will hear you,
even though his seat in glory is far removed,
and then your present multitude of pains
will seem like child's play. My poor friend, give up
this angry mood of yours and look for means
of getting yourself free of trouble. Maybe
what I say seems to you both old and commonplace;
but this is what you pay, Prometheus, for
that tongue of yours which talked so high and haughty:
you are not yet humble, still you do not yield
to your misfortunes, and you wish, indeed,
to add some more to them; now, if you follow
me as a schoolmaster you will not kick
against the pricks, seeing that he, the King,
that rules alone, is harsh and sends accounts
to no one's audit for the deeds he does.
Now I will go and try if I can free you:
do you be quiet, do not talk so much.
Since your mind is so subtle, don't you know
that a vain tongue is subject to correction?

Prometheus

I envy you, that you stand clear of blame,
yet shared and dared in everything with me!
Now let me be, and have no care for me.
Do what you will, Him you will not persuade;
He is not easily won over: look,
take care lest coming here to me should hurt you.

Oceanos

You are by nature better at advising
others than yourself. I take my cue
from deeds, not words. Do not withhold me now
when I am eager to go to Zeus. I'm sure,

I'm sure that he will grant this favor to me,
to free you from your chains.

Prometheus

I thank you and will never cease; for loyalty
is not what you are wanting in. Don't trouble,
for you will trouble to no purpose, and no help
to me—if it so be you want to trouble.
No, rest yourself, keep away from this thing;
because I am unlucky I would not,
for that, have everyone unlucky too.
No, for my heart is sore already when
I think about my brothers' fortunes—Atlas,
who stands to westward of the world, supporting
the pillar of earth and heaven on his shoulders,
a load that suits no shoulders; and the earthborn
dweller in caves Cilician, whom I saw
and pitied, hundred-headed, dreadful monster,
fierce Typho, conquered and brought low by force.
Once against all the Gods he stood, opposing,
hissing out terror from his grim jaws; his eyes
flashed gorgon glaring lightning as he thought
to sack the sovereign tyranny of Zeus;
but upon him came the unsleeping bolt
of Zeus, the lightning-breathing flame, down rushng,
which cast him from his high aspiring boast.
Struck to the heart, his strength was blasted dead
and burnt to ashes; now a sprawling mass
useless he lies, hard by the narrow seaway
pressed down beneath the roots of Aetna: high
above him on the mountain peak the smith
Hephaestus works at the anvil. Yet one day
there shall burst out rivers of fire, devouring
with savage jaws the fertile, level plains
of Sicily of the fair fruits; such boiling wrath
with weapons of fire-breathng surf, a fiery
unapproachable torrent, shall Typho vomit,
though Zeus's lightning left him but a cinder.

But all of this you know: you do not need me
to be your schoolmaster: reassure yourself
as you know how: this cup I shall drain myself
till the high mind of Zeus shall cease from anger.

Oceanos

Do you not know, Prometheus, that words are healer of the sick temper?

Prometheus

Yes, if in season due one soothes the heart with them, not tries violently to reduce the swelling anger.

Oceanos

Tell me, what danger do you see for me in loyalty to you, and courage therein?

Prometheus

I see only useless effort and a silly good nature.

Oceanos

Suffer me then to be sick of this sickness, for it is a profitable thing, if one is wise, to seem foolish.

Prometheus

This shall seem to be my fault.

Oceanos

Clearly your words send me home again.

Prometheus

Yes, lest your doings for me bring you enmity.

Oceanos

His enmity, who newly sits on the all-powerful throne?

Prometheus

His is a heart you should beware of vexing.

Oceanos

Your own misfortune will be my teacher, Prometheus.

Prometheus

Off with you, then! Begone! Keep your present mind.

Oceanos

These words fall on very responsive ears. Already my four-legged bird is pawing the level track of Heaven with his wings, and he will be glad to bend the knee in his own stable.

Chorus

STROPHE

I cry aloud, Prometheus, and lament your bitter fate,
my tender eyes are trickling tears:
their fountains wet my cheek.
This is a tyrant's deed; this is unlovely,
a thing done by a tyrant's private laws,
and with this thing Zeus shows his haughtiness
of temper toward the Gods that were of old.

ANTISTROPHE

Now all the earth has cried aloud, lamenting:
now all that was magnificent of old
laments your fall, laments your brethren's fall
as many as in holy Asia hold
their stablished habitation, all lament
in sympathy for your most grievous woes.

STROPHE

Dwellers in the land of Colchis,
maidens, fearless in the fight,
and the host of Scythia, living
round the lake Maeotis, living
on the edges of the world.

ANTISTROPHE

And Arabia's flower of warriors
and the craggy fortress keepers
near Caucasian mountains, fighters
terrible, crying for battle,
brandishing sharp pointed spears.

STROPHE

One god and one God only I have seen
before this day, in torture and in bonds
unbreakable: he was a Titan,
Alas, whose strength and might
ever exceeded; now he bends his back
and groans beneath the load of earth and heaven.

ANTISTROPHE

The wave cries out as it breaks into surf;

the depth cries out, lamenting you; the dark
Hades, the hollow underneath the world,
sullenly groans below; the springs
of sacred flowing rivers all lament
the pain and pity of your suffering.

Prometheus

Do not think that out of pride or stubbornness I hold my peace;
my heart is eaten away when I am aware of myself, when I
see myself insulted as I am. Who was it but I who in truth dis-
pensed their honors to these new gods? I will say nothing of
this; you know it all; but hear what troubles there were
among men, how I found them witless and gave them the use
of their wits and made them masters of their minds. I will tell
you this, not because I would blame men, but to explain the
goodwill of my gift. For men at first had eyes but saw to no
purpose; they had ears but did not hear. Like the shapes of
dreams they dragged through their long lives and handled all
things in bewilderment and confusion. They did not know of
building houses with bricks to face the sun; they did not
know how to work in wood. They lived like swarming ants in
holes in the ground, in the sunless caves of the earth. For
them there was no secure token by which to tell winter not
the flowering spring nor the summer with its crops; all their
doings were indeed without intelligent calculation until I
showed them the rising of the stars, and the settings, hard to
observe. And further I discovered to them numbering, pre-
eminent among subtle devices, and the combining of letters
as a means of remembering all things, the Muses' mother,
skilled in craft. It was I who first yoked beasts for them in the
yokes and made of those beasts the slaves of trace chain and
pack saddle that they might be man's substitute in the hard-
est tasks; and I harnessed to the carriage, so that they loved
the rein, horses, the crowning pride of the rich man's luxury.
It was I and none other who discovered ships, the sail-driven
wagons that the sea buffets. Such were the contrivances that I
discovered for man—alas for me! For I myself am without
contrivance to rid myself of my present affliction.

Chorus

What you have suffered is indeed terrible. You are all astray and bewildered in your mind, and like a bad doctor that has fallen sick himself, you are cast down and cannot find what sort of drugs would cure your ailment.

Prometheus

Hear the rest, and you will marvel even more at the crafts and resources I contrived. Greatest was this: in the former times if a man fell sick he had no defense against the sickness, neither healing food nor drink, nor unguent; but through the lack of drugs men wasted away, until I showed them the blending of mild simples [herbs] wherewith they drive out all manner of diseases. It was I who arranged all the ways of seercraft, and I first adjudged what things come verily true from dreams; and to men I gave meaning to the ominous cries, hard to interpret. It was I who set in order the omens of the highway and the flight of crooked-taloned birds, which of them were propitious or lucky by nature, and what manner of life each led, and what were their mutual hates, loves, and companionships; also I taught of the smoothness of the vitals and what color they should have to pleasure the gods and the dappled beauty of the gall and the lobe. It was I who burned thighs wrapped in fat and the long shank bone and set mortals on the road to this murky craft. It was I who made visible to men's eyes the flaming signs of the sky that were before dim. So much for these. Beneath the earth, man's hidden blessing, copper, iron, silver, and gold — will anyone claim to have discovered these before I did? No one, I am very sure, who wants to speak truly and to the purpose. One brief word will tell the whole story: all arts that mortals have come from Prometheus.

Chorus

Therefore do not help mortals beyond all expediency while neglecting yourself in your troubles. For I am of good hope that once freed of these bonds you will be no less in power than Zeus.

Prometheus

Not yet has fate that brings to fulfilment determined these

things to be thus. I must be twisted by ten thousand pangs and agonies, as I now am, to escape my chains at last. Craft is far weaker than necessity.

Chorus

Who then is the steersman of necessity?

Prometheus

The triple-formed Fates and the remembering Furies.

Chorus

Is Zeus weaker than these?

Prometheus

Yes, for he, too, cannot escape what is fated.

Chorus

What is fated for Zeus besides eternal sovereignty?

Prometheus

Inquire of this no further, do not entreat me.

Chorus

This is some solemn secret, I suppose, that you are hiding.

Prometheus

Think of some other story: this one it is not yet the season to give tongue to, but it must be hidden with all care; for it is only by keeping it that I will escape my despiteful bondage and my agony.

Chorus

STROPHE

May Zeus never, Zeus that all
the universe controls, oppose
his power against my mind:
may I never dallying
be slow to give my worship at
the sacrificial feasts
when the bulls are killed beside
quenchless Father Ocean:
may I never sin in word:
may these precepts still abide
in my mind nor melt away.

ANTISTROPHE

It is a sweet thing to draw out

a long, long life in cheerful hopes,
and feed the spirit in the bright
benignity of happiness:
but I shiver when I see you
wasted with ten thousand pains,
all because you did not tremble
at the name of Zeus: your mind
was yours, not his, and at its bidding
you regarded mortal men
too high, Prometheus.

STROPHE

Kindness that cannot be requited, tell me,
where is the help in that, my friend? What succor
in creatures of a day? You did not see
the feebleness that draws its breath in gasps,
a dreamlike feebleness by which the race
of man is held in bondage, a blind prisoner.
So the plans of men shall never
pass the ordered law of Zeus.

ANTISTROPHE

This I have learned while I looked on your pains,
deadly pains, Prometheus.
A dirge for you came to my lips, so different
from the other song I sang to crown your marriage
in honor of your couching and your bath,
upon the day you won her with your gifts
to share you bed—of your own race she was,
Hesione—and so you brought her home.

[*Enter* IO, *a girl wearing horns like an ox.*]

Io

What land is this? what race of men? Who is it
I see here tortured in this rocky bondage?
What is the sin he's paying for? Oh tell me
to what part of the world my wanderings have brought me.
O, O, O,
there it is again, there again — it stings me,
the gadfly, the ghost of earth-born Argos:

keep it away, keep it away, earth!
I'm frightened when I see the shape of Argos,
Argos the herdsman with ten thousand eyes.
He stalks me with his crafty eyes: he died,
but the earth didn't hide him; still he comes
even from the depths of the Underworld to hunt me:
he drives me starving by the sands of the sea.

The reed-woven pipe drones on in a hum
and drones and drones its sleep-giving strain:
O, O, O,
Where are you bringing me, my far-wandering wanderings?
Son of Kronos, what fault, what fault
did you find in me that you should yoke me
to a harness of misery like this,
that you should torture me so to madness
driven in fear of the gadfly?
Burn me with fire: hide me in earth: cast me away
to monsters of the deep for food: but do not
grudge me the granting of this prayer, King.
Enough have my much wandering wanderings
exercised me: I cannot find
a way to escape my troubles.
Do you hear the voice of the cow-horned maid?

Prometheus

Surely I hear the voice, the voice of the maiden, gadfly-
haunted, the daughter of Inachus? She set Zeus's heart on fire
with love and now she is violently exercised running on
courses overlong,
driven by Hera's hate.

Io

How is it you speak my father's name?
Tell me, who are you? Who are you? Oh
who are you that so exactly accosts me by name?
You have spoken of the disease that the Gods have sent to me
which wastes me away, pricking with goads,
so that I am moving always
tortured and hungry, wild bounding,

quick sped I come,
a victim of jealous plots.
Some have been wretched
before me, but who of these
suffered as I do?
But declare to me clearly
what I have still to suffer: what would avail
against my sickness, what drug would cure it:
Tell me, if you know:
tell me, declare it to the unlucky, wandering maid.

Prometheus

I shall tell you clearly all that you would know, weaving you no riddles, but in plain words, as it is just to open the lips to friends. You see before you him that gave fire to men, even Prometheus.

Io

O spirit that has appeared as a common blessing to all men, unhappy Prometheus, why are you being punished?

Prometheus

I have just this moment ceased from the lamentable tale of my sorrows.

Io

Will you then grant me this favor?

Prometheus

Say what you are asking for: I will tell you all.

Io

Tell who it was that nailed you to the cliff.

Prometheus

The plan was the plan of Zeus, and the hand the hand of Hephaestus.

Io

And what was the offense of which this is the punishment?

Prometheus

It is enough that I have told you a clear story so far.

Io

In addition, then, indicate to me what date shall be the limit of my wanderings.

Prometheus

Better for you not to know this than know it.

Io

I beg you, do not hide from me what I must endure.

Prometheus

It is not that I grudge you this favor.

Io

Why then delay to tell me all?

Prometheus

It is no grudging, but I hesitate to break your spirit.

Io

Do not have more thought for me than pleases me myself.

Prometheus

Since you are so eager, I must speak; and do you give ear.

Chorus

Not yet: give me, too, a share of pleasure. First let us question
her concerning her sickness, and let her tell us of her desperate fortunes. And then let you be our informant for the sorrows that still await her.

Prometheus

It is your task, Io, to gratify these spirits, for besides other
considerations they are your father's sisters. To make wail
and lament for one's ill fortune, when one will win a tear
from the audience, is well worthwhile.

Io

I know not how I should distrust you: clearly
you shall hear all you want to know from me.
Yet even as I speak I groan in bitterness
for that storm sent by God on me, that ruin
of my beauty; I must sorrow when I think
who sent all this upon me. There were always
night visions that kept haunting me and coming
into my maiden chamber and exhorting
with winning words. "O maiden greatly blessed,
why are you still a maiden, you who might
make marriage with the greatest? Zeus is stricken
with lust for you; he is afire to try

the bed of love with you: do not disdain him.
Go, child, to Lerna's meadow, deep in grass,
to where your father's flocks and cattle stand
that Zeus's eye may cease from longing for you."
With such dreams I was cruelly beset
night after night until I took the courage
to tell my father of my nightly terror.
He sent to Pytho many an embassy
and to Dodona seeking to discover
what deed or word of his might please the God,
but those he sent came back with riddling oracles
dark and beyond the power of understanding.
At last the words came clear to Inachus
charging him plainly that he cast me out
of home and country, drive me out footloose
to wander to the limits of the world;
if he should not obey, the oracle said,
the fire-faced thunderbolt would come from Zeus
and blot out his whole race. These were the oracles
of Loxias, and Inachus obeyed them.
He drove me out and shut his doors against me
with tears on both our parts, but Zeus's bit
compelled him to do this against his will.
Immediately my form and mind were changed
and all distorted; horned, as you see,
pricked on by the sharp biting gadfly, leaping
in frenzied jumps I ran beside the river
Kerchneia, good to drink, and Lerna's spring.
The earth-born herdsman Argos followed me
whose anger knew no limits, and he spied
after my tracks with all his hundred eyes.
Then an unlooked-for doom, descending suddenly,
took him from life: I, driven by the gadfly,
that god-sent scourge, was driven always onward
from one land to another: that is my story.
If you can tell me what remains for me,
tell me, and do not out of pity cozen

with kindly lies: there is no sickness worse
for me than words that to be kind must lie.

Chorus

Hold! Keep away! Alas!
never did I think that such strange
words would come to my ears:
never did I think such intolerable
sufferings, an offense to the eye,
shameful and frightening, so
would chill my soul with a double-edged point.
Alas, Alas, for your fate!
I shudder when I look on Io's fortune.

Prometheus

You groan too soon: you are full of fear too soon: wait till you
hear besides what is to be.

Chorus

Speak, tell us to the end. For sufferers it is sweet to know beforehand clearly the pain that still remains for them.

Prometheus

The first request you made of me you gained
lightly: from her you wished to hear the story
of what she suffered. Now hear what remains,
what sufferings this maid must yet endure
from Hera. Do you listen, child of Inachus,
hear and lay up my words within your heart
that you may know the limits of your journey.
First turn to the sun's rising and walk on
over the fields no plough has broken: then
you will come to the wandering Scythians
who live in wicker houses built above
their well-wheeled wagons; they are an armed people,
armed with the bow that strikes from far away:
do not draw near them; rather let your feet
touch the surf line of the sea where the waves moan,
and cross their country: on your left there live
the Chalybes who work with iron: these
you must beware of; for they are not gentle,

nor people whom a stranger dare approach.
Then you will come to Insolence, a river
that well deserves its name: but cross it not—
it is no stream that you can easily ford—
until you come to Caucasus itself,
the highest mountains, where the river's strength
gushes from its very temples. Cross these peaks,
the neighbors of the stars, and take the road
southward until you reach the Amazons,
the race of women who hate men, who one day
shall live around Thermodon in Themiscyra
where Salmydessos, rocky jaw of the sea,
stands sailor-hating, stepmother of ships.
The Amazons will set you on your way
and gladly: you will reach Cimmeria,
the isthmus, at the narrow gates of the lake.
Leave this with a good heart and cross the channel,
the channel of Maeotis: and hereafter
for all time men shall talk about your crossing,
and they shall call the place for you Cow's-ford.*
Leave Europe's mainland then, and go to Asia.
[*To the* CHORUS.]
Do you now think this tyrant of the Gods
is hard in all things without difference?
He was a God and sought to lie in love
with this girl who was mortal, and on her
he brought this curse of wandering: bitter indeed
you found your marriage with this suitor, maid.
Yet you must think of all that I have told you
as still only in prelude.

Io

O, O

Prometheus

Again, you are crying and lamenting: what will you do when
you hear of the evils to come?

---

*Cow's-ford: Bosporus.

Chorus

Is there still something else to her sufferings of which you will speak?

Prometheus

A wintry sea of agony and ruin.

Io

What good is life to me then? Why do I not throw myself at once from some rough crag, to strike the ground and win a quittance of all my troubles? It would be better to die once for all than suffer all one's days.

Prometheus

You would ill bear my trials, then, for whom Fate reserves no death. Death would be a quittance of trouble: but for me there is no limit of suffering set till Zeus fall from power.

Io

Can Zeus ever fall from power?

Prometheus

You would be glad to see that catastrophe, I think.

Io

Surely, since Zeus is my persecutor.

Prometheus

Then know that this shall be.

Io

Who will despoil him of his sovereign scepter?

Prometheus

His own witless plans.

Io

How? Tell me, if there is no harm to telling.

Prometheus

He shall make a marriage that shall hurt him.

Io

With god or mortal? Tell me, if you may say it.

Prometheus

Why ask what marriage? That is not to be spoken.

Io

Is it his wife shall cast him from his throne?

Prometheus

She shall bear him a son mightier than his father.

Io

Has he no possibility of escaping this downfall?

Prometheus

None, save through my release from these chains.

Io

but who will free you, against Zeus's will?

Prometheus

Fate has determined that it be one of your descendants.

Io

What, shall a child of mine bring you free?

Prometheus

Yes, in the thirteenth generation.

Io

Your prophecy has now passed the limits of understanding.

Prometheus

Then also do not seek to learn your trials.

Io

Do not offer me a boon and then withhold it.

Prometheus

I offer you then one of two stories.

Io

Which? Tell me and give me the choice.

Prometheus

I will: choose that I tell you clearly either what remains for
you or the one that shall deliver me.

Chorus

Grant her one and grant me the other and do not deny us the
tale. Tell her what remains of her wanderings: tell us of the
one that shall deliver you. That is what I desire.

Prometheus

Since you have so much eagerness, I will not
refuse to tell you all that you have asked me.
First to you, Io, I shall tell the tale
of your sad wanderings, rich in groans—inscribe
the story in the tablets of your mind.
When you shall cross the channel that divides
Europe from Asia, turn to the rising sun,

to the burnt plains, sun-scorched; cross by the edge
of the foaming sea till you come to Gorgona
to the flat stretches of Kisthene's country.
There live the ancient maids, children of Phorcys:
these swan-formed hags, with but one common eye,
single-toothed monsters, such as nowhere else
the sun's rays look on nor the moon by night.
Near are their winged sisters, the three Gorgons,
with snakes to bind their hair up, mortal-hating:
nor mortal that but looks on them shall live:
these are the sentry guards I tell you of.
Hear, too, of yet another gruesome sight,
the sharp-toothed hounds of Zeus, that have no bark,
the vultures—them take heed of—and the host
of one-eyed Arimaspians, horse-riding,
that live around the spring which flows with gold,
the spring of Pluto's river: go not near them.
A land far off, a nation of black men,
these you shall come to, men who live hard by
the fountain of the sun where is the river
Aethiops—travel by his banks along
to a waterfall where from the Bibline hills
Nile pours his holy waters, pure to drink.
This river shall be your guide to the triangular
land of the Nile and there, by Fate's decree,
there, Io, you shall find your distant home,
a colony for you and your descendants.
If anything of this is still obscure
or difficult ask me again and learn
clearly: I have more leisure than I wish.

Chorus

If there is still something left for you to tell her of her ruinous
wanderings, tell it; but if you have said everything, grant us
the favor we asked and tell us the story too.

Prometheus

The limit of her wanderings complete
she now has heard: but so that she may know

that she has not been listening to no purpose
I shall recount what she endured before
she came to us here: this I give as a pledge,
a witness to the good faith of my words.
The great part of the story I omit
and come to the very boundary of your travels.
When you had come to the Molossian plains
around the sheer back of Dodona where
is the oracular seat of Zeus Thesprotian,
the talking oaks, a wonder past belief,
by them full clearly, in no riddling terms,
you were hailed glorious wife of Zeus that shall be:
does anything of this wake pleasant memories?
Then, goaded by the gadfly, on you hastened
to the great gulf of Rhea by the track
at the side of the sea: but in returning course
you were storm-driven back: in time to come
that inlet of the sea shall bear your name
and shall be called Ionian, a memorial
to all men of your journeying: these are proofs
for you, of how far my mind sees something farther
than what is visible: for what is left,
to you and you this I shall say in common,
taking up again the track of my old tale.
There is a city, furthest in the world,
Canobos, near the mouth and issuing point
of the Nile: there Zeus shall make you sound of mind
touching you with a hand that brings no fear,
and through that touch alone shall come your healing.
You shall bear Epaphos, dark of skin, his name
recalling Zeus's touch and his begetting.
This Epaphos shall reap the fruit of all
the land that is watered by the broad flowing Nile.
From him five generations, and again
to Argos they shall come, against their will,
in number fifty, women, flying from
a marriage with their kinsfolk: but these kinsfolk

their hearts with lust aflutter like the hawks
barely outdistanced by the doves will come
hunting a marriage that the law forbids:
the God shall grudge the men these women's bodies,
and the Pelasgian earth shall welcome them
in death: for death shall claim them in a fight
where women strike in the dark, a murderous vigil.
Each wife shall rob her husband of his life
dipping in blood her two-edged sword: even so
may Love come, too, upon my enemies.
But one among these girls shall love beguile
from killing her bedfellow, blunting her purpose:
and she shall make her choice — to bear the name
of coward and not murder: this girl,
she shall in Argos bear a race of kings.
To tell this clearly needs a longer story,
but from her seed shall spring a man renowned
for archery, and he shall set me free.
Such was the prophecy which ancient Themis
my Titan mother opened up to me;
but how and by what means it shall come true
would take too long to tell, and if you heard
the knowledge would not profit you.

Io

Eleleu, eleleu
It creeps on me again, the twitching spasm,
the mind-destroying madness, burning me up
and the gadfly's sting goads me on —
steel point by no fire tempered —
and my heart in its fear knocks on my breast.
There's a dazing whirl in my eyes as I run
out of my course by the madness driven,
the crazy frenzy; my tongue ungoverned
babbles, the words in a muddy flow strike
on the waves of the mischief I hate, strike wild
without aim or sense.

Chorus

STROPHE

A wise man indeed he was
that first in judgment weighed this word
and gave it tongue: the best by far
it is to marry in one's rank and station:
let no one working with her hands aspire
to marriage with those lifted high in pride
because of wealth, or of ancestral glory.

ANTISTROPHE

Never, never may you see me,
Fates majestic, drawing nigh
the bed of Zeus, to share it with the kings:
nor ever may I know a heavenly wooer:
I dread such things beholding
Io's sad virginity
ravaged, ruined; bitter wandering
hers because of Hera's wrath.

EPODE

When a match has equal partners
then I fear not: may the eye
inescapable of the mighty
Gods not look on me.
That is a fight that none can fight: a fruitful
source of fruitlessness: I would not
know what I could do: I cannot
see the hope when Zeus is angry
of escaping him.

Prometheus

Yet shall this Zeus, for all his pride of heart
be humble yet: such is the match he plans,
a marriage that shall drive him from his power
and from his throne, out of the sight of all.
So shall at last the final consummation
be brought about of Father Kronos' curse
which he, driven from his ancient throne, invoked
against the son deposing him: no one

of all the Gods save I alone can tell
a way to escape this mischief: I alone
know it and how. So let him confidently
sit on his throne and trust his heavenly thunder
and brandish in his hand his fiery bolt.
Nothing shall all of this avail against
a fall intolerable, a dishonored end.
So strong a wrestler Zeus is now equipping
against himself, a monster hard to fight.
This enemy shall find a plan to best
the thunderbolt, a thunderclap to best
the thunderclap of Zeus: and he shall shiver
Poseidon's trident, curse of sea and land.
So, in his crashing fall shall Zeus discover
how different are rule and slavery.

Chorus
You voice your wishes for the god's destruction.
Prometheus
They are my wishes, yet shall come to pass.
Chorus
Must we expect someone to conquer Zeus?
Prometheus
Yes; he shall suffer worse than I do now.
Chorus
Have you no fear of uttering such words?
Prometheus
Why should I fear, since death is not my fate?
Chorus
But he might give you pain still worse than this.
Prometheus
Then let him do so; all this I expect.
Chorus
Wise are the worshipers of Adrasteia.
Prometheus
Worship him pray; flatter whatever king
is king today; but I care less than nothing
for Zeus. Let him do what he likes,

let him be king for his short time: he shall not
be king for long.
            Look, here is Zeus's footman,
this fetch-and-carry messenger of him,
the New King. Certainly he has come here
with news for us.

Hermes
                You, subtle-spirit, you
bitterly overbitter, you that sinned
against the immortals, giving honor to
the creatures of a day, you thief of fire:
the Father has commanded you to say
what marriage of his is this you brag about
that shall drive him from power — and declare it
in clear terms and no riddles. You, Prometheus,
do not cause me a double journey; these
[*Pointing to the chains.*]
will prove to you that Zeus is not softhearted.

Prometheus
Your speech is pompous sounding, full of pride,
as fits the lackey of the Gods. You are young
and young your rule and you think that the tower
in which you live is free from sorrow: from it
have I not seen two tyrants thrown? the third,
who now is king, I shall yet live to see him
fall, of all three most suddenly, most dishonored.
Do you think I will crouch before your Gods,
— so new — and tremble? I am far from that.
Hasten away, back on the road you came.
You shall learn nothing that you ask of me.

Hermes
Just such the obstinacy that brought you here,
to this self-willed calamitous anchorage.

Prometheus
Be sure of this: when I set my misfortune
against your slavery, I would not change.

Hermes
It is better, I suppose, to be a slave

to this rock, than Zeus's trusted messenger.

Prometheus
Thus must the insolent show their insolence!

Hermes
I think you find your present lot too soft.

Prometheus
Too soft? I would my enemies had it then,
and you are one of those I count as such.

Hermes
Oh, you would blame me too for your calamity?

Prometheus
In a single word, I am the enemy
of all the Gods that gave me ill for good.

Hermes
Your words declare you mad, and mad indeed.

Prometheus
Yes, if it's madness to detest my foes.

Hermes
No one could bear you in success.

Prometheus
                                                  Alas!

Hermes
Alas! *Zeus* does not know the word.

Prometheus
Time in its aging course teaches all things.

Hermes
But you have not yet learned a wise discretion.

Prometheus
True: or I would not speak so to a servant.

Hermes
It seems you will not grant the Father's wish.

Prometheus
I should be glad, indeed, to requite his kindness!

Hermes
You mock me like a child!

Prometheus
                              And are you not
a child, and sillier than a child, to think

that I should tell you anything? There is not
a torture or an engine wherewithal
Zeus can induce me to declare these things,
till he has loosed me from these cruel shackles.
So let him hurl his smoky lightning flame,
and throw in turmoil all things in the world
with white-winged snowflakes and deep bellowing
thunder beneath the earth: me he shall not
bend by all this to tell him who is fated
to drive him from his tyranny.

Hermes
Think, here and now, if this seems to your interest.

Prometheus
I have already thought — and laid my plans.

Hermes
Bring your proud heart to know a true discretion —
O foolish spirit — in the face of ruin.

Prometheus
You vex me by these senseless adjurations,
senseless as if you were to advise the waves.
Let it not cross your mind that I will turn
womanish-minded from my fixed decision
or that I shall entreat the one I hate
so greatly, with a woman's upturned hands,
to loose me from my chains: I am far from that.

Hermes
I have said too much already — so I think —
and said it to no purpose: you are not softened:
your purpose is not dented by my prayers.
You are a colt new broken, with the bit
clenched in its teeth, fighting against the reins,
and bolting. You are for too strong and confident
in your weak cleverness. For obstinacy
standing alone is the weakest of all things
in one whose mind is not possessed by wisdom.
Think what a storm, a triple wave of ruin
will rise against you, if you will not hear me,

and no escape for you. First this rough crag
with thunder and the lightning bolt the Father
shall cleave asunder, and shall hide your body
wrapped in a rocky clasp within its depth;
a tedious length of time you must fulfill
before you see the light again, returning.
Then Zeus's winged hound, the eagle red,
shall tear great shreds of flesh from you, a feaster
coming unbidden, every day: your liver
bloodied to blackness will be his repast.
And of this pain do not expect an end
until some God shall show himself successor
to take your tortures for himself and willing
go down to lightless Hades and the shadows
of Tartarus' depths. Bear this in mind
and so determine. This is no feigned boast
but spoken with too much truth. The mouth of Zeus
does not know how to lie, but every word
brings to fulfilment. Look, you, and reflect
and never think that obstinacy is better
than prudent counsel.

Chorus

Hermes seems to us
to speak not altogether out of season.
He bids you leave your obstinacy and seek
a wise good counsel. Hearken to him. Shame
it were for one so wise to fall in error.

Prometheus

Before he told it me I knew this message:
but there is no disgrace in suffering
at an enemy's hand, when you hate mutually.
So let the curling tendril of the fire
from the lightning bolt be sent against me: let
the air be stirred with thunderclaps, the winds
in savage blasts convulsing all the world.
Let earth to her foundations shake, yes to her root,
before the quivering storm: let it confuse

the paths of heavenly stars and the sea's waves
in a wild surging torrent: this my body
let Him raise up on high and dash it down
into black Tartarus with rigorous
compulsive eddies: death he cannot give me.

Hermes

These are a madman's words, a madman's plan:
is there a missing note in this mad harmony?
is there a slack chord in his madness? You,
you, who are so sympathetic with his troubles,
away with you from here, quickly away!
lest you should find your wits stunned by the thunder
and its hard deafening roar.

Chorus

                               Say something else
different from this: give me some other counsel
that I will listen to: this word of yours
for all its instancy is not for us.
How dare you bid us practice baseness? We
will bear along with him what we must bear.
I have learned to hate all traitors: there is no
disease I spit on more than treachery.

Hermes

Remember then my warning before the act:
when you are trapped by ruin don't blame fortune:
don't say that Zeus has brought you to calamity
that you could not foresee: do not do this:
but blame yourselves: now you know what you're doing:
and with this knowledge neither suddenly
nor secretly your own want of good sense
has tangled you in the net of ruin, past
all hope of rescue.

Prometheus

Now it is words no longer: now in very truth
the earth is staggered: in its depths the thunder
bellows resoundingly, the fiery tendrils
of the lightning flash light up, and whirling clouds

carry the dust along: all the winds' blasts
dance in a fury one against the other
in violent confusion: earth and sea
are one, confused together: such is the storm
that comes against me manifestly from Zeus
to work its terrors. O Holy mother mine,
O Sky that circling brings the light to all,
you see me, how I suffer, how unjustly.

The Vertical Axis
or
The Ambiguities of Prometheus
by Jan Kott

Marx called Prometheus "the loftiest saint and martyr in the philosophical calendar."[1] "The patron saint of the proletariat" is a contemporary view of Prometheus, quoted by Thomson.[2] In no other Greek tragedy has "the above," in its double sense and symbolic meaning of the gods and naked force, been attacked so ferociously. "I am the enemy of all the gods that gave me ill for good." Io the poor heifer hates her persecutor with all her bleeding body. To her both predictions are directed; but her only hope is he who will topple Zeus off his throne: of the Son as Redeemer for her is the Son as Revenger.

Io
Can Zeus ever fall from power?
Prometheus
You would be glad to see that catastrophe, I think.
Io
Surely, since Zeus is my persecutor.
Prometheus
Then know that this shall be.

Everyone hates Zeus: Prometheus, Io and the abused forces of nature. Everyone except police officials, the political intriguer Oceanus and the messenger boy Hermes. In Aeschylus the Chorus is never only a witness and commentator on events, and *Prometheus Bound* is the only tragedy in which the Chorus perishes with the hero. The Chorus of sea nymphs, representing the elements of water and air, have come to express their compassion for Prometheus. The Chorus, terrified at first at the openness of the rebellion, gradually learns the bitter history of the world. Prometheus, who taught men courage, now does so again through this assembly of girls and birds. He has revolutionized the Chorus.

Hermes

> You,
> you, who are so sympathetic with is troubles,
> away with you from here, quickly away!
> lest you should find your wits stunned by the thunder
> and its hard deafening roar.

Chorus

> ...How dare you bid us practise baseness? We
> will bear along with him what we must bear.
> I have learnt to hate all traitors.

In the cosmic perspective there is a choice between two as yet unborn sons of Zeus: the son of the New Covenant and the son "stronger than the father." In the dramatic perspective of *Prometheus Bound* the choice is between loyalty to oneself and betrayal, courage and cowardice, inflexible determination and resignation. In political categories it is a choice between a revolutionary program and compromise.[3] "There is significance in revelling," Mao writes in his *Red Book*. The choices open to Prometheus are the options of a prisoner. "Such is the reward," Hephaestus tells him, "you reap of your man-loving disposition. For you, a God, feared not the anger of the Gods, but gave honors to mortals beyond what was just." But what is the scale that enables us to define what is "just" and what is an abuse of the just; what is "due" and what is more than due in relations between guard and prisoner, between the above and the below? Prometheus, wrote Marx, did not want to be "the tyrant's slave and the executioner's henchman." In the same introduction to his doctoral dissertation, dated "March 1841," he goes on to say:

> Prometheus' confession: "I am the enemy of all the gods,"
> is a confession of faith in philosophy, its notion directed
> against all gods of heaven and earth, who do not recognize
> human consciousness as the highest deity. This deity will
> not suffer any rivals.

This Marxian manifesto of Prometheanism seems far closer to the unbound and romantic Prometheus figures of Goethe and Shelley than to the severe and realistic anthropology of Aeschylus.[4] In the real world, split into the above and the below, Aeschylus says that the only choice is between reconciliation and a new tyranny, between compromise and a new son "stronger than the father." And yet "every ruler is harsh whose rule is new." Aeschylus, it seems, knew very well that heaven is never empty for long and that a new god occupies the place of every fallen one.

Goethe's, Byron's and Shelley's Prometheus figures were brothers of Satan.[5] But angels had fallen from heaven because of the sin of pride. Lucifer is the Prince of Reason. The last deity of all, the one that "will not suffer rivals," one that seems even more cruel than the former, is the arrogance of reason. This deity considers itself to have mastered destiny, to be able to change and direct it. "Freedom is the recognition of necessity," Marx wrote. The Hegelian realization of the realm of reason and Marxian "historic necessity" are among those "blind hopes" Prometheus offered to men.[6]

"What is a man's freedom," says a tortured prisoner in Malraux's *Times of Contempt*, "if not consciousness and organization of his destinies?" "I liberated the mortals," says Prometheus at the opening of the tragedy, "from going shattered to death." And just before the end, a moment before being thrown into Tartarus, he exclaims defiantly: "Why should I fear, since death is not my fate?" Martyrs of all faiths have said they were immortal; revolutionaries have gone to their deaths declaring that theirs was the victory beyond the grave. In nineteenth-century interpretations, Prometheus was Saint Satan, Saint Carbonarius, Saint Proletarian. He liberated the spirit, or humanity. Fate, destiny, historic necessity — all in their different ways contributed to the passage of time, the working-out of morality, rationality, meaning. Theogony changes into theodicy. The capture of heaven, or of history, was to be the recompense for all sufferings. But what if the hope of Io stung by the invisible gadfly and the hope of Prometheus thrown down into Tartarus were blind, too?

Chorus
What is fated for Zeus besides eternal sovereignty?
Prometheus
Inquire of this no further, do not entreat me.

Chorus
   This is some solemn secret, I suppose, that you are hiding.

Shortly before the end, Prometheus says, "Time in its aging course teaches all things." The sacred Iranian book *Bundahisn* says something very similar: "Time is more powerful than the two Creations."[7] But what is it exactly that time teaches? The ambiguity of the Aeschylean Prometheus consists in the co-existence of two kinds of time. There is the didactic time of theophany, in which the end of cosmogony and history will be Athens and the Great Conciliation, just as it was to be the Prussian state for Hegel; and there is time without hope, in which Prometheus is thrown, once and for all, into Tartarus to the accompaniment of heavenly fireworks. For the optimistic nineteenth-century poets and philosophers, Prometheus was ultimately to triumph, and suffering was the price of progress. The tragedy of Prometheus was that he had come too early. But closer to our experience is Camus' bitter interpretation: Prometheus' greatness is his revolt without hope:

   ... A revolution is always accomplished against the gods, beginning with the revolution of Prometheus, the first of modern conquerors. It is man's demands made against his fate; the demands of the poor are but a pretext ...
   Yes, man is his own end. And he is his only end. If he aims to be something, it is in this life ... Conquerors sometimes talk of vanquishing and overcoming. But it is always 'overcoming oneself' that they mean ... Every man has felt himself to be the equal of a god at certain moments. At least, this is the way it is expressed. But this comes from the fact that in a flash he felt the amazing grandeur of the human mind. The conquerors are merely those among men who are conscious enough of their strength to be sure of living constantly on those heights and fully aware of that grandeur...
   There they find the creature mutilated, but they also encounter there the only values they like and admire, man and his silence ...[8]

One can express this in yet another way. The greatness of Prometheus is hopeful despair or desperate hope. "Being deprived of hope," Camus concludes, "is not despairing."[9] But this is still not the bitterest interpretation of Prometheus' fate.

In Cicero's treatise, which contains one of the few fragments preserved of the two lost parts of the trilogy, Prometheus is depicted as unable to bear his endless torture any longer, so that he wishes only for human death: *"amore mortis terminum anquirens mali"* (yearning for death as end to misery).[10] The time of one human life's duration is a time of suffering and waiting for our own death.

There is also another conclusion of the tragedy of "the absurd rebel." In one of Pindar's odes, which is perhaps connected with the end of Prometheus' tragedy, the eagle who guards Zeus's thunder once fell asleep as the Muses sang to the accompaniment of Apollos' lyre. It was the eagle that every morning flew to the rocks of the Caucasus to feed on Prometheus' liver.[11]

> On the sceptre of Zeus the eagle sleeps,
> Drooping his swift wings on either side.[12]

The eagle fell asleep to the sweet sounds of music, and anger departed from among the Olympians. This is the fourth and last form of time, that of forgetfulness and the passing into nothingness.

Kafka must have known Cicero's treatise and Pindar's ode because in his notebook he set down the four legends[13] of Prometheus:

According to the first, because he had betrayed the gods to men he was chained to a rock in the Caucasus and the gods sent eagles that devoured his liver, which always grew again.

According to the second, Prometheus in his agony, as the beaks hacked into him, pressed deeper and deeper into his rock until he became one with it.

According the the third, in the course of thousands of years his treachery was forgotten, the gods forgot, the eagles forgot, he himself forgot.

According the the fourth, everyone grew weary of what had

become meaningless. The gods grew weary, the eagles grew weary, and the wound closed wearily.

What remained was the inexplicable range of mountains. Legend tries to explain the inexplicable. Since it arises out of a foundation of truth, it must end in the realm of the inexplicable.

Kafka, with his incomparable intelligence, realized that when topocosm has lost its meaning, all that can be left of it are the desolate mountains between heaven and earth. But this is not the end of the Prometheus myth. In the entire history of drama there are only two works in which the hero cannot leave his place from the beginning to the end of the play.[14] The first is *Prometheus Bound*. In the other, the heroine is buried in the earth, first up to her waist, then up to her neck. There is no chorus. There is only a paralyzed man who cannot approach her. All that is left of the external world of objects is a parasol and a big black handbag containing toilet articles and a revolver. The woman kisses the revolver and puts it aside; soon it is too late — she is buried up to her neck, with her hands in the earth. She has to live until she dies. Time is measured with bells. The below and the above continue to exist; but the earth is merely a heap of sand, and the sky is empty without a single cloud. The only action is being buried in the earth, deeper and deeper. This is the fifth form of time: sinking into the earth, which means no more than sinking into the earth.

There is no need for Zeus any more. Beckett's *Happy Days* is the final version of the Prometheus myth.

1. In the introduction to his doctoral dissertation; Marx Engels, *Werke*, Erganzungsband, Vol. I (Berlin, Dietz-Verlag, 1968), p. 262 ff.
2. George D. Thomson, *Aeschylus and Athens: A Study in the Social Origins of Drama* (London, Lawrence & Wishart, 1941), p. 316.
3. Shelley's preface to his *Prometheus Unbound* is characteristic: "But, in truth, I was averse from a catastrophe so feeble as that of reconciling the Champion with the Oppressor of mankind. The moral interest of the fable, which is powerfully sustained by the sufferings and endurance of Prometheus, would be annihilated if we could conceive of him as unsaying his high language and quailing before his successful and perfidious adversary" (Shelley's *Prometheus Unbound*, edited by Lawrence J. Zillman [Seattle, University of Washington Press, 1969], p. 35).

4. Cf. Kerenyi, *Prometheus*, p. 17: "Goethe's Prometheus is no God, no Titan, no man, but the immortal prototype of man as the original rebel and affirmer of his fate: the original inhabitant of the earth, seen as an antigod, as Lord of the Earth." Goethe wrote about himself: "I cut myself off, like Prometheus, from the gods." And this is how he ended his celebrated ode on Prometheus, published in 1785 (quoted in Kerenyi, p. 6):

> Here I sit, shaping man
> After my image,
> A race that is like me,
> To suffer, to weep,
> To rejoice and be glad,
> And like myself
> To have no regard for You.

Marx, of course, knew Goethe's ode by heart.

5. In the same preface by Shelley: "The only imaginary being resembling in any degree Prometheus is, Satan; and Prometheus is, in my judgement, a more poetical character than Satan, because, in addition to courage, and majesty, and firm and patient opposition to omnipotent force, he is susceptible of being described as exempt from the taints of ambition, envy, revenge, and a desire for personal aggrandizement, which, in the hero of *Paradise Lost*, interfere with the interest" (Shelley, *op. cit.*, pp. 35, 37).

6. Cf. Eliade, *The Sacred and the Profane*, p. 203: "Modern nonreligious man assumes a new existential situation; he regards himself solely as the subject and agent of history, and he refuses all appeal to transcendence...Man *makes himself*, and he only makes himself completely in proportion as he desacralizes himself and the world. The sacred is the prime obstacle to his freedom. He will become himself only if he is totally demysticized. He will not be truly free until he has killed the last god."

7. Eliade, *Cosmos and History*, p. 125.

8. Albert Camus, *The Myth of Sisyphus*, translated by Justin O'Brien (New York, Knopf, 1955), p. 65.

9. Amazingly and disturbingly close to Camus is the interpretation of the Prometheus myth by the Neo-Platonists, in Marsilio Ficino and in the famous panels of Piero de Cosimo. Panofsky, *op. cit.* (pp. 50-51): "The later mythographers, especially Boccaccio, have always insisted on the fact that, while Vulcan personified the *ignis elementatus*, that is, the physical fire which enables mankind to solve its practical problems, the torch of Prometheus lighted at the wheels of the sun's chariot /*'rota solis, id est e gremio Dei'*/ carries the 'celestial fire' which stands for the 'clarity of knowledge' infused into the heart of the ignorant,' and that this very clarity can only be attained at the expense of happiness and peace of mind...In Piero's Strasburg panel this idea is beautifully expressed by the triumphal gesture of the statue which

forms a striking contrast with the tortured position of Prometheus. The punishment of the latter symbolizes the price which mankind has to pay for its intellectual awakening, that is...to be tortured by our profound meditation, and to recover only to be tortured again." This is already a pre-existentialist interpretation; Prometheus' torture is "unhappy awareness."

10. Cicero, *Tusculan Disputations* ii, 10.
11. See John H. Finley, Jr., *Pindar and Aeschylus*, Martin Classical Lectures, XIV (Cambridge, Mass., Harvard University Press, 1955), p. 231.
12. *Pythian* I, 6-7, in *The Odes of Pindar*, translated by C. M. Bowra (Penguin Classics; Baltimore, Penguin Books, 1969), p. 131.
13. Franz Kafka, *Wedding Preparations in the Country and Other Posthumous Prose Writings*, translated by Ernst Kaiser and Eithne Wilkins (London, Secker & Warburg, 1954), p. 95.
14. "Or take Beckett's *Happy Days:* has there been a comparable stasis, a comparable shape of action since the *Prometheus?*" George Steiner in reply to an *Arion* questionnaire, "The Classics and the Man of Letters," *Arion*, Vol. III (Winter 1964), p. 82.

Sophocles
OEDIPUS
THE KING

**Translated by
Kenneth Cavander**

Characters	*Oedipus, King of Thebes*
	Priest
	Creon, brother of Jocasta
	Teiresias, an old blind prophet
	Jocasta, wife of Oedipus
	Messenger
	Shepherd
	Servant

[In front of the palace of Oedipus at Thebes. Near the altar stands the PRIEST *with a large crowd of supplicants. Enter* OEDIPUS.]*

Oedipus

My children, why do you crowd and wait at my altars?
Olive branches . . . and wreaths of sacred flowers —
Why do you bring these, my people of Thebes? Your streets
Are heavy with incense, solemn with prayers for healing,
And when I heard your voice, I would not let
My messengers tell me what you said. I came
To be your messenger myself, Oedipus, whose name
Is greatest known and greatest feared.

[To PRIEST.]*

Will you tell me, then? You have dignity enough
To speak for them all — is it fear that makes you kneel
Before me, or do you need my help? I am ready,
Whatever you ask will be done . . . Come, I am not cold
Or dead to feeling — I will have pity on you.

Priest

King Oedipus, our master in Thebes, if you will look
At your altars, and at the ages of those who kneel there,
You will see children, too small to fly far from home;
You will see old men, slow with the years they carry,
And priests — I am a priest of Zeus; and you will see
The finest warriors you have; the rest of your people
Kneel, praying, in the open city, in the temples
Of Athene, and in the shrine where we keep a flame
Always alive and the ash whispers the future.
Look about you. The whole city drowns
And cannot lift its hand from the storm of death
In which it sinks: the green corn withers
In the fields, cattle die in the meadows,
Our wives weep in agony, and never give birth!
Apollo brings his fire like a drover and herds us
Into death, and nature is at war with herself.
Thebes is sick, every house deserted, and the blind

Prison of the dead grows rich with mourning
And our dying cries.
Eternal powers control our lives, and we do not
Think you are their equal; yet we pray to you, as your children,
Believing that you, more than any man, may direct
Events, and come to terms with the powers beyond us.
When the savage riddle of the Sphinx enslaved
Thebes, you came to set us free. We
Were powerless, we could not tell you how to answer her.
And now they say, and it is believed, that you
Were close to God when you raised our city from the dead.
Oedipus, we pray to your power, which can overcome
Sufferings we do not understand; guard us
From this evil. In heaven and earth there must
Be some answer to our prayer, and you may know it.
You have struggled once with the powers above us and been
Victorious; we trust that strength and believe your words.
Oedipus, you are the royal glory of Thebes —
Give us life; Oedipus — think. Because
You overpowered the evil in the Sphinx
We call you savior still. Must we remember
Your reign for the greatness in which you began, and the sorrow
In which you ended? The country is sick, and you
Must heal us. You were once our luck, our fortune, the augury
Of good we looked for in the world outside. Fulfil
That augury now. You are the king of Thebes, but consider:
Which is it better to rule — a kingdom? Or a desert?
What is a castle or a ship if there are
No men to give it life? Emptiness! Nothing!

Oedipus

My children, I know your sorrows, I know why
You have come, and what you ask of me. I see
The pain of sickness in you all, and yet in all
That sickness, who is so sick as I? Each
Of you has one sorrow, his grief is his own —
But I must feel for my country, for myself,
And for you. That is why you did not find me

Deaf or indifferent to your prayers. No,
I have spent many tears, and in my thoughts
Traveled long journeys. And then I saw
That we could be saved in one way only;
I took that way and sent Creon, my brother-
In-law, to the Oracle of Apollo; there
The god will tell him how I can save the city —
The price may be an act of sacrifice, or perhaps
A vow, a prayer, will be enough . . . But the days
Run on and the measure of time keeps pace with them
And I begin to fear. What is he doing?
I did not think he would stay so long — he should not
Stay so long! . . . But when he comes I will do
Whatever the god commands; if I disobeyed
It would be a sin.

Priest

Heaven listened then;
This messenger says that Creon is returning.

Oedipus

My lord Apollo, let his news be the shining sun
That answers our prayers and guides us out of death!

Priest

I can see him no . . . the news must be good.
Look, there is a crown of bay thick with flowers
Covering his hair.

Oedipus

At last we shall know the truth.
If I shout, he will hear me . . . Creon!
My brother, son of Menoeceus, Lord of Thebes,
What answer does Apollo send to us? Do you bring
An answer?

[*Enter* CREON.]

Creon

Our danger is gone. This load of sorrow
Will be lifted if we follow the way
Where Apollo points.

Oedipus

What does this mean? I expected

Hope, or fear, but your answer gives me neither.
Creon
I am ready to tell you my message now, if you wish;
But they can hear us, and if we go inside . . .
Oedipus
Tell me now and let them hear! I must not think
Of myself; I grieve only when my people suffer.
Creon
Then this is what I was told at Delphi:
Our land is tainted. We carry the guilt in our midst.
A foul disease, which will not be healed unless
We drive it out and deny it life.
Oedipus
                                    But how
Shall we be clean? How did this happen to us?
Creon
The crime of murder is followed by a storm.
Banish the murder and you banish the storm, kill
Again and you kill the storm.
Oedipus
                                    But Apollo means
One man — who is this man?
Creon
                                    My lord,
There was once a king of Thebes; he was our master
Before you came to rule our broken city.
Oedipus
I have heard of him . . . I never saw your king.
Creon
Now that he is dead your mission from the god
Is clear: take vengeance on his murderers!
Oedipus
But where are they now? The crime is old,
And time is stubborn with its secrets. How
Can you ask me to find these men?
Creon
The god said

You must search in Thebes; what is hunted can
Be caught, only what we ignore escapes.

Oedipus

Where was the murder? Was Laius killed in the city?
Or did this happen in another country?

Creon

He was travelling
To Delphi, he said. But he never returned to the palace
He left that day.

Oedipus

Did no one see this?
A messenger? The guard who watched his journey? You could
Have questioned them

Creon

They were all killed, except
One. He ran home in terror, and could only
Repeat one thing.

Oedipus

What did he repeat?
Once we have learnt one thing, we may learn the rest.
This hope is the beginning of other hopes.

Creon

He said they met some robbers who killed the king.
He talked of an army, too strong for the servants of Laius.

Oedipus

Robbers would not dare to kill a king — unless
They had bribes. They must have had bribes from the city!

Creon

We suspected that, but with Laius dead
We were defenseless against our troubles

Oedipus

Were
Your troubles so great that they prevented you
From knowing the truth? Your king had been murdered . . . !

Creon

The the Sphinx
Had a riddle to which there was no answer, and we thought

Of our closest sorrows. We had no time for other
Mysteries.
Oedipus
But I will begin again, and make your mysteries
Plain. Apollo was right, and you were right,
To turn my thoughts to the king who died. Now
You will see the measure of my power; I come to defend you,
Avenging your country and the god Apollo.
[*Aside.*]
If I can drive out this corruption and make the city
Whole, I shall do more than save my people,
Who are my friends, but still my subjects — I shall save
Myself. For the knife that murdered Laius may it
Drink from my heart, and the debt I pay to him
Lies to my own credit.
My children, quickly, leave this altar and take
Your branches. I will have the people of Thebes assembled
To hear that I shall do all the god commands.
And in the end we shall see my fortune smiling
From heaven, or my fall.
[*Exit.*]
Priest
Let us go, my sons; our king has given the order
We came to hear. May Apollo, who sent this answer
From his oracle, come to lay our sickness
To rest, and give us life.
[*Exeunt* PRIEST, CREON, *and some of the elders. Enter* CHORUS.]
Chorus
From golden Delphi Apollo replies to Thebes
And the words of heaven send a warning.
As a lyre is strung and tightened, so we
Are tightened by fear.
As a lyre trembles, so we tremble at the touch of fear.
Apollo, god of healing, god of newness,
We fear you, and the commands you send to humble us.
Do you ask a new submission? Or is your command
The same as we hear in every wind, and every season, and
every year?

Only the child of golden hope, whose voice
Will never die, only the spirit of truth can tell us.
First in my prayers is the goddess Athene, the daughter of
    Zeus;
Second, her sister Artemis, who is queen in Thebes,
For she sits at our country's heart, pure and honored,
In a temple like the sun. And third in our prayer
Is Phoebus Apollo, whose arm reaches over all the world.
Come three times to drive our wrongs before you!
If ever in the past, when evil and blindness
Rose like a wave, when grief was burning in our city,
If ever you banished that grief,
Come now to help us.
There is no numbering our sorrows;
The whole country is sick, and mortal will and human mind
Are no weapons to defend us.
The great earth whom we call our mother
Is barren and dead; women weep in the pain of childbirth
But they fall sick and die.
Look, can you see the dying go following each other,
Gliding like gentle birds, quicker
Than the restless flash of fire that will never sleep,
The dying on their flight to the shore
Where evening sits like a goddess?
The city of the dying goes countless away
And the children of life fall to the earth,
The toys of death,
With no pity and no remembering tears.
In the rest of our city wives and mothers
Stand grey at the altars,
Which tell us of a certainty resisting the seas of doubt;
They weep, pray, plead for release
From the harsh revenge which heaven brings.
A cry for healing rises and burns above the still crown
That mourns in the city.
Send us strength that will look kindly on us,
Golden daughter of Zeus.

Ares, the god of war, confront us, bitter in his cruelty,
And his shout burns like fire;
But his war is fought with no armor, and Ares
Carries no shield, for he brings his conflict
Into the moment of our birth and death.
Oh turn him flying down the winds, turn him
Back and dash him from our country
Into the wide chambers where Amphitrite sleeps,
Or to the lonely cliffs of Thrace where the seas
Allow no guests. For Ares comes to finish
The deadly work left undone by the night.
Zeus, you are the lord of lightning, lord of fire,
Strike to protect us.
We pray for Artemis to bring her chaste fires,
Which we see her carry like a shining torch across
The mountains where the wolf runs.
I call you, the god with the golden crown,
Born in our country, Bacchus,
With the fire of wine in your cheek,
And the voice of wine in your shout,
Come with your pine branch burning, and your Maenads
Following the light, the fire of heaven's madness
In their eyes, come to guard us against the treacherous power
Who goes to war with justice and the harmony of heaven!

[*Enter* OEDIPUS.]

Oedipus

Yo have told me of your need. Are you content
To hear me speak, obey my words, and work
To humor the sickness? . . . Then you will thrust away
The weight with which you struggle, and fulfill
Your need. I am a stranger to this story,
And to the crime; I have no signs to guide me,
And so if I am to trap his murderer, my hunt
Must follow every hope. I am speaking, then,
To every citizen of Thebes, and I shall not
Exempt myself, although I am a citizen only
In name, and not in blood.

Whoever knows the murderer of Laius, son
Of Labdacus, must make his knowledge mine.
It is the king's command! And if he is afraid,
Or thinks he will escape, I say to him, "Speak!
You will go into exile, but you will go unharmed —
Banishment is all you have to fear."
Or if you know the assassin comes from another
Country, you must not be silent. I shall pay
The value of your knowledge, and your reward
Will be more than gratitude.
But if I find only silence, if you are afraid
To betray a friend or reveal yourself, and lock
The truth away, listen, this is my decree:
This murderer, no matter who he is, is banished
From the country where my power and my throne
Are supreme. No one must shelter him or speak to him;
When you pray to heaven, he must not pray with you;
When you sacrifice, drive him away, do not
Give him holy water, beat him from your doors!
He carries the taint of corruption with him — for so
The god Apollo has revealed to me . . . You see
How I serve the god and revenge the king who dies!
I curse that murderer; if he is alone, I curse him!
If he shares his guilt with others, I curse him! May
His evil heart beat out its years in sorrow,
Throughout his life may he breathe the air of death!
If I give him shelter, knowing who
He is, and let him feel the warmth of my fire,
I ask this punishment for myself.
This must be done! In every word I speak
I command obedience, and so does the god Apollo,
And so does your country, which a barren sickness
And an angry heaven drag to death. But even
If it is not a god that comes to punish you
It would be shame to leave your land impure.
Your king was killed — he was a royal and noble
Man; hunt his murderer down!

I live in Laius' palace, my queen was once
The queen of Laius, and if his line had prospered
His children would have shared my love.
But now time has struck his head to earth
And in revenge I will fight for him as I
Would fight for my own father. My search will never
End until I take in chains the murderer
Of Laius, son of Labdacus. I pray heaven
That those who will not help me may watch the soil
They have ploughed crumble and turn black, let them see
Their women barren, let them be destroyed by the fury
That scourges us, but may it rage more cruelly!
And for all the Thebans who will obey me gladly
I ask the strength of justice, and the power of heaven.
So we shall live in peace; so we shall be healed.

Chorus

Your curse menaces me, my lord, if I lie.
I swear I did not kill him, nor can I tell
Who did. Apollo sent the reply, and Apollo
Should find the murderer.

Oedipus

Yes, we believe
It is Apollo's task — but we cannot make
The gods our slaves; we must act for ourselves.

Chorus

Our next
Hope then, must be . . .

Oedipus

And every hope
You have. When I search, nothing escapes.

Chorus

We know a lord who sees as clearly as the lord
Apollo — Teiresias; we could ask Teiresias, my king,
And be given the truth.

Oedipus

Creon told me, and his advice
Did not lie idle for want of action. I have sent

Two servants . . . It is strange they are not here.

Chorus

And there are the old rumors — but they tell us nothing . . .

Oedipus

What do these rumors say? I must know
Everything.

Chorus

They say some travelers killed him.

Oedipus

I have heard that too. But the man who saw those travelers
Was never seen himself.

Chorus

The murdered will leave our country;
There is a part of every man that is ruled
By fear, and when he hears your curse . . .

Oedipus

A sentence
Holds no terror for the man who is not afraid
To kill.

Chorus

But now he will be convicted. Look,
They are leading your priest to you; Teiresias comes.
When he speaks, it is the voice of heaven
That we hear.

[*Enter* TEIRESIAS, *guided by a boy.*]

Oedipus

Teiresias, all things lie
In your power, for you have harnessed all
Knowledge and all mysteries; you know what heaven
Hides, and what runs in the earth below, and you
Must know, though you cannot see, the sickness with which
Our country struggles. Defend us, my lord, and save us —
We shall find no other defense or safety.
For Apollo — and yet you must have heard the message —
Apollo, whom we asked in our doubt, promised release —
But on one condition: that we find the murderers
Of Laius, and banish them, or repay the murder.

Teiresias, the singing birds will tell you of the future,
You have many ways of knowing the truth. Do not grudge
Your knowledge, but save yourself and your city, save me,
For murder defiles us all. Think of us
As your prisoners, whose lives belong to you!
To have the power and use that power for good
Is work to bring you honor.

Teiresias
When truth cannot help
The man who knows, then it brings terror. I knew
That truth, but I stifled it. I should not have come.

Oedipus
What is it? You come as sadly as despair.

Teiresias
Send me away, I tell you! Then it will be easy
For *you* to play the king, and I the priest.

Oedipus
This is no reply. You cannot love Thebes — your own
Country, Teiresias if you hide what the gods tell you.

Teiresias
I see your words guiding you on the wrong
Path; I pray for my own escape.

Oedipus
Teiresias!
You do not turn away if you know the truth; we all
Come like slaves to a king with our prayers to you.

Teiresias
But you come without the truth, and I can never
Reveal my own sorrows, lest they become
Yours.

Oedipus
You cannot? Then you know and will not tell us!
Instead, you plan treason and the city's death.

Teiresias
I mean to protect us both from pain. You search
And probe, and it is all wasted. I will not tell you!

Oedipus
You demon! You soul of evil! You would goad

A thing of stone to fury. Will you never speak?
Can you feel, can you suffer? Answer me, and end this!

Teiresias

You see wrong in my mood, you call me evil — blind
To the mood that settles in you and rages there.

Oedipus

Rages! Yes, that is what your words
Have done, when they shout your contempt for Thebes.

Teiresias

The truth will come; my silence cannot hide it.

Oedipus

And what must come is what you must tell me.

Teiresias

I can tell you no more, and on this answer let
Your fury caper like a beast.

Oedipus

It is
A fury that will never leave me. Listen, I know
What you are. I see now that you conspired to plan
This murder, and you committed it — all but the stroke
That killed him. If you had eyes, I would have said
The crime was yours alone.

Teiresias

Oedipus, I warn you!
Obey your own decree and the oath you swore.
Never from this day speak to me, or to these nobles;
You are our corruption, the unholiness in our land.

Oedipus

How you must despise me to flaunt your scorn like this,
Thinking you will escape. How?

Teiresias

I have escaped.
I carry the truth: it is my child, and guards me.

Oedipus

Truth! Who taught you? Heaven never taught you!

Teiresias

You taught me; you forced me to the point of speech.

Oedipus
Repeat your words, I do not remember this speech.
Teiresias
You did not understand? Or do you try to trap me?
Oedipus
I know nothing! Repeat your truth!
Teiresias
I said, you are the murderer you are searching for.
Oedipus
Again you attack me, but I will not forgive you again!
Teiresias
Shall I say more to make your anger sprawl?
Oedipus
All you have breath for — it will all be useless.
Teiresias
Then . . . you live with your dearest one in burning
Shame, and do not know it; nor can you see
The evil that surrounds you.
Oedipus
Do you think
You will always smile in freedom if you talk like this?
Teiresias
If truth can give strength, I will
Oedipus
It can —
But not to you; you have no truth. Your senses
Have died in you — ears: deaf! eyes: blind!
Teiresias
Yes, be bitter, mock at me, poor Oedipus.
Soon they will all mock as bitterly as you.
Oedipus
You live in perpetual night; you cannot harm
Me, nor anyone who moves in the light.
Teiresias
Your downfall
Will come, but I will not be the cause. Apollo
Is a great power; he watches over the end.

Oedipus

Did you or Creon plan this?

Teiresias

Creon is not

Your enemy; you carry your enemy with you — in your soul.

Oedipus

We have wealth and power, the mind reaches higher, grows,
Breaks its own fetters, our lives are great and envied,
And the world rewards us — with spitefulness and hate!
Consider my power — I did not come begging, the city
Laid its submission in my hands as a gift.
Yet, for this power, Creon, my trusted, my first
Friend, goes like a thief behind my back,
Tries to exile me, and sends this wizard,
This patcher of threadbare stories, this cunning peddler
Of the future, with no eyes except
For money, and certainly no eyes for mysteries.
Tell me, tell me, when did you ever foretell the truth?
When the Sphinx howled her mockeries and riddles
Why could you find no answer to free the city?
Her question was too hard for the simple man,
The humble man; only heaven's wisdom could find
A reply. But you found none! Neither your birds
Above you, nor the secret voice of your inspiration
Sent you knowledge — then we saw what you were!
But I came, ignorant Oedipus, and silenced her,
And my only weapon was in my mind and my will;
I had no omens to teach me. And this is the man
You would usurp! You think when Creon is king
You will sit close to the throne; butl I think
Your plans to drive the accursed away will return
To defeat you, and to defeat their architect.
You are old, Teiresias, or else your prophetic wisdom
Would have been your death.

Chorus

Your majesty, what he has said
And your reply — they were both born in anger.

We do not need this wildness; we ask the best
Fulfilment of Apollo's commands. This must be the search.
Teiresias [*To* OEDIPUS.]
You flourish your power; but you must give me the right
To make my reply, and that will have equal power.
I have not lived to be your servant, but Apollo's;
Nor am I found in the list of those whom Creon
Protects. You call me blind, you jeer at me —
I say your sight is not clear enough to see
Who shares your palace, nor the room in which you walk,
Nor the sorrow about you. Do you know who gave you birth?
You are the enemy of the dead, and of the living,
And do not know it. The curse is a two-edged sword,
From your mother, from your father; the curse will hunt you,
Like a destruction, from your country. Now
You have sight, but then you will go in blindness;
When you know the truth of your wedding night
All the world will hear your crying to rest,
Every hill a Cithaeron to echo you.
You thought that night was peace, like a gentle harbor —
But there was no harbor for that voyage, only grief.
Evil crowds upon you; you do not see
How it will level you with your children and reveal
Yourself as you truly are. Howl your abuse
At Creon and at me . . . All men must suffer,
Oedipus, but none will find suffering more terrible
Than you.
Oedipus
Must I bear this? Must I be silent?
Die! Go to your death! Leave my palace now!
Get away from me!
Teiresias
Yet you called me here, or I would not have come.
Oedipus
If I had known you would talk in the raving language
Of a madman, I would never have sent for you.
Teiresias
I am no more than you see. You see a madman,

The parents who gave you life saw a prophet.
Oedipus
My parents? Wait! Who were my parents?
Teiresias
Today will be your parent, and your murderer.
Oedipus
Always riddles, always lies and riddles!
Teiresias
You were best at solving riddles, were you not?
Oedipus
When you think of my greatness, it inspires your mockery.
Teiresias
That greatness has conspired to be your traitor.
Oedipus
I saved this country, I care for nothing else.
Teiresias
Then I shall go. . . [*To his guide:*] Boy, lead me away.
Oedipus
Yes, lead him . . . You come and trouble me — you are nothing
But hindrance to my plans. Go, and I shall be safe.
Teiresias
I came to speak, and I shall not leave until I speak.
I need not cower at your frown, you cannot
Harm me. This man for whom you search,
Whom you threaten, and to the people call "the murderer
Of Laius," this man is here, a stranger, a foreigner;
But he will see his Theban blood, though he will not
Have any joy at the discovery.
He will be blind — though now he sees; a beggar —
Though now he is rich, and he will go feeling
Strange ground before him with a stick.
He is a father to children — then he will
Be called their brother; he is his mother's son —
Then he will be called her husband, then
He will be called his father's murderer.
Consider this when you walk between your palace walls;
If you find I have been false to you, then say

That all my prophetic wisdom is a lie.
[*Exeunt all but the* CHORUS.]
Chorus
>   In the rock at Delphi there is a cave
>   Which is the mouth of heaven; now
>   The cave warns us of one man, whose hands are red
>   With murder, and whose actions
>   Break the unspoken laws that shackle us.
>   Time tells him now to escape,
>   Faster than the jostling horses of the storm,
>   For Apollo, the son of Zeus, leaps down on him,
>   Armed with lightning, dressed in fire,
>   And the terrible avengers follow where he goes,
>   The Furies who never mistake and are never cheated.
>   From the snow of Parnassus over Delphi the message
>   Gleamed and came shining to Thebes.
>   We must all hunt the murderer
>   Who hides from justice. Like a lonely bull
>   He crosses and crosses our country, through the harsh forests,
>   The hollows of the mountains, and the rocks.
>   Sadly thinking and alone,
>   Sadly trying to escape
>   The words that came from Delphi, the heart of the world.
>   But their wings are always beating in his head.
>   The wisdom of the priest sets fear, fear, beating in our blood;
>   Truth or lies, nothing comforts, nothing denies.
>   The world is built out of our beliefs,
>   And when we lose those beliefs in doubt,
>   Our world is destroyed, and the present and the past
>   Vanish into night.
>   We must have proof, a certainty that we can touch
>   And feel, before we turn against Oedipus.
>   The land is peopled with rumors and whispers —
>   They cannot make us avenge King Laius,
>   Whose death is guarded by such mystery.
>   All that men may do is watched and remembered
>   By Zeus, and by Apollo. But they are gods;

Can any man, even the prophet,the priest,
Can even he know more than us?
And if he can, who will be judge of him, and say he lied
Or spoke the truth?
Yet wisdom may come to us, not the wisdom that sees
How the world is ruled, but the wisdom that guides
The modest life. In this alone we may excel.
But the proof must be clear and certain,
Before I can accuse Oedipus.
Remember that the Sphinx came flying
To meet him, evil beyond our comprehension,
And we saw his wisdom then, we knew and felt
The goodness of his heart towards our country.
Thoughts cannot be guilty traitors to such a man.

[*Enter* CREON.]

Creon

Lords of Thebes, this message has called me here
In terror . . . These crimes of which our king accuses me —
No one would dare to think of them! If he
Believes I could wrong him, or even speak of wrong,
At such a time, when we are in such sorrow,
Let me die! I have no wish to live out my years
If I must live them suspected and despised.
I will not bear this slander, which is no trifle
To forget, but the greatest injury — the name
Of traitor. The people will call me that, even
You will call me that!

Chorus

His fury mastered him;
Perhaps he did not mean the charge.

Creon

He said
To you all — you all heard — that the priest
Had been told to lie, and that I had planned the answer?

Chorus

He said that, but I know he did not mean it.

Creon

And when he

Accused me, he seemed master of his thoughts, and there was
Reason in his voice?

Chorus

I cannot remember,
I do not observe my king so closely . . . But here
He comes from the palace himself to meet you.

[*Enter* OEDIPUS.]

Oedipus

So,
My citizen, you have come to your king? Your eyes have great
Courage — they can look on my palace out of a murderer's
Face, a robber's face! Yes, I know you;
You blaze, you thief of power...In heaven's name
Tell me: when you planned to kill me, did you think I had
Become a coward or a fool? Did you think I would not
Notice your treason stalking me? Or were you sure
That if I knew, I would not dare defense?
See your insane attempt! You try to capture
Power, which must be hunted with armies and gold;
But no one will follow you, no one will make
You rich!

Creon

Wait! You have accused, but you must not judge
Until you have heard my defense; I can reply.

Oedipus

You talk with the fangs of cleverness; but how
Can I understand? I understand only
That you are my enemy, and dangerous.

Creon

There is one thing I must say; hear it first.

Oedipus

One thing you must not say: "I am innocent."

Creon

You are stubborn, Oedipus, your will is too hard;
It is nothing to treasure, and you are wrong to think it is.

Oedipus

Treason, crimes against a brother, will not

Escape justice: you are wrong to think they will.

Creon

I do not quarrel with your talk of justice.
But tell me how I have harmed you: what is my crime?

Oedipus

Did you persuade me — perhaps you did not — to send for
The priest whom we used to worship for his wisdom?

Creon

And I still have faith in that advice.

Oedipus

How long
Is it since Laius . . .

Creon

What has Laius to do
With this? I do not see . . .

Oedipus

Since he was hidden
From the living sun, since he was attacked and killed?

Creon

The years are old and the time is long since then.

Oedipus

Was Teiresias already a priest and prophet then?

Creon

As wise as now, and no less honored and obeyed.

Oedipus

But at the time he did not mention me?

Creon

I did not hear him . . .

Oedipus

But surely you tried to find
The murderer?

Creon

We searched, of course, we could discover
Nothing.

Oedipus

If I was guilty, why did Teiresias
Not accuse me then? He must have known, for he is wise.

Creon

I do not know. If I cannot know the truth
I would rather be silent.

Oedipus

But there is one truth
You will confess to; none knows it better . . . ?

Creon

What is that? I shall deny nothing . . .

Oedipus

That only by some insidious plan of yours
Could Teiresias ever say I murdered Laius!

Creon

If he says that, I cannot unsay it for him;
But give me an answer in return for mine.

Oedipus

Question till you have questions left;
You cannot prove me a murderer.

Creon

Now,
You have married my sister?

Oedipus

I do not deny it; the truth
Was in your question.

Creon

You and she rule
This country, you are equal?

Oedipus

If she has a wish
I grant it all to her.

Creon

And am I not
Considered equal to you both?

Oedipus

Yes, there your friendship
Shows the face of evil it concealed.

Creon

No, reason to yourself as I have reasoned.

First, imagine two ways of ruling, each
Bringing equal power. With one of these fear
Never leaves you, but with the other you sleep
Calm in the night. Who do yo think
Would not choose the second? I feel no ambition
To be the king, when I have the power of a king.
For I have my place in the world, I know it, and will not
Overreach myself. Now, you give me all
I wish, and no fear comes with the gift;
But if I were king myself, much more would be forced
Upon me. Why should I love the throne better
Than a throne's power and a throne's majesty
Without the terrors of a throne? Now,
I may smile to all, and all will bow to me;
Those who need you petition me,
For I am their hopes of success. Is this such a worthless
Life that I should exchange it for yours? Treason
Is for those who cannot value what they have.
I have never had longing thoughts about your power,
Nor would I help a man who had. Send
To Delphi, make a test of me, ask the god
Whether my message was true, and if you find
I have plotted with your priest, then you may kill me —
I will be your authority, I will assent
When you decree my death. But do not accuse me
Yet, when you know nothing. You wrong your friends
To think them enemies, as much as you do wrong
To take enemies for friends. Think, be sure!
You banish life from your body — and life you love
Most dearly — by banishing a good friend.
Time will set this knowledge safely in your heart;
Time alone shows the goodness in a man —
One day is enough to tell you all his evil.

Chorus

My king, a cautious man would listen; beware
Of being convinced too quickly. Suddenness is not safety.

Oedipus

When the attack is quick and sudden, and the plot

Runs in the darkness, my thoughts must be sudden
In reply. If I wait, sitting in silence,
He will have done his work, and I lost
My chance to begin.

Creon
Your decision then! Will you
Banish me?

Oedipus
No, not banishment; I
Will have your life! You must teach men the rewards
That I keep for the envious and the cruel.

Creon
Will you not listen to persuasion and the truth?

Oedipus
You will never persuade me that you speak the truth.

Creon
No, I can see you are blind to truth.

Oedipus
I see
Enough to guard my life.

Creon
My life is as precious
To me.

Oedipus
But you are a traitor!

Creon
You know nothing!

Oedipus
Yet the king must rule

Creon
Not when the king is evil.

Oedipus
My city! My city!

Creon
It is my city too, do not forget that!

Chorus
Stop, my lords! Look, here is Jocasta coming to you

From the palace, at the moment when she may help you
To bring this quarrel to rest.

[*Enter* JOCASTA.]

Jocasta

My lords, it is pitiful to hear your senseless voices
Shouting and wrangling. Have you no shame? Our country
Is sick, and you go bustling about your private
Quarrels. My king, you must to inside, and you,
Creon, go to the palace. At this time
We have no troubles except the plague; all
Others are pretence.

Creon

My sister, your sovereign, Oedipus,
Condemns me cruelly in his efforts to be just.
He will banish me, or murder me; in both he does wrong.

Oedipus

No, I have found a traitor, my queen, who plots
Against my life.

Creon

Never let me breathe
In freedom again, let me die under your curse,
If I am guilty of those crimes!

Jocasta

Oh, Oedipus,
Believe him. Believe him for the sake of those words
That heaven witnessed; you have a duty to that oath,
And to me, and to your people.

Chorus

Obey her, my lord, I beg you; do not be harsh,
Be wise.

Oedipus

Must I be ruled by you?

Chorus

Creon was always wise and faithful in the past; his oath was
    great
And you must respect it.

Oedipus

You know what you are asking?

Chorus
I know.

Oedipus
Tell me, what do you advise?

Chorus
He is your friend — that is a truth
As simple as the light of day;
But only confused and uncertain rumors call him traitor;
No cause to rob him of his honor.

Oedipus
But listen, in asking this, you ask
For my banishment, or for my death.

Chorus
No! By the sun who is prince of the sky!
If that was ever my intention,
I pray for death, without friends on earth,
Without love in heaven,
Death in pain and misery.
Now, now, when the decaying earth eats our lives
Away, will you add your quarrels to all
That we already suffer?

Oedipus
Let him go then; I shall die, I do not care;
I shall be driven into banishment and disgrace.
I do this for love and pity of you. For him, I feel none;
Wherever he goes, he cannot escape my hatred.

Creon
For you submission is a torment — you do not hide it.
And when you force your way against the world
You crush us all beneath you. Such natures
Find their own company most terrible to bear.
It is their punishment.

Oedipus
Leave my sight, then! Leave me to myself!

Creon
I shall leave you. In all the time you knew me,
You never understood me...They see my innocence.

[*Exit.*]

Chorus

My queen, take our king to the palace now.

Jocasta

I must know what has happened.

Chorus

Doubt and suspicion. Oedipus spoke without thinking;
He was unjust, and Creon cannot bear injustice.

Jocasta

Both were to blame?

Chorus

Yes.

Jocasta

What was said?

Chorus

The country is weary with sickness already;
I am content, content to go no further
And let the evil rest.

Oedipus

You see what you have done, you good,
Good adviser? My temper was a spear
And you have turned the edge and blunted it.

Chorus

Your majesty, I have repeated many times —
But I tell you again;
I would have been robbed of all my senses,
Emptied of all my reason,
If I cause your death.
You came like the wind we pray for in danger,
When the storm was conquering us with sorrows,
And carried our country into safety. Again
You may bring a spirit to guide us.

Jocasta

But I still do not know why you were quarrelling, my king,
And I must know, for they talked of your death.

Oedipus

Jocasta,
You may command me when even my people may not,

And I let Creon go. But he had conspired
Against me . . .

Jocasta

Treason! Is this true? Can you prove it?

Oedipus

He says I am Laius' murderer.

Jocasta

How
Can he know? Has he always known, or has someone told
him?

Oedipus

He sent that priest Teiresias, the wicked Teiresias.
Creon's lips do not commit themselves to words!

Jocasta

Then set all this talk aside and listen. I
Will teach you that no priest, no holy magic
Can know your future or your destiny, and my proof
Is as short as the stroke of a knife. Once, an oracle
Came to Laius — I will not say it was from
Apollo — but from Apollo's priests. It told him
He was destined to be murdered by the son that I
Would bear to him. But Laius, so they say,
Was murdered by robbers from another country at a place
Where three roads meet. A son was born
To us, but lived no more than three days. Yes,
Laius pinned his ankles together and sent him
Away to die on a distant, lonely mountain.
Once he was there, no power could make him a murderer,
Nor make Laius die at the hands of his son —
And he feared that above anything in the world.
You see how you may rely upon priests and their talk
Of the future. Never notice them! When God wishes
The truth discovered, he will easily work his will.

Oedipus

As I listened, my queen, my thoughts went reaching out
And touched on memories that make me shudder . . .

Jocasta

What memories? You stare as if you were trapped.

Oedipus
　　You said — I heard you say — that Laius' blood
　　Was spilt at a place where three roads meet.
Jocasta
　　We were all told that, and no one has denied it.
Oedipus
　　And where is the place where this happened?
Jocasta
　　The country
　　Is called Phocis; the roads splits, to Delphi
　　And to Daulia.
Oedipus
　　When did all this happen?
Jocasta
　　The city was given the news a little before
　　You became king of Thebes.
Oedipus
　　God,
　　What do you hold prepared for me?
Jocasta
　　Oedipus!
　　What made you frown when I talked of your becoming king?
Oedipus
　　Do not ask me yet . . . Laius — what was he like?
　　His appearance, his age, describe them to me.
Jocasta
　　He was tall, his hair beginning to be flecked with a down
　　Of white; he was built like you . . .
Oedipus
　　Stop! You torture me!
　　I have hurled myself blindly against unthinking
　　Fury and destruction!
Jocasta
　　How? I cannot bear
　　To watch you, my lord.
Oedipus
　　So little hope is frightening.

Listen, Teiresias the priest was not blind!
But one more answer, one more, will be better proof.

Jocasta

I dare not answer; but if my answers help you,
Ask.

Oedipus

When he left Thebes, was he alone,
Or did he have a company of men at arms
So that all could recognize he was a king?

Jocasta

No, five were all the travellers, and one
Was a herald. A single chariot carried Laius . . .

Oedipus

Yes! Not I see the truth . . . Who told you this?

Jocasta

A servant, the only man who returned alive.

Oedipus

Is he still in the palace with us?

Jocasta

No, after
He escaped, and found that you were king, and Laius
Dead, he implored me by my duty to a suppliant
To send him away. To the country, he said, herding
Sheep on the hillsides, where he could never see
The city he had left . . . And I let him go; he was
A good servant, deserving more than this
Small favor.

Oedipus

He must be found at once;
Can this be done?

Jocasta

Yes, but why do you want him?

Oedipus

My queen, as I look into myself I begin to fear;
I had no right to say those things, and so
I must see this man.

Jocasta

He will come. But I

Expect to be told your sorrow, my king, when they weigh
So heavily.

Oedipus

And I will not refuse you, Jocasta.
I have come to face such thoughts, and who should hear
Of them before you? I walk among
Great menaces.
My father is king of Corinth — Polybus; my mother —
Merope from Doris. In Corinth I was called
Their prince, their greatest noble, until
This happened to me — it was strange, yet not
So strange as to deserve my thoughts so much.
A man, stuffed with wine at a feast, called out
To me as he drank. He said I was a son only
In the imagination of my father. Anger
And pain would not let me rest that day; the next
I went to my parents and questioned them. They answered
The drunkard harshly for his insulting story,
And for their sakes I was glad he lied. Yet I always
Felt the wound, and the story spread in whispers.
At last I went to Delphi — my parents did not know —
But Apollo thought me unworthy of an answer
To that question. Instead he foretold many trials,
Many dangers, many sorrows. I was to be
My mother's husband, I was to murder my own
Father, my children would carry the guilt and none
Would dare look on them. When I heard this
I ran from my home and afterwards knew the land
Only by the stars that stood above it.
Never must I see the shame of that evil prophecy
Acted out my me in Corinth. I travelled
Until I came to this place where you say your king
Was killed . . . My wife, this is the truth . . . I will tell you . . .
My journey brought me to the meeting of three roads;
And there a herald, and an old man who rode
A chariot drawn by mares, came towards me . . .
Jocasta, the rider was like the man you described!

He and the herald, who went in front tried
To force me out of their path. In a rage I struck
The one who touched me, the servant at the wheel.
The old man watched me, and waited till I was passing;
Then from the chariot he aimed at the crown of my head
With the twin prongs of his goad. It was a costly
Action! Slashing with my stick I cut at him
And my blow tumbled him backwards out of the chariot —
Then I killed them all! If this man I met may be said
To resemble Laius, to be, perhaps, Laius,
I stand condemned to more sorrows than any man,
More cursed by an evil power than any man.
No one in Thebes, no stranger, may shelter me
Or speak to me; they must hunt me from their doors.
And I, it was I, who cursed myself, cursed myself!
And the dead king's pillow is fouled by the touch
Of my murdering hands. Is the evil in my soul?
Is my whole nature tainted? Must I go into exile,
Never see my people again, nor turn home
And set foot in Corinth? — for if I do, I must wed
My mother, and kill my father — Polybus, who gave me
Life and youth. Can you see this happen, and then
Deny that a cruel power has come to torture me?
No! You heavens, you pure light and holiness!
Let me die before that day, hide me before
I feel that black corruption in my soul!

Chorus

My king, this if a frightening story. But hope,
Until you hear from the man who saw what happened.

Oedipus

Yes, that is all the hope I have. Oedipus
Waits for one man, and he is a shepherd.

Jocasta

What makes you so eager for him to come?

Oedipus

I reason like this. We may find that his story
Matches yours. Then I shall be as free

As if this had never happened.

Jocasta

Was there anything in what
I said that could have such power?

Oedipus

You said
He told you robbers murdered Laius. If he still
Say's "robbers" and not "a robber," I am innocent.
One man cannot be taken for many.
But if he says a murderer, alone,
the guilt comes to rest on me.

Jocasta

But we all
Heard him say "robbers"; that is certain. He cannot
Unsay it. I am not alone, for the whole city heard.
But even if he swerves a little from his old account,
That will not prove you Laius' murderer,
Not in truth, not in justice. For Apollo said
He was to be killed by a son that was born to me . . .
And yet my son, poor child, could not have killed him,
For he died first . . . but that shows the deceit
Of prophecies. They beckon at you, but I
Would fix my eyes ahead, and never look at them!

Oedipus

You are right. Nevertheless send someone
To bring me that servant; do not forget.

Jocasta

                                              Yes,
I will send now. Let us go to the palace;
I would do nothing that could harm or anger you.

[*Exeunt all but the* CHORUS.]

Chorus

All actions must beware of the powers beyond us, and each word
Must speak our fear of heaven. I pray
That I may live every hour in obedience.
The laws that hold us in subjection
Have always stood beyond our reach, conceived

In the high air of heaven. Olympus
Was their sire, and no woman on earth
Gave them life. They are laws
That will never be lured to sleep in the arms of oblivion,
And in their strength heaven is great and cannot grow old.
Yet man desires to be more than man, to rule
His world for himself.
This desire, blown to immensity
On the rich empty food of its ambition,
Out of place, out of time,
Clambers to the crown of the rock, and stands there,
Tottering; then comes the steepling plunge down to earth,
To the earth where we are caged and mastered.
But this desire may work for good
When it fights to save a country, and I pray
That heaven will not weaken it then.
For then it comes like a god to be our warrior
And we shall never turn it back.
Justice holds the balance of all things,
And we must fear her.
Do not despise the frontiers in which we must live,
Do not cross them, do not talk of them,
But bow before the places where the gods are throned.
Time will come with cruel vengeance on the man
Who disobeys; that is the punishment
For those who are proud and are more than men —
They are humbled.
If a man grows rich in defiance of this law,
If his actions trespass on a world that he should fear,
If he reaches after mysteries that no man should know,
No prayer can plead for him when the sword of heaven is
    raised.
If he were to glory in success
All worship would fall dumb.
Delphi is the heart of the world and holds its secrets;
The temple of Zeus, and Olympia, command our prayers;
But we shall never believe again

Until the truth of this murder is known.
Let us be sure of our beliefs, give us proof.
Zeus, you may do your will; do not forget that you are im-
mortal,
Your empire cannot die; hear our prayers.
For the oracle given to Laius in the years of the long past
Is dying and forgotten, wiped from the memory,
Apollo's glory turns to shadows,
And all divinity to ruin.

[*Enter* JOCASTA.]

Jocasta

My lords, I have been summoned by my thoughts
To the temples of the gods, and I have brought
These garlands and this incense for an offering.
Oedipus is like a lonely bird among
The terrors that flock about his mind. He forgets
His wisdom, and no longer thinks the past will guide him
When he tries to foresee the future. Instead, he is
The slave of any word that talks of fear.
I try to reach him, to make him see that there is hope,
But it is useless; I have failed. And so I turn
To you, Apollo, nearest to us in Thebes,
A suppliant with prayers and gifts. Resolve this doubt
By sending the truth. He is the guide and master
Of our ship. What shall we do when even he
Is struck into bewilderment?

[*Enter* MESSENGER.]

Messenger

I do not know this country. Will you show me the palace
Of King Oedipus? I must find King Oedipus . . .
Do you know where he is?

Chorus

This is his palace, sir.
He is inside, and you see his queen before you.

Messenger

Heaven give her and all she loves riches
And happiness if she is the queen of such a king.

Jocasta

I return your greeting. You have spoken well and deserve
Well wishing. But what do you want with Oedipus?
Or do you bring a message for us?

Messenger

A message
Of good, for your palace and your husband, my queen.

Jocasta

What is it? Who sent you here?

Messenger

I come from Corinth.
My story may be quickly told. You will be glad, of course,
For the news is glad, and yet . . . yet you may grieve.

Jocasta

Well, what is this story with a double meaning?

Messenger

The people of Corinth — it was already announced
There — will make Oedipus their king.

Jocasta

But why?
Your king is Polybus. He is wise, revered . . .

Messenger

But no longer our king. Death hugs him to the earth.

Jocasta

Is this true? Polybus is dead?

Messenger

By my hopes of living out my years, it is true.

Jocasta

Servant, go, tell this to your master. Run!

[*Exit* SERVANT.]

Where are the prophecies of heaven now? Always
Oedipus dreaded to kill this man, and hid
From him. But look, Polybus has been murdered
By the careless touch of time, and not by Oedipus.

[*Enter* OEDIPUS.]

Oedipus

Dear Jocasta, dear wife, why have you called me

Here from the palace?

Jocasta

This man brings a message;
Listen, and then ask yourself what comes
Of the oracles from heaven that used to frighten us.

Oedipus

Who is this man? What has he to say to me?

Jocasta

He comes from Corinth, and his message is the death
Of Polybus. You will never see Polybus again!

Oedipus

You said that, stranger? Let me hear you say that plainly.

Messenger

Since you force me to give that part of my message first,
I repeat, he walks among the dead.

Oedipus

A plot?
Or did sickness conspire to kill him?

Messenger

A small
Touch on the balance sends old lives to sleep.

Oedipus

So, my poor father, sickness murdered you.

Messenger

And many years had measured out his life.

Oedipus

Oh look, look, who would listen to Apollo
Talking in his shrine at Delphi, or notice birds
That clamor to the air? They were the signs
That told me — and I believed — that I would kill
My father. But now he has the grave to protect him,
While I stand here, and I never touched a sword . . .
Unless he died of longing to see me —
Then perhaps he died because of me. No!
Polybus lies in darkness, and all those prophecies
Lie with him, chained and powerless.

Jocasta

I told you long ago how it would happen . . .

Oedipus
Yes, but I was led astray by fears.

Jocasta
Then think no more of them; forget them all.

Oedipus
Not all. The marriage with my mother — I think of it.

Jocasta
But is there anything a man need fear, if he knows
That chance is supreme throughout the world, and he cannot
See what is to come? Give way to the power
Of events and live as they allow! It is best.
Do not fear this marriage with your mother. Many
Men have dreams, and in those dreams they wed
Their mothers. Life is easiest, if you do not try
To oppose these things that seem to threaten us.

Oedipus
You are right, and I would agree with all
You say, if my mother were not alive. And though
You are right, I must fear. She is alive.

Jocasta
Think of your father, and his grave.
There is a light to guide you.

Oedipus
It does guide me!
I know he . . . But she is alive and I am afraid.

Messenger
You are afraid of a woman, my lord?

Oedipus
Yes,
Merope — Polybus was her husband.

Messenger
How can you be afraid of her?

Oedipus
A prophecy warned me.
To beware of sorrow . . .

Messenger
Can you speak of it, or are you

Forbidden to talk of these things to others?

Oedipus

No,

I am not forbidden. The Oracle At Delphi
Has told me my destiny — to be my mother's husband
And my father's murderer. And so I left
Corinth, many years ago and many
Miles behind me. The world has rewarded me richly,
And yet all those riches are less than the sight
Of a parent's face.

Messenger

And you went into exile because
You feared this marriage?

Oedipus

And to save myself from becoming
My father's murderer.

Messenger

Then, my king,
I ought to have freed you from that fear since I
Wished to be thought your friend.

Oedipus

Your reward
Will be measured by my gratitude.

Messenger

I had hoped for reward
When you returned as king of your palace in Corinth.

Oedipus

I must never go where my parents are.

Messenger

My son,
You do not know what you say; I see you do not.

Oedipus

How, sir? Tell me quickly.

Messenger

. . . If you live in exile
Because of Polybus and Merope.

Oedipus

Yes, and I live

In fear that Apollo will prove he spoke the truth.

Messenger
And it is from your parents that the guilt is to come?

Oedipus
Yes, stranger, the fear never leaves my side.

Messenger
You have no cause to be afraid — do you know that?

Oedipus
No cause? But they were my parents — that is the cause!

Messenger
No cause, because they were not your parents, Oedipus.

Oedipus
What do you mean? Polybus was not my father?

Messenger
As much as I, and yet no more than I am.

Oedipus
How could my father be no more than nothing?

Messenger
But Polybus did not give you life, nor did I.

Oedipus
Then why did he call me son?

Messenger
Listen, you were
A gift that he took from my hands.

Oedipus
A child
Given him by a stranger? But he loved me
Dearly.

Messenger
He had no children, and so consented.

Oedipus
So you have me to . . . Had you bought me for your slave?
Where did you find me?

Messenger
You were lying beneath the trees
In a glade upon Cithaeron.

Oedipus
What were you doing on Cithaeron?

Messenger
> My flocks were grazing in the mountains;
> I was guarding them.

Oedipus
> Guarding your flocks — you were
> A shepherd, a servant?

Messenger
> It was in that service that I saved
> Your life, my child.

Oedipus
> Why? Was I hurt or sick
> When you took me home?

Messenger
> Your ankles will be my witness
> that you would not have lived.

Oedipus
> Why do you talk
> Of that? The pain is forgotten!

Messenger
> Your feet were pierced
> And clamped together. I set you free.

Oedipus
> The child
> In the cradle had a scar — I still carry
> The shame of it.

Messenger
> You were named in remembrance
> Of that scar.

Oedipus
> In heaven's name, who did this?
> My mother? My father?

Messenger
> I do not know. The man
> Who gave you to me knows more of the truth.

Oedipus
> But you said you found me! Then it was not true . . .
> You had me from someone else?

Messenger
>Yes, another
>Shepherd gave me the child.

Oedipus
>Who? Can you
>Describe him?

Messenger
>They said he was a servant of Laius.

Oedipus
>Laius, who was once king of Thebes?

Messenger
>Yes,
>This man was one of his shepherds.

Oedipus
>Is he still
>Alive, could I see him?

Messenger
>Your people here
>Will know that best.

Oedipus
>Do any of you,
>My friends, know the shepherd he means? Has he
>Been seen in the fields, or in the palace? Tell me,
>Now! It is time these things were known!

Chorus
>I think
>He must be the man you were searching for, the one
>Who left the palace after Laius was killed.
>But Jocasta will know as well as I.

Oedipus
>My wife, you remember the man we sent for a little
>Time ago? Is he the one this person means?

Jocasta
>Perhaps . . . But why should he . . . Think nothing of this!
>Do not idle with memories and stories . . .

Oedipus
>No, I have been given these signs, and I must

Follow them, until I know who gave me birth.

Jocasta

No! Give up this search! I am tortured and sick
Enough. By the love of heaven, if you value life . . .

Oedipus

Courage! You are still a queen, though I discover
That I am three times three generations a slave.

Jocasta

No, listen to me, I implore you! You must stop!

Oedipus

I cannot listen when you tell me to ignore the truth.

Jocasta

But I know the truth, and I only ask you to save
Yourself.

Oedipus

I have always hated that way to safety!

Jocasta

But evil lies in wait for you . . . Oh, do not let him
Find the truth!

Oedipus

Bring this shepherd to me,
And let her gloat over the riches of her ancestry.

Jocasta

My poor child! Those are the only words
I shall ever have for you . . . I can speak no others!

[*Exit* JOCASTA.]

Chorus

What is the torment that drives your queen so wildly
Into the palace, Oedipus? Her silence threatens
A storm. I fear some wrong . . .

Oedipus

Let the storm
Come if it will. I must know my birth,
I must know it, however humble. Perhaps she,
For she is a queen, and proud, is ashamed
That I was born so meanly. But I consider
Myself a child of Fortune, and while she brings me

Gifts, I shall not lack honor. For she has given me
Life itself; and my cousins, the months, have marked me
Small and great as they marched by. Such
Is my ancestry, and I shall be none other —
And I will know my birth!

Chorus

There are signs
Of what is to come, and we may read them,
Casting our thoughts into the future,
   And drawing in new knowledge.
For we have seen how the world goes
And we have seen the laws it obeys.
Cithaeron, mountain of Oedipus, the moon
Will not rise in tomorrow's evening sky
Before our king calls you his true father,
His only nurse and mother — and then
You will have your greatest glory.
You will be honored with dances and choirs
For your gentle kindness to our king — Hail
To the god Apollo! May he be content
With all our words.
Pan walks among the mountains, and one
Of the immortal nymphs could have lain with him;
Who was the goddess who became your mother, Oedipus?
Or was she the wife of Apollo, for he loves
The wild meadows and the long grass.
Or was it the prince of Cyllene, Hermes?
Or Bacchus, whose palace is the mountain top?
Did he take you as a gift from the nymphs of Helicon,
With whom he plays through all his immortal years?

Oedipus

I never knew the shepherd or encountered him,
My people, but the man I see there must be
The one we have been seeking. His age answers
My riddle for me; it holds as many years
As our messenger's. And now I see that those
Who lead him are my servants. But you have known him

Before, you can tell me whether I am right.

Chorus

Yes, we recognize him — the most faithful
Of Laius' shepherds.

Oedipus

And you, Corinthian,
You *must* tell me first. Is this the man you mean?

Messenger

It is; you see him there.

[*Enter* SHEPHERD.]

Oedipus

You, sir, come to me,
Look me in the eyes, and answer all my questions!
Did you once serve Laius?

Shepherd

Yes, and I was born
In his palace; I was not brought from another country . . .

Oedipus

Your life? How were you employed?

Shepherd

Most
Of my life I watched his flocks.

Oedipus

And where
Was their pasture? They had a favorite meadow?

Shepherd

Sometimes Cithaeron, sometimes the places near.

Oedipus

Do you recognize this man? Did you see him on Cithaeron?

Shepherd

Why should anyone go there? Whom do you mean?

Oedipus

Here! Standing beside me. Have you ever met him?

Shepherd

I do not think so . . . My memory is not quick.

Messenger

We should not wonder at this, your majesty;

But I shall remind him of all he has forgotten.
I know that he remembers when for three
Whole years I used to meet him near Cithaeron,
Six months, from each spring to the rising of the Bear;
I had a single flock and he had two.
Then, in the winters, I would take my sheep to their pens
While he went to the fields of Laius . . . Did this happen?
Have I told it as it happened, or have I not?

Shepherd

The time is long since then . . . yes, it is the truth.

Messenger

Good; now, tell me: you know the child you gave me . . . ?

Shepherd

What is happening? What do these questions mean?

Messenger

Here is the child, my friend, who was so little then.

Shepherd

Damnation seize you! Can you not keep your secret?

Oedipus

Wait, Shepherd! Do not find fault; as I listened
I found more fault in you than in him.

Shepherd

What
Have I done wrong, most mighty king?

Oedipus

You will not
Admit the truth about that child.

Shepherd

He wastes
His time. He talks, but it is all lies.

Oedipus

When it would please me, you will not speak; but you will
When I make you cry for mercy . . .

Shepherd

No, my king,
I am an old man — do not hurt me!

Oedipus [*To guards.*]

Take his arms and tie them quickly!

Shepherd
> But why,
> Poor child? What more do you want to know?

Oedipus
> You gave
> The boy to this Corinthian?

Shepherd
> Yes I did . . .
> And I should have prayed for death that day.

Oedipus
> Your prayer will be answered now if you lie to me!

Shepherd
> But you will surely kill me if I tell the truth.

Oedipus
> He will drive my patience to exhaustion!

Shepherd
> No!
> I told you now, I did give him the child.

Oedipus
> Where did it come from? Your home? Another's?

Shepherd
> It was not mine, it was given to me.

Oedipus
> By someone
> In the city? . . . I want to know the house!

Shepherd
> By all that is holy,
> No more, your majesty, no more questions!

Oedipus
> You die
> If I have to ask again!

Shepherd
> The child was born
> In the palace of King Laius.

Oedipus
> By one of his slaves?
> Or was it a son of his own blood?

Shepherd

My king,

How shall I tell a story of such horror?

Oedipus

And *how* shall I hear it? And yet I must, must hear.

Shepherd

The child was called his son. But your queen in the palace

May tell you the truth of that most surely.

Oedipus

Jocasta gave you the child?

Shepherd

Yes, my king.

Oedipus

Why? What were you to do?

Shepherd

I was to destroy him.

Oedipus

The poor mother asked that?

Shepherd

She was afraid.

A terrible prophecy . . .

Oedipus

What?

Shepherd

There was a story

That he would kill his parents.

Oedipus

Why did you give

The child away to this stranger?

Shepherd

I pitied it,

My lord, and I thought he would take it to the far land

Where he lived. But he saved its life only for

Great sorrows. For if you are the man he says,

You must know your birth was watched by evil powers.

Oedipus

All that was foretold will be made true! Light,

Now turn back and die; I must not look on you!
See, this is what I am; son of parents
I should not have known, I lived with those
I should not have touched, and murdered those
A man must not kill!

[*Exit* OEDIPUS.]

Chorus

Every man who has ever lived
Is numbered with the dead; they fought with the world
For happiness, yet all they won
Was a shadow that slipped away to die.
And you, Oedipus, are all those men. I think of the power
Which carried you to such victories and such misery
And I know there is not joy or triumph in the world.

Oedipus aimed beyond the reach of a man
And fixed with his arrowing mind
Perfection and rich happiness.
The Sphinx's talons were sharp with evil, she spoke in the
    mysteries
Of eternal riddles, and he came to destroy her,
To overcome death, to be a citadel
Of strength in our country.
He was called our king, and was
The greatest noble in great Thebes.
And now his story ends in agony.
Death and madness hunt him,
Destruction and sorrow haunt him.
Now his life turns and brings the reward of his greatness . . .
Glorious Oedipus, son, and then father,
In the same chamber, in the same silent room,
Son and father in the same destruction;
Your marriage was the harvesting of wrong.
How could it hold you where your father lay,
And bear you in such silence for such an end?

Child of Laius, I wish, I wish I had never known you,
For now there is only mourning, sorrow flowing

From our lips.
And yet we must not forget the truth;
If we were given hope and life, it was your work.
[*Enter* SERVANT.]
Servant

My lords of Thebes, on whom rest all the honors
Of our country, when you hear what has happened,
When you witness it, how will you bear your grief
In silence? Weep, if you have ever loved
The royal house of Thebes. For I do not think
The great streams of the Phasis or the Ister
Could ever wash these walls to purity. But all
The crimes they hide must glare out to the light,
Crimes deliberate and considered. The sorrows
We choose ourselves bring the fiercest pain!

Chorus

We have seen great wrongs already, and they were frightening.
Do you bring new disasters?

Servant

I bring a message
That I may tell, and you may hear, in a few
Swift words. Jocasta is dead.

Chorus

Then she died in grief. What caused her death?

Servant

It was her own will. Of that terrible act
The worst must remain untold, for I did not watch it.
Yet you will hear what happened to our poor queen
As far as memory guides me. When she went
Into the domed hall of the palace, whirled
On the torrent of her grief, she ran straight
To her marriage chamber, both hands clutched at her hair,
Tearing like claws. Inside, she crashed shut the door
And shrieked the name Laius, Laius who died
So long ago. She talked to herself of the son
She once bore, and of Laius murdered by that son;
Of the mother who was left a widow, and became

Wife and mother again in shame and sorrow.
She wept for her marriage, in which her husband gave
To her a husband, and her children, children.
How her death followed I cannot tell you . . .
We heard a shout, and now Oedipus blazed
And thundered through the door. I could not see
How her sorrow ended, because he was there,
Circling in great mad strides, and we watched
Him. He went round each begging to each
Of us; he asked for a sword, he asked to go
To his wife who was more than a wife, to his mother in whom
His birth and his children's birth, like two harvests
From the same field, had been sown and gathered. His grief
Was a ranging madness, and some power must have guided
　　him —
It was none of us who were standing there. He gave
A cry full of fear and anguish, then, as if
A ghost was leading him he leaped against the double
Doors of Jocasta's room. The hinges tilted
Full out of their sockets, and shattered inside
The chamber — and there we saw his wife, hanging
By her throat in the grip of a tall rope. And when
He saw her, he shrieked like wounded beast, wrenched loose
The knot that held her, and laid her on the ground.
What followed was terrible to watch. He ripped
The gold-worked brooches from her robes — she wore them
As jewels — and raised them above his head. Then he plunged
　　them
Deep into the sockets of his eyes, shouting
That he would never look upon the wrongs
He had committed and had suffered. Now
In his blackness he must see such shapes as he deserved
And never look on those he loved. Repeating
This like a chant, he lifted his hands and stabbed
His eyes, again and again. We saw his eyeballs
Fill with tears of blood that dyed his cheeks,
And a red stream pouring from his veins, dark

As the blood of life, thick as storming hail.
Yes, this is a storm that has broken, a storm
That holds the queen and the king in its embrace.
They were rich and fortunate, and they were so
As we should wish to be. Now, in one day,
See how we must mourn them. The blind rush
To death, the shame, all the evils that we
Have names for — they have escaped none!

Chorus

Has our poor king found ease for his sorrow yet?

Servant

He shouts at us to open the doors and show
To all Thebes the murderer of his father
And his mother's . . . his words are blasphemous,
I dare not speak them . . . He will be driven from Thebes,
Will not stay beneath this curse that he called upon
Himself. Yet he needs help and a guide. No one
Could bear that agony . . . But he comes himself to show you;
The great doors of the palace open, and what you will see
Will turn you away in horror — yet will ask for pity.

[*Enter* OEDIPUS.]

Chorus

This suffering turns a face of terror to the world.
There is no story told, no knowledge born
That tells of greater sorrow.
Madness came striding upon you, Oedipus,
The black, annihilating power that broods
And waits in the hand of time . . .
I cannot look!
We have much to ask and learn and see.
But you blind us with an icy sword of terror.

Oedipus

Where will you send this wreckage and despair of man?
Where will my voice be heard, like the wind drifting emptily
On the air. Oh you powers, why do you drive me on?

Chorus

They drive you to the place of horror,

That only the blind may see,
And only the dead hear of.

Oedipus

Here in my cloud of darkness there is no escape,
A cloud, thick in my soul, and there it dumbly clings;
That cloud is my own spirit
That now wins its fiercest battle and turns back
To trample me . . . The memory of evil can tear
Like goads of molten fire, and go deep,
Infinity could not be so deep.

Chorus

More than mortal in your acts of evil.
More than mortal in your suffering, Oedipus.

Oedipus

You are my last friend, my only help; you have
Waited for me, and will care for the eyeless body
Of Oedipus. I know you are there . . . know . . .
Through this darkness I can hear your voice.

Chorus

Oedipus, all that you do
Makes us draw back in fear. How could you take
Such vivid vengeance on your eyes: What power lashed you on?

Oedipus

Apollo, my lords, Apollo sent this evil on me.
I was the murderer; I struck the blow. Why should I
Keep my sight? If I had eyes, what could delight them?

Chorus

It is so; it is as you say.

Oedipus

No, I can look on nothing . . .
And I can love nothing — for love has lost
Its sweetness, I can hear no voice — for words
Are sour with hate . . . Take stones and beat me
From your country. I am the living curse, the source
Of sickness and death!

Chorus

Your own mind, reaching after the secrets

Of gods, condemned you to your fate.
If only you had never come to Thebes . . .

Oedipus

But when my feet were ground by iron teeth
That bolted me in the meadow grass.
A man set me free and ransomed me from death.
May hell curse him for that murderous kindness!
I should have died then
And never drawn this sorrow on those I love
And on myself . . .

Chorus

Our prayers echo yours.

Oedipus

Nor killed my father,
Nor led my mother to the room where she gave me life.
But now the gods desert me, for I am
Born of impurity, and my blood
Mingles with those who gave me birth.
If evil can grow with time to be a giant
That masters and usurps our world,
That evil lords its way through Oedipus.

Chorus

How can we say that you have acted wisely?
Is death no better than a life in blindness?

Oedipus

Do not teach me that this punishment is wrong —
I will have no advisers to tell me it is wrong!
Why choke my breath and go among the dead
If I keep my eyes? For there I know I could not
Look upon my father or my poor mother . . .
My crimes have been too great for such a death.
Or should I love my sight because it let me
See my children? No, for then I would
Remember who their father was. My eyes
Would never let me love them, nor my city,
Nor my towers, nor the sacred images
Of gods. I was the noblest lord in Thebes,

But I have stripped myself of Thebes, and become
The owner of all miseries. For I commanded
My people to drive out the unclean thing, the man
Heaven had shown to be impure in the house
Of Laius.
I found such corruption in me — could I see
My people and not turn blind for shame? . . .
My ears are a spring, and send a river
Of sound through me; if I could have dammed that river
I would have made my poor body into a bolted prison
In which there would be neither light nor sound.
Peace can only come if we shut the mind
Away from the sorrow in the world outside.
Cithaeron, why did you let me live? Why
Did you not kill me as I lay there? I would
Have been forgotten, and never revealed the secret
Of my birth. Polybus, Corinth, the palace
They told me was my father's, you watched over
My youth, but beneath that youth's nobility lay
Corruption — you see it in my acts, in my blood!
There are three roads, a hidden valley, trees,
And a narrow place where the roads meet — they
Drink my blood, the blood I draw from my father —
Do they remember me, do they remember what I did?
Do they know what next I did? . . . The room, the marriage
Room — it was there I was given life, and now
It is there I give the same life to my children.
The blood of brothers, fathers, sons, the race
Of daughters, wives, mothers, all the blackest
Shame a man may commit . . . But I must not name
Such ugly crimes. Oh, you heavens, take me
From the world and hide me, drown me in oceans
Where I can be seen no more! Come, do not fear
To touch a single unhappy man. Yes, a man,
No more. Be brave, for my sufferings can fall to no one
But myself to bear!

Chorus
Oedipus, Creon came

While you were praying; he brings advice and help.
You can protect us no more, and we turn to him.

Oedipus

What can I say to Creon? I have given him
No cause to trust me or to listen. In all I said
Before, he has seen that I was wrong.

[*Enter* CREON *with* ANTIGONE *and* ISMENE.]

Creon

I have not come scorning or insulting you, Oedipus,
For those wrongs [*To servants.*] Have you no shame before
Your countrymen? At least show reverence to the sun's
Flame that sends us life, and do not let
This curse lie open to disfigure heaven.
Neither earth, nor the pure falling rain, nor light
May come near it. Take him to the palace now!
When evil grows in the family, only the family
May hear of it and look without pollution.

Oedipus

Creon, I thought . . . but now you have struck those fears
Away — you will be a gentle king.
But I ask one thing, and I ask it to help you,
Not myself, for I am hated by powers too strong
For us.

Creon

What do you ask so eagerly?

Oedipus

Banish me from the country now. I must go
Where no one can see or welcome me again.

Creon

I would have done so, Oedipus, but first
I must know from Apollo what he commands.

Oedipus

But we have heard all his answers — destroy the
Parricide, the unholiness, destroy me!

Creon

So it was said . . . And yet we are in such danger;
It is better to hear what we must do.

Oedipus

Why need you
Go to Delphi for my poor body?

Creon

Delphi will never deceive us; you know it speaks
The truth.

Oedipus

But Creon, I command you! . . . I will kneel
And pray to you . . . Bury my queen as you wish
In her royal tomb; she is your sister
And it is her right. But as for myself, I
Must never think of entering my father's city
Again, so long as its people live. Let me
Have no home but the mountains, where the hill
They call Cithaeron, my Cithaeron, stands.
There my mother and my father, while
They lived, decreed I should have my grave.
My death will be a gift from them, for they
Have destroyed me . . . And . . . yet I know that sickness
Cannot break in and take my life, nothing
May touch me. I am sure of this, for each moment
Is a death, and I am kept alive only
For the final punishment . . . But let it go,
Let it go, I do not care what is done with me.
Creon, my sons will ask nothing more from you;
They are men, wherever they go they will take what they need
From life. But pity my two daughters, who will have
No love. All that was owned by me, they shared,
And . . . when I banqueted, they were always beside me.
You must become their father . . . But let me touch them
And talk to them of our sorrows. Come, my lord,
Come, my noble kinsman, let me feel them
In my arms and believe they are as much my own
As when I saw . . . I cannot think . . . Their weeping,
Their dear voices are near. Creon has pitied me
And given me my children. Is this true?

Creon

I sent for them; I know what joy they would give you

And how you loved them once. Yes, it is true.

Oedipus

May heaven bless your life, and may the power
Watching us, guard you more safely on the throne
Than me. My children, where are you? Come near, come
To my hands; they are your brother's hands and they
Went searching out and took your father's seeing
Eyes to darkness. I did not know my children,
And did not ask, but now the world may see
That I gave you life from the source that gave me mine.
Why is there no light? I cannot see you! . . . And tears
Come when I think of the years you will have to live
In a cruel world. In the city they will shun you,
Fear your presence; when they feast and dance in the streets
You will not be allowed to watch, and they
Will send you weeping home. And when you come
To the years of marriage, children, who will there be
So careless of his pride as to accept the shame
That glares on my birth and on yours? "Your father
Killed his father!" "Your father gave life where he
Was given life, you are children where he was once
A child." That will be your humiliation!
And who will wed you?
No one, my daughters, there will be no one, and I see
You must pine to death in lonely childlessness.
Creon, you are their father, you alone.
For they have lost their parents. Do not let them go
Into beggary and solitude — their blood is yours.
I have nothing, but do not afflict them with
My poverty. Have pity on them. See, so young
And robbed of all except your kindliness.
Touch me once, my lord, and give your consent.
My children, I would have said much to comfort
And advise you — but how could you understand?
But pray, you must pray to live as the world allows
And find a better life than the father whom you follow.

Creon

No more now. Go inside the palace.

Oedipus
It is hard, but I must obey.
Creon
All things are healed
By time.
Oedipus
But Creon, I demand one thing before
I go.
Creon
What do you demand?
Oedipus
Banishment!
Creon
Only heaven can answer your prayer. When Apollo . . .
Oedipus
But Apollo can only detest me.
Creon
Then your prayer will be
The sooner heard.
Oedipus
You mean what you say?
Creon
I cannot
Promise, when I see nothing certain.
Oedipus
Now!
Exile me now!
Creon
Go then, and leave your children.
Oedipus
You must not take them from me!
Creon
You give
Commands as if you were king. You must remember
Your rule is over, and it could not save your life.
Chorus
Men of Thebes, look at the king who ruled

Your country; there is Oedipus.
He knew how to answer the mystery
Of evil in the Sphinx, and was our greatest lord.
We saw him move the world with his will, and we envied him.
But look, the storm destroys him, the sea
Has come to defeat him.
Remember that death alone can end all suffering;
Go towards death, and ask for no greater
Happiness than a life
In which there has been no anger and no pain.

Oedipus the King
by Tom F. Driver

Oedipus the King[1] was produced in about 427 B.C. when Sophocles was, to the best of our knowledge, some sixty-eight years old. If sixty-eight seems an advanced age for a playwright to be creating his masterpiece, we must remember that George Bernard Shaw wrote *Saint Joan* when he was sixty-seven.

Sophocles when he wrote the play was at the height of his powers. He had already written *Ajax, Antigone,* and *Electra,* which we still possess, and others perhaps just as great which are now lost. He had learned much from other playwrights including Aeschylus (who had died some thirty years before) but he had gone beyond the others in at least two important respects: (1) He had introduced the use of three principal actors rather than the two that Aeschylus had at first employed.[2] (2) While he had not surpassed Aeschylus in depiction of human character, he had managed to make character and dramatic action interdependent to a degree that Aeschylus had not achieved, and probably had not even attempted.

The play was first performed, as were all the Greek tragedies we possess, at the festival known as the City Dionysia, held annually at Athens in the spring of the year. The Theater of Dionysus, parts of which still exist, was a large and splendid amphitheater. Its central feature was the circular playing-space on the ground level known as the *orchestre,* where the chorus sang and danced. At the back of this was a low stage used for some, but not all, the scenes, and a small wooden building called the *skene* that served both as a scenic background (in this case the palace) and as a shelter into which the actors could retire. In the front center of the audience were the prominent seats of the judges, since the plays were entered in competition. The principal seat was reserved for the priest of Dionysus. The altar of the god, once in the center of the *orchestre* had been moved to another part of the grounds. The benches for the audience, reaching more than half way around the *orchestre* and banked on the side of the hill, were sufficient to accommodate 17,000 spectators. In other words, they would hold the entire adult nonslave population of the city and numerous visitors from the countryside.

In comparison with our modern playhouses the Theater of Dionysus, open to the sky, was vast, formal, and ritualistic. Greek drama strove to *present* the shape of human action rather than to *represent* the appearance of things. The actors, arbitrarily costumed in long robes, wore heavy masks on their faces. Their height was increased by tall headdresses called *onkoi* and high-soled boots called *kothornoi*. They spoke a complicated verse that approached song. All the stage conventions, consonant with the Greek conventions of dramaturgy, were pointed toward suggesting ontological reality more than physical reality. It is strictly within this context that Sophocles turns his attention, as he partly does, toward human character and psychology.

The story of Oedipus was well known to Sophocles's audience. Laius, king of Thebes, was warned by an oracle that his son Oedipus would grow up to slay his father and wed his mother. The parents decided to do away with the child by exposing him on the hillside. However, the shepherd who was entrusted with this task took pity on the infant and gave him to another shepherd who took him out of the country. Oedipus grew up in Corinth supposing himself the son of the king of that region. In time he heard what the oracle had prophesied for him. In an effort to escape his fate he journeyed toward Thebes. On the way he encountered an old man in a chariot at the crossroads. An argument flared up over the right of way, Oedipus found himself attacked, and in the skirmish he killed the old man. Arriving at Thebes, he became a hero by delivering the city from the power of the Sphinx, and as a result he was made king and took the queen, Jocasta, for his wife. Later a plague came to Thebes. The queen's brother, Creon, was sent to consult the oracle at Delphi (Putho) to find the cause and remedy for the disaster, and the oracle reported that the slayer of Laius dwelt within the city and that the plague would not be lifted until the criminal was discovered and expunged. In the ensuing investigation it came to light that the offender was King Oedipus himself. Mad with horror, Jocasta killed herself. Oedipus put out his eyes and went into voluntary exile. Creon became the king, and for a time life grew calm again in Thebes.

What happens in *Oedipus the King*, however, is not the story as I have told it. What happens is the *uncovering* of the story, which is a different matter. They play starts when Creon is returning from his mission to the oracle. It ends a few hours later with the catastrophe. In the center Sophocles has placed the most fearsome and the most masterful of all detective stories. The action is a "finding out" and it is propelled relentlessly by a quartet of converging forces: (1) the desire of the people of Thebes to end the plague that is ravaging the city; (2) the injunction of the oracle to find the criminal; (3) Oedipus's own nature, which prompts him to expose the truth come what may; and (4) the workings of fate, which seem like chance.

The truth sought and found in the play is more than a mere sequence of facts. It is essentially truth about the cosmos and the gods. Sophocles expressed himself in religious terms, and we may suppose that he, like Shakespeare, is more at home with religious conservatism than with religious controversy. Shakespeare is not Marlowe and Sophocles is not Euripides. Yet in spite of the religious expression in *Oedipus the King* we are nearer the mark when we say that the truth uncovered in it is philosophical. To be more precise, it is ontological. It has to do with the reality of unseen things. It has to do with the way things are. In the broadest sense it is moral, but the play is not a morality play, and it holds no lesson that might profit a man in planning his affairs or in saving his soul.

The gods of Sophocles are not akin to the God we are used to hearing about in Biblical monotheism. That God transcends His creation and rules absolutely over it. Hence He can judge and can give mercy. The gods of Sophocles (for which we ought to use his own word *theoi*) are the forces which everywhere and at all times operate within the cosmos, giving it its manifest consistency and order. They are imminent rather than transcendent. They do not judge; they merely function, as all forces do. Judgment is the work of Fate (*moira*) and means simply to give to a man his apportioned lot. If Oedipus, wittingly or unwittingly, offends the *theoi* opposing incest and patricide, he must eventually suffer, for redress will come. If it were not so, moral chaos would result; yet in a world maintained by a balance of forces among the *theoi*, chaos is unthinkable. Every detail of *Oedipus the King* is contrived so as to reinforce the conception of order disturbed and order restored. The play itself is such a masterpiece of orderly construction that its very form mirrors the cosmic order which it exists to disclose.

Readers of *Oedipus the King* differ according to whether they regard Sophocles's cosmic vision as one of comfort or despair. If comfort depends upon hope, there is none of it in the play. On the other hand, if despair springs from chaos, there is none of that either. The fact is that the play's very affirmation is the product of its uncompromising bleakness. It has the comfort of moral certainty, but not the comfort that springs from renewal.

Oedipus the King is not to be read in light of *Oedipus at Colonus*, written some twenty years later. The presuppositions of the latter play are different, and its spirit of beatitude is new. *Oedipus at Colonus* is shot through with benevolent thoughts about the future. *Oedipus the King* knows no future. If we break down the play into its several parts, taking note of the major incidents in the plot and the structural sections of the play, we arrive at the following outline.[3]

INCIDENTS OF THE PLOT	STRUCTURAL SECTION
a. Introduction: we learn of the plague, the remedy prescribed by the oracle, and therefore the problem confronting Oedipus and Thebes.	Prologue
b. The *agon* (conflict) with Teiresias, in which the play's ending is revealed.	Episode 1
c. Oedipus is thrown off the track by his suspicion of Creon.	Episode 2
d. Oedipus learns he probably slew Laius.	Episode 3
e. Jocasta tells of exposing her infant son.	Episode 3

INCIDENTS OF THE PLOT	STRUCTURAL SECTION
f. Oedipus tells how and why he left Corinth, to avoid the prediction of the oracle.	Episode 3
g. The Corinthian Messenger brings the information that Oedipus is not Polybus's son.	Episode 4
h. The herdsman bring the knowledge that Oedipus was the infant exposed by Jocasta.	Episode 5
i. Jocasta hangs herself.	Episode 6
j. Oedipus blinds himself.	Episode 6
k. Lament. Oedipus is visited by his children and asks for exile.	Ode 7 and Episode 7

In this outline *d*, *e*, *f*, *g*, and *h* tell of events that took place in the past.[4] This is expository material. In this play, however, it becomes the very goal of the action, not its springboard. In the center of the play the past is imbedded.

Formally, then, the present embraces the past. Yet as the play proceeds this formal arrangement is reversed. In a play shot through with irony, the basic irony is this: while the form of the play shows the past enclosed within the present, the action shows that in reality the present is enclosed within the past.

The deeper the play probes into the past, the more violent the present becomes, as if to know the past were to shake the foundations of the present. The conception is similar to that informing *The Iceman Cometh* and *Long Day's Journey Into Night*, by Eugene O'Neill, whose understanding of time is Grecian. In *Oedipus the King* every decision except one that affects the outcome of things was made in the past, before the action of the play begins. The one decision made in the present is Oedipus's to persevere, against the warnings of Teiresias and Jocasta, in his search for the truth. This means that the one decisive act we are shown is the decision to recover the past. In the denouement we have a suicide, a self-blinding (perhaps a symbol of self-mutilation, itself a kind of death), and an exile. For Oedipus, the future is obliterated by the past and plunges into darkness.

Thebes, on its part, returns to a state of health and calm. Order is restored. Yet the city, though it has escaped catastrophe, has lost something of its heart. The chorus of Theban citizens closes the play in a minor key:

Men of Thebes, look at the king who ruled
Your country; there is Oedipus.
He knew how to answer the mystery
Of evil in the Sphinx, and was our greatest lord.
We saw him move the world with his will, and we envied him.
But look the storm destroys him, the sea
Has come to defeat him.
Remember that death alone can end all suffering;
Go towards death, and ask for no greater
Happiness than a life
In which there has been no anger and no pain.

The achievement of the Greek thinkers was that they discovered new ways to see the constants that lie within life's apparently random change. What is given immediately to our experience is variety and mutation, and this produces unbearable anxiety unless some pattern of consistency can be found within it. The peoples of the eastern Mediterranean, who cradled our civilization, sought to transcend the flux through the elaboration of various myths and rituals. The Greeks did also, and it became their privilege eventually to transmute the myths and rituals into philosophy and literature of such universal appeal that time has not rendered them obsolete. The Greeks fought against time and won. They did it, strangely, by shutting out the future. The future is the enemy of timelessness, as the past, which is fixed, and the present, which is ineffable, are not.

Between the Greek hostility to temporal change and the Christian espousal of it because God is thought to redeem time, there is little room for compromise. We may not agree with Reinhold Niebuhr that the Greek drama is populated by "real persons engaged in actual history — betrayed into evil by — their freedom over natural impulses."[5] That is to Christianize the plays and to give them an insight into what we call the Biblical view of morality which they possessed only dimly if at all. Their concern, we may say more accurately, was not man but the cosmic conditions to which man was subject.

The Greek view of man's lot will be especially attractive, however, in any age which, having ceased to believe that time is being redeemed, fears to contemplate the future. In several dramatists, such as O'Neill, Williams, and sometimes Ibsen, the Greek view of time returns. Though the view is dark, and though it lends little support to social reform, it is preferable to chaos. It has, besides, the effect of making one intensely aware of the light of the sun. That is why, when we look at the *Oedipus the King* of Sophocles, we do not think so much about the dark that surrounds it as about the luminosity that shines from all its surfaces.

1. The name sometimes appears as *Oedipus Rex* or *Oedipus Tyrannus*, a form Latinized from the Greek: Οἰδίπους Τύραννος.
2. The actors customarily played more than one role. In this play, for instance, one actor probably played Oedipus, while a second played the Priest, Jocasta, and the servant of Laius, leaving the third to play Creon, Teiresias, and the two messengers. The point of Sophocles's using the third actor was not that it made everyone's work easier but that it enabled him to write scenes with three characters speaking instead of only two, which was of course a great dramatic and psychological advantage.
3. Greek tragedies are divided into odes and episodes and sometimes prologue and epilogue. The prologue is that which comes before the first choric ode. Thereafter the episodes alternate with the odes—i.e., scenes among the actors, in which the chorus also may take part, alternating with the choric odes, which are distinct. The epilogue is whatever follows the last ode.
4. This outline appears in *The Sense of History in Greek and Shakespearean Drama*, by Tom F. Driver (New York: Columbia University Press, 1960, p. 156). The book includes an extended discussion of the treatment of time in *Oedipus the King* and other Greek tragedies.
5. *The Self and the Dramas of History*, by Reinhold Niebuhr (New York: Charles Scribner's Sons, 1955, p. 78).

Sophocles
ANTIGONE

**Translated by
Dudley Fitts
and
Robert Fitzgerald**

Characters   *Antigone*

                    Ismene

                    Eurydice

                    Creon

                    Haimon

                    Teiresias

                    A Sentry

                    A Messenger

                    Chorus

SCENE: *Before the palace of* CREON, *King of Thebes. A central double door, and two lateral doors. A platform extends the length of the facade, and from this platform three steps lead down into the "orchestra," or chorus-ground.*

TIME: *Dawn of the day after the repulse of the Argive army from the assault on Thebes.*

PROLOGUE [ANTIGONE *and* ISMENE *enter from the central door of the Palace.*]

Antigone
Ismene, dear sister,
You would think that we had already suffered enough
For the curse on Oedipus
I cannot imagine any grief
That you and I have not gone through. And now —
Have they told you of the new decree of our King Creon?

Ismene
I have heard nothing: I know
That two sisters lost two brothers, a double death
In a single hour; and I know that the Argive army
Fled in the night; but beyond this, nothing.

Antigone
I thought so. And that is why I wanted you
To come out there with me. There is something we must do.

Ismene
Why do you speak so strangely?

Antigone
Listen, Ismene
Creon buried our brother Eteocles
With military honors, gave him a soldier's funeral,
And it was right that he should; but Polyneices,
Who fought as bravely and died as miserably, —
They say that Creon has sworn
No one shall bury him, no one mourn for him,
But his body must lie in the fields, a sweet treasure
For carrion birds to find as they search for food.

That is what they say, and our good Creon is coming here
To announce it publicly; and the penalty —
Stoning to death in the public square!

     There it is,
And now you can prove what you are
A true sister, or a traitor to your family.

Ismene
Antigone, you are mad! What could I possibly do?

Antigone
You must decide whether you will help me or not.

Ismene
I do not understand you. Help you in what?

Antigone
Ismene, I am going to bury him. Will you come?

Ismene
Bury him! You have just said the new law forbids it.

Antigone
He is my brother. And he is your brother, too.

Ismene
But think of the danger! Think what Creon will do!

Antigone
Creon is not strong enough to stand in my way.

Ismene
Ah sister!
Oedipus dies, everyone hating him
For what his own search brought to light, his eyes
Ripped out by his own hand; and Jocasta died,
His mother and wife at once: she twisted the cords
That strangled her life; and our two brothers died,
Each killed by the other's sword. and We are left:
But oh, Antigone,
Think how much more terrible than these
Our own death would be if we should go against Creon
And do what he has forbidden! We are only women,
We cannot fight with men, Antigone!
The law is strong, we must give in to the law
In this thing, and in worse. I beg the Dead

To forgive me, but I am helpless: I must yield
To those in authority. And I think it is dangerous business
To be always meddling.

Antigone

If that is what you think,
I should not want you, even if you asked to come.
You have made your choice, you can be what you want to be.
But I will bury him; and if I must die,
I say that this crime is holy: I shall lie down
With him in death, and I shall be as dear
To him as he to me.

It is the dead,
Not the living, who make the longest demands
We die for ever . . .

You may do as you like,
Since apparently the laws of the gods mean nothing to you.

Ismene

They mean a great deal to me; but I have no strength
To break laws that were made for the public good.

Antigone

That must be your excuse, I suppose. But as for me,
I will bury the brother I love.

Ismene

Antigone,
I am so afraid for you!

Antigone

You need not be
You have yourself to consider, after all.

Ismene

But no one must hear of this, you must tell no one!
I will keep it a secret, I promise!

Antigone

Oh tell it! Tell everyone!
Think how they'll hate you when it all comes out
If they learn that you knew about it all the time!

Ismene

So fiery! You should be cold with fear.

Antigone

Perhaps. But I am doing only what I must.

Ismene

But can you do it? I say that you cannot.

Antigone

Very well: when my strength gives out, I shall do no more.

Ismene

Impossible things should not be tried at all.

Antigone

Go away, Ismene

I shall be hating you soon, and the dead will too,

For your words are hateful. Leave me my foolish plan

I am not afraid of the danger; if it means death,

It will not be the worst of deaths—death without honor.

Ismene

So then if you feel that you must.

You are unwise,

But a loyal friend indeed to those who love you.

[*Exit into the Palace.* ANTIGONE *goes off, L. Enter the* CHORUS.]

PARODOS

Chorus

STROPHE 1

Now the long blade of the sun, lying

Level east to west, touches with glory

Thebes of the Seven Gates. Open, unlidded

Eye of golden day! O marching light

Across the eddy and rush of Dirce's stream,

Striking the white shields of the enemy

Thrown headlong backward from the blaze of morning!

Choragos

Polyneices their commander

Roused them with windy phrases,

He the wild eagle screaming

Insults above our land,

His wings their shields of snow,

His crest their marshalled helms.

Chorus

ANTISTROPHE 1

Against our seven gates in a yawning ring
The famished spears came onward in the night;
But before his jaws were sated with our blood,
Or pinefire took the garland of our towers,
He was thrown back; and as he turned, great Thebes —
No tender victim for his noisy power —
Rose like a dragon behind him, shouting war.

Choragos

For God hates utterly
The bray of bragging tongues;
And when be beheld their smiling,
Their swagger of golden helms,
The frown of his thunder blasted
Their first man from our walls.

Chorus

STROPHE 2

We heard his shout of triumph high in the air
Turn to a scream; far out in a flaming arc
He fell with his windy torch, and the earth struck him.
And others storming in fury no less than his
Found shock of death in the dusty joy of battle.

Choragos

Seven captains at seven gates
Yielded their clanging arms to the god
That bends the battle-line and breaks it.
These two only, brothers in blood,
Face to face in matchless rage,
Mirroring each the other's death,
Clashed in long combat.

Chorus

ANTISTROPHE 2

But now in the beautiful morning of victory
Let Thebes of the many chariots sing for joy!
With hearts for dancing we'll take leave of war
Our temples shall be sweet with hymns of praise,
And the long night shall echo with our chorus.

SCENE I
Choragos
> But now at last our new King is coming
> Creon of Thebes, Menoiceus' son.
> In this auspicious dawn of his reign
> What are the new complexities
> That shifting Fate has woven for him?
> What is his counsel? Why has he summoned
> The old men to hear him?

[*Enter* CREON *from the Palace, C. He addresses the* CHORUS *from the top step.*]

Creon
> Gentlemen: I have the honor to inform you that our Ship of State, which recent storms have threatened to destroy, has come safely to harbor at last, guided by the merciful wisdom of Heaven. I have summoned you here this morning because I know that I can depend upon you: your devotion to King Laius was absolute; you never hesitated in your duty to our late ruler Oedipus; and when Oedipus died, your loyalty was transferred to his children. Unfortunately, as you know, his two sons, the princes Eteocles and Polyneices, have killed each other in battle; and I, as the next in blood, have succeeded to the full power of the throne.
>
> I am aware, of course, that no Ruler can expect complete loyalty from his subjects until he has been tested in office. Nevertheless, I say to you at the very outset that I have nothing but contempt for the kind of Governor who is afraid, for whatever reason, to follow the course that he knows is best for the State; and as for the man who sets private friendship above the public welfare, — I have no use for him, either. I call God to witness that if I saw my country headed for ruin, I should not be afraid to speak out plainly; and I need hardly remind you that I would never have any dealings with an enemy of the people. No one values friendship more highly than I; but we must remember that friends made at the risk of wrecking our Ship are not real friends at all.

These are my principles, at any rate, and that is why I have
made the following decision concerning the sons of Oedipus:
Eteocles, who dies as a man should die, fighting for his country, is to be buried with full military honors, with all the ceremony that is usual when the greatest heroes die; but his
brother Polyneices, who broke his exile to come back with
fire and sword against his native city and the shrines of his
fathers' gods, whose one idea was to spill the blood of his
blood and sell his own people into slavery — Polyneices, I say,
is to have no burial: no man is to touch him or say the least
prayer for him; he shall lie on the plain, unburied; and the
birds and the scavenging dogs can do with him whatever they
like.

This is my command, and you can see the wisdom behind it.
As long as I am King, no traitor is going to be honored with
the loyal man. But whoever shows by word and deed that he
is on the side of the State, — he shall have my respect while
he is living, and my reverence when he is dead.

Choragos
If that is your will, Creon son of Menoiceus,
You have the right to enforce it: we are yours.

Creon
That is my will. Take care that you do your part.

Choragos
We are old men: let the younger ones carry it out.

Creon
I do not mean that: the sentries have been appointed.

Choragos
Then what is it that you would have us do?

Creon
You will give no support to whoever breaks this law.

Choragos
Only a crazy man is in love with death!

Creon
And death it is; yet money talks, and the wisest
Have sometimes been known to count a few coins too many.

[*Enter* SENTRY *from L.*]

Sentry

I'll not say that I'm out of breath from running, King, because
every time I stopped to think about what I have to tell you, I
felt like going back. And all the time a voice kept saying,
"You fool, don't you know you're walking straight into trouble?"; and then another voice: "Yes, but if you let somebody
else get the news to Creon first, it will be even worse than
that for you!" But good sense won out, at least I hope it was
good sense, and here I am with a story that makes no sense at
all; but I'll tell it anyhow, because, as they say, what's going
to happen's going to happen, and —

Creon

Come to the point. What have you to say?

Sentry

I did not do it. I did not see who did it. You must not punish
me for what someone else has done.

Creon

A comprehensive defense! More effective, perhaps,
If I knew its purpose. Come: what is it?

Sentry

A dreadful thing . . . I don't know how to put it —

Creon

Out with it!

Sentry

Well, then;
The dead man —
Polyneices —

[*Pause. The* SENTRY *is overcome, fumbles for words.* CREON *waits
impassively.*]

out there —
someone, —
New dust on the slimy flesh!

[*Pause. No sign from* CREON.]

Someone has given it burial that way, and
Gone . . .

(*Long pause.* CREON *finally speaks with deadly control.*]

Creon

And the man who dared to this?

Sentry

> I swear I
> Do not know! You must believe me!
>> Listen:
> The ground was dry, not a sign of digging, no,
> Not a wheeltrack in the dust, no trace of anyone.
> It was when they relieved us this morning: and one of them,
> The corporal, pointed to it.
>> There it was,
> The strangest —
>> Look
> The body, just mounded over with light dust: you see?
> Not buried really, but as if they'd covered it
> Just enough for the ghost's peace. And no sign
> Of dogs or any wild animal that had been there.
> And then what a scene there was! Every man of us
> Accusing the other: we all proved the other man did it,
> We all had proof that we could not have done it.
> We were ready to take hot iron in our hands,
> Walk through fire, swear by all the gods,
> *It was not I!*
> *I do not know who it was, but it was not I!*

[CREON's *rage has been mounting steadily, but the* SENTRY *is too
intent upon his story to notice it.*]

> And then, when this came to nothing, someone said
> A thing that silenced us and made us stare
> Down at the ground: you had to be told the news,
> And one of us had to do it! We threw the dice,
> And the bad luck fell to me. So here I am,
> No happier to be here than you are to have me
> Nobody like the man who brings bad news.

Choragos

> I have been wondering, King: can it be that the gods have
> done this?

Creon   [*Furiously.*]

> Stop!
> Must you doddering wrecks

Go out of your heads entirely? "The gods!"
Intolerable!
The gods favor this corpse? Why? How had he served them?
Tried to loot their temples, burn their images,
Yes, and the whole State, and its laws with it!
Is it your senile opinion that the gods love to honor bad men?
A pious thought!—

    No, from the very beginning
There have been those who have whispered together,
Stiff-necked anarchists, putting their heads together,
Scheming against me in alleys. These are the men,
And they have bribed my own guard to do this thing.
Money!

[*Sententiously.*]

There's nothing in the world so demoralizing as money.
Down go your cities,
Homes gone, men gone, honest hearts corrupted,
Crookedness of all kinds, and all for money!

[*To* SENTRY.]

    But you — !
I swear by God and by the throne of God,
The man who has done this thing shall pay for it!
Find that man, bring him here to me, or your death
Will be the least of your problems: I'll string you up
Alive, and there will be certain ways to make you
Discover your employer before you die;
And the process may teach you a lesson you seem to have
    missed:
The dearest profit is sometimes all too dear:
That depends on the source. Do you understand me?
A fortune won is often misfortune.

Sentry

    King, may I speak?

Creon

    Your very voice distresses me.

Sentry

    Are you sure that it is my voice, and not your conscience?

Creon

    By God, he wants to analyze me now!

Sentry

    It is not what I say, but what has been done, that hurts you.

Creon

    You talk too much.

Sentry

       Maybe, but I've done nothing.

Creon

    Sold your soul for some silver: that's all you've done.

Sentry

    How dreadful it is when the right judge judges wrong!

Creon

    Your figures of speech
    May entertain you now; but unless you bring me the man,
    You will get little profit from them in the end.

[*Exit* CREON *into the Palace.*]

Sentry

    "Bring me the man" — !
    I'd like nothing better than bringing him the man!
    But bring him or not, you have seen the last of me here.
    At any rate, I am safe!

[*Exit* SENTRY.]

ODE I
Chorus

STROPHE 1

Numberless are the world's wonders, but none
More wonderful than man; the stormgray sea
Yields to his prows, the huge crests bear him high;
Earth, holy and inexhaustible, is graven
With shining furrows where his plows have gone
Year after year, the timeless labor of stallions.

ANTISTROPHE 1

The lightboned birds and beasts that cling to cover,
The lithe fish lighting their reaches of dim water,
All are taken, tamed in the net of his mind;

The lion on the hill, the wild horse wind-maned,
Resign to him; and his blunt yoke has broken
The sultry shoulders of the mountain bull.
STROPHE 2
Words also, and thought as rapid as air,
He fashions to his good use; statecraft is his,
And his the skill that deflects the arrows of snow,
The spears of winter rain: from every wind
He has made himself secure — from all but one
In the late wind of death he cannot stand.
ANTISTROPHE 2
O clear intelligence, force beyond all measure!
O fate of man, working both good and evil!
When the laws are kept, how proudly his city stands!
When the laws are broken, what of his city then?
Never may the anarchic man find rest at my hearth,
Never be it said that my thoughts are his thoughts.

SCENE II

[*Re-enter* SENTRY *leading* ANTIGONE.]

Choragos

What does this mean? Surely this captive woman
Is the Princess, Antigone. Why should she be taken?

Sentry

Here is the one who did it! We caught her
In the very act of burying him. — Where is Creon?

Choragos

Just coming from the house.

[*Enter* CREON, *C.*]

Creon

What has happened?
Why have you come back so soon?

Sentry   [*Expansively.*]

O King.
A man should never be too sure of anything:
I would have sworn
That you'd not see me here again: your anger
Frightened me so, and the things you threatened me with;

But how could I tell then
That I'd be able to solve the case so soon?
No dice-throwing this time: I was only too glad to come!
Here is this woman. She is the guilty one
We found her trying to bury him.
Take her, then; question her; judge her as you will.
I am through with the whole thing now, and glad of it.

Creon
But this is Antigone! Why have you brought her here?

Sentry
She was burying him, I tell you!

Creon [*Severely.*]
  Is this the truth?

Sentry
I saw her with my own eyes. Can I say more?

Creon
The details: come, tell me quickly!

Sentry
  It was like this
After those terrible threats of yours, King,
We went back and brushed the dust away from the body.
The flesh was soft by now, and stinking.
So we sat on a hill to windward and kept guard.
No napping this time! We kept each other awake.
But nothing happened until the white round sun
Whirled in the center of the round sky over us
Then, suddenly,
A storm of dust roared up from the earth, and the sky
Went out, the plain vanished with all its trees
In the stinging dark. We closed our eyes and endured it.
The whirlwind lasted a long time, but it passed;
And then we looked, and there was Antigone!
I have seen
A mother bird come back to a stripped nest, heard
Her crying bitterly a broken note or two
For the young ones stolen. Just so, when this girl
Found the bare corpse, and all her love's work wasted,
She wept, and cried on heaven to damn the hands

That had done this thing.
>   And then she brought more dust
And sprinkled wine three times for her brother's ghost.
We ran and took her at once. She was not afraid,
Not even when we charged her with what she had done.
She denied nothing.
>   And this was a comfort to me,
And some uneasiness: for it is a good thing
To escape from death, but it is no great pleasure
To bring death to a friend.
>   Yet I always say
There is nothing so comfortable as your own safe skin!

Creon [*Slowly, dangerously.*]
>   And you, Antigone,
You with your head hanging, — do you confess this thing?

Antigone
>   I do. I deny nothing.

Creon [*To* SENTRY.]
>   You may go.

[*Exit* SENTRY.]

[*To* ANTIGONE.]
>   Tell me, tell me briefly
Had you heard my proclamation touching this matter?

Antigone
>   It was public. Could I help hearing it?

Creon
>   And yet you dared defy the law.

Antigone
>   I dared.
It was not God's proclamation. That final Justice
That rules the world below make no such laws.
Your edict, King, was strong,
But all your strength is weakness itself against
The immortal unrecorded laws of God.
They are not merely now: they were, and shall be,
Operative for ever, beyond man utterly.
I knew I must die, even without your decree

I am only mortal. And if I must die
Now, before it is my time to die,
Surely this is no hardship: can anyone
Living, as I live, with evil all about me,
Think Death less than a friend: This death of mine
Is of no importance; but if I had left my brother
Lying in death unburied, I should have suffered.
Now I do not.
      You smile at me. Ah Creon,
Think me a fool, if you like; but it may well be
That a fool convicts me of folly.

Choragos
Like father, like daughter: both headstrong, deaf to reason!
She has never learned to yield.

Creon
      She has much to learn.
The inflexible heart breaks first, the toughest iron
Cracks first, and the wildest horses bend their necks
At the pull of the smallest curb.
      Pride? In a slave?
This girl is guilty of a double insolence,
Breaking the given laws and boasting of it.
Who is the man here,
She or I, if this crime goes unpunished?
Sister's child, or more than sister's child,
Or closer yet in blood — she and her sister
Win bitter death for this!
[*To* SERVANTS.]
      Go, some of you,
Arrest Ismene. I accuse her equally.
Bring her: you will find her sniffling in the house there.
Her mind's a traitor: crimes kept in the dark
Cry for light, and the guardian brain shudders;
But how much worse than this
Is brazen boasting of barefaced anarchy!

Antigone
Creon, what more do you want than my death?

Creon
> Nothing.
> That gives me everything.

Antigone
> Then I beg you: kill me.
> This talking is a great weariness: your words
> Are distasteful to me, and I am sure that mine
> Seem so to you. And yet they should not seem so:
> I should have praise and honor for what I have done.
> All these men here would praise me
> Were their lips not frozen shut with fear of you.
> [*Bitterly.*]
> Ah the good fortune of kings.
> Licensed to say and do whatever they please!

Creon
> You are alone here in that opinion.

Antigone
> No, they are with me. But they keep their tongues in leash.

Creon
> Maybe. But you are guilty, and they are not.

Antigone
> There is no guilt in reverence for the dead.

Creon
> But Eteocles — was he not your brother too?

Antigone
> My brother too.

Creon
> And you insult his memory?

Antigone [*Softly.*]
> The dead man would not say that I insult it.

Creon
> He would: for you honor a traitor as much as him.

Antigone
> His own brother, traitor or not, and equal in blood.

Creon
> He made war on his country. Eteocles defended it.

Antigone
> Nevertheless, there are honors due all the dead.

Creon

But not the same for the wicked as for the just.

Antigone

Ah Creon, Creon,

Which of us can say what the gods hold wicked?

Creon

An enemy is an enemy, even dead.

Antigone

It is my nature to join in love, not hate.

Creon [*Finally losing patience.*]

Go join them, then; if you must have your love,

Find it in hell!

Choragos

But see, Ismene comes

[*Enter* ISMENE, *guarded.*]

Those tears are sisterly, the cloud

That shadows her eyes rains down gentle sorrow.

Creon

You too, Ismene,

Snake in my ordered house, sucking my blood

Stealthily — and all the time I never knew

That these two sisters were aiming at my throne!

Ismene,

Do you confess your share in this crime, or deny it?

Answer me.

Ismene

Yes, if she will let me say so. I am guilty.

Antigone [*Coldly.*]

No, Ismene. You have no right to say so.

You would not help me, and I will not have you help me.

Ismene

But now I know what you meant; and I am here

To join you, to take my share of punishment.

Antigone

The dead man and the gods who rule the dead

Know whose act this was. Words are not friends.

Ismene

Do you refuse me, Antigone? I want to die with you

I too have a duty that I must discharge to the dead.

Antigone
You shall not lessen my death by sharing it.

Ismene
What do I care for life when you are dead?

Antigone
Ask Creon. You're always hanging on his opinions.

Ismene
You are laughing at me. Why, Antigone?

Antigone
It's a joyless laughter, Ismene.

Ismene
But can I do nothing?

Antigone
Yes. Save yourself. I shall not envy you.
There are those who will praise you; I shall have honor, too.

Ismene
But we are equally guilty!

Antigone
No more, Ismene.
You are alive, but I belong to Death.

Creon [*To the* CHORUS.]
Gentlemen, I beg you to observe these girls
One has just now lost her mind; the other,
It seems, has never had a mind at all.

Ismene
Grief teaches the steadiest minds to waver, King.

Creon
Yours certainly did, when you assumed guilt with the guilty!

Ismene
But how could I go on living without her?

Creon
You are.
She is already dead.

Ismene
But your own son's bride!

Creon
There are places enough for him to push his plow.

I want no wicked women for my sons!
Ismene
O dearest Haimon, how your father wrongs you!
Creon
I've had enough of your childish talk of marriage!
Choragos
Do you really intend to steal this girl from your son?
Creon
No; Death will do that for me.
Choragos
Then she must die?
Creon [*Ironically.*]
You dazzle me.
— But enough of this talk!
[*To* GUARDS.]
You, there, take them away and guard them well:
For they are but women, and even brave men run
When they see Death coming.
[*Exeunt* ISMENE, ANTIGONE, *and* GUARDS.]

ODE II
Chorus
STROPHE 1
Fortunate is the man who has never tasted God's vengeance!
Where once the anger of heaven has struck, that house is
   shaken
For ever: damnation rises behind each child
LIke a wave cresting out of the black northeast,
When the long darkness under sea roars up
And bursts drumming death upon the windwhipped sand.
ANTISTROPHE 1
I have seen this gathering sorrow from time long past
Loom upon Oedipus' children: generation from generation
Takes the compulsive rage of the enemy god.
So lately this last flower of Oedipus' line
Drank the sunlight! but now a passionate word
And a handful of dust have closed up all its beauty.

STROPHE 2

> What mortal arrogance
> Transcends the wrath of Zeus?
> Sleep cannot lull him, nor the effortless long months
> Of the timeless gods: but he is young for ever,
> And his house is the shining day of high Olympos.
> > All that is and shall be,
> > And all the past, is his.
> No pride on earth is free of the curse of heaven.

ANTISTROPHE 2

> The straying dreams of men
> May bring them ghosts of joy:
> But as they drowse, the waking embers burn them;
> Or they walk with fixed eyes, as blind men walk.
> But the ancient wisdom speaks for our own time
> > *Fate works most for woe*
> > *With Folly's fairest show.*
> Man's little pleasure is the spring of sorrow.

SCENE III
Choragos

> But here is Haimon, King, the last of all your sons.
> Is it grief for Antigone that brings him here,
> And bitterness at being robbed of his bride?

[*Enter* HAIMON.]

Creon

> We shall soon see, and no need of diviners.
> > — Son,
> You have heard my final judgement on that girl
> Have you come here hating me, or have you come
> With deference and with love, whatever I do?

Haimon

> I am your son, father. You are my guide.
> You make things clear for me, and I obey you.
> No marriage means more to me that your continuing wisdom.

Creon

> Good. That is the way to behave: subordinate
> Everything else, my son, to your father's will.

This is what a man prays for, that he may get
Sons attentive and dutiful in his house,
Each one hating his father's enemies,
Honoring his father's friends. But if his sons
Fail him if they turn out unprofitably,
What has he fathered but trouble for himself
And amusement for the malicious?
    So you are right
Not to lose your head over this woman.
Your pleasure with her would soon grow cold, Haimon,
And then you'd have a hellcat in bed and elsewhere.
Let her find her husband in Hell!
Of all the people in this city, only she
Has had contempt for my law and broken it.

Do you want me to show myself weak before the people?
Or to break my sworn word? No, and I will not.
The woman dies.
I suppose she'll plead "family ties." Well, let her.
If I permit my own family to rebel,
How shall I earn the world's obedience?
Show me the man who keeps his house in hand,
He's fit for public authority.
    I'll have no dealings
With law-breakers, critics of the government:
Whoever is chosen to govern should be obeyed —
Must be obeyed, in all things, great and small,
Just and unjust! O Haimon,
The man who knows how to obey, and that man only,
Knows how to give commands when the time comes.
You can depend on him, no matter how fast
The spears come: he's a good soldier, hell stick it out.
Anarchy, anarchy! Show me a greater evil!
This is why cities tumble and the great houses rain down;
This is what scatters armies!
No, No: Good lives are made so by discipline.
We keep the laws then, and the lawmakers,
And no woman shall seduce us. If we must lose,

Let's lose to a man, at least! Is a woman stronger than we?

Choragos

Unless time has rusted my wits,
What you say, King, is said with point and dignity.

Haimon   [*Boyishly earnest.*]

Father:
Reason is God's crowning gift to man, and you are right
To warn me against losing mine. I cannot say —
I hope that I shall never want to say! — that you
Have reasoned badly. Yet there are other men
Who can reason, too; and their opinions might be helpful.
You are not in a position to know everything
That people say or do, or what they feel:
Your temper terrifies them — everyone
Will tell you only what you like to hear.
But I, at any rate, can listen; and I have heard them
Muttering and whispering in the dark about this girl.
They say no woman has ever, so unreasonably,
Died so shameful a death for a generous act
"She covered her brother's body. Is this indecent?
She kept him from dogs and vultures. Is this a crime?
Death? — She should have all the honor that we can give her!"
This is the way they talk out there in the city.
You must believe me:
Nothing is closer to me than your happiness.
What could be closer? Must not any son
Value his father's fortune as his father does his?
I beg, you do not be unchangeable
Do not believe that you alone can be right.
The man who thinks that,
The man who maintains that only he has the power
To reason correctly, the gift to speak, the soul —
A man like that, when you know him, turns out empty.
It is not reason never to yield to reason!
In flood time you can see how some trees bend,
And because they bend, even their twigs are safe,
While stubborn trees are torn up, roots and all.

And the same thing happens in sailing
Make your sheet fast, never slacken, — and over you go,
Head over heels and under: and there's your voyage.
Forget you are angry! Let yourself be moved!
I know I am young; but please let me say this:
The ideal condition
Would be, I admit, that men should be right by instinct;
But since we are all to likely to go astray,
The reasonable thing is to learn from those who can teach.

Choragos
You will do well to listen to him, King,
If what he says is sensible. And you, Haimon,
Must listen to your father. — Both speak well.

Creon
You consider it right for a man of my years and experience
To go to school to a boy?

Haimon
It is not right
If I am wrong. But if I am young, and right,
What does my age matter?

Creon
You think it right to stand up for an anarchist?

Haimon
Not at all. I pay no respect to criminals.

Creon
Then she is not a criminal?

Haimon
The City would deny it, to a man.

Creon
And the City proposes to teach me how to rule?

Haimon
Ah. Who is it that's talking like a boy now?

Creon
My voice is the one voice giving orders in this City!

Haimon
It is no City if it takes orders from one voice.

Creon
The State is the King!

Haimon

 Yes, if the State is a desert.

[*Pause.*]

Creon

 This boy, it seems, has sold out to a woman.

Haimon

 If you are a woman: my concern is only for you.

Creon

 So? Your "concern"! In a public brawl with your father!

Haimon

 How about you, in a public brawl with justice?

Creon

 With justice, when all that I do is within my rights?

Haimon

 You have no right to trample on God's right.

Creon [*Completely out of control.*]

 Fool, adolescent fool! Taken in by a woman!

Haimon

 You'll never see me taken in by anything vile.

Creon

 Every word you say is for her!

Haimon [*Quietly, darkly.*]

  And for you.

 And for me. And for the gods under the earth.

Creon

 You'll never marry her while she lives.

Haimon

 Then she must die. But her death will cause another.

Creon

 Another?

 Have you lost your senses? Is this an open threat?

Haimon

 There is no threat in speaking to emptiness.

Creon

 I swear you'll regret this superior tone of yours!

 You are the empty one!

Haimon

  If you were not my father,

I'd say you were perverse.
Creon
You girlstruck fool, don't play at words with me!
Haimon
I am sorry. You prefer silence.
Creon
Now, by God — !
I swear, by all the gods in heaven above us,
You'll watch it, I swear you shall!
[*To the* SERVANTS.]
Bring her out!
Bring the woman out! Let her die before his eyes!
Here, this instant, with her bridegroom beside her!
Haimon
Not here, no; she will not die here, King.
And you will never see my face again.
Go on raving as long as you've a friend to endure you.
[*Exit* HAIMON.]
Choragos
Gone, gone.
Creon, a young man in a rage is dangerous!
Creon
Let him do, or dream to do, more than a man can.
He shall not save these girls from death.
Choragos
These girls?
You have sentenced them both?
Creon
No, you are right.
I will not kill the one whose hands are clean.
Choragos
But Antigone?
Creon [*Somberly.*]
I will carry her far away
Out there in the wilderness, and lock her
Living in a vault of stone. She shall have food,
As the custom is, to absolve the State of her death.

And there let her pray to the gods of hell
They are her only gods
Perhaps they will show her an escape from death,
Or she may learn,
    though late,
That piety shown the dead is pity in vain.
[*Exit* CREON.]

ODE III
Chorus
STROPHE
Love, unconquerable
Waster of rich men, keeper
Of warm lights and all-night vigil
In the soft face of a girl
Sea-wanderer, forest-visitor!
Even the pure Immortals cannot escape you,
And mortal man, in his one day's dusk,
Trembles before your glory.
ANTISTROPHE
Surely you swerve upon ruin
The just man's consenting heart,
As here you have made bright anger
Strike between father and son —
And none has conquered but Love!
A girls' glance working the will of heaven:
Pleasure to her alone who mocks us,
Merciless Aphrodite.

SCENE IV
Choragos   [*As* ANTIGONE *enters guarded.*]
But I can no longer stand in awe of this,
Nor, seeing what I see, keep back my tears.
Here is Antigone, passing to that chamber
Where all find sleep at last.
Antigone
STROPHE 1
Look upon me, friends, and pity me

Turning back at the night's edge to say
Good-bye to the sun that shines for me no longer;
Now sleepy Death
Summons me down to Acheron, that cold shore
There is no bridesong here, nor any music.

Chorus

Yet not unpraised, not without a kind of honor,
You walk at last into the underworld;
Untouched by sickness, broken by no sword.
What woman has ever found your way to death?

Antigone

ANTISTROPHE 1

How often I have heard the story of Niobe,
Tantalos' wretched daughter, how the stone
Clung fast about her, ivy-close: and they say
The rain falls endlessly
And sifting soft snow; her tears are never done.
I feel the loneliness of her death in mine.

Chorus

But she was born of heaven, and you
Are woman, woman-born. If her death is yours,
A mortal woman's, is this not for you
Glory in our world and in the world beyond?

Antigone

STROPHE 2

You laugh at me. Ah, friends, friends,
Can you not wait until I am dead? O Thebes,
O men many-charioted, in love with Fortune,
Dear springs of Dirce, sacred Theban grove,
Be witnesses for me, denied all pity,
Unjustly judged! and think a word of love
For her whose path turns
Under dark earth, where there are no more tears.

Chorus

You have passed beyond human daring and come at last
Into a place of stone where Justice sits.
I cannot tell

What shape of your father's guilt appears in this.
Antigone
ANTISTROPHE 2
You have touched it at last: that bridal bed
Unspeakable, horror of son and mother mingling
Their crime, infection of all our family!
O Oedipus, father and brother!
Your marriage strikes from the grave to murder mine.
I have been a stranger here in my own land:
All my life
The blasphemy of my birth has followed me.
Chorus
Reverence is a virtue, but strength
Lives in established law: that must prevail.
You have made your choice,
Your death is the doing of your conscious hand.
Antigone
EPODE
Then let me go, since all your words are bitter,
And the very light of the sun is cold to me.
Lead me to my vigil, where I must have
Neither love nor lamentation; no song, but silence.
[CREON *interrupts impatiently*.]
Creon
If dirges and planned lamentations could put off death,
Men would be singing for ever.
[*To the* SERVANTS.]
        Take her, go!
You know your orders: take her to the vault
And leave her alone there. And if she lives or dies,
That's her affair, not our: our hands are clean.
Antigone
O tomb, vaulted bride-bed in eternal rock,
Soon I shall be with my own again
Where Persephone welcomes the thin ghosts underground
And I shall see my father again, and you, mother,
And dearest Polyneices—

dearest indeed
To me, since it was my hand
That washed him clean and poured the ritual wine
And my reward is death before my time!
And yet, as men's hearts know, I have done no wrong,
I have not sinned before God. Or if I have,
I shall know the truth in death. But if the guilt
Lies upon Creon who judged me, then, I pray,
May his punishment equal my own.

Choragos

O passionate heart,

Creon

Her guards shall have good cause to regret their delaying.

Antigone

Ah! That voice is like the voice of death!

Creon

I can give you no reason to think you are mistaken.

Antigone

Thebes, and you my fathers' gods,
And rulers of Thebes, you see me now, the last
Unhappy daughter of a line of kings,
Your kings, led away to death. You will remember
What things I suffer, and at what men's hands,
Because I would not transgress the laws of heaven.

[*To the* GUARDS, *simply*.]

Come: let us wait no longer.

[*Exit* ANTIGONE, L., *guarded*.]

ODE IV

Chorus

STROPHE 1

All Danae's beauty was locked away
In a brazen cell where the sunlight could not come:
A small room, still as any grave, enclosed her.
Yet she was a princess too,
And Zeus in a rain of gold poured love upon her.
A child, child,

No power in wealth or war
Or tough sea-blackened ships
Can prevail against untiring Destiny!
ANTISTROPHE 1
And Dryas' son also, that furious king,
Bore the god's poisoning anger for his pride
Sealed up by Dionysos in deaf stone,
His madness died among echoes.
So at the last he learned what dreadful power
His tongue had mocked
For he had profaned the revels,
And fired the wrath of the nine
Implacable Sisters that love the sound of the flute.
STROPHE 2
And old men tell a half-remembered tale
Of horror done where a dark ledge splits the sea
And a double surf beats on the gray shores:
How a king's new woman, sick
With hatred for the queen he had imprisoned,
Ripped out his two sons' eyes with her bloody hands
While grinning Ares watched the shuttle plunge
Four times: four blind wounds crying for revenge,
ANTISTROPHE 2
Crying, tears and blood mingled. — Piteously born,
Those sons whose mother was of heavenly birth!
Her father was the god of the North Wind
And she was cradled by gales,
She raced with young colts on the glittering hills
And walked untrammeled in the open light
But in her marriage deathless Fate found means
To build a tomb like yours for all her joy.

SCENE V

[*Enter blind* TEIRESIAS, *led by a boy. The opening speeches of*
TEIRESIAS *should be in singsong contrast to the realistic lines
of* CREON.]

Teiresias

This is the way the blind man comes, Princes, Princes,

Lock-step, two heads lit by the eyes of one.

Creon

What new thing have you to tell us, old Teiresias?

Teiresias

I have much to tell you: listen to the prophet, Creon.

Creon

I am not aware that I have ever failed to listen.

Teiresias

Then you have done wisely, King, and ruled well.

Creon

I admit my debt to you. But what have you to say?

Teiresias

This, Creon: you stand once more on the edge of fate.

Creon

What do you mean? Your words are a kind of dread.

Teiresias

Listen, Creon

I was sitting in my chair of augury, at the place
Where the birds gather about me. They were all a-chatter,
As is their habit, when suddenly I heard
A strange note in their jangling, a scream, a
Whirring fury; I knew that they were fighting,
Tearing each other, dying
In a whirlwind of wings clashing. And I was afraid,
I began the rites of burnt-offering at the altar, But Hephaistos
failed me: instead of bright flame,
There was only the sputtering slime of the fat thighflesh
Melting: the entrails dissolved in gray smoke,
The bare bone burst from the welter. And no blaze!
This was a sign from heaven. My boy described it,
Seeing for me as I see for others.
I tell you Creon, you yourself have brought
This new calamity upon us. Our hearths and altars
Are stained with the corruption of dogs and carrion birds
That glut themselves on the corpse of Oedipus' son.
The gods are deaf when we pray to them, their fire
Recoils from our offering, their birds of omen

Have no cry of comfort, for they are gorged
With the thick blood of the dead.

    O my son,
These are no trifles! Think: all men make mistakes,
But a good man yields when he know his course is wrong,
And repairs the evil. The only crime is pride.
Give in to the dead man, then: do not fight with a corpse —
What glory is it to kill a man who is dead?
Think, I beg you
It is for your own good that I speak as I do.
You should be able to yield for your own good.

Creon

It seems that prophets have made me their especial province.
All my life long
I have been a kind of butt for the dull arrows
Of doddering fortune-tellers!

    No, Teiresias
If your birds — if the great eagles of God himself
Should carry him stinking bit by bit to heaven,
I would not yield. I am not afraid of pollution
No man can defile the gods.

    Do what you will,
Go into business, make money, speculate
In India gold or that synthetic gold from Sardis,
Get rich otherwise than by my consent to bury him.
Teiresias, it is a sorry thing when a wise man
Sells his wisdom, lets out his words for hire!

Teiresias

Ah Creon! Is there no man left in the world —

Creon

To do what? — Come, let's have the aphorism!

Teiresias

No man who know that wisdom outweighs any
wealth?

Creon

As surely as bribes are baser than any baseness.

Teiresias

You are sick, Creon! You are deathly sick!

Creon

As you say: it is not my place to challenge a prophet.

Teiresias

Yet you have said my prophecy is for sale.

Creon

The generation of prophets has always loved gold.

Teiresias

The generation of kings has always loved brass.

Creon

You forget yourself! You are speaking to your King.

Teiresias

I know it. You are a king because of me.

Creon

You have a certain skill; but you have sold out.

Teiresias

King, you will drive me to words that —

Creon

Say them, say them!

Only remember: I will not pay you for them.

Teiresias

No, you will find them too costly.

Creon

No doubt. Speak

Whatever you say, you will not change my will.

Teiresias

Then take this, and take it to heart!
The time is not far off when you shall pay back
Corpse for corpse, flesh of your own flesh.
You have thrust the child of this world into living night,
You have kept from the gods below the child that is theirs
The one in a grave before her death, the other,
Dead, denied the grave. This is your crime
And the Furies and the dark gods of Hell
Are swift with terrible punishment for you.
Do you want to buy me now, Creon?

Not many days,

And your house will be full of men and women weeping,

And curses will be hurled at you from far
Cities grieving for sons unburied, left to rot
Before the walls of Thebes.
These are my arrows, Creon: they are all for you.
But come, child: lead me home.

[*To* BOY:]
Let him waste his fine anger upon younger men.
Maybe he will learn at last
To control a wiser tongue in a better head.

[*Exit* TEIRESIAS.]

Choragos
The old man has gone, King, but his words
Remain to plague us. I am old, too,
But I cannot remember that he was ever false.

Creon
That is true . . . It troubles me.
Oh it is hard to give in! but it is worse
To risk everything for stubborn pride.

Choragos
Creon: take my advice.

Creon
What shall I do?

Choragos
Go quickly: free Antigone from her vault
And build a tomb for the body of Polyneices.

Creon
You would have me do this?

Choragos
Creon, yes!
And it must be done at once: God moves
Swiftly to cancel the folly of stubborn men.

Creon
It is hard to deny the heart! But I
Will do it: I will not fight with destiny.

Choragos
You must go yourself, you cannot leave it to others.

Creon
I will go.

— Bring axes, servants
Come with me to the tomb. I buried her, I
Will set her free.
    Oh quickly!
My mind misgives —
The laws of the gods are mighty, and a man must
serve them
To the last day of his life!

[*Exit* CREON.]

PAEAN
Choragos
    God of many names
    STROPHE 1
Chorus
        O Iacchos
        son
of Cadmeian Semele
        O born of the Thunder!
Guardian of the West
        Regent
of Eleusis' plain
        O prince of maenad Thebes
and the Dragon Field by rippling Ismenos
    ANTISTROPHE 1
Choragos
    God of many names
Chorus
        the flame of torches
flares on our hills
        the nymphs of of Iacchos
dance at the spring of Castalia
from the vine-close mountain
        come ah come in ivy
Evohe evohe! sings through the streets of Thebes
    STROPHE 2
Choragos
    God of many names

290 *Sophocles*

Chorus

      Iacchos of Thebes
   heavenly Child
      of Semele bride of the Thunderer!
   The shadow of plague is upon us
      come
   with clement feet
      oh come from Parnasos
   down the long slopes
      across the lamenting water

Choragos

   Io Fire! Chorister of the throbbing stars!
   O purest among the voices of the night!
   Thou son of God, blaze for us!

Chorus

   Come with choric rapture of circling Maenads
   Who cry *Io Iacche!*
      God of many names!

EXODOS

[*Enter* MESSENGER, L.]

Messenger

   Men of the line of Cadmos, you who live
   Near Amphion's citadel:
      I cannot say
   Of any condition of human life " This is fixed,
   This is clearly good, or bad." Fate raises up,
   And Fate casts down the happy and unhappy alike
   No man can foretell his Fate.
      Take the case of Creon
   Creon was happy once, as I count happiness
   Victorious in battle, sole governor of the land,
   Fortunate father of children nobly born.
   And now it has all gone from him! Who can say
   That a man is still alive when his life's joy fails?
   He is a walking dead man. Grant him rich,
   Let him live like a king in his great house

If his pleasure is gone, I would not give
So much as the shadow of smoke for all he owns.
Choragos
Your words hint at sorrow: what is your news for us?
Messenger
They are dead. The living are guilty of their death.
Choragos
Who is guilty? Who is dead? Speak!
Messenger
  Haimon.
Haimon is dead; and the hand that killed him
Is his own hand.
Choragos
  His father's? or his own?
Messenger
His own, driven mad by the murder his father had done.
Choragos
Teiresias, Teiresias, how clearly you saw it all!
Messenger
This is my news: you must draw what conclusions you
can from it.
Choragos
But look: Eurydice, our Queen
Has she overheard us?
[*Enter* EURYDICE *from the Palace,* C.]
Eurydice
I have heard something, friends
As I was unlocking the gate of Pallas' shrine,
For I needed her help today, I heard a voice
Telling of some new sorrow. And I fainted
There at the temple with all my maidens about me.
But speak again: whatever it is, I can bear it
Grief and I are no strangers.
Messenger
  Dearest Lady,
I will tell you plainly all that I have seen.
I shall not try to comfort you: what is the use,

Since comfort could like only in what is the not true?
The truth is always best.
    I went with Creon
To the outer plain where Polyneices was lying,
No friend to pity him, his body shredded by dogs.
We made our prayers in that place to Hecate
And Pluto, that they would be merciful. And we bathed
The corpse with holy water, and we brought
Fresh-broken branches to burn what was left of it,
And upon the urn we heaped up a towering barrow
Of the earth of his own land.
    When we were done, we ran
To the vault where Antigone lay on her couch of stone.
One of the servants had gone ahead,
And while he was yet far off he heard a voice
Grieving within the chamber, and he came back And told
Creon. And as the King went closer,
The air was full of wailing, the words lost,
And he begged us to make all haste. "Am I a prophet?"
He said, weeping, "And must I walk this road,
The saddest of all that I have gone before?
My son's voice calls me on. Oh quickly, quickly!
Look through the crevice there, and tell me
If it is Haimon, or some deception of the gods!"
We obeyed; and in the cavern's farthest corner
We saw her lying
She had made a noose of her fine linen veil
And hanged herself. Haimon lay beside, her,
His arms about her wait, lamenting her,
His love lost under ground, crying out
That his father had stolen her away from him.
When Creon saw him the tears rushed to his eyes
And he called to him: "What have you done, child?
Speak to me.
What are you thinking that makes your eyes so strange?
O my son, my son, I come to you on my knees!"
But Haimon spat in his face. He said not a word,
Staring —

And suddenly drew his sword
And lunged. Creon shrank back, the blade missed; and the boy,
Desperate against himself, drove it half its length
Into his own side, and fell. And as he died
He gathered Antigone close in his arms again,
Choking, his blood bright red on her white cheek.
And now he lies dead with the dead, and she is his
At last, his bride in the houses of the dead.

[*Exit* EURYDICE *into the Palace.*]

Choragos

She has left us without a word. What can this mean?

Messenger

It troubles me, too; yet she knows what is best,
Her grief is too great for public lamentation,
And doubtless she has gone to her chamber to weep
For her dead son, leading her maidens in his dirge.

Choragos

It may be so: but I fear this deep silence

[*Pause.*]

Messenger

I will see what she is doing. I will go in.

[*Exit* MESSENGER *into the Palace.*]

[*Enter* CREON *with attendants, bearing* HAIMON's *body.*]

Choragos

But here is the King himself: oh look at him,
Bearing his own damnation in his arms.

Creon

Nothing you say can touch me any more.
My own blind heart has brought me
From darkness to final darkness. Here you see
The father murdering, the murdered son —
And all my civic wisdom!
Haimon my son, so young, so young to die,
I was the fool, not you; and you died for me.

Choragos

That is the truth; but you were late in learning it.

Creon

    This truth is hard to bear. Surely a god
    Has crushed me beneath the hugest weight of heaven,
    And driven me headlong a barbaric way
    To trample out the thing I held most dear.
    The pains that men will take to come to pain!

[*Enter* MESSENGER *from the Palace.*]

Messenger

    The burden you carry in your hands is heavy,
    But it is not all: you will find more in your house.

Creon

    What burden worse than this shall I find there?

Messenger

    The Queen is dead.

Creon

    O port of death, deaf world,
    Is there no pity for me? And you, Angel of evil,
    I was dead, and your words are death again.
    Is it true, boy? Can it be true?
    Is my wife dead? Has death bred death?

Messenger

    You can see for yourself.

[*The doors are opened, and the body of* EURYDICE *is disclosed within.*]

Creon

    Oh pity!
    All true, all true, and more than I can bear!
    O my wife, my son!

Messenger

    She stood before the altar, and her heart
    Welcomed the knife her own hand guided,
    And a great cry burst from her lips for Megareus dead,
    And for Haimon dead, her sons; and her last breath
    Was a curse for their father, the murderer of her sons.
    And she fell, and the dark flowed in through her closing eyes.

Creon

    O God, I am sick with fear.

Are there no swords here? Has no one a blow for me?
Messenger
    Her curse is upon you for the deaths of both.
Creon
    It is right that it should be. I alone am guilty.
    I know it, and I say it. Lead me in,
    Quickly, friends.
    I have neither life nor substance. Lead me in.
Choragos
    You are right, if there can be right in so much wrong.
    The briefest way is best in a world of sorrow.
Creon
    Let it come,
    Let death come quickly, and be kind to me.
    I would not ever see the sun again.
Choragos
    All that will come when it will; but we, meanwhile,
    Have much to do. Leave the future to itself.
Creon
    All my heart was in that prayer!
Choragos
    Then do not pray any more: the sky is deaf.
Creon
    Lead me away. I have been rash and foolish.
    I have killed my sons and my wife.
    I look for comfort; my comfort lies here dead.
    Whatever my hands have touched has come to nothing.
    Fate has brought all my pride to a thought of dust.
[*As* CREON *is being led into the house, the* CHORAGOS *advances
    and speaks directly to the audience.*]
Choragos
    There is no happiness where there is no wisdom;
    No wisdom but in submission to the gods.
    Big words are always punished,
    And proud men in old age learn to be wise.

The Secret Cause
by *Normand Berlin*

Sophocles' *Antigone* has been the focus of much critical attention. It is a play that can be approached from different angles and it raises wide-ranging issues and questions. A popular play in university courses, it allows the teacher to demonstrate the relevance of ancient drama to our contemporary situation. *Antigone* dramatizes problems that always seem modern: the conflict between the state and individual conscience; the clash between written and unwritten laws; the claims of family affection vs. the claims of political stability. In addition, students of drama have posed and attempted to answer more academic questions: Is Antigone an ideal tragic heroine? Whose tragedy is it — Antigone's or Creon's? How "romantic" is the play? Does the play conform to Aristotelian principles? Or, on the other hand, is it an excellent example of Hegelian tragedy?

One of the results of such heavy attention is that Antigone's tragedy has been sentimentalized. This is understandable, because her youth, her sex, her betrothal to Haemon (Creon's son and therefore the son of her executioner), her fate-crossed birth — we can never forget she is Oedipus' daughter — her family affections, her defiant personality, all of these have helped make her a popular tragic heroine and have prompted modern dramatists, like Jean Anouilh, to retell her story. But these same considerations, based on her charismatic character, combined with the relevant issues that the play raises, have diverted attention from the exact nature of the tragedy. William Arrowsmith is surely correct in asserting that we are not "stirred" by the usual interpretations of the play, and that these interpretations have neglected the play's "turbulence," its emotional experience.[1] I would like to help correct this situation by concentrating on what I see as the essential core of Sophocles' play, what makes it a tragedy, what gave it a potency before we moderns pounced upon its "relevance," and what is the deeper reason for the play's hold on the imagination: its presentation of the radical contradictions of man's experience, Sophocles' handling of the vital and shifting relationship of love and death and the gods; in short, the play's confrontation with the secret cause.

The first appearance of the titular figure in a Greek tragedy presents his character note. We are dealing with masks, of course, and the mask, necessarily immobile, freezes the character into a stance, at least when the character first enters. As the play progresses, we may see a different mask, or we may discern more clearly what is *behind* the mask, but the mask, in its first appearance, it not meant to deceive us. (I see it as a truth-teller, comparable to the Shakespearean soliloquy.) When we first see Oedipus in *Oedipus Rex* he is a concerned, pious king. When we first see Antigone in her play, she is a defiant, fiery young woman, filled with love for brother, loyalty to family, anger against Creon, and piety toward the gods. Between her entrance, with Ismene, from the central door of the palace to her departure alone as she takes her long walk across the large pit of the Greek amphitheater, Sophocles offers us her entire present being and a sense of her past.

Her first words to Ismene, her "dear sister," bring up the "curse of Oedipus," which has informed her past life and which she will confront directly just before going to her death. She tells Ismene of Creon's decree that Polyneices, their dead brother, cannot be buried on penalty of death, and she expresses her horror that his body is food for carrion birds. There is no hesitation in her voice when she asserts "there is something we must do" and in her straight-forward challenge to Ismene: by helping with the burial, "you can prove what you are: / A true sister, or a traitor to your family."[2] Ismene thinks Antigone is "mad," a word that pinpoints Antigone's irrational, instinctive defiance of Creon's decree. It is difficult to interpret Antigone's attitude toward the decree as incorrect because Sophocles seems relentless in presenting her act of burial in the most praiseworthy terms. She is obeying divine laws; the "crime" of burying the body is "holy"; if the act means death, "it will not be the worst of deaths—death without honor." What she says to Ismene now, we, as audience know to be right because we, like Antigone, instinctively recoil from the idea of an unburied dead body; we, like Antigone, realize the outrage to humanity when the body of a man is left for carrion. We are willing, therefore, to take Antigone's comments on "the laws of the gods" to be true as well. But if we have any doubts that the *human* thing to do coincides with the wishes of the gods, the sentry's report to Creon dispels them. The sentry, naturally troubled because what he has to say may reflect on him, fearfully presents the details of the symbolic burial of Polyneices: "someone" has put "new dust on the slimy flesh," just enough dust "for the ghost's peace"; there was "not a sign of digging, no, / Not a wheeltrack in the dust, no trace of anyone" and "no sign / Of dogs or any wild animal." The sentry does not know "how to put it," and for good reason—the burial is inexplicable if we think in terms of a mortal's having buried the body. The question, Who buried Polyneices? is answered immediately by the question of the leader of the chorus: "Can it be that the gods have done this?" Sophocles is calculatingly placing this burial in the context of mystery, and raising a question that he answers with a question, the interrogative mood of the tragedy always with us. The chorus leader's questions must be taken seriously, very seriously, especially because Creon the tyrant rejects it so vehemently. The gods are operating in this burial, just as they are operating in Antigone's entire life. It seems that Antigone and the gods are working together in burying a body, and that they are working together in challenging Creon's inhuman and ungodly decree.

The rightness and essential piety of Antigone's attitude toward the burial, as she utters it to Ismene, seem irrefutable. But the *way* she voices her attitude toward Ismene must give us pause. Her family affections, her great love for a dear brother, make her defiant and fearless, heroic qualities indeed. However, this defiance and fearlessness seem so heightened in the face of a death to come that Antigone appears inhuman. Ismene stresses the point: "You are mad"; "think of the danger"; "we are only women"; "I am so afraid for you!"; "you should be cold with fear." And inhuman too, or at least cold and forbidding, are Antigone's words, which are first of sarcasm and then of hatred, to a sister who rejects her offer of complicity: "Go away, Ismene: /I shall be hating you soon, and the dead will too, / For your words are hateful." Ismene leaves the stage praising Antigone as "a loyal friend indeed to those who love you." No words come from Antigone as she takes her long walk to the dead body of Polyneices. Her righteous cause of burying a beloved brother has produced a coldness of heart for a dear sister.

Later, Antigone will not allow Ismene, who now realizes her duty to the dead, to die with her. "You shall not lessen my death by sharing it." Ismene rightly feels that she is being mocked. Family affection stifles family affection. Here is the first of many paradoxes in the play: love has led to a negation of love; a cause based on love has made "a stone of the heart," to use Yeats' phrase when he was describing another cause. This is what causes do. Which of us does not hear the words, "It is the cause, it is the cause," as Othello for the sake of justice is ready to murder Desdemona. Sophocles forces us very early in the play, in this first exchange between sisters, to think of the terrible paradox of love leading to a denial of love.

The coldness and fiery defiance that we associate with Antigone return to the stage in the person of Creon. They are, after all, related to each other, and they are both related, we can never forget, to the fiery Oedipus. But Antigone's coldness still clings to a cause that is right; Creon's always clings to a cause that is wrong. Perhaps one should not be too dogmatic about right and wrong in so complex a play, but, many critics notwithstanding, Creon is the unequivocal tyrant of the play, relentlessly narrow in his views and destructive in his behavior. He stands firmly against every idea of compassion and love; he goes against every principle of democracy in government; he epitomizes the principle of calculation.[3] In short, he represents hatred in a play about love. It is difficult, therefore, to accept the Hegelian interpretation of *Antigone* as a clash between two rights, what Hegel calls "the equal validity of both powers engaged in conflict."[4] The neatness of Hegel's tragic formula does not fit the tragedy that he seems to have based it on. Creon's cause has no validity, as it is presented in the play. The issue of the validity of the claims of the state vs.

the claims of family and individual is always a debatable one, and helps explain the popularity of the play, but it is not an issue in *this* play. Creon is clearly a tyrant, and his denial of the gods and of love will cause his eventual suffering in terms of the coldest kind of poetic justice. To think of Creon as the possible tragic hero, as many have, seems a gross misreading of the play. And to see a resemblance between Creon and his brother-in-law and nephew Oedipus in anything more than their anger is forgetting the important issue of piety to the gods. Creon works against the gods and is punished—as if a logical equation is being worked out. Oedipus works with the gods and for the gods but is their victim—thereby producing the large inexplicable questions about man's relationship to the gods. And this brings us back to the tragic heroine, Antigone, who in burying Polyneices is doing the work of the gods.

When the sentry appears a second time, he brings Antigone with him, whom he has caught placing dust on the stinking corpse and sprinkling wine three time "for her brother's ghost." Even in this second burial the gods seem to have been at work. These are the sentry's words:

> But nothing happened until the white round sun
> Whirled in the center of the round sky over us:
> Then, suddenly,
> A storm of dust roared up from the earth, and the sky
> Went out, the plain vanished with all its trees
> In the stinging dark. We closed our eyes and endured it.
> The whirlwind lasted a long time, but is passed;
> And then we looked, and there was Antigone!

Antigone's act is given a macrocosmic dimension. This is no ordinary burial; the gods who helped to accomplish the first burial seem to be watching this second burial.

In her agon with Creon, Antigone denies nothing, reaffirms that "unrecorded laws of God," asserts that "there is no guilt in reverence for the dead," and is sure that she will have "praise and honor" for what she has done. Here too she seems to welcome death. She knows she must die eventually — "I am only mortal"

— so sees no hardship in dying now, before her time, for the pious act of burying her brother. In fact, in a world of evil, she sees death as a "friend." Her last phrase in this scene is " . . . I belong to Death." Headstrong, bitter in her condemnation of Creon, cold to Ismene, weary of words, and intellectually accepting the death that she knows is the price of her action, Antigone displays an "inflexible heart," to use Creon's phrase. But she is attached to a pious cause, and, cold though she is in her behavior, she is acting in behalf of love. Surely her most important line in this entire encounter with Creon is: "It is my nature to join in love, not hate."

Love is the power that informs the play.[5] It is the essential instinctive motive of Antigone when she buries Polyneices; the reason Ismene asks to share her sister's fate; the bond between Antigone and Haemon; the force that prompts Haemon to rebel against his father and then to kill himself; the idea that even Creon asserts when he suggests that love can only exist within an orderly society.[6] (Obviously, Creon has his private notion of what love is, for he emerges as the apostle of hate. Throughout, he denies love or cheapens it; he has no understanding of its hidden power or mystery.) Love is what connects Antigone's human act of burying Polyneices with her pious obedience to the gods. In the third choric ode, the chorus sings about love's power, informing us of "a girl's glance working the will of heaven." This ode concludes with an important idea, usually neglected in discussions of the play. Love is "pleasure to her alone who mocks us, / Merciless Aphrodite." Love, we know, causes pain and suffering, it causes hardness of heart, it brings about the death of Antigone, the deaths of Haemon and Eurydice, and the living death of Creon. It has awesome power over men and gods. But it is a "pleasure" to the goddess Aphrodite who "mocks" us. Here is a note of cruelty, the kind of mocking cruelty that is often associated with the gods, and in this play is associated with mortals as well. Ismene felt she was being mocked by Antigone; Creon mocked his son's love, the chorus, and the gods; Antigone, when going to her death, will feel she is mocked by the chorus and the gods. A tragic heroine, a tyrant, and a goddess all mock, all look at those around them from a heightened position, but only the goddess prevails, for the tyrant and heroine are themselves mocked—Creon when he is justly punished by the gods for his impiety, Antigone when she for the first time in the play (and the last time that we see her) displays confusion and anxiety and doubt. Only the immortals can *remain* mockers; the heightened mortals, because they are human, must fall *down* to their humanity and must eventually become the victims of the gods' mockery. But in the fall to humanity, the wounded and mocked mortals rise in our estimation, achieving dignity. Creon does not rise much because of his narrow tyranny and lovelessness, although he does learn, too late, that he was a "fool," that he is guilty of the deaths around him, but that some of the guilt rests on the gods who crushed him, driving him headlong to barbarism. Antigone rises enormously, for in her confusion at being mocked and in her horror at facing death alone, she appears to take upon herself "the mystery of things," and she is never more human and, paradoxically, more heightened than in her last moments.

Sophocles carefully prepares for Antigone's last appearance on stage. She enters just as the chorus completes its ode on love with the words on the mocking, merciless Aphrodite. Indeed, love has brought her to the final scene and she will feel mocked. Antigone's words:

> Look upon me, friends, and pity me
> Turning back at the night's edge to say
> Good-by to the sun that shrines for me no longer;
> Now sleepy Death
> Summons me down to Acheron, that cold shore:
> There is no bridesong there, nor any music.

Here is the first time that Antigone displays fear in the face of death; her words betray the softer emotions of a young girl going to her end. She realizes that she is on the edge of night, having come to her boundary situation, and she knows that the night she is entering contains neither light nor song. Her loneliness seems to overwhelm her as she goes on to mention the story of Niobe, "how the stone / Clung fast about her." When the chorus mentions her "glory" because she is dying with "a kind of honor," Antigone thinks herself mocked. "You laugh at me. Ah, friends, friends, / Can you not wait until I am dead?" When the chorus, pursuing the idea of justice, mentions her father's guilt, Antigone, in moving terms, recalls, for us and for herself, her dark beginnings, mentioned in her first speech and surely always lurking in her mind.

> You have touched it at last: that bridal bed
> Unspeakable, horror of son and mother mingling:
> Their crime, infection of all our family!
> O Oedipus, father and brother!
> Your marriage strikes from the grave to murder mine.
> I have been a stranger here in my own land:
> All my life
> The blasphemy of my birth has followed me.

It is unjust that an innocent girl is suffering for her father's sin, and this injustice reminds us that her father too was an innocent sufferer, and that the gods continue to play their demonic and inexplicable role. However, the chorus, forever upholding established law, denies her innocence: "You have made your choice, / Your death is the doing of your conscious hand." The coldness of the sentiment—precisely echoing the coldness that Antigone herself displayed to Ismene: ("You have made your choice") — leads Antigone to despair.

> Then let me go, since all your words are bitter,
> And the very light of the sun is cold to me.
> Lead me to my vigil, where I must have
> Neither love nor lamentation; no song, but silence.

She laments her isolation, the condition of most tragic heroes, and she sees herself not only alone but neither pitied nor loved. Her act of love in burying Polyneices, a pious act in her eyes, is branded as impious and wrong. Small wonder that she refuses to address the chorus any longer, finding some consolation in speaking directly to her tomb of death, believing she will soon be "with her own again," especially with Polyneices for whom she is dying. She reasserts her innocence: "And yet, as men's hearts know,

I have done no wrong. / I have not sinned before God." Her tone, in the Fitts-Fitzgerald translation, must betray her deep disappointment with the gods. Knox's translation makes her sense of being deserted by the gods more explicit: "Why should I in my misery look to the gods anymore? Which of them can I call my ally?"[7] Revealing human disappointment, terrible loneliness in the face of death, Antigone is mocked not only by the people around her, but by the gods, including the merciless Aphrodite. Once again, the gods in Sophoclean tragedy are wearing masks impossible to penetrate, performing actions that seem unjust. It is natural for a confused young woman on the brink of death to question their enigmatic ways. She is not shouting against the gods as her father — a larger tragic hero — had, but rather, in her quiet shudder and lonely desperation, she is reminding us and herself of their injustice.

But the scene does not end on this note of disappointment. Antigone prays that if Creon is guilty in his actions, his punishment should equal hers, and she leaves the stage still defiantly expressing the piety of her act, this time to her native Thebes:

> Thebes, and you my fathers' gods,
> And ruler of Thebes, you see me now, the last
> Unhappy daughter of a line of kings,
> Your kings, led away to death. You will remember
> What things I suffer, and at what men's hands,
> Because I would not transgress the laws of heaven.

She walks to her death in the tomb, and as she departs we surely feel the rightness in her questioning of the gods, the power of her instinctive love, and the heroism of her unshakable defiance. The chorus immediately sings an ode about others who have journeyed to darkness — Danae, Lycurgus, and the sons of Cleopatra. The choice of these particular figures from the past and the search for the ode's unity and relevance to Antigone has produced some interesting critical commentary,[8] but no critic, to my knowledge, has noticed the thread of mockery connecting each of the allusions. The innocent Danae was hidden by her father in a gravelike chamber "where the sunlight could not come" so that she could not bear a son who, according to an oracle, would kill his grand-father. But Zeus visited her in a shower of gold, pouring "love" upon her, thereby mocking the merely human precautions of Da-nae's father. The guilty Lycurgus was entombed in a dungeon by Dionysus because "his tongue had mocked" the power of that powerful god. And, most appropriate to Antigone's story, the two sons of imprisoned Cleopatra had their eyes "ripped out" by a vi-cious woman filled with hatred "while grinning Ares watched." Cleopatra was "of heavenly birth" but "in her marriage deathless Fate found means / To build a tomb like yours for all her joy." These three stories extend the idea of entombment, as Antigone goes to her tomb. They remind us that gods and men have mocked Antigone. And, in the ode's climactic story, we are forced to remember the curse on Oedipus' house, his blinding and jour-ney from light to dark, and — specifically touching Antigone's story at *this* moment — the children who were victims of fate and human cruelty. The chorus, never directly showing pity for Antigone or expressing horror at her situation, sings an ode that manages to evoke both tragic emotions. The ode is bathed in darkness — in the situations it presents and in the language it uses. Therefore — here Sophocles seems most brilliant in his grasp of tragic movement — as Antigone walks to her death, we the audience also lean toward night and mystery. From the ques-tions on the behavior of the gods, from the darkness of their mocking, from the mystery of a potent love, the play moves to-ward the darkness of cruelty, the mystery of Oedipus' story, and finally, the darkness and mystery of death.

Before we learn the specific nature of Antigone's death, how-ever, an unexpected god, mentioned in the ode just discussed, takes on some significance. After Teiresias reveals the anger of the gods at Creon's refusal to bury Polyneices, whose rotting corpse is polluting Thebes, the chorus, who supported Creon throughout the play, either out of fear or because of respect for law, now insists that Creon listen to Teiresias, that he immedi-ately free Antigone and bury Polyneices. Creon readily agrees, ut-tering that "the laws of the gods are mighty," and leaves the stage. The chorus then sings a hymn — not to Apollo, whose priest they just heard, who is traditionally concerned with the pollution of a state, and who seems the logical recipient of their prayers — but to Dionysus. Dionysus, true to his nature, seems intrusive here. Of course, we can explain his presence by saying that he is the bringer of good gifts; the chorus, after all, is praying for deliverance from the pestilence. And we can add to this that Dionysus is a Theban god, a god of local patriotism. But the power of the chorus's hymn, as I read it, rests on its strongly *emotional* appeal to a mysterious force, a god born of Thunder to a mortal woman, the god who punished Lycurgus, the god of wine and dance and rapture, the "purest among the voices of the night!" This is the figure who occupies the mid-region between man and god; he connects the two, just as Antigone's act of burial connects the human impulse to the godly wish. He reminds us of the connection between Antigone and Oedipus, both of whom descended from Dionysus. But most important, at this high point in the drama, he makes us acknowledge the emotional life, the irrational and instinctive love that informs Antigone's entire being. He allows us to understand the limitations of narrow reason and cold calculation, associated with Creon. Dionysus is the god whom Oedipus discovered within himself and who must intrude into the story of Oedipus' daughter — a heroine who acted madly and instinctively out of love, and who, at the very moment the chorus is singing its song to the potent voice of the night, is herself rushing to the night of the dead.

The rest of the play seems to belong to Creon, and for this reason many have seen him as the tragic hero. I have already indicated why this is a misguided view. Antigone's play ends with Creon's punishment in order to demonstrate that Antigone was right in her action, that she indeed worked for the gods, who now punish her adversary. The result of Antigone's action is the defeat of a tyrant, and we must understand this clearly. As the miseries of Creon pile up, as he goes on his very speedy journey to suffering and wisdom, the image of Antigone, who helped bring him to his living death, haunts the stage. Haemon kills himself for love of Antigone and he does so in her tomb. Antigone, still independent, listening to her own deathly drummer, has hanged herself in the tomb. Creon's punishment is speedily dramatized in an atmosphere of the strict justice of the gods, a dramatically disappointing but absolutely necessary acting out of poetic justice. The echoes of Antigone's end in the tomb, and her life before that, fill the last part of the play up to Creon's very last line: "Fate has brought all my pride to a thought of dust." The dust that first the gods and then Antigone spread on Polyneices' body is recalled here and we are back to the play's beginning. Between that dust and his "thought of dust" a young woman has traveled her fated journey to death.

Antigone's act of burying her brother is prompted by the deep sources of her personal motivation, based on love, but in this act we also see the workings of the gods. It is the cause that gives Antigone stature; and it is the cause that makes her godlike in her sureness of self, in her cold rejection of Ismene, in her relentless defiance of the tyrant Creon. When Antigone is mocked, when she realizes the gods have left her, when she clearly confronts the curse on her family, when she feels most abandoned and most alone, then she becomes most human and, in her descent, rises in our estimation. She regains her humanity, retains her dignity, and reminds us once again that love was the source of her action, but this time a love that seems more precious and powerful because it forces her to face the mystery of death. In Sophocles' treatment of the Antigone story, when the mystery of love touches the mystery of death, tragedy is born. And in this tragedy, Sophocles prods us into asking the important existential questions: Why does a pious act based on love lead to death? Why do the gods mock those who are pious? Why does love lead to a denial of love? Why are the promptings of love and the workings of the gods darker than the dark earth of Antigone's tomb? What is behind such radical contradictions in man's existence?

Uncertainty, a radical uncertainty, lodges at the deepest roots of our human experience. The deeper we get, the darker the terrain; the darker the terrain, the more uncertain our vision and our footing. That is why Oedipus needs a stick and that is why Antigone—abandoned and mocked, facing her own death for the first time—shudders in horror, revealing her humanity and revealing the enormous power of love that can propel a fearful woman on a journey to night. The dark seed of Antigone's shudder, like the dark root of Oedipus' scream of anguish, touches mystery, the secret cause.

1. William Arrowsmith, "The Criticism of Greek Tragedy," in *Tragedy: Vision and Form*, ed. Robert W. Corrigan (San Francisco: Chandler, 1965), pp. 320-21.
2. Sophocles, *Antigone*, p. 186, in the Fitts-Fitzgerald text.
3. Richmond Y. Hathorn discusses this principle in *Tragedy, Myth and Mystery*, pp. 66-78.
4. Friedrich Hegel, *The Philosophy of Fine Art*, quoted in Corrigan, p. 438.
5. H.D.F. Kitto, (*Form and Meaning*, pp. 138-78), Richmond Hathorn, and William Arrowsmith argue effectively for the importance of love.
6. To my knowledge, Arrowsmith is alone in mentioning Creon's belief that love can only exist in a stable society. In Corrigan, p. 328.
7. Bernard M.W. Knox, *The Heroic Temper*, p. 106.
8. See especially Kitto, *Form and Meaning*, pp. 171-73, and S.M. Adams, *Sophocles the Playwright* (Toronto: University of Toronto Press, 1957), p. 55.

Euripides
MEDEA

Translated by
Michael Townsend

Characters	*Nurse*

Pedagogue

Medea

Chorus of the women of Corinth

Creon

Jason

Aigeus

Messenger

First Child ⎫ *the children of*

Second Child ⎭ *Jason and Medea*

[*Before Jason's house at Corinth.*]
Nurse

 Everything's gone wrong — my darling mistress upset
 And the atmosphere all full of bitterness.
 Oh I wish the good ship Argo hadn't managed
 To nip between the dark Symplegades . . .
 Or (come to that) if only that pine tree
 Had never been cut down on Pēlion;
 And if only, if only those hearty Heroes
 Had not rowed the thing across the sea
 To get the golden fleece for Pelias.
 For then my mistress wouldn't have fallen in love
 With Jason and sailed with him to Iolchus city;
 She wouldn't have made the daughters of Pelias kill him,
 She wouldn't have had to flee to Corinth here,
 She wouldn't have done all that she did for Jason,
 She wouldn't have been so darned complaisant to Jason.
 Oh, being a good wife is a fine thing . . .
 As long as it doesn't come to a bust-up.
  And now of course Jason has let her down,
 Her and the children too. He's going to marry
 The daughter of King Creon, — getting in
 With the royal family, that's his idea.
 And so Medea's shouting to high heaven
 About his marriage oaths and the joining of hands,
 And what can be a more solemn bond than that?
 She's pestering the gods to bear witness
 To the way Jason shows his gratitude.
 It's affected her, she's given herself up
 To grief, — lies there weeping, takes no food.
 Ever since she heard of how her husband wronged her,
 She hasn't lifted her face from the ground.
 You'd think she was a rock or a wave in the sea, —
 She takes no notice of her friends at all.
 Just turns her head occasionally to mutter
 Bitter regretful words about her father,

Who she adored, and about her old home —
You see she left all that to go with Jason,
And now look how Jason has treated her.
She's found out too late there's nothing like
One's own home country, — staying at home is best.
Even hates her children, cannot bear
The sight of them. I'm worried about her.
She's a strong character and she won't take
Bad treatment lying down. She may
Be planning something desperate, — I know her.
Creep into the bride's bedroom at night
And thrust a knife into the girl's heart.
Or kill the king; kill her husband too.
She is a fighter. No one get her down.
I'll stop; here come the children back
From playing with their hoops. They haven't noticed
Their mother's troubles. Why should they? They're young.

Pedagogue

Hullo, old thing, you old piece of furniture,
What are you doing here all by yourself
Indulging in a monologue of complaints?
Doesn't Medea want you to be with her?

Nurse

Well, you're the pedagogue of Jason's children,
So you must know, if a servant's any good,
He takes to heart the misfortunes of his owners.
I felt I simply had to come out here
And give vent to my feelings about Medea.

Pedagogue

Poor soul, and is she still crying then?

Nurse

What blissful ignorance, she's hardly started.

Pedagogue

I shouldn't comment on my betters, but
It's silly taking on like that, when you think
She hasn't heard half of her troubles yet.

Nurse

There's something else? Well, tell me. Come on, tell me.

Pedagogue
>Nothing. I didn't mean what I said.

Nurse
>Don't try to hide it. I'm a servant, too.
>Please . . . I won't pass it on to anyone.

Pedagogue
>Down by the laundry-stones in the river,
>Where the old men come to sit and have their gossip,
>I heard it, overheard somebody talking.
>These kids — Creon's going to exile them;
>Medea too. That's only what I heard;
>I most sincerely hope it isn't true.

Nurse
>But Jason can't allow it; his own children.

Pedagogue
>That marriage is a dead letter, my dear.
>Old ties are being cut. A new wife now.

Nurse
>It'll be the end if we've got to bear
>This new blow, before she's weathered the old.

Pedagogue
>Of course it isn't right for her to hear
>The news now, so you keep quiet about it.

Nurse
>Are you listening, children? Such a father you've got!
>Damnation take him — no, he's still my master.
>A traitor to his family he is.

Pedagogue
>You don't know much about human nature.
>Everyone looks after himself before
>Anyone else. Whether they use lawful
>Or unlawful means, it's just the same. Their dad
>Wants a new wife; so, the kids have had it.

Nurse
>Now run along, children, into the house.
>Don't let them near their mother while she's in
>This state. I've seen her eyes like the eyes

Of a bull, looking at them; obviously thinking
Of doing something. I'm sure she won't let
Her anger die without doing someone harm.
I only hope it's no one that I like.

Medea [*Inside.*]

Oh, I feel miserable.
I want, I want to die.

Nurse

Do you hear that, children? Mother
Is whipping herself to a fury.
Hurry, into the house with you.
Don't go near her, my dears.
Go on, go on, hurry.
Soon it'll be worse,
And what will she do then?
She's a deep one, a deep one;
There's no stopping her.

Medea

Oh, weep, I want to weep.
Oh the children, to hell with them.
To hell with their mother, to hell with
Their father, to hell with the lot.

Nurse

Oh, lordie me.
It isn't the kiddies' fault.
Why do you hate them?
I'm worried about you, dears,
Worried. Being a royal
Person she's used to getting
Whatever she wants. Me,
I'd rather be humbly born
And safe. I'd rather be safe.

Chorus

Medea, — we couldn't help
Hearing her shouts and cries.
Tell us what is the matter.
We come as friends, you know.

Nurse

> We aren't a family any more.
> He's all wrapped up in his new
> Connection, the king's daughter;
> And she's gone to her bedroom,
> Given way to self-pity,
> Won't listen to her friends.

Medea

> Oh, blast, the ruddy lightning,
> I wish it would strike me down.
> I want to die and end it all,
> I can't stand my life.

Chorus

> Good heavens, what a thing
> To say. And shouting like that.
> Death will come in time;
> Why rush it? You poor thing,
> Your husband's sex life
> Is his affair; and God
> Will punish him for you.
> No sense in your getting
> Upset about it. Forget it.

Medea

> Artemis, I'm asking you,
> And Themis, Divine Justice,
> Witness what I'm going through,
> In spite of the oaths he took.
> I'd like to see him
> And his bride and the whole house
> Ground to powder. Father,
> At Colchis my old home,
> I left you and killed
> My brother, to go with him.

Nurse

> Hark at her, serious now,
> And testifying the gods.
> She's getting obsessed now.

Chorus

Surely we can help her —
Bring her out, we'll speak to her.
There's nothing like a friend
For helping you out of depression.
I refuse to let her down.

Nurse

Get her out? I can't.
But I'll try, for her sake.
She glares so, when any
Of us servants try to speak.
It's funny to think that men of old
Invented songs for banquets
And festivals and joyful occasions,
But didn't think of making music
To be a medicine for wounded feelings.
That would have been a discovery, now.
For hurt feelings, if not mended,
Bring death and disaster to whole families.

Chorus

It's Themis she calls upon;
For it was the oaths he swore by Themis
That made her embark in a little boat
And set out at night on the limitless sea,
The great salt road that leads to every land.

Medea

Ladies of Corinth, I've come out, you see.
I've come out, in a way, to defend myself.
When someone isn't seen for a long time,
Well, folk soon begin to imagine the worst.
A typically unfair attitude,
I suppose, condemning people in their absence.
I stayed indoors; a foreigner like me
With much to learn about your ways should not
Go barging about and antagonizing people.
Let's face it, this thing that's happened to me
Has knocked me all of a heap. I stopped caring,

My friends, — I can call you my friends, can't I?
I didn't want to live. You imagine what it's like,
To find that the man who was all your life to you
Has been a complete traitor and let you down.
My husband, yes, my husband.
     Aren't we of all god's creatures the most unlucky,
We women? First we have to buy our husbands, —
Actually pay for a man to lord it over us . . .
Think yourself lucky if you get a good one;
It isn't done for *women* to divorce,
Oh no. And what preparation do we get
For marriage? None. If you do find you're able
To live with him, you're lucky. If you don't,
You've had it. Compare us with a man;
If a man no longer fancies the wife he has,
He's off, and battens on to another woman.
But we're chained to one person; everything
Depends on him. Oh I know what they say, —
We live a safe, comfortable life at home,
While they go out to war, risk life and limb,
Fighting with swords and spears to protect us.
I'd far rather serve in the front line
A dozen times, than go through childbirth once!
     It isn't the same for me as it is for you.
This is your country, your families are here,
Your homes are here, and all your friends are round you.
I am alone, a displaced person, stateless.
How am I to defend myself against
My husband? Mother, brother, I have no one,
No relative to whom to turn for refuge.
So may I ask this one favor of you;
If I get a chance to pay him back,
Don't tell. Women don't like violence,
But when their husbands desert them, that is different.

Chorus
We won't tell anyone. You're justified
In trying to pay him back. We don't blame you

For being depressed. Here comes the king,
Creon; it looks as though something is up.

Creon

Now listen here. It's you I'm talking to,
You with the long face, Medea; I've decreed
You must leave the country, take your children with you,
And be quick about it. You've got me to deal with, —
There's no way out, I'm not going home
Until I personally see you across the border.

Medea

I'm finished.
Why are my enemies so implacable?
Why have I deserved this, may I ask?

Creon

Frankly, I'm scared you'll kill my daughter.
You're clever and you've been jilted, that's enough.
I've heard you've been making threats against us,
Me and my daughter and Jason. I'm not waiting
Until you get your chance. Hate me then.
If I took pity on you, I'd regret it.

Medea

Oh, heavens.
It's not the first time I've suffered from gossip.
A sensible man doesn't bring up clever children.
Aren't clever people hated? They're lazy;
A nuisance and an embarrassment to the dim;
While those who think themselves bright are jealous of them.
This has happened to me, — and yet I'm not really clever.
Apparently you're afraid of me. Now why?
Why should I be so crazy as to offend
A king? Have you provoked me? You've given
Your daughter to the man of your choice.
It's my husband I hate. As for you,
You've acted sensibly; I've nothing against you.
Good luck to you; I won't stand in your way.
So please let me stay on in this country.
There'll be no more threats — I know when I'm beaten.

Creon

That little speech just makes me trust you less.
When you seen tame you are most dangerous.
Get out, out now. Enough of making speeches.
Dammit, it is decided, you must go.
How can I let you stay when you hate me?

Medea

Oh, please. I beg you in your daughter's name.

Creon

You're wasting time. I will not change my mind.

Medea

You'll kick me out, won't even take pity on me?

Creon

I'm bound to put my family before you.

Medea

Your family; I can't return to mine.

Creon

The best things in life, family and country.

Medea

It's love, love that causes all the trouble.

Creon

But luck, just luck, has a lot to do with it.

Medea

Oh god, remember who did this to me.

Creon

Come on, get moving. Don't make it hard for me.

Medea

Hard for you, you? Isn't it hard on me?

Creon

I'll have to get my men to manhandle you.

Medea

Please don't do that. Look, Creon, I implore you —

Creon

I see you're going to insist on being a nuisance.

Medea

I'll go. No, I'll go. It's not that I want.

Creon

Then what are you clinging to me for?

Medea

> Just let me stay today, just this one day;
> To get my mind accustomed to exile and
> Prepare my children for the journey. Oh,
> Their father will not trouble himself about them.
> If not on me, at least have pity on
> The children. You have children of your own.

Creon

> I never was a tyrannical sort of man.
> Mildness has been my undoing many a time.
> I'm wrong to do it, — you can have your wish.
> Stay for today if you're so bent on it:
> You can't do much damage in a day.
> But listen here, if you're not over the border
> Tomorrow, then by Heaven you will die.

Chorus

> Poor dear, how sorry I am
> For you. You've nowhere to go.
> I don't know what you can do.

Medea

> Things certainly look bad, I'll not deny it.
> But don't imagine it will end this way.
> They haven't won yet, those marriage-makers;
> I can see a few clouds on their horizon.
> You don't honestly think I'd go crawling
> To a man like that, if it weren't for a purpose.
> Good lord, I shouldn't have spoken to him or touched him.
> The poor fool, if only he'd thrown me out
> He could have demolished all my plans.
> But now he's given me a day, a day;
> And in this day I'll turn them into corpses,
> The three of them, the father, the daughter, and him.
>   I have so many ways I can put them to death.
> I can't make up my mind which I shall use,
> My friends. Set fire to the bridal chamber,
> Or tiptoe up beside the bed they sleep in
> And stab them, ram a dagger into the heart?

No.
I might be caught trying to get in,
Then I'd be executed, my enemies
Would think it a great joke. I won't risk that.
Best stick to what I know; let it be poison.
Yes.
There they lie dead. Now who will take me in?
What country is bound by the laws
Of hospitality to give me asylum?
None. So they'll get me in the end.
Maybe some chance of asylum will turn up,
And if it does I'll do the deed by stealth.
But if there's no hope of any refuge,
I'll kill them openly, with a sword or something.
I'll show them I have guts; they don't wrong me
And get away with it. To action then,
Medea, and keep your courage high.
You mustn't disgrace your family
And allow yourself to be a subject for jokes
At your husband's wedding. Use your brains;
Women are better than men at planning evil.

Chorus
Are rivers flowing in reverse?
Has everything gone upside-down?
It should. For, in spite of what poets try
To tell us about the perfidiousness
Of women, a man this time
Has broken faith.

All pious restraints are shattered, all sense of shame
Has left the earth and flown up into the sky.
And you, Medea, are caught
In a strange land, a refugee,
Alone and husbandless.

You can't return again
To your father's home from which you sailed away,
Across the sea, between the clashing rocks,

> To what? To this, to a usurped marriage,
> To a home auctioned to royal bidders,
> To the faithlessness of men.

Jason

> It's not the first time I've seen it happen —
> If one gives way to temper, one regrets it.
> If only you could have contained yourself
> And submitted to the plans of your betters,
> You could have kept your home here in this city.
> But you had to give vent to empty threats;
> And so you've been exiled. Now I don't mind
> What you take it into your head to say against me.
> but the things you've been saying about Creon —
> Just count yourself lucky you're still alive.
> I did my very best to soften his wrath,
> But what could I do when you kept on
> Insulting and cursing? He is the king, you know.
> But forget all that; I am not the man
> To let down those I care for, my dear.
> I've come to see that you're provided for
> (Oh, and the children) now you're going into exile.
> You see, your hating me doesn't alter things;
> I still can't ever feel ill will towards you.

Medea

> You evil creature, how dare you come here?
> How dare you show yourself after what you've done?
> How dare you look me in the face? It isn't
> Self-confidence or courage makes you do it;
> It's sheer hypocrisy. But I'm glad you've come.
> It will relieve me to speak my mind;
> And I rejoice that what I say will hurt you.
>
> I'll go through it all in order of time.
> First, as your fellow sailors in Argo know,
> I saved your life,
> When you were sent to yoke the fire dragons
> And sow the seed that bore fighting men.
> And that snake, the snake that never slept,

That sinuous sentry coiled around the fleece,
Who killed it? I did. Saved you again.
Having betrayed my father and family,
I left all I had to go with you
To Iolchus. Was that self-interest,
Or was it passion, my passion for you?
Then I killed Pelias, made his children kill him,
And devastated that whole family for you.
When I've done that and that and that for you,
You reject me and get another wife!
And we have children. If we'd had no children,
Your itch for another woman might be excused.
And the marriage vows you swore, — do you understand
You've broken them? Or do you think
The gods you swore by then have disappeared?
Or that the rules we live by have changed?
To think of my right hand here, and the times you clung to it;
And these knees of mine, your arms round them.
You've played on my heart, and cheated my hopes.
I feel I've been made foul by your touch.
　　But let me speak to you as to a friend —
You're not my friend, but that's on your conscience.
Where should I go? To my father's house?
Him I betrayed and abandoned for you.
To the daughters of Pelias? They'd be glad
To have me back, their father's murderess.
It's like this, you see. Those I should love
Have made themselves accursed, while others
Who'd normally be my friends I've alienated
For your sake. I do congratulate you,
On being a wonderful husband to me, —
You've deprived me of every friend I had,
And got me and our children deported.
I hope your new bride enjoys the thought;
These children wandering homeless, vagrant beggars.
　　And what of me, who saved your life so often?
O god, you made a touchstone for gold,

And anyone can tell the counterfeit.
But men, why did you make no sign
By which debased men could be distinguished?
Chorus
There is no bitterness to be compared
With that between two people who once loved.
Jason
I see I should have come prepared to argue.
And I see that I'll need all my skill
To steer a course against this hurricane
Of words. Well now, you lay a lot of stress
On your feelings for me, and I'll confess
The goddess of love proved the savior
Of my nautical venture in the Argo.
Your head was easily turned — why not admit it? —
And the crush you had on me saved my life.
But do we have to be a bore about that?
I'd be the first to acknowledge the benefit.
On the other hand, I think I can prove
That you've received more than you gave.
You're living in a civilized country now
Instead of in the wilds; and you've had
The blessings of our way of life in which
The rule of law puts right in front of might.
Your gifts, too, are appreciated here
By people of culture. If you'd still been living
Out there in the back of beyond, do you think
You'd be the talk of the town as you are here?
That's life, that is, to be on everyone's lips;
I'd rather have that than a houseful of gold
Or the poetic genius of Orpheus.
        That's what I have to say about your help
To me in my adventures. I wouldn't have spoken;
But you're determined to have an argument.
As for your rude remarks about my marriage
To the king's daughter, I can prove to you
That this act of mine is a wise one,

And not only wise but reasonable,
And not only reasonable but beneficial
To you and to my children — now hold on,
Hold on, I say. When I got here from Iolchus,
I was a fugitive, remember, an exile.
I had a lot to contend with, — what could be better
As a solution than to marry
The king's daughter? It's not that I find you
No longer attractive, it's not that I want more children,
It's just the most important reason of all, —
I want . . . us to live well, not be in want
And without friends as other exiles are;
I want to bring up my children in a way that's worthy
Of my family. When I beget more children,
Their money will be available to these.
So we'll be well off. Have I done wrong?
What's the matter with that? I know what's wrong, —
It's the fact that you no longer share my bed.
You women are all the same, if bed's all right,
You think everything else can go to the wind.
But if there's any infringement of your bed-rights,
Then fair is foul and all hell's let loose.
Why can't men get children some other way,
Without women? What a picnic life would be
If women didn't exist.

Chorus

You're very plausible, but let's face it,
You can't get away from the fact
That you've done wrong and let your wife down.

Medea

I seem not to see things as others do;
I'd double the punishment for those
Who sin and then try to get off
By clever talk. Their tongues encourage them
To take a risk in evildoing; like you,
You think you can wrap me up with words,
But there's one thing that knocks you out cold, —

If your motives had really been so good
You'd have spoken to me before about this marriage,
Not acted in this hold-in-the-corner fashion.

Jason

That's rich — how would you have reacted to that,
When you can't see for your anger even now?

Medea

Why not admit you didn't like the thought
Of being married to someone of my race,
To a barbarian, a non-Greek?

Jason

For heaven's sake, I swear to you
There's nothing personal in my marrying
The king's daughter. How often must I tell you
I did it to save you from want
And give these children and our family
The protection of having royal brothers?

Medea

I don't want money and misery.
I don't want affluence that makes me sick.

Jason

I hope you won't regret saying that;
There's worse things than being comfortably off.

Medea

You can afford to be supercilious;
You've seen to it that you're provided for.
It's me that's friendless, homeless, and deserted.

Jason

By your own choice — you've no one else to blame.

Medea

I chose it? How? Have I married again, betrayed you?

Jason

By uttering those threats against Creon.

Medea

He's not the only one I've got it in for.

Jason

I can't go on arguing like this.

Look, if there's anything at all you need
For yourself or the children in exile,
Speak up. I'll do anything to help you.
I'll write to my friends abroad; they will
Look after you, I'm sure. Don't be a fool
And say no, my dear. Forget your anger;
It will be better for you if you do.

Medea

I won't accept your friends' hospitality.
I won't accept anything from you; don't offer.
The gifts of an evil man have no value.

Jason

All right then; I hope it's understood
(And I pray the gods to bear witness)
That I'm willing to do anything for you.
But you will not let your friends help you,
So you'll only have yourself to blame for that.

Medea

Be on your way. Your new little wife
Is calling you; you've been away too long.
Go forward into matrimony together;
I think you won't enjoy it, so help me god.

Chorus

There's nothing so lovely as love if it isn't obsessive:
I like a sensible passion without high feelings,
Without insatiable quarrels and battles in bed.

There's no virtue in love that's too possessive;
So, Aphrodite, the arrows you dip in desire
Do not aim them, do not aim them at my head.

As I think of my home, my country,
I'm frightened of being homeless, homeless,
When life reaches ahead like a monotonous road.

I know what it is at first hand,
And I'd rather die than live like that.
You've had nobody, nobody to share your heavy load.

May he die with no joy at his end,
The man who won't be troubled
To unlock the keys of his heart and make a friend.
Aigeus
Hullo, Medea, how are you? I hope
You're well. I like to hear good news of my friends.
Medea
Aigeus, hullo. . . . I hope you're well, too.
What brings you here? Where have you come from?
Aigeus
I'm on my way back from the Delphic oracle.
Medea
And what made you want to go there?
Aigeus
To find out how I can have children.
Medea
No children yet? Should have had some by now.
Aigeus
No children, due to some unlucky chance.
Medea
I take it your married, anyhow.
Aigeus
Oh yes, indeed, I am married all right.
Medea
And what did Phoebus tell you about children?
Aigeus
Something too deep for human intelligence.
Medea
Would you mind telling me what it was?
Aigeus
Be glad to, — it needs a clever brain.
Medea
Let's hear it then, if you say you don't mind.
Aigeus
Something about not opening my wineskin . . .
Medea
Before doing what, before arriving where?

Aigeus
Before I get back to my home again.
Medea
So then, why are you traveling this way?
Aigeus
You've heard of Pittheus, king of Troezene?
Medea
I've heard of him, a very religious man.
Aigeus
I want to tell the oracle to him.
Medea
A good idea, he's expert at such things.
Aigeus
And he's an old friend of mine as well.
Medea
Well than, good luck, I hope you succeed.
Aigeus
Look,
I can tell from your face you're upset.
Medea
Aigeus, it is my husband — rotten all through. . . .
Aigeus
What's that? What's he done to upset you?
Medea
He's wronged me, without justification.
Aigeus
What has he done? Please be more explicit.
Medea
He's put another wife in my place.
Aigeus
He had the temerity to do that?
Medea
He certainly did, chucked me over completely.
Aigeus
Infatuated, or to get away from you?
Medea
Must be a great passion to make a man unfaithful.

Aigeus

If he's no good, you're well rid of him.

Medea

But he's married into a royal family.

Aigeus

And what's his name, the father-in-law?

Medea

It's Creon, the king of Corinth here.

Aigeus

No wonder you're worried, in that case.

Medea

Worried? I'm finished. It's exile for me.

Aigeus

By whose command are you being banished?

Medea

Creon, Creon wants to throw me out.

Aigeus

Jason's not stopping him? Worse and worse.

Medea

He pretends he's not pleased, but you can see
He wants me to go. Now I beg you
By your knees, by your beard, have pity on me,
Have pity on me in my great misfortune,
Don't stand and watch me being made destitute,
But give me a refuge in your country
And in your home. I hope, in return,
That you'll have children and die a happy man.
In fact, you don't know how lucky you are,
For I can make sure you have children,
Since I know the medicines you need.

Aigeus

I've several good reasons for saying yes, —
The main one being that it's what god commands.
But also what you said about children,
That weights with me. I'm obsessed about this,
This being childless. You come to my country,
And I'll give you hospitality.

Once in my palace, you shall have asylum;
I'll not surrender you to anyone.
But leave Corinth yourself — I won't take you;
I don't want to offend the people here.

Medea

I'll do that. But I'd like one more thing, —
Will you bind your undertaking with a promise?

Aigeus

Isn't my undertaking good enough?

Medea

Of course, it is. But look at it this way.
There's Pelias's and Creon's families
Against me, people of wealth and influence.
And I am weak. If you were bound by oaths,
You couldn't possibly give me up to them.
But if you just assented, took no oath,
It's possible you might be persuaded. . . .

Aigeus

Oh, I don't mind doing it, if you're set on it.
It'll be an added reason for me to give
Your enemies for not surrendering you.
And you'll feel more secure. What gods do you want?

Medea

Swear to me by the Earth and by the Sun,
And by the whole family of gods.

Aigeus

To do what, or refuse what? Spell it out.

Medea

Never to eject me from your country,
Nor to surrender me to anyone
Who demands my extradition.

Aigeus

I swear by Earth, Sun, and all the gods,
To abide by the terms you have spoken.

Medea

That's it. Now what sanctions if you break it?

Aigeus

The sanctions usual for impious men.

Medea

> That's fine, fine. Go on your way, good luck.
> I'll see you in Athens as soon as I can,
> When I've . . . done what I want to do here first.

Chorus

> May Hermes guide you
> To your home, Aigeus.
> And may you achieve
> All you have set your heart on.
> You've acted like a good man and true.

Medea

> By Zeus, by Justice, by the light of the sun,
> We're on the way, we're on the way, my friends.
> We're going to beat them, going to lick them, lick them.
> That man who's just left, he's giving me
> A harbor just where I wanted it.
> A home for me in Athens, — now my plans
> Have a secure place to anchor in.
> It's time I told you all I have in mind;
> You listen, and remember I'm not joking.
>
> I'll send one of my servants to Jason,
> And ask him to come and see me.
> And when he comes, I'll speak him soft words, —
> Say I agree with him about his marriage,
> Say I approve and I'm glad he thought of it.
> I'll ask him to let the kids stay on,
> Not so they can be a laughingstock
> But so I can use them to kill the bride.
> I'll send them carrying in their little hands
> Some gifts for the bride, thank-you presents
> For being allowed to stay, a gold tiara
> And a nice dress. Just let her put them on,
> And she'll die horribly; so will anyone
> Who touches her. Such poisons I've put on them.
> I don't like what I must do then;
> I'm going to kill the children, my children.
> And don't try to change my mind — you can't.

What havoc in Jason's family then!
Next, leave the country — can't stay on and face
The consequences of murdering my children.
I love my children. . . . it is dreadful, dreadful
What I will do to them. But what else
Will teach these people that I won't be laughed at?
    What's stopping me? I've nothing to live for;
No home, country, or anywhere where I
Can forget my troubles. . . . my big mistake
Was leaving my family to follow
A smooth-tongued foreigner . . . but I'll pay him back,
He won't see his children by me again,
And he won't have any children by his bride
Because she's going to die of my poisons —
A nasty death for a nasty little girl.
Nobody shoves me around, understand.
I won't be treated as a nonentity.
I am a person, someone to reckon with;
A good friend, and a good hater; these are
The characteristics that make people famous.

Chorus

Since I am privileged to know your plans,
I'd like to speak as one who wishes you well, —
It's against human nature, don't do it.

Medea

There's no way round it. Oh, I don't blame you —
You haven't suffered like I have, have you?

Chorus

I don't believe it — kill your own children?

Medea

I will. Just imagine Jason's face.

Chorus

And just imagine what you'll feel like.

Medea

What's stopping me? This talk is wasting time.
You, off to Jason and ask him to come.
I know I can trust you not to speak;

You're a woman like me, a loyal servant too.
Chorus
Athens, always a happy city,
Her kings descended from the gods,
Her land sacred, unravaged by hostile affray,
Her people drinking knowledge, walking
Serenely, where the light of day
Is brightest in the world.

Athens, where the nine Pierian Muses
Were born, where Aphrodite
Draws fertile water from Cephisus stream
And sends a breath of sweet breezes over the fields.

And her sons, the Loves,
That dwell with Wisdom,
That work all kinds of goodness,
Run her errands over the land, while she wreathes
A fragrant crown of roses for her hair.

How can such a land, such a city
Give refuge to a murderess, a killer
Of her own children, an infanticide?
Don't kill them, I beg you, don't.
Could any woman have
The hardihood? Their blood
On her hands, their cries
For mercy. . . . When she looks
At them, she won't dare.
Jason
You asked for me; I come. However much
You hate me, I'm still very much your servant.
What do you want now? I am all attention.
Medea
Oh Jason, Jason, can you ever forgive me
For what I said to you? You've shown me
So much kindness, how can I ask you
To bear with my bad temper too?
When you'd gone away, I began thinking

And realized just how wrong I'd been.
You are a silly fool (I said to myself)
Antagonizing those who are trying to help you.
Your husband's doing his very best for you,
Seeing to it that your children will have brothers
In the royal family. You and your children
Are going into exile; you'll need help.
Isn't it obvious you must stop being angry,
And accept the benefits that are being offered?
You've nothing to gain by being obstinate
And alienating your husband and the king.
So now I think you're right; I was mad.
I ought to support you in your plans,
Applaud your marriage and encourage it.
However, — you know what women are like.
I rely on you not to behave like that;
You won't act childishly just because I have.
There now, I admit I was wrong,
And I believe you've acted for the best.
    Children, children, come out here, will you?
Your daddy's here; say hello to him
With me. We're all friends again now.
Take his hand, that's right . . . Oh, for a moment
I was reminded of — forget about it.
Oh children, shall I see you, in the long days ahead,
Stretching out your hands just like that?
Silly old me, I'm still nervous
And liable to burst into tears at nothing —
Must be the aftereffects of our quarrel.

Chorus

The tears are running down my cheeks as well.
I pray that now we won't have any more trouble.

Jason

Bravo, you're not afraid to change your mind.
Don't worry about the past, — I don't blame you,
The female mind is easily upset.
But recognizing what's right, upon reflection, —

It takes a sensible woman to do that.
And, children, daddy's going to look after you.
I'm sure we'll see you with your new brothers,
Among the flower of the land. Just keep on
Growing up like you are; leave the rest
To me. I tell you what, I see you already
As fine young men, ruling the roost here,
And striking terror into my enemies.
      Hullo, what's the matter with you, there?
Don't try to look away; I can see.
Why on earth aren't you happy with what I'm saying?

Medea

Nothing. Only thinking about the children.

Jason

Well then, cheer up. I'll see that they're all right.

Medea

Cheer up, yes I will. I believe you.
It's just that, being a woman, I have to cry.

Jason

Must you go on? No need to cry about them.

Medea

I gave them birth. When you spoke about their future,
I wondered . . . wondered if it could be true.
      Now let's get down to business; the king
Wants me to quit the country, and I agree
That I mustn't stay here and embarrass him.
So I'll be off; but what about the children?
Can't you ask Creon to let them stay?
If they don't stay, how can you look after them?

Jason

I don't know if he'll allow it; I can try.

Medea

I know, get your new wife to ask him.

Jason

Good idea, I think she could persuade him.

Medea

Of course, she can, if she's at all a woman.

And I can help. I'll send her lovely presents,
Some really lovely things, a gossamer dress
And a gold tiara. The children will take them.
One of you servants, bring my gifts out here.
Won't she be pleased, first getting married to you
And then receiving these gifts, costumes that
My grandfather handed down as heirlooms.
      Now, children, take these presents carefully
And give them to the bride, the lucky bride.

Jason

Now, please, this is pointless; you can't afford it.
Keep these things for yourself; you're going to need them.
It's not as though the royal palace is short
Of clothes and gold trinkets. And I'm sure
She'd prefer to do it simply for my sake.

Medea

I must insist. There's something very persuasive
About a gift; the proverb says that even
The gods can't say no to a gift.
They're more persuasive than words. Why, good heavens,
It isn't much to give to help my children:
A bit of gold, — I'd give my life if necessary.
All right then, children, go to the big, rich house
And ask to see your father's new wife,
My mistress; ask her nicely to let you stay.
And give her the gifts, and (remember)
Make sure that she takes them herself.
      Well, skip along then. I shall count on you
To come back with good news for your mother.

Chorus

I've given up hope for the children's lives;
They're walking to their doom,
With death as a gift for the bride, and she'll accept it.
She'll put hell's regalia on her head.

The beauty of the garments will woo her to the dark,
And she'll be dressed as a bride among the lifeless ones.
The heiress-hunter, all unknowing,

Has brought death to his bride and his sons.

I'm sorry too for the mother who is going
To kill her children. All
Because she was wrongly repudiated, all
Because her husband lives with another woman.

Pedagogue
Madam, the children have been excused from exile.
And the princess was delighted with your presents.
It looks as though they've nothing against the children.
Hey.
Why do you stand like that? Thought you'd be pleased.

Medea
Damn.

Pedagogue
I wonder if you heard me correctly.

Medea
Damn, damn.

Pedagogue
What have I said? Thought it was good news.

Medea
I heard what you said. Don't get upset.

Pedagogue
Can't see why you're depressed, why you're crying.

Medea
Old fellow, there are plenty of reasons.
It's god's will, and my personality.

Pedagogue
Oh cheer up. You'll see our children again.

Medea
And when I see them, what will they be like?

Pedagogue
You're not the first woman to lose her children.
We must all learn to bear our troubles lightly.

Medea
You're right there. Look, isn't it time you went
Indoors to look after the children's food?
     Oh, children, this is the parting of the ways.

You have a home still and a country, where
You'll live your lives out with no mother by you.
While I must go away, to a strange land,
And never see you grown up, never see you
Enjoying your prime, marrying —
When they raise the bridal torches at your weddings,
The flames will not show your mother's face.
Oh, I could be happy if I had no spirit.
So it was all for nothing that I brought you up,
My children, all for nothing that I've slaved
And undergone the pangs of childbirth for you.
There was a time when I would dream about you
Looking after me when I was old
And being at my bedside when I died.
Those were pleasant thoughts, — all finished now.
Since I must leave you and live in misery
And you'll be . . . in a different sphere of life . . .
And never set eyes on mummy again.
Don't look at me like that please, please don't smile,
Don't smile at me.
Oh, what can I do? I haven't the courage.
I can't do it. I've changed my mind.
I'll take them away with me instead.
It's their faces, — I can't hurt myself
As much as this, just to punish Jason.
I've changed my mind, definitely changed my mind.
    What's the matter with me? My persecutors
Will laugh at me for not hitting back.
I'll get on with the job. Silly scruples!
Run along into the house, children.
Don't do it. Leave them alone, leave them alone.
They'll be company, company for me in exile.
    Shall I let my enemies humiliate them?
There's no escaping it; it must be done.
I've gone too far already; the princess
Has put my things on and will be dead by now.
So I must travel on, on a hard, hard road,

And send these off on a yet harder road.
Children, out here a moment. Give us your hands,
Give us your hands to kiss. Dear little hands,
Dear little heads, dear little handsome faces,
God bless you, in the place where you're going.
Your father's lost you your opportunities here.
What soft skin you have, children, how sweet
Your breath is, how I love
The way you push against me. Go away,
Into the house; I can't bear looking at you.
I'll take them away with me instead.
It's too much: I know what I'm doing,
I know it's wrong; but my resentment is
Too strong for anything else. In life, the worst
Disasters come from passions like this of mine.

Chorus

Be childless, childless, if you want
The best chance of happiness.
Children are sweet as the buds in spring,
But I've noticed that those who have them
Have nothing but trouble all their lives.

Trouble to bring them up well, trouble
To leave them a decent fortune when you die.
And after all your trouble, you still don't know
Good or evil, which way their characters will go.

Even supposing all these turn out well —
They are reared, provided for, and their natures are good,
Death comes at any time and sweeps them away to hell.

Medea

I'm waiting. Any moment I expect
To hear how things have gone for me at the palace.
Ah, here comes one of Jason's servants now.
He's blown; I reckon he has a story of horror.

Messenger

You've got a nerve. Still here, after what you've done?
Get into the fastest carriage you've got

And get out, get out quick. Don't hang around —
Medea

Oh yet? And why the need for this hasty exit?
Messenger

The king's daughter's dead; and Creon too.
And it's your poisons that have killed them both.
Medea

Great news! The very best news possible.
And you, sir, count yourself my friend for life.
Messenger

Well, you're a crazy one all right, you are.
You've killed two people of the royal family
And stand there giggling. Aren't you afraid?
Medea

My dear friend, I won't bother to argue.
Don't fret yourself. Relax, and let us have it —
The full story, exactly how they died.
Don't spare the details, — the more horrible the better.
Messenger

We were so happy, all us servants were,
Following with the children and their father
To the palace, because the word had got about
That you and Jason had got reconciled.
We were so pleased, we kissed the kiddies' hands
And their curly heads, for joy.
Now when the princess saw us coming along,
You could see her face light up when she saw Jason,
But when she noticed the children, she turned away
And made a face, — obviously annoyed.
But your husband said "Don't be angry with them.
I love them, so you should love them too.
Look, they're bringing gifts; please accept them,
And ask your father to excuse them from exile.
They're only little children, after all;
Will you do that for them, for my sake?"
     Soon as she saw the clothes, she couldn't resist them,
So she agreed to everything Jason said.

The moment Jason and the kids had left,
She couldn't wait to put the finery on;
She puts your dress on and the gold tiara,
And starts fixing her hair in a mirror
Goggling and grinning away at her reflection.
Now when she reckoned that she'd got it right,
She starts off through the palace to show herself,
Mincing along, thoroughly pleased with herself
And looking down all the time to check
The way the dress hung. And then it happened, —
She turned pale and ran back, shaking,
And only just got to her chair before she fell.
Her skin was white, her eyeballs stuck out,
And there was froth on her mouth. One of her servants,
An old woman, thought she was having a fit
And screamed. That started it. All the rest
Began screaming too. And, besides the screams,
The house banged like a drum to their footsteps,
As they ran, one to the king, another to
The bridegroom, to tell them what had happened.
The girl sat quiet with her eyes half closed
For a minute; but then she jumped up yelling.
That gold tiara (crazy as it may seem)
Had burst into flames, and the dress
Of muslin was eating into her flesh
Like acid. She ran up and down
Trying to shake the tiara off her head,
But it stuck all the more. And of course
The flames got bigger, with her shaking her head.
In the end she fell to the ground, unrecognizable
To anyone except her own father.
Talk about the pretty face she once had, —
You couldn't even see where her eyes were.
The marrow ran from her bones like the sap
You see coming out of a log on the fire.
It was a horrible sight. We daren't touch
The corpse; not after seeing what we'd seen.

Then in came her father. First thing he sees
Is the corpse; he cries out and bends down
And embraces and kisses it and says
"Oh no, my poor girl, who's done this?
What happened, what god have I offended?
This makes me childless now, an old man.
Oh god, why can't I die with you, my child?"
And then he tried to get up, but found
His body was stuck fast to the corpse
Like ivy to a laurel-tree. It was awful
To watch him keep trying to raise himself.
The more force he used, the more he tore
His flesh from the bones. So in the end
He gave up trying and died, — couldn't fight any more.
And so they lie together, two corpses,
A young girl and her father, — a terrible sight.
    And as for you, I'd rather not speak.
You'll know what to do, if you've any sense.
This all agrees with what I think about life —
That happiness is a shadow, — just a shadow.
Some men may be more fortunate than others
As chance has it; but no one's happy — no one.

Chorus
A bad day for Jason, and he deserves it,
But I'm very sorry for Creon's daughter;
She suffered because she married Jason.

Medea
My friends, I've decided what to do.
I must get a move on, kill the children, and quit
The country as soon as I possibly can.
If I dither around, I merely leave them
For someone else, some enemy, to kill.
They're bound to die; so it is only right
That she who gave them life should take it away.
All right, get on with it, get on with it.
It's got to be done, — do it without flinching.
Whatever I do, my life will be unhappy.

I'll armor my heart with callousness,
And take the sword in my hand, — try to forget
That they are my children and that I love them.
I only need forget for a short time,
And then I can remember all my life.

[*Leaves.*]

Chorus

Oh Sun, you can see
Everything, see what Medea is doing,
And stop her. She is your descendant,
So the curse of murder will be on your family.
All her labor for her children — in vain.
All the long toil of birth — gone to waste.
All the love she lavished — thrown away.
What anger she must feel, to make her kill.

[*Indoors, the children scream.*]

The children! The devil, she's doing it.

First Child

Help, what can I do? She's going to catch me.

Second Child

I can't help you, brother. We're going to be killed.

Chorus

We must rescue them. How to get in?

Child

Oh, rescue us before it's too late.
Any second now the sword'll get us.

Chorus

The woman must be made of steel or stone
To do such a thing.

I know only one woman in history
Who killed her own children. Ino, it was,
Her that was made mad by Hera and sent
Out from her home to wander around the world.
Poor Ino threw herself into the sea,
And her two children with her. That was
Jealousy again. Women's favors
Cause trouble, trouble, trouble all the time.

Jason

    She still here, Medea? . . . You know what she's done.
    You've been standing here, — know where she is?
    Run off, has she? She'd need to be clever
    And hide herself in the earth or fly like a bird
    To escape the vengeance of the royal house.
    But I'm not so concerned about her;
    She'll get her deserts from those she's wronged.
    No, it's my children, — I've come to save them.
    I'm afraid the relatives of those who died
    May want to kill them for what their mother's done.

Chorus

    Oh Jason, you don't know half your troubles;
    Or so I infer from your words.

Jason

    What's that? You mean she wants to kill me?

Chorus

    Your children, they're dead. Medea's killed them.

Jason

    What's that? Impossible. Are you trying to scare me?

Chorus

    You must accept the fact that they're dead.

Jason

    Where are they, indoors or outside?

Chorus

    If you can open the doors, you'll see their bodies.

Jason

    Get these doors open, men, break them open.
    My children are inside, and that woman.

Medea [*Appearing above, in the chariot of the Sun.*]

    For god's sake leave the wretched doors alone.
    If you want to talk to me, talk away.
    But don't come any closer, — this chariot's fast,
    The chariot of the Sun, on one can catch it.

Jason

    You've murdered your own children, you bitch.
    Aren't you ashamed to be alive?

I was made to take you from your savage country
Into civilization, after you'd betrayed
Your father and killed your own brother.
The curse from those crimes has turned on me.
Now you've married me, you've gone and killed
Your children, out of sexual jealousy.
A Greek woman wouldn't have dreamed of it.
You're not a woman, you're an animal.
I'd curse you, but I see you're past cursing;
There's no insult so foul you'd even feel it.
Oh god, I'm unhappy. I've lost my wife,
And lost the children I've watched grow up for years.

Medea

I can't be bothered to reply to you.
I'm satisfied that god knows it all, —
The way you've repaid what I did for you.
Call me what names you like, I don't mind.
There's only one thing that matters to me.
I've got my revenge, got my revenge
On you. You can't sit and enjoy yourself
And laugh over the trick you played me now.
And Creon and his daughter, who banished me,
They've suffered, they've not got away with it either.

Jason

This tragedy affects you as well.

Medea

I don't mind crying, as long as you don't laugh.

Jason

Poor children, what an evil mother you had.

Medea

Poor children, their father's behavior killed them.

Jason

Did I take a sword and murder them?

Medea

Your arrogant behavior was instrumental.

Jason

Let's get it right, you killed them out of jealousy?

Medea

You think it's nothing to a woman, to be rejected?

Jason

A woman can be sensible; but you're mad.

Medea

They're dead, aren't they? You don't like it, do you?

Jason

The guilt of their murder is on your head.

Medea

The gods know who started all the trouble.

Jason

They know one thing, that you're a murderess.

Medea

I hate you, why don't you go away?

Jason

I will, but I'd like one thing first.

Medea

What is it? Perhaps I would permit it.

Jason

Let me have the bodies to lament and bury.

Medea

No! I say no. I'll bury them myself, —
I'll bury them with this hand of mine.
I'll take them to Hera's sacred precinct,
Where no one can desecrate their grave.
And in this land of Corinth, in after time,
There'll be an annual ceremony in remembrance
Of this act of mine; great events
Lodge deep in the memory of men.
I'm off now to be the guest of Aigeus
At his palace in Athens. As for you,
The best thing for you would be to go
And crack your skull on a bit of Argo's wreckage
Then crawl away into a corner and die.

Jason

May the murder curse destroy you.

Medea

                           Hark at you, who's listening

To your words, a liar's words?

Jason

Well spoken, murderess.

Medea

Go home and put your wife to bed.

Jason

I'm going, and the children?

Medea

No wife, no children. Never mind, it's worse when you're older.

Jason

Oh children, how I loved you.

Medea

I loved them, you did not.

Jason

And, loving them, you killed them?

Medea

I did it for your sake.

Jason

I want just to kiss the boys.

Medea

Just found out you like them?
A while ago, you banished them.

Jason

I only want to touch them.

Medea

You want to; and you won't. Because I won't allow it.

Jason

Oh god, is she human? At least I can lament them,
The children that I fathered, to be murdered by you.

Chorus

God in heaven has dominion
Over so many events.
He can frustrate what seems inevitable,
And bring to pass the thing that you least expect.

A Greek Theater of Ideas
by William Arrowsmith

Several years ago I made a plea that scholars and critics should recover a feeling for what I called turbulence in Greek tragedy.[1] By turbulence I meant both "the actual disorder of experience as that experience gets into Greek drama" and "the impact of ideas under dramatic test." What I want to do here is to take up the turbulence of ideas, as I see those ideas expressed by Euripidean drama, with the purpose of showing that the Greeks possessed a theater which we should have no difficulty in recognizing as a genuine theater of ideas. By theater of ideas I do not mean, of course, a theater of intellectual *sententiae* or Shavian "talk" or even the theater of the sophist-poet; I mean a theater of dramatists whose medium of thought was the stage, who used the whole machinery of the theater as a way of *thinking*, critically and constructively, about their world.

In such a theater I assume that the emphasis will be upon ideas rather than character and that a thesis or problem will normally take precedence over development of character or heroism; that aesthetic or formal pleasure will be secondary to intellectual rigor and thought; and that the complexity of ideas presented may require severe formal dislocations or intricate blurrings of emotional modes and genres once kept artistically distinct. It is also likely that the moral texture of an action will be "difficult," and that moral satisfaction will not come easily or even at all; that problems may be left unresolved; that is, that the effect of a play may very well be discomfort or even pain, and that the purpose of this discomfort will be to influence the social rather than the individual behavior of the spectator. Beyond this, I would expect such a theater to be commonly concerned with the diagnosis and dramatization of cultural crisis, and hence that the universe in which the dramatic action takes place would tend to be either irrational or incomprehensible. All of these characteristics are, of course, abstracted at random from the historical theater of ideas from Hebbel to the present, but in their ensemble they serve to give at least a general sense of the kind of theater of ideas I have in mind.

That such a theater — so specifically modern and anti-traditional a theater — existed among the Greeks is not, I believe, exactly an article of faith among scholars and critics. To be sure, the Greek theater, like any other great theater, made abundant use of ideas, and the Athenians regarded the theater, not as entertainment, but as the supreme instrument of cultural instruction, a democratic *paideia* complete in itself. Aeschylus, for instance, uses ideas with stunning boldness, showing in play after play how the great post-Hesiodic world order could be compellingly and comprehensively adapted to Athenian history and society; and his theater not only provides a great, and new, theodicy, but dramatically creates the evolving idea of Athens as the supreme achievement of the mind of Zeus and the suffering of mankind. As for Sophocles, I am not of those who believe that he, like Henry James, possessed a mind so fine that no idea could violate it. In Oedipus, for instance, we have Sophocles' image of heroic man, shorn of his old Aeschylean confidence in himself and his world, and relentlessly pursuing the terrible new truth of his, and human, destiny. Oedipus looks into the abyss that yawns beneath him — the frightful knowledge of his nature which fifth-century man had learned from the war, the plague and the atrocities, the sophistic revolution and the collapse of the old world-order — and dashes out his eyes at the unbrookable sight. Similarly in Sophocles' Ajax I think we are meant to see a somewhat earlier symbol of the old aristocratic ethos; caught in new and anti-heroic circumstances which degrade him and make him ludicrous, Ajax consistently prefers suicide to a life of absurdity in an alien time.[2] But all this is merely to say that Sophocles, like Aeschylus, uses the perceptions of cultural crisis as framing dramatic ideas or symbolically, not that his theater is in any meaningful sense a theater of ideas. Clearly it is to Euripides — the innovator and experimentalist, the anti-traditional "immoralist" and "stage-sophist" — that we must look for any valid fifth-century theater of ideas.

That the second half of the fifth century B.C. was a period of immense cultural crisis and political convulsion is, fortunately for my purpose here, beyond any real doubt. The evidence itself needs only the barest rehearsal, but it should at least be *there*, the real though sketchy weather of my argument. Let me therefore brush it in.

There is, first of all, the breakdown of the old community, the overwhelming destruction of that mythical and coherent world-order which Werner Jaeger has described so fully in *Paideia*. Political convulsion — stasis and revolution — broke out everywhere. If civil war was nothing new among the Greek city-states, civil war on the fifth-century scale was absolutely unprecedented in its savagery: city against city, man against man, father against son. Under such conditions the whole kinship structure on which the polis was theoretically and constitutionally founded was irretrievably weakened. In culture the sophistic revolution ushered in something like a transvaluation of morals. In society there was the rise of a new bourgeoisie provided with new sanctions and new theories of human nature, as well as a politically conscious proletariat. In the arts restless innovation was the rule, and throughout the Hellenic world — in literature, thought, and politics — there took place a vast debate whose very terms vividly report the schism in the culture, especially in the great argument between *physis* (nature) and *nomos* (custom, tradition, and law). Men begin to wonder now whether the laws of the state and the state itself, once thought divinely established, are any longer related to *physis* at large or to human *physis* in particular. Thus the great experience of the late fifth century is what can be called "the loss of innocence." Sophocles, Euripides, Aristophanes, and Thucydides are all, each in his different way, haunted by the disappearance of the old integrated culture and the heroic image of man that had incarnated that culture. There is a new spirit of divisiveness abroad in the Hellenic world; appearance and reality, nature and tradition, move steadily apart under the destructive pressure of war and its attendant miseries. Subjected to harsh necessity, human nature now shows itself in a new nakedness, but also in a startling new range of behavior, chaotic and uncontrollable. . . .

How did this convulsion of a whole culture affect the idea of a theater as we find that idea expressed by Euripides?

The immediate, salient fact of Euripides' theater is the assumption of a universe devoid of rational order or of an order incomprehensible to men. And the influence of Aristotle is nowhere more obvious that in the fact that this aspect of Euripides' theater is the one least often recognized or acted upon by critics. Yet it is stated both explicitly and implicitly from play to play throughout Euripides' lifetime. "The care of god for us is a great thing," says the chorus of Hippolytus, "if a man believe it. . . . So I have a secret hope of someone, a god, who is wise and plans; / but my hopes grow dim when I see / the actions of men and their destinies. / For fortune always veers and the currents of life are shifting, / shifting, forever changing course." "O Zeus, what can I say?" cries Talthybius in *Hecuba*. "That you look on men and care? Or do we, holding that the gods exist, / deceive ourselves with unsubstantial dreams / and lies, while random careless chance and change / alone control the world?" Usually desperate, feeble, and skeptical in the first place, it is the fate of these hopes to be destroyed in action. In *Heracles* the fatal chaos of the moral universe is shown formally; a savage reversal which expresses the flaw in the moral universe splits the entire play into two contrasting actions connected only by sequence. Thus the *propter hoc* structure required by Aristotelian drama is in Euripides everywhere annulled by *created* disorder and formal violence. What we get is *dissonance, disparity, rift, peripeteia;* in Euripides a note of firm tonality is almost always the sign of traditional parody; of the false, the unreal, or lost innocence remembered in anguish. What this assumption of disorder means is: first, that form is not organic; second, that character is not destiny, or at best that only a part of it is; and third, that Aristotelian notions of responsibility, tragic flaw, and heroism are not pertinent.

The central dissonance assumes a variety of forms. But the commonest is a carefully constructed clash between myth (or received reality) on the one hand, and fact (or experienced reality) on the other. Λόγῳ μέν . . . ἔργῳ δέ, as the Greeks put it, contrasting theory (*logos*) and fact (*ergon*), appearance (or pretence) and reality, legend and truth. In *Alcestis*, for instance, Euripides juxtaposes the traditional, magnanimous Admetus with the shabby egotist who results when a "heroic" character is translated into realistic fifth-century terms. By making Alcestis take Admetus at his own estimate, Euripides delays the impact of his central idea — the exposure of Admetus' *logos* by his *ergon* — until the appearance of Pheres, whose savage "realistic" denunciation of his son totally exposes the "heroic" Admetus. By a similar translation, Euripides' Odysseus becomes a demagogue of *realpolitik*, Agamemnon a pompous and ineffectual field marshal, and Jason a vulgar adventurer. It was, of course, this technique of realism, this systematic exposure and deflation of traditional heroism, which earned Euripides his reputation for debasing the dignity of the tragic stage. And in some sense the charge is irrefutable. Euripides' whole bent is clearly anti-traditional and realistic; his sense of rebelliousness is expressed beyond doubt by the consistency with which he rejects religious tradition, by his restless experiments with new forms and new music, and by his obvious and innocent delight in his own virtuosity — his superior psychology and his naturalistic stagecraft. With justifiable pride he might have seen himself as a dramatic pioneer, breaking new ground, and courageously refusing to write the higher parody of his predecessors which his world — and ours — have demanded of him. There must be, I imagine, very few theaters in the world where the man who writes of "people as they are" is automatically judged inferior to the man who writes of "people as they should be."

But it would be wrong to assume that realism was the whole story or that Euripides was drawn to realism because he knew it would offend the worthies of his day. For it was life, not Euripides, which had abandoned the traditional forms and the traditional heroism. What Euripides reported, with great clarity and honesty, was the widening gulf between reality and tradition; between the operative and the professed values of his culture; between fact and myth; between *nomos* and *physis*; between life and art. That gulf was the greatest and most evident reality of the last half of the fifth century, *the* dramatic subject par excellence, and it is my belief that the theater of Euripides, like Thucydides' history, is a radical and revolutionary attempt to record, analyze and assess that reality in relation to the new view of human nature which crisis revealed. To both Thucydides and Euripides, the crisis in culture meant that the old world order with its sense of a great humanity and its assumption of an integrated human soul was irrecoverably gone. The true dimensions of the human psyche, newly exposed in the chaos of culture, forbade any return to the old innocence or heroism. Any theater founded on the old psyche or the old idea of fate was to that extent a lie. The task imposed upon the new theater was not merely that of being truthful, of reporting the true dimensions and causes of the crisis, but of coping imaginatively and intellectually with a change in man's very condition.

It is for this reason that Euripides' theater almost always begins with a severe critique of tradition, which necessarily means a critique of his predecessors. Such programmatic criticism is what we expect from any new theater, and in the case of Greek theater, where the dramatist is official *didaskalos*, charged with the *paideia* of his people, it was especially appropriate. Aeschylus and Sophocles were not merely great theatrical predecessors; they were the moral tutors of Athens and their versions of the myths embodied, as nothing else did, the values of tradition and the old *paideia*. Given such authority and power, polemic and criticism were only to be expected, the only possible response; indeed, were it not for the fact that Euripides' criticism has generally been construed as cultural *lèse-majesté*, the point would hardly be worth making. When Shakespeare or Ibsen or Shaw or Brecht criticizes the theater of his immediate predecessors, we applaud; this is what we expect, the aggressive courage a new theater requires. When Euripides does it, it becomes somehow sacrilege, a crime against the classics. We respond, if at all, with outraged traditionalism, automatically invoking that double standard which we seem to reserve for the classics, that apparent homage which turns out to be nothing but respect for our own prejudices. . . .

The point here, I believe, is both important and neglected. Let me try to restate it. Euripides' favorite technique for demonstrating the new dissonance in Athenian culture, the disparity between putative values and real values, is simply realism of the pattern λόγῳ μέν . . . ἔργῳ δέ. But it is balanced at times by the converse technique — allowing the myth to criticize the everyday reality — ἔργῳ μέν . . . λόγῳ δέ. And these exceptions are important, since they show us that Euripides' realism is not a matter of simple anti-traditionalism, but consistent dramatic technique. What is basic is the mutual criticism, the mutual exposure that occurs when the incongruities of a given culture — its actual behavior and its myth — are juxtaposed in their fullness. That this is everywhere the purpose of Euripidean drama is clear in the very complaints critics bring against the plays: their tendency to fall into inconsistent or opposed parts (*Heracles, Andromache*); their apparent multidimensionality (*Alcestis, Heracles*), the frequency of the *deus ex machina*. This last device is commonly explained by a hostile criticism as Euripides' penchant for archaism and aetiology, or as his way of salvaging botched plays. Actually it is *always* functional, a part of the very pattern of juxtaposed incongruities which I have been describing. Thus the appearance of any god in a Euripidean play is invariably the sign of *logos* making its epiphany, counterpointing *ergon*. Most Euripidean gods appear only in order to incriminate themselves (or a fellow god), though some — like Athena in the *Iphigenia in Tauris* — criticize the action and the reality which the action mirrors. But it is a variable, not a fixed, pattern, whose purpose is the critical counterpointing of the elements which Euripides saw everywhere sharply and significantly opposed in his own culture: myth confronted by behavior, tradition exposed by, or exposing, reality; custom and law in conflict with nature. What chiefly interested him was less the indictment of tradition, though that was clearly essential, than the *confrontation*, the *dramatic juxtaposition*, of the split in his culture. This was his basic theatrical perception, *his* reality, a perception which makes him utterly different from Aeschylus and Sophocles, just as it completely alters the nature of his theater.

Is that theater merely analytical then, a dramatic description of a divided culture? I think not. Consider this statement: "As our knowledge becomes increasingly divorced from real life, our culture no longer contains ourselves (or only contains an insignificant part of ourselves) and forms a social context in which we are not 'integrated.' The problem thus becomes that of again reconciling our culture with our life, by making our culture a living culture once more. . . ." That happens to be Ionesco on Artaud, but it could just as well be Euripides' description of the nature and purpose of his own theater. The reconciliation of life and culture is, of course, more than any theater, let alone a single dramatist, can accomplish; and it is perhaps enough that the art of a divided culture should be diagnostic, should describe the new situation in its complexity. Only by so doing can it redefine man's altered fate. It is my own conviction that Euripidean theater is critical and diagnostic, and that, beyond this, it accepts the old artistic burden of constructive order, does not restrict itself to analysis alone. But what concerns me at the moment is the way in which his basic theatrical perceptions altered his theater.

First and most significant after the destruction of *propter hoc* structure is the disappearance of the hero. With the sole exception of *Heracles* — Euripides' one attempt to define a new heroism — there is no play which is dominated by the single hero, as is Sophocles' *Oedipus* or *Ajax*.

Corresponding to the disappearance of the hero is Euripides' "fragmentation" of the major characters. What we get is typically an agon or contest divided between two paired characters (sometimes there are three): Admetus and Alcestis; Jason and Medea; Hippolytus and Phaedra; Andromache and Hermione; Pentheus and Dionysus, etc. In such a theater, the Aristotelian search for a tragic hero is, of course, meaningless. But the significance of the fragmentation is not easy to assess; it is not enough to say merely that Euripides was temperamentally drawn to such conflicts because they afforded him opportunities for psychological analysis. What is striking about the consistently paired antagonists one finds in Euripides is, I think, their obsessional nature. They function like obsessional fragments of a whole human soul; Hippolytus as chastity, Phaedra as sexuality. The wholeness of the old hero is now represented divisively, diffused over several characters; the paired antagonists of the Euripidean stage thus represent both the warring modes of a divided culture and the new incompleteness of the human psyche. Alternatively, as in the *Bacchae*, they embody the principles of conflicting ideas: Pentheus as *nomos*, Dionysus as *physis*.

This fragmentation is also the sign of a new psychological interest. That the convulsion of the late fifth century had revealed new dimensions in the human psyche is sharply expressed by Thucydides, and just as sharply by Euripides. Indeed, Euripides' interest in abnormality and mental derangement is so marked that critics have usually seen it as the very motive of his drama. This, I think, is a mistake. The interest in psychology is strong, but it is always secondary; the real interest lies in the analysis of culture and relationship between culture and the individual. If I am correct in assuming that Euripides' crucial dramatic device is the juxtaposition and contrast of *logos* and *ergon*, then it follows that the characters of his plays must bear the burden of the cultural disparity involved. I mean: if a myth is bodily transplanted from its native culture to a different one, then the characters of the myth must bear the burden of the transplantation, and that burden is psychological strain. Consider, for example, Euripides' Orestes, a man who murders his mother in an Argos where civil justice already exists; or the heroic Jason translated into the context of a fifth-century Corinth; or an Odysseus or Hermione or Electra cut off from the culture in which their actions were once meaningful or moral, and set in an alien time which *immoralizes* or *distorts* them. The very strain that Euripides succeeds in imposing upon his characters is the mark of their modernity, their involvement in a culture under similar strain. And it is the previously unsuspected range of the human psyche, the discovery of its powers, its vulnerability to circumstance, its incompleteness, and its violence, that interest Euripides, not the psychological process itself. The soliloquy in which Medea meditates the murder of her children is much admired; but Euripides' dramatic interest is in the collapse or derangement of culture — the gap between *eros* and *sophia* — that makes the murder both possible and necessary.

Side by side with cultural strain is the striking loneliness of

the Euripidean theater. Loneliness is, of course, a feature of traditional tragedy, but the difference between Euripides and his predecessors in this respect is marked. In Aeschylus the loneliness of
human fate if effectively annulled by the reconciliation which
closes trilogies and creates a new community in which god and
man become joint partners in civilization. In Sophocles the sense
of loneliness is extremely strong, but it is always the dis-
tinguishing mark of the hero, the sign of the fate which makes
him an outcast, exiled from the world to the world's advantage
and his own anguish. But in Euripides loneliness is the common
fate. Insofar as the characters are fragmented and obsessional,
their loneliness is required. The one thing they normally cannot
do is communicate, and typically, even such communications as
occur (for instance, Heracles' moving reunion with his children)
are liable to almost certain destruction by the malevolence of
fate. Again and again Euripides gives us those exquisite, painterly
groupings which stress the impassable gulf which separates the
old from the young, man from god, woman from man, and even
hero from hero. The climax of the *Heracles* comes when Heracles, touched by Theseus' *philia*, makes his great decision to
live; but the understanding is then immediately and deliberately
clouded as Theseus fails to understand the enormous range of his
friend's new heroism. The touch is typically and revealingly Euripidean. The gulf seems to close only to widen out again.

From the point of view of traditional tragedy nothing is more
strikingly novel than the Euripidean fusion and contrast of comic
and tragic effects. Thus at any point in a tragedy the comic, or
more accurately, the pathetic or ludicrous, can erupt with poig-
nant effect, intensifying the tragic or toughening it with parody.
Nor is this a device restricted to Euripides' so-called "romantic"
plays or his tragicomedies; it occurs even in the most powerful
and serious tragedies. Tiresias and Cadmus in the *Bacchae*, for instance, are seen simultaneously as tragic and comic, that is, directly pathetic and incongruous: two old mummers of ecstasy;
they try to dance for Dionysus as the god requires, but their bodies, like their minds, are incapable of expressing devotion except
as a ludicrous mimicry. Aegeus, in *Medea*, has puzzled traditional

interpretation from Aristotle on, precisely because he is Euripides' pathetic and ironic embodiment of Athens — that Athens which the chorus hails later as the place

> where Cypris sailed,
> and mild sweet breezes breathed along her path,
> and on her hair were flung the sweet-smelling garlands
> of flowers of roses by the Lovers, the companions
> of Wisdom, her escort, the helpers of men
> in every kind of *arete*.

The irony is not, of course, the cutting irony of exposure, but the gentler irony that comes when *logos* and *ergon* of things not too far apart are juxtaposed: we feel it as a light dissonance. Which is merely another way of saying that the new element of the comic in Euripidean tragedy is just one more instance of the dramatist's insistence upon preserving the multiplicity of possible realities in the texture of his action. In the traditional drama, such dissonance is rightly avoided as an offence against seriousness and tragic dignity; Euripides significantly sees both tragedy and comedy as equally valid, equally necessary. A drama of truth will contrive to contain them both; the complex truth requires it.

It is for this same reason that Euripides accentuates what might be called the multiple moral dimension of his characters. Every one of them is in some sense an exhibit of the sophistic perception that human character is altered by suffering or exemption from suffering; that every human disposition contains the possibilities of the species for good or evil. Aristotle objects, for instance, that Euripides' Iphigenia changes character without explanation. And so, in fact, she does, and so does Alcmene in *Heraclidae*. They change in this way because their function is not that of rounded characters or "heroes" but specifications of the shaping ideas of the play. Besides, if Heraclitus was right, and character is destiny, then the complex or even contradictory destiny which Euripidean drama assumes and describes must mean complex and contradictory characters. But the one kind of character which Euripides' theater cannot afford is that splendid integrated self-knowledge represented by the "old fantastical Duke of dark corners" in *Measure for Measure*; Euripides' theater is all Angelos, Lucios, and Claudios — average, maimed, irresolute, incomplete human nature. The case of Heracles himself, the most integrated hero Euripides ever created, is darkened by Euripides' insistence that we observe, without passing judgment, that even the culture-hero has murder in his heart. This fact does not, of course, compose a tragic flaw, but rather what Nietzsche called "the indispensable dark spring" of action. Moral judgment is, as Euripides tried to show, no less precarious and difficult than the comprehensive description of reality. How could it be otherwise?

This does not mean that Euripides avoids judgment or that his plays are attempts to put the problematic in the place of dramatic resolution. It means merely that his theater everywhere insists upon scrupulous and detailed recreation of the complexity of reality and the difficulty of moral judgment. The truth is concealed, but not impenetrably concealed. There can be little doubt, for instance, that Euripides meant his *Medea* to end in a way which must have shocked his contemporaries and which still shocks today. His purpose was, of course, not merely to shock, but to force the audience to the recognition that Medea, mortally hurt in her *eros*, her defining and enabling human passion, must act as she does, and that her action has behind it, like the sun, the power of sacred *physis*. There is no more savage moral oxymoron in Greek drama. But if Euripides here speaks up for *physis* against a corrupt *nomos*, he is capable elsewhere of defending *nomos* and insisting that those who prostrate themselves before *physis*, like the Old Nurse in Hippolytus, are the enemies of humanity. Necessity requires submission, but any necessity that requires a man to sacrifice the morality that makes him human, must be resisted to the end, even if it cost him — as it will — his life. Better death than the mutilation of his specifically human skill, that *sophia* which in Euripides is mankind's claim to be superior to the gods and necessity. Only man in this theater makes morality; it is this conviction, the bedrock classical conviction, that provides the one unmistakable and fixed reference point in Euripides' dramatic world. Above that point all truths are purposely played off against one another in endless and detailed exactness of observation.

Within this new context of changed reality, Euripides' whole theater of ideas is set. . . .

Finally, consider the *Medea*. Traditionally classified as psychological tragedy, it is better interpreted as a genuine drama of ideas. Superficially it is a critique of relations between men and women, Greeks and barbarians, and of an *ethos* of hard, prudential self-interest as against passionate love. At a profounder level it is a comprehensive critique of the quality and state of contemporary culture. Like the *Bacchae*, Euripides' other great critique of culture, the *Medea* is based upon a central key term, *sophia*. Inadequately translated "wisdom," *sophia* is an extremely complex term, including Jason's cool self-interest, the magical and erotic skills of the sorceress Medea, and that ideal Athenian fusion of moral and artistic skills which, fostered by *eros*, creates the distinctive *arete* of the civilized polis. This third sense of *sophia* — nearly synonymous with "civilization" and specifically including the compassion[3] for the suppliant and the oppressed for which Athens was famous and which Aegeus significantly shows to Medea — is the standard by which the actions of Jason and Medea are to be judged. Thus the vivid harmony of *eros* and *sophia* which Athens represents is precisely what Jason and Medea are not. Jason's calculating, practical *sophia* is, lacking *eros*, selfish and destructive; Medea's consuming *eros* and psychological *sophia* (an emotional cunning which makes her a supreme artist of revenge) is, without compassion, maimed and destructive. They are both destroyers, destroyers of themselves, of others, of *sophia*, and the polis.[4] And it is this *destructiveness* above all else which Euripides wants his audience to observe: the spirit of brutal self-interest and passionate revenge which threatens both life and culture, and which is purposely set in sharp contrast to life-enhancing Athens where the arts flourish, were *eros* collaborates with *sophia*, and where creative *physis* is gentled by just *nomoi*. Behind Jason and Medea we are clearly meant to see that spreading spirit of expedience and revenge which, unchecked by culture or religion, finally brought about the Peloponnesian War and its attendant atrocities. For it cannot be mere coincidence that a play like this was performed in the first year of the war.

What of Medea herself? Upon our understanding of her depends the final interpretation of the play. Thus those who find in Medea a barbarian woman whose lack of self-control, hunger for revenge, and male courage set her in firm contrast to the Corinthian women of the chorus, with their Greek praise of *sophrosune* and their fear of excess, usually see the play as a psychological tragedy of revenge. Against this interpretation there are decisive arguments. For one thing, Euripides takes pains to show that Medea is not at all pure barbarian femininity, but rather a barbarian woman who has been partially and imperfectly Hellenized. Thus Medea's first appearance is an intentionally striking one, dominated by her attempt to pass for Greek, to say the right thing; she talks, in fact, the stock language of Greek women, *hesuchia* and *sophrosune*. Now this may be a pose, but it may just as well be genuine cultural imitation, the sort of thing a barbarian woman in Corinth might be expected to do. But the point is important for, if I am right, this play records the loss of the civilized skills through the conflict of passion; and for this reason Euripides first shows us his Medea making use of those civilized virtues which, in the throes of passion, she promptly loses, reverting to barbarism. Euripides' point is not that Medea *qua* barbarian is different in nature from Greek women, but that her inhibitions are weaker and her passions correspondingly nearer the surface. Thus she can very quickly be reduced to her essential *physis*, and it is this nakedness of *physis*, shorn of all cultural overlay, that Euripides wants displayed. Unimpeded *eros* (or unimpeded hatred) can be shown in Medea with a concentration and naturalness impossible in a Greek woman, not because Greek women were less passionate, but because their culture required them to repress their passions. If culture is truly effective, the control of passion eventually becomes true self-mastery (*sophrosune*); where culture is less effective or out of joint (as in the Corinth of this play), *physis* is checked only by fear, and reveals itself in resentment of the punishing authorities and ready sympathy with those who rebel against them. Hence the profound resentment which the chorus in this play feels against male domination. This — and not mere theatrical convention or necessity — is why Medea can so easily convince the chorus to become her accomplices in her "crusade" against Jason and male society. Their control over their passions, while greater than Medea's perhaps, is still inadequate and precarious (as their bitter resentment of men makes clear); and Medea's revenge arouses their fullest sympathy, just as war evokes the barbarian in an imperfectly civilized man. And this is Euripides' point, that "one touch of nature" makes kin of Hellene and barbarian. In Medea's barbarism we have a concentrated image of human *physis* and a symbol of the terrible closeness of all human nature to barbarism. In her inadequate *sophrosunē* and her imperfect *sophia* is represented the norm of Hellenic, and most human, society. Thus when Jason cries out, "No Greek woman would have dared this crime," we are meant, not to agree, but to wonder and doubt, and finally to disbelieve him.

The validity of that doubt and disbelief is immediately confirmed by the appearance of the golden chariot of the Sun in which Medea makes her escape to Athens. In this chariot Euripides does two related things: first restates, vividly and unmistakably, the triumph of Medea over Jason, and secondly he provides the whole action with a symbolic and cosmological framework which forces the private agon of Jason and Medea to assume a larger public significance. And by showing Medea, murderess and infanticide, as rescued by the Sun himself — traditionally regarded as the epitome of purity, the unstained god who will not look upon pollution — he drives home his meaning with the shock of near sacrilege. As for the chariot of the Sun, it is the visible cosmic force which blazes through Medea's motives and which her whole *pathos* expresses: the blinding force of life itself, stripped of any mediating morality or humanizing screen; naked, unimpeded, elemental *eros*; intense, chaotic, and cruel; the primitive, premoral, precultural condition of man and the world. If that force vindicates Medea as against Jason, her ardor as against his icy self-interest, it is only because her *eros* is elemental and therefore invincible. But she is vindicated only vis-à-vis Jason; and she is not *justified* at all. Of justification there can be no question here, not only because *eros* is, like any elemental necessity, amoral and therefore unjustifiable, but also because Euripides clearly believes the loss of *sophia* to be a tragic defeat for man and human culture.

In the agon of Jason and Medea, passion, vengeance, and self-interest expel *sophia*. That agon, as we have seen, stands for the Peloponnesian War — the war which Euripides, like Thucydides, feared would expel *sophia* from civilized cities, thereby barbarizing and brutalizing human behavior. At any time, in both individuals and cities, *sophia* is a delicate and precarious virtue; if anywhere in the Hellenic world, *sophia* flourished in Athens, but even there it bloomed precariously (how precariously the plague which overtook the city in the following year proved). And with the coming of Medea to Athens, Euripides seems to imply, comes the spirit of vengeance and passion, endangering *sophia*, that *sophia* whose creation and growth made Athens, in Thucydides' phrase, "the education of Hellas." For Hellas and humanity a new and terrible day dawns at the close of the *Medea*. . . .

In any traditional perspective, Euripidean theater is complex and uncomfortably strange, almost exasperating to a taste founded on Aeschylus and Sophocles. Its premises, as we have seen, are unlike, and almost the inversion of, those of the traditional Greek theater. Typically it likes to conceal the truth beneath strata of irony because this is the look of truth: layered and elusive. For the same reason it presents its typical actions as problems and thereby involves the audience in a new relation, not as worshippers but as jurors who must resolve the problem by decision. But because the problem is usually incapable of outright resolution, is in fact tragic, the audience is compelled to forfeit the only luxury of making a decision — the luxury of *knowing* that one has decided wisely. Something — innocence, comfort, complacency — is always forfeited, or meant to be forfeited, by the audience of jurors. This suggests that the essential anagnorisis of Euripidean theater is not between one actor and another but between the audience and its own experience, as that experience is figured in the plays. Anagnorisis here is knowing moral choice, exercised on a problem which aims at mimicking the quandary of a culture. As such, it is a pattern of the way in which the psyche is made whole again, and the hope of a culture.

1. See "The Criticism of Greek Tragedy," in *The Tulane Drama Review*, III, No. 3 (Spring, 1959), 31 ff.
2. Compare Ajax' situation with Thucydides' statement in the Corcyraean excursus: "The ancient simplicity into which honor so largely entered was laughed down and disappeared."
3. Cf. Euripides' *Electra*, 294-96, where Orestes says: "Compassion is found in men who are *sophoi*, never in brutal and ignorant men. And to have a truly compassionate mind is not without disadvantage to the *sophoi*."
4. Just as Medea and Jason between them destroy Creon and his daughter Glauke, so Medea, once she is domiciled in Athens, will attempt to murder Theseus, the son whom Aegeus so passionately desires — a fact which Athenians could be expected to know and hold against Medea, especially in view of Aegeus' generosity to her. Wherever Medea goes, the polis, as represented by the ruling family, is threatened.

Euripides
THE BAKKHAI

**Translated by
Robert Bagg**

THE BAKKHAI

Characters   *Dionysos*

Chorus of Asian Bakkhai

Leader of the Chorus

Tiresias, a blind prophet

Kadmos, ex-king and founder of Thebes

Pentheus, young king of Thebes

Soldier

Herdsman

Messenger

Agave, daughter of Kadmos, mother of Pentheus

[Before the royal palace at Thebes. Two doors open in the facade;
a great one leads to the royal apartments, a rougher one to a
stable which serves also as a jail. At center stage but near the
main door is an altar and smouldering ruins of a house, both
enclosed by a thick mesh of grapevines. This is Semelê's
tomb. DIONYSOS *enters. He is in his late teens, with curly*
long blond hair and a soft unmuscular body. He wears an ivy
crown, a fawn or leopard skin cloak and carries a thyrsos, *the*
long fennel stalk with ivy braided into its tip. His style is one
of radiant, uncanny calm, but touched with sudden bursts of
excitement and irony which hint at the fury to come.

Dionysos
I'm back! — a god standing on ground
where I was born, in Thebes.
Lightning ripped me
from the pregnant body
of Kadmos' daughter, Semelê.
That blast of flame was my midwife.
I am Dionysos, the son of Zeus.

You see me now at the rivers,
Dirce and Ismenus, but my godhead
you cannot see, because I've changed it
for *this:* the body of a man.
There — by the palace — is my mother's tomb:
the lightning girl.
Those glowing ruins were her house, once.
Now they're proof that the fire of Zeus
never dies down, proof that Hera —
still murderous
toward my mother — still rages
white hot under those ashes.
I'm pleased by what Kadmos has built
for his daughter: this tombsite,
a sacred place no one enters.
I wreathe it myself with clustering
green growing vines.

I first gave joy to the people
far from here, in the golden deserts
of Phrygia and Lydia.
Then I left, circling
over the Persian steppes
where blazing sun beats down,
past Baktrian fortress towns
and the Medes' gale-brewing wastes.
I crossed lucky Arabia
to the salt sea, where I found
a great mix of Levantines and Greeks —
who rub shoulders the length of that swarming
Mediterranean coast, and who pack
towering seaports with the crush of life.
Everywhere on my march here
I taught my holy dances, my mysteries,
and everywhere, the people knew I was god.

From Asia I came on to Thebes,
my first Greek city, to make shrill
barbarian joy flare up in her women.
I bound fawnskin to their bodies,
armed them all with my green fennel wand —
in battle it's an ivied spear.

My purpose is to end the lies
told by Semelê's own sisters,
who had least right to speak them.
They swore to Thebes that Zeus was not
my father, that some man she'd loved
made Semelê pregnant, and that her claim
Zeus fathered her child was a gamble
Kadmos forced her to take —
a blasphemy, her sisters crowed,
which made Zeus in a flash of rage
crush out her life.

Semelê's sisters lied, now they suffer.
My frenzy touched their minds, it drives them

outdoors, to roam the mountains
dressed in my sacred gear,
stupefied by my power.
I've emptied Thebes of her women,
but only her women,
and I control their madness.
They perch high up on the bare rocks,
the well-born and the dirt poor —
a pack that Kadmos' own daughters join
under the blue-green pines.

Like it nor not, this town
must learn to perfection
all my mysteries have to teach.
When the shock of my power
dawns on its people, they will believe:
that my mother was honest
and that I am the god she bore to Zeus.

By now the old king, Kadmos, has given up
his throne and its honors to his grandson:
Pentheus, a young man spoiling
to fight gods, who picks me as the god
he would like most to challenge.
He spills wine offerings to some gods
but excludes *me* from that honor.
Nor does he speak the name
"Dionysos" in his prayers.

Therefore: What happens next
will be my demonstration —
to him and to Thebes — that I was born a god.
When my worship here runs smoothly
I'll move on — to surprise some other
country with my divinity.

Should Thebes turn against me, by sending troops
to sweep my Bakkhai off the mountain — I'll
face their army in battle,
my own maenads raging at my back.

But to make my plans work
I need this human disguise — Thebes
must think I'm a man.

Let's go! my
women who adore me!
After following me across Asia,
down Tmolus, the mountain wall
that guards Lydia, and after sharing
my marches and my rests,
you're part of me!
Give me the drums
Goddess Rhea and I
taught you to beat in Phrygia —
there's the palace: pound the drums!
Hound Pentheus with your booms!
Turn the whole city
out to watch.
         Meanwhile
climbing straight up
Cithaeron's ravines,
I'll overtake my Bakkhai
dancing on the heights —
I'll run them
wild with ecstasy!

[DIONYSOS *runs off. The* CHORUS *enters chanting, shaking tam-
borines, clapping them to a stirring beat. They wear fawnskins, ivy garlands, and carry the long wands of fennel.*]

Chorus

We ran down Tmolus, our holy mountain
and crossed Asia, moving fast
to do sweet work for the God Who Cries Out —
all the labor we give him, he gives back
     as joy! — roared out
in our dances so lightly run
     to Bakkhos!

Who's with us
    out here in the streets?

Who's there
    in the dark house?
Come! All of you! Keep your
mouths quiet and your minds pure.
Hear us sing
    to Dionysos the living god
truths that will never die.

Bless the man, bless his luck,
who learns the mysteries of god:
he lives in sacred joy.

Bless the dancers
who give body and soul to Bakkhos!
We take them
with us into the holy body of god.
Bakkhos will dance
steep mountain joy into our spirits
until we are pure.
We keep Great Mother Kybele's rites —
twisting the ivy into our hair,
lifting the green wand
to Dionysos our god.

Go out
into the hills, Bakkhai! Find him!
Bring home the God Who Cries Out,
down from the Phrygian hills.
Find dancing room for the Zeuschild
through the wide streets of Greece.
Bring the god home whose mother
suffered the lightning's
brutal contractions,
which drove the foetus out of her body —
but Zeus, with a god's quick hand,
opens his own thigh, recovers his son,
then shuts with golden pins
his flesh over Bakkhos.

Hera never saw him, but the Fates did —
the child grew ripe in their care, till Zeus
gave birth to his bull-horned son,
the god, and crowned him with serpents.
From that time to ours
all god-maddened women
wear earthcrawling snakes in their hair.

Thebans,
weave ivy through your hair
for Semelê, whom you raised.
Bright berries and bryony flowers
will burst you all into bloom.
Pick springs from the oak and fir,
tuft your brown skins of fawn
with soft white wool —
these will put you in mind
of Bakkhos.

Guard the violence in your green wand,
respect its holy power.
This land will be dancing
when god runs his pack
out to the mountain, pulling the women
free of their looms,
their minds stung wild
by Bakkhos.

We honor you,
holy island of Crete
where Zeus was born,
we salute you, Kuretes,
who raised him
in your black caves —
there the dancing Korybantes
first stretched
resilient hide over drums
and struck
the tense beat of Bakkhos —

they blew the flute's
sweet piercing voice
to lift and lighten the beat,
then handed on
that beating drum
to Rhea, our goddess mother,
who taught it to carry
the joysongs of maenads —
but raving satyrs
captured the drum,
now it beats through
their orgies, which Dionysos
delights in, every other year.

The mountain goes sweet with Bakkhos!
He's there in the maenad,
his fawnskin's on her body —
out of the running pack
she drops to the earth!
She kills in blood, she devours in joy
the raw flesh of a goat, and is hurled
back to the mountains
of Phrygia and Lydia,
cried on by the Loud God, whose cry
runs through her.

Beneath her the meadow is running with milk
running with wine
running slowly
with the nektar of bees.

And the man turned god!
Turned Bakkhos himself!
holds up the flaming pine
whose smoke
is Syrian incense,
running and wavering
he floats
red sparks and milky smoke behind him,

his great voice
fires the stragglers,
roaring his strength into them —
then shakes his airy curls
in the mountain wind.

His shout thunders over
the maenads' cries
of rising joy:
"Faster, my Bakkhai!
you glitter again
with gold that pours
down our mountain —
dance the god's dances,
pound the god's drum.
Pour glory on him!
The joy in your voices
swells up
through his booming voice —
yell out the wild Phrygian cry!"

Lotus flutes whistle their sweet holy notes,
the running women veer in their flight
to the mountain!
To the mountain!

Waves of joy shake the maenad —
like a colt grazing near its mare
nimble and skittering
she breaks leaping away.

[TIRESIAS *enters, a white-bearded blind prophet in Bakkhic dress. He carries a green wand which he uses to test his way. His voice bellows.*]

Tiresias

Who's in charge of these gates? Find me Kadmos,
Agenor's son! That immigrant from Sidon
who built Thebes her stone battlements.
Tell him Tiresias is waiting. He'll know why.
We're both old men, but we've said

we'll do it — now we will: dress in fawnskins,
tie ourselves green wands of ivy
and crown our heads with its tendrils.

[KADMOS *emerges from the palace. He, too, wears Dionysos'*
ritual garb.]

Kadmos

Dear old friend!
That voice! Even indoors
I knew it was yours: a voice
wise as the man.

               So here I am,
committed to Bakkhos, wearing his gear.
My daughter had a son who's now a god.
We'll do our part to enlarge his power.
Tiresias, you're wise enough to know where
god's people are dancing — instruct me,
one old man to another.

                     We'll go there! —
tossing our heads, making the grey hair fly.
We'll never tire — not if we leap and whirl
all night, then spend the whole next day
drumming the ground with our green wands.
It's pure joy to forget how old I am.

Tiresias

I feel the same — young and ready to dance.

Kadmos

Shall we ride a chariot into the hills?

Tiresias

No! That would not show respect for the god.
We'd better go out there on foot.

Kadmos

Then let me guide you, old man,
I'll lead you like a child.

Tiresias

No, Bakkhos will move us with easy strides.

Kadmos

Who else in Thebes will dance for Bakkhos?

Tiresias
No one else. We're two sane men in a mad city.
Kadmos
Then let's not linger *here!* Take my hand.
Tiresias
You take mine, friend. We're well matched.
Kadmos
I know what I am — a man who must die.
I can't afford to take any god lightly.
Tiresias
You won't hear me asking which gods exist
or cross-examining their actions.
I hold with those hardy traditions
we inherit from our fathers —
their roots go deep, they're old as time.
The wisest man living, though he brings
to bear his keenest logic,
will never break their grip on our lives.

Now this ivy in my hair will shock those
who think old men should act their age.
But Bakkhos has no law which says
that young men must dance and old men can't dance —
this gods excludes no one. He wants honor
from each of us, he wants our joy,
all we can give him.
Kadmos
                    Tiresias, because you're blind,
let *me* be the seer for a change.
                                   I see
Pentheus coming here in a hurry, Echion's boy,
in whose hands I put the power of Thebes.
He looks upset, there must be news.
[PENTHEUS *enters. He, too, is in his late teens, quick and assured
    of mind and body. Friends and servants accompany him. He
    does not notice* TIRESIAS *and* KADMOS *for some time.*]
Pentheus
The crisis broke while I was abroad. Word reached me

that something new and evil is at work here.
It harms our women, who desert their families
to prowl out there in the mountain forests.
They claim possession by Bakkhos, the sudden god —
is he a god? — whom they worship with a lewd
hypnotic dance. Packs of these women
drink wine from brimming bowls, then creep off
to isolated nooks where they give sex
freely to any lusty male who wants them.
They exalt this activity by calling it
a maenad's offering to the new god Bakkhos,
but it's pure Aphrodite they adore.
I have arrested a handful already,
they're tied up now in the public stable
out of harm's way. My next move
will be to track down the women
still out there on the mountain
and drag them back in iron nets.
That should end with dispatch
this outbreak of Bakkhos.

A stranger, they tell me, has slipped into town,
a smooth-talking spellbinder, from Lydia,
with long curly blond hair. And it's *perfumed!*
He's rosy-cheeked, and his bright insinuating eyes
promise our women more of Aphrodite's joy
than they can stand. Day and night he bothers them,
he dangles his rituals and they swarm to him.
But once he's penned in my jail
I'll have his head cut from his body,
his wand will stop its pounding,
his tossing hair will lie still.
This stranger tells us Dionysos is a god,
a "god" that Zeus — supposedly —
carried in his thigh. Here's the truth:
he's a "god" lightning burned up with his mother
as punishment for her great lie —
that she had slept with Zeus.

No matter who this stranger is,
we should hang him for blasphemy.
[PENTHEUS *at last notices* KADMOS *and* TIRESIAS *who have been listening to him with amazement.*]
Now that is a remarkable sight!
      Tiresias,
the master of portents, in a spotted fawnskin.
Grandfather Kadmos — should we all laugh? —
dancing, parading with a wand! It's painful
to watch old men go soft in the head.
Please, Grandfather, take the ivy off.
Drop the wand.
      Tiresias!
All this must be your work.
You promote a new god to our people
in order to get rich — by selling
bird prophecies and prodding the future
from the organs of burning beasts.
If you weren't such a weak old man
I'd lock you in the stable with the Bakkhai
for sponsoring their filthy rituals.
Show me a bowl foaming with wine
among feasting women — and I'll show you proof
nothing's healthy in that festival.

Leader

That's blasphemy! You are sneering at the gods,
Pentheus, and at Kadmos, who sowed the snaketeeth
which shot up into men. Why does Echion's son
want to humiliate his own people?

Tiresias

When a wise man takes hold of a valid case
we expect him to argue well. Now your tongue
is lively, you sound impressive, but something's
missing: intelligence. You talk nonsense.
A man who persuades us because his speech
is poised and aggressive, is a civic
menace when he lacks judgment.

Now the new god you laugh at —
his future power throughout Greece will be vast,
I can't even predict myself how vast.
                                    Young fellow,
mankind is blessed with two supreme natural powers:
Earth power and Liquid power. Demeter,
or Goddess Earth — call her whichever you like —
gave us our dry life-nourishing bread.
Another god then came to complete her good work:
Semelê's child Bakkhos,
who found a vital juice in the grape cluster —
wine! — when men drink their fill, it stops grief
by drowning the day's troubles in sleep.
How else could we ease the ache of living?
What's more, we sprinkle drops of this god
to summon other gods when we need their help.
Always, the good life flows through Bakkhos.
     Now, from this god, the truth of prophecy
speaks — for the ecstasy of maenads and the madman's
delirium are both visionary.
When Bakkhos comes rushing into their bodies
they're raving mad, but what they say comes true.
In wartime, Bakkhos even gives Ares a hand.
Picture an army aligned for battle.
Suddenly it panics, men drop their weapons and run
before a single spear has been thrown.
That swift fever of dread is also Bakkhos.
I promise you, Dionysos will climb Delphi! Someday
you will see him leap and his maenad packs
racing across the high ground between crags,
carrying pine torches and the sacred wand.
O I think Bakkhos will succeed in Greece!
Believe me, Pentheus, don't be so sure
that brute force is what governs human life.
Your mind is riddled with sick fantasies
which you act on as though they made sense.
You would do better to welcome this god.

Open the gates. Pour wine in his honor.
Learn his dances, wear his crown.
As for that point which upsets you
the most — sex: Dionysos will not suppress
lust in a woman: her own character must.
Even at the peak of Bakkhic abandon
a chaste woman remains perfectly chaste.
Now, when the whole city turns out to praise you,
Pentheus, doesn't that lift your spirits?
Try to grasp that this god also loves praise.
Therefore, Kadmos and I, though it makes
you laugh, will put his ivy on and dance.
Pair of old fools? No doubt. But dance we must,
by god we'll dance! I will not cross a god
no matter what arguments you bully me with.
You have a raging brain fever — and no drug
will cure it. But I think something will.

Leader

Tiresias, you are Apollo's prophet,
but he'll agree with you — that Bakkhos
is no less powerful a god.

Kadmos

You listen to Tiresias, son. He's right.
Don't turn your back on our fathers' ways —
stay here with us. Collect your wits — and start
thinking like a king. Suppose it's true
that Bakkhos is no real god —
proclaim him one. It's a fine distinguished lie!
Our Semelê then becomes a god's mother,
a cult will honor her, and her good luck
will shower prestige on our whole family.
Remember how your cousin Actaeon died.
Out there, on those same wooded hillsides,
he told the world he could outhunt Artemis.
His own man-eating hounds ripped him apart.
Something like that might happen to you.
Don't let it.

Here, I'll crown you with ivy.
We'll honor this god of ours together.

Pentheus

Don't touch me with that crown! Go out there,
wallow in Bakkhos yourself. But don't smear
your crazy squalor off on me. Your folly
I will punish at its source: this teacher of yours.
Men, go at once to where this prophet
cuts open birds. Take iron poles and rock
his altar over on its side. Smash it.
Leave his whole operation rubble.
Scatter his holy ribbons
into the teeth of the wind — that will rip
the old prophet where it hurts.
The rest of you patrol the town and drag back
the stranger with a girlish body — the one who
inflames and corrupts all our women.
When you've caught him, lash his hands, lead him here.
I have his sentence ready: we'll stone him
to death. He'll be stunned when he finds out
how we Thebans celebrate Bakkhos.

Tiresias

You crazy fool! You don't know the risk your words take.
Did I say you were mindless? That's wrong.
You're a maniac. Kadmos, pray for this boy.
However savage he is, we'll pray that god
has no evil surprise for Thebes.
Pick up your wand, we'll leave.
We'll travel holding each other up, because
two stumbling old men make a shameful sight.
But we'll accept what comes. Let Bakkhos,
son of Zeus, know we are his slaves.
                                        Kadmos,
Pentheus' name means grief —
take care he doesn't force
that grief on your own flesh and blood.
That's not my prophecy, that's common sense.

When that fool speaks, his folly shouts.
[TIRESIAS *and* KADMOS *leave on the road toward Cithaeron.*
PENTHEUS *goes into the palace.*]
Chorus

>   Lady Holiness, even among gods
>   you are a power,
>   a queen,
>   and the dark beat of your gold wings
>   wheeling
>   sends a chill over the earth.
>
>   Did you hear Pentheus
>   sneer at the Loud One? —
>   his insolence
>   does this to Semelê's child,
>   who, when the Blessed gather to feast,
>   their shoulders in roses,
>   lavender bloom on their hair,
>   see our god
>   for what he is: a Prince!
>   With open hands he gives us
>   mountain dancing, joy
>   that makes us whole,
>   flutes running with laughter,
>   and wine that puts an end
>   to all our troubles, wine
>   flashing, pouring out
>   wherever the gods feast.
>   There the ivy dancers
>   coming to rest, drink sleep
>   from the swirling bowl.
>
>   A reckless mouth and a mad
>   defiant mind
>   ruin a man —
>   but restraint and good sense
>   protect him: though far off
>   in the brilliant sky,

the gods watch us:
cleverness is not wisdom,
nor is the flash of pride
that tempt mankind out of its depth.
Life passes so fast —
knowing that, who would chase
greatness, and lose the sweet life
already in our hands?
Men die on the track
of such glory — but I call
what they do madness.

If only I were there
    on Cyprus
Aphrodite's island,
where little Loves,
    calling
    dance, dance!
distract us all day long.
Take me to the town
    of Paphos
where no rain falls,
but the far-off
barbarian Nile
with its hundred mouths
washes the Paphian shore
until she breeds green life.

Take me to charmed
    Pieria, where
on the foothills of Olympos
    the Muses live.
Take me to the home
    of the Graces,
    to the woods
where Desire runs — there
when you dance, god's in you,
    your voice roars,

it summons him, the God Who
Cries Out! to your joy.
Let's go where the wild dance
is loved, let's go where it's welcome!

Our god delights
in festive good times,
but he loves also
Peace, who makes men rich
and saves the young men's lives.
He gives wine freely
to the powerful, the poor:
its pleasure
drowns all their pain.

But god hates any man
who does not fill his nights
with pleasure, his days with calm.
Watch out
for the arrogant thinker:
he's dangerous,
he never lets up.

I believe only
what common men of plain good sense
believe: anything they do
I will do.

[*Enter* SOLDIER *with bound* DIONYSOS; PENTHEUS *emerges
from palace.*]

Soldier

He's some fierce beast you made us hunt,
Pentheus! We caught him with no trouble.
He went tame on us, wouldn't run,
just held his wrists out — like this.

                                                                     No sign
of fear in that rosy wine-drinker's face.
He smiled as we tied him up,
advising me at every step.
"Lead me to Pentheus," he said.

He made our work very easy.
I was ashamed, and told him, "Stranger,
Pentheus ordered your arrest. Blame him.
I carry out the order, but I don't like it."
There's something else. Those captured madwomen
you chained in the stable — they're free, they're dancing
back up the mountain, chasing Loud Bakkhos, their god.
All the shackles let go of their ankles,
the locked bolts loosened and dropped off the doors
with no blow from any human hand.
That stranger brings so many miracles to Thebes
he overflows with them. Now he's all your worry.

Pentheus

Untie him — let him test our net if he wants.
He's fast — but is he faster than I am?
I don't think so.

[PENTHEUS *silently examines* DIONYSOS.]

Your body's not bad looking, Stranger —
to women, at least. That's the real point,
isn't it, of your trip to Thebes?
Of course it is: look at this wavy hair
at your cheeks. *I'm lovely*, it says, *Touch me!*
I don't think wrestling is your sport.
Nor did your creamy skin just happen.
You hid it from the sun, to save its pale beauty
for hunting Aphrodite in the dark.
(*Belligerently.*) Who are you? Born where?

Dionysos

No famous place.
Have you heard of Tmolus,
the mountain covered with flowers?

Pentheus

I know that its stone arms
ring the town of Sardis.

Dionysos

Now you know where I'm from:
the Lydian mountains.

Pentheus
Who ordered these rituals of yours into Greece?

Dionysos
Bakkhos, the child of Zeus,
delivers them himself.

Pentheus
So Lydia has its own version of Zeus
to father its bastard gods?

Dionysos
Our Zeus is your Zeus — he slept with Semelê.

Pentheus
Were you dreaming when god possessed you?
Or face to face?

Dionysos
                              Face to face —
with a god who gave me ritual power.

Pentheus
Tell me about these mysteries of yours.

Dionysos
I couldn't tell *you*. You're not one of *us*.

Pentheus
What does this ritual do — I mean
for those who join it?

Dionysos
We keep that knowledge to ourselves.
But it's worth having.

Pentheus
You tell me nothing with so much cunning
it makes me ache to hear more.

Dionysos
The orgies of god are hard on heretics.

Pentheus
You've seen the god up close — what is he like?

Dionysos
That's not for *me* to say. He can look like — anyone.

Pentheus
You start to say something
but your words lead nowhere.

Dionysos
Authentic wisdom stupefies a fool.

Pentheus
Is Thebes the first place you've brought this god?

Dionysos
No, our dancing joy has swept Asia.

Pentheus
Asians aren't Greeks — what do they know?

Dionysos
This time, they've caught on much faster than you.
They respond differently to life.

Pentheus
These rituals — do they happen in daylight? Or at night?

Dionysos
Mostly at night. Darkness helps us to feel holy.

Pentheus
You mean it helps you to rape women.

Dionysos
A worse outrage
can happen in broad daylight.

Pentheus
You'll pay dearly for that cynical wit.

Dionysos
Provoking god, you'll find, exacts its own price.

Pentheus
For someone dressed like a mild
priest of Bakkhos, you talk remarkably tough.
But it's all talk.

Dionysos
                              Then what will you do
to punish me? Will it be savage?

Pentheus
First I'll clip your delicate curls.

Dionysos
My hair is divine — I grow it for god.

[PENTHEUS *supervises his men, who cut off* DIONYSOS' *curls.*]

Pentheus
Give me that wand.

Dionysos
Take it yourself: it's the wand Dionysos uses.
[PENTHEUS *seizes the wand.*]
Pentheus
Now we can drive you down to the stable,
bolt it, and post guards.
Dionysos
             When I wish to go free
god will turn me loose.
Pentheus
             Then go rally your Bakkhai *now*,
whip them into a frenzy yelling for Bakkhos.
Dionysos
He is so close, he sees
what I suffer with his own eyes.
Pentheus
Then why can't I see him? Where is this god?
Dionysos
Where I am. You can't see him
because you have no faith.
Pentheus
I've seen enough of your contempt. So has Thebes.
Take him.
Dionysos
           Men, don't use force on me.
Don't offend wisdom
to obey that blind fool.
Pentheus
And I say: chain him! You have no power,
you're not in command here. I am.
Dionysos
Why, you're not even in command
of your own life!
             You don't know
what you are doing, or who you are.
Pentheus
I am Pentheus, son of Echion and Agave.

Dionysos

No, *sorrow* is what your name means,
Pentheus. And *pain*. It fits.

Pentheus

Move him out, lock him in a horse stall —
he'll find enough darkness down there
for the kind of dancing he likes to much.
As for your women accomplices, who help you
carry out this evil nightmare, I've just
made them my slaves.
I might sell them,
or I might work them at my palace looms.
But I'll have peace. No more drums!
No more stamping feet.

Dionysos

I'm ready. I'll go now —
though I cannot be hurt
by an act which cannot take place.
But you, Pentheus, can be certain
that the god you call "dead" —
is Dionysos the Evenhanded
who will make you answer for every
outrage you do him. Insofar
as your ropes punish me,
they punish also him, the living god.

[SOLDIERS *escort* DIONYSOS *off*; PENTHEUS *follows*.]

Chorus

Queen Dirce,
child of the great river
Achelaus — are you still
the charming rivergirl
who bathed our god?
Cleansing the foetus
Zeus fathered,
the son he pulled from his own
everblazing fire,
and as he did, cried:

"Dithyrambos, my son!
     Live here
in my male womb.
I name you *Bakkhos* —
     Thebans
will know you by that name."

Now tell us, Dirce,
why you shun us, and turn your back
when we dance on your banks!
We bring you maenads wearing flowers,
and still you tell us: No,
still you slide coolly away.

But as sure as there is
     pleasure in grapes
Bakkhos presses into wine,
your neglect of the God
Who Cries Out
     will end:
                    and soon.

There is evil in Pentheus' blood —
the bestial earth blazes in his face,
an inhuman face
like those his giant fathers had,
those butchers who were beaten
when they tried to fight gods.

He's a crude beast: *we*
are the god's servants,
yet we are the ones
Pentheus wants to enslave.
He's thrown our companion,
shackled, into a dark cell.

Dionysos, son of Zeus —
how can you stand to watch
this bully using force
against us, your teachers of joy?

Come down from Olympos, Lord,
armed with your wand
flashing gold —
stop his abuse,
end his murdering days.

Where are you?
Loud One!
Somewhere on Nysa
the beast-loving mountain, leading
packs of maenads with your wand?
Or running the Corycian highlands?
Or gone to the vast wood on Olympos
where Orpheus once
plucking music from his lyre
moved the trees! moved the wild beasts!
spellbound
toward his singing.

Now the god turns to you
graceful Pieria,
he dances down your slopes
to join his Bakkhic enjoyers —
he splashes across
fastflowing Axios,
he's driving his maenads
on over Lydias,
the riverfather
who makes men rich, makes them happy,
whose waters carry gold,
making that land of fast horses
glow.

[*An earthquake. Blasts of lightning.*]

Dionysos [*Gives a great yell.*]
Hear me, Bakkhai!
Bakkhai!
Do you hear my shout?

Chorus [*Speaking individually.*]
— Whose voice are we hearing?

— Where is it coming from?
— Is it you, Loud One?
— The god who comes when we call
now calls for us!
Dionysos   [*Another yell.*]
The son of Zeus, the son of Semelê
calls you now!
Chorus
— Lord, we are here.
— Master, come down,
be with us! Loud One!
Dionysos
Poseidon, tear the earth!
Break up the world's floor, here, now!
Chorus
— The palace totters, it's going down!
— Look, its front cracks, it's splitting open!
— Dionysos is in there. I feel him.
— Worship him, adore him!
— O I do! I do!
— Watch those columns! They've
broken loose from the roof.
— The Loud One is roaring
his great roar of triumph!
Dionysos
Lightning, strike this place!
Burn Pentheus' palace to the ground.
Burn it!
Chorus
Look! Fire blazes up
over Semelê's tomb,
where she was killed by Zeus! —
that's the lightning that killed her!
Flat on the ground, Maenads.
Bakkhos is coming! The son of Zeus!
He's left the high soaring palace
rubble lying crushed in a field.
[*The* CHORUS *falls face down.* DIONYSOS *reappears disguised still*

as his own priest, now in an openly exhilarated mood.]

Dionysos

You lovely terrified Bakkhai from Asia!
What knocked you down? Rise up,
take heart. The panic is over.
That was *Bakkhos* who sent the earthquake
rolling through Pentheus' palace.

Leader

It's you! You light up our holy lives
with joy when you shout like a god!
You'll save us now, but without you
we were alone and defenseless.
To see you unharmed is a great relief.

Dionysos

You must have been sunk in gloom
when they hauled me into that stable.

Leader

How could we help it? Who could protect us
while you were locked in that jail?
How did you escape that godless man?

Dionysos

I freed myself. Gently, without exertion.

Leader

Didn't he lash ropes around your arms?

Dionysos

He did, convinced he had me in his grip.
He tied me up, though, without
touching me — hallucination
fed his desires. That
was how I humiliated him.
Down in the stables where he led me
a bull faced him — he roped it, thinking
the bull was me, hauling on the noose
that held the bull's hooves and knees,
breathing hard, raging, drenched
with sweat, his teeth grinding into his lip.
I sat and quietly watched. Then Bakkhos

came from nowhere, he rocked the building,
he blew flames back to life
on his mother's tomb —
the palace seemed to catch fire —
but it burned in *his* mind only.
He scrambled here, raced there, screaming for water,
for bucketfuls of River — which his slaves brought
until the palace was awash with confusion.
Then Pentheus quit fighting fire
to chase me, hacking with his dark sword
after me through the palace. The God Who
Cries Out obliged him — maybe this happened,
it could be merely my speculation —
by shining a phantom ME out in the courtyard.
Pentheus lunged at it, murdering this man-sized glow
which sparkled as he cut what seemed to be my throat.
Not yet satisfied, Dionysos humbled him
once more: he smashed the palace into dust —
the fool's reward for jailing me. Exhausted,
Pentheus dropped his blade and collapsed.
He's a *man*, that's all. And he tried to fight god.
I was calm when I went outside to find you.
Pentheus' fury ceased to concern me.
Now I hear boots tramping —
he's about to come through that door
gasping with rage. But I'll deal with him calmly —
a cool head and an even temper
are indispensable to a wise man.

[PENTHEUS *appears, dazed, in the palace doorway.*]

Pentheus

Something horrible had me in there.
The stranger's gone — where?
He was chained!
Look! There he is.
Why are you here?
Why aren't you back inside?

Dionysos

You're staggering with rage. Stand still, calm down.

Pentheus

    How did you do that — escape me?

    What happened to your chains?

Dionysos

    I told you — next time, listen —

    that I'd be set free by someone.

Pentheus

    Who? I can't keep up with all your

    sudden explanations. Who?

Dionysos

    The god who taught men to use grapes.

Pentheus

    Put men on the towers and seal off the city.

Dionysos

    I'm not impressed. Gods hurdle over walls.

Pentheus

    You are clever — everywhere except where it counts.

Dionysos

    That is just where my cleverness counts the most.

[DIONYSOS *looks offstage at the* HERDSMAN *approaching.*]

    This man brings you news from the mountain.

    Listen to him. And don't be anxious

    about us: we won't run. We're here to stay.

[*A young* HERDSMAN *enters from Cithaeron.*]

Herdsman

    Pentheus, Master of Thebes,

    I live on Cithaeron where it snows

    bright flurries the year round . . .

Pentheus

    If you have news, Herdsman, tell it.

Herdsman

    I've seen those holy women who ran

    half-naked and frantic out of your gates,

    covering ground like a flight of spears.

    I've come down to tell you, and Thebes,

    that what your women are doing in the hills

    outstrips miracles, it's so strange, so horrible!

Will I be safe telling you the whole story?
Or should I cut it short? Pentheus,
you're an impatient master, who might
flare up at a man whose news you hated.
They say you can get angry like a king.

Pentheus

Speak freely. There's no need to fear me,
I don't punish innocent people.
But the more evil I hear about those maenads
the harder I'll be on *him* — that man there — all
their vile magic comes from him.

Herdsman

The sun had just come up, burning the chill
off the mountain pastures. My cattle were climbing
through steep rock country, when I spot
three packs of those dancing women —
Autonoë led one, your mother, Agave,
led the second, the third was Ino's —
all sleeping where exhaustion dropped them:
some with their backs leaning on fir boughs,
or their heads resting on piles of oak leaves.
No question they were carefree, king, but not vulgar,
not drunk, as you told it — or looking for sex.
They weren't led through the woods by love-flutes.
Your mother Agave heard my cows lowing —
she stood up yelling
over her sleepers a great holy cry
to wake them up: their bodies shivered, they rubbed
their eyes until the bloom of sleep was gone,
then jumped up lightly to their full height —
old women, young women, and girls
not yet married — all moving
in perfect formation.
                              My god it was eerie.
First, they loosened their hair
down their backs and hitched their fawnskins up,
if the straps had slipped overnight.

Then I saw,
like belts around each woman, *live snakes*
who twisted up to lick their cheeks!
And mothers whose new babies were back home
eased their aching breasts by picking up
gazelles and wild wolf cubs to suckle
with white human milk.
                            Soon they were working
leaf-garlands into each other's hair —
of ivy, oak and bryony flowers.
                            Then one struck her wand
to a rock — out jumps icy springwater!
Another pushed hers gently into the pasture
feeling for Bakkhos — she found the god
who made wine flood up right there!
Women eager for milk raked the meadow
with their fingers until it oozed out
fresh and white.
                            Raw honey was dripping
in sweet threads from their wands.
Had you been there watching, Pentheus,
you would have dropped to your knees
blessing this god you've been cursing.
We herdsmen met to trade miracles
all morning. We'd listen amazed, or outdo
each other's stories if we could.
                            Then a drifter
who had learned how to talk fast in the city
saw his chance: "Listen, you mountain men," he said,
"if we hunt down Agave, the king's mother,
pull her clear of that dancing mob, Pentheus
will credit us with a great favor."
Good plan — or so it seemed then. We tunneled
through underbrush, elbowing up for an ambush.
At a signal from somewhere, the maenads
lifted their wands, dancing and chanting
Bakkhos, Child of Zeus, O God Who Cries Out,

their voices swelling together, then the whole
mountain started to dance for Bakkhos,
even the wild birds and squirrels filled with god
as they rushed past, shrilling for joy!
When Agave leaps my way, I scramble from my bush
grappling for her, but she shouts,
"Over here! Sisters! My baying pack!
Men are hunting us! We'll fight them
with our wands!"
                                    If we hadn't run hard
they would have torn us apart.
Armed with nothing but their bare hands
they charged into the midst of our cattle
who were chewing grass in a peaceful meadow.
You could see one girl hold by the legs
ripped halves of a shrieking heifer,
others tore into cows, sending cleft hooves
and rib-clusters spinning out into the trees
which caught shredded flesh and dripped blood.
Even some proud stud bulls
whose rage boiled under their horns, stumbled
and sank when the girls attacked —
a blur of hands, you couldn't count them all,
stripped off their coats of hide and flesh
faster than you could shut your royal eyes,
sir.
        Then they ran so fast, they flew,
lifted like birds over the valley,
skimming the wheat along the river Asopus.
They landed on those villages in the foothills,
Hysia and Erythrae, like enemy raiders
grabbing everything — even children
from their homes.
                            The booty stuck to their backs —
ironware, bronze — nothing fell to the ground.
Fire sizzled and flashed in their hair,
but they weren't burned.

The mountain people were enraged.
They rushed for their weapons and waded in.
What happened was awful, hard to believe.
How could the men's tough sharp spears
not draw blood from a single maenad? —
while the women, hurling their green wands,
wounded the men until they turned tail and ran.
Men beaten by females! — but I think some god
helped the women.
    Now the maenads headed back
to the springs where they woke — those springs
Bakkhos set flowing, and they scrubbed
the blood off. Snakes licked the gore
crusted over their cheeks
until the maenads' faces glowed.

King, whoever this god is, welcome him.
Give him the city. He has power — *of all kinds* —
but his great strength is wine that cures heartache.
Lose wine, and we'd lose the love goddess next —
we'd lose it all — whatever gives men joy.
[*Exit* HERDSMAN.]
Leader
Truth isn't what this tyrant wants to hear —
I'm shaking — but he must be told:
No god is greater than Dionysos!
Pentheus
Here comes the Bakkhic savagery, raging
out of control, burning its way here.
Now it's close. If we don't act now
Greece will look at us with disgust.
Soldier! Muster our heavy infantry
outside the Elektran Gates. Commit
our horsemen, the fastest we have.
Hold ready the light infantry
and the long-range archers.
Thebes, we're going to war against the Bakkhai!
I've had enough. We are humiliated

when we let women act like this.

Dionysos

Pentheus, you'll reject my advice,
but even though you wrong me, I'll
warn you again: don't use force against a god.
Keep the peace. The Loud One won't let you
clear his maenads off that mountain —
too much joy is echoing all over it.

Pentheus

Don't lecture me and don't provoke me.
You're free now. Keep this up and you won't be.

Dionysos

If I were a man enraged at a god — as you are —
I'd call off my rebellion. Why don't you
make a sacrifice to this god?

Pentheus

I'll burn him an offering — one he deserves —
the corpses of his women, after I myself
have made the bloodiest slaughter
Cithaeron has ever seen.

Dionysos

You will all run terrified for your lives.
The maenads' wands wave your bronze shields aside.

Pentheus

This stranger wears me down. No matter who holds
the upper hand, he never shuts his mouth.

Dionysos

Friend, there is still time to make peace.

Pentheus

How? By letting female slaves dictate to me?

Dionysos

I'll lead your women home unharmed.

Pentheus

You're damned shrewd! — talking me into some trap.

Dionysos

What trap? My shrewdness could be your salvation.

Pentheus

I think you and your maenads

plot no end of Bakkhic joy.
Dionysos
No, that it something that I plot with god.
Pentheus
Bring my weapons. You — we're through talking.
Dionysos
Are we! Would you like to see maenads
sitting together, up there on the mountain?
Pentheus
I would give all the gold I have to see that.
Dionysos
So, suddenly you're passionate to see them?
Pentheus
If they were drunk, I wouldn't like that. But . . .
Dionysos
But you'd enjoy it, though it hurt you to see it?
Pentheus
I would. I'll keep quiet and watch from a pine.
Dionysos
They'll corner you, no matter how softly you sneak up.
Pentheus
Then I should go in the open. Good point.
Dionysos
Are you ready to go? I'll lead you.
Pentheus
Get me there quickly. Waiting is torture.
Dionysos
First, clothe your body in a fine linen dress.
Pentheus
A dress? Why are you disguising my sex?
Dionysos
To save your life. The maenads kill all men.
Pentheus
Splendid! Your cunning is right on target.
Dionysos
Dionysos himself put that thought in my head.

Pentheus
How does your strategy work out in practice?
Dionysos
I'll go inside with you and dress you up.
Pentheus
Me, in a woman's gown? That would embarrass me.
Dionysos
Then you're not keen to see maenads up close?
Pentheus
But I am! Tell me again how I must dress.
Dionysos
I'll find you some elegant long hair.
Pentheus
And then? You're changing me — how far will this go?
Dionysos
I'll bind your hair and drop skirts to your feet.
Pentheus
Is that all? Anything else?
Dionysos
                                              I'll give you
a green wand to hold and a fawn to wear.
Pentheus
That's what your *women* wear! Not me. I can't do it.
Dionysos
People will die if you battle the maenads.
Pentheus
That's right. Maybe we should reconnoiter first.
Dionysos
It makes more sense than to kill and be killed.
Pentheus
How shall I walk through Thebes without being seen?
Dionysos
I'll see that we travel through deserted streets.
Pentheus
That's a relief. The maenads *must not laugh at me.*
I'm going indoors now to think things through.
Dionysos
I'm ready for whatever you decide.

Pentheus
>When I come out, I'll either be fighting, or I'll
>put myself in your hands.

[PENTHEUS *goes into the palace.*]

Dionysos
>Women, no need to aim our net —
>he plunges into it. He'll see the Bakkhai,
>but it will cost him his life.
>Dionysos, I leave the rest to you.
>You're near, I think. Take your revenge.
>First, destroy Pentheus' mind by flooding it
>with perverse hallucination. Sane,
>he'd never wear a woman's dress;
>delirious, he cannot resist wearing it.
>When I lead him through town I want the Thebans
>to laugh at his womanly shape — to repay us
>for all the ugly bullying we took from him.
>Now I'll go in to help him dress in the clothes
>he'll wear on his passage to Hades, sent there
>by his mother, whose own hands will butcher him.
>He shall then *know* Dionysos, the son of Zeus
>and the extremest of gods — pure terror
>to humankind, and yet, pure loving kindness.

[DIONYSOS *follows into the palace.*]

Chorus
>Will I ever again
>arch my throat back
>>with joy
>>>to dance
>>barefoot
>in the dark dew of heaven
>the nightlong dance
>>>>>ever again
>be the fawn bounding
>>out —
>>>>into the sheer
>green joy of a meadow

away from the hunters, away
from the beaters closing in,
        away
from the closing nets,
from the hounds
the huntsman shouts
racing toward my scent!

        Out there
I'm the fawn rushing
like a gust
        of wind
into the march grass —
arriving, at last, among ferns
far back in the shadow of the forest,
where no men are.

What is wisdom?
                When the gods
crush our enemies, their heads cowed
under the hard fist of our power,
that is glory!
                — and glory
always is the prize men crave.

The gods work slowly,
but you can trust them —
their power breaks all
mad arrogant men
who love foolishness
and pay no mind to the gods —

but the gods are devious
and in no hurry —
                they put
an impious man at his ease, then
hunt him down.
                Therefore:
let no one

do or conceive
anything
the ancient law forbids.

It costs little to believe,
    that, whatever divinity is,
it is power;
it costs little to believe
    those laws
which time seasons, strengthens
    and lets stand —
such laws are Nature herself
    coming to flower.

What is wisdom?
              When the gods
crush our enemies, their heads cowed
under the hard fist of our power,
that is glory!
            — and glory
always is the prize men crave.

    The stormblown sailor
swept into harbor is blessed with luck,
so is the cornered man who fights free;
one man defeats another,
some in this venture, some in that.
Men grown rich, or take power,
ten thousand men want ten thousand things,
most see their hopes
go to ruin, a few see them all
come true — but the man whose life
    right now, this day
brings joy to his heart —
is happy beyond harm.

[DIONYSOS *steps out from the palace, looks behind him and calls*
    to PENTHEUS, *who hesitates inside.*]

Dionysos
              Come on out!

Aren't you the man so eager to see
what he shouldn't? I mean you, Pentheus.
Don't hide indoors, let's have a look at you.
If you like evil so much, show us
[PENTHEUS *emerges wearing a maenad's clothes — long gown,*
false curls, a fawnskin and fennel wand.]
how you dress for it.
                              Ah! As a woman, a maenad,
one of the Bakkhai! You won't find it hard
to infiltrate your mother's pack —
you could pass for any of Kadmos' daughters.

Pentheus

I think I'm seeing two suns
on fire in heaven, and Thebes
doubles into two cities,
her seven gates are now fourteen —
and you trot like a bull, with horns
sprouting from your head!
Or were you always . . . animal?
There's no question you're a bull now.

Dionysos

What you see is the god — not hostile,
but helping us, since we've appeased him.
Your eyes now see what they must.

Pentheus

Don't I have great presence when I move?
Tell me who I look like. Like mother? Or my aunts?

Dionysos

I look at you, but I see all those women.
                                          Wait,
let's tuck back this curl. It's springing loose.

Pentheus

Inside I was dancing, throwing my head back
like a maenad, and it shook out.

Dionysos

                              Let it be
my job to make it behave. Hold still.

Pentheus
Please fix it. I want you to take care of me.
Dionysos
Your belt's not snug. Look how your gown bunches
over your ankles.
Pentheus
It's bunched on the right,
but on my left side it falls perfectly.
Dionysos
When you see the Bakkhai, you'll find them
surprisingly good at what they do —
so good, you'll admit I'm your best friend.
Pentheus
How does
a maenad hold her wand? Right-handed? Or like this?
Dionysos
Shift it to your right hand. Now thrust in time
with your right foot, and keep it high.
I'm glad you've dropped your old rigid ways.
Pentheus
Could I carry Cithaeron and the maenads on my shoulders?
Dionysos
You could. You can do anything you wish,
now that your sick mind has gone sane.
Pentheus
Will be need a crowbar? Or just my bare hands?
Shall I armlock the peak and wrench it loose?
Dionysos
Don't, you'll crush the nymphs' caves and hurt
the woodlands where Pan plays his pipes.
Pentheus
You're right. We must not use crude strength
to overpower the women. I'll gain my end
by hiding in a fir tree.
Dionysos
We'll make this ambush
worthy of a skillful maenad-watcher like you.

Pentheus

> I see maenads spring up and down
> in their tickets like netted birds,
> caught up in sex and loving it.

Dionysos

> You have found your life's work: to witness
> exactly that! You will catch them in the act —
> or it could be *your* face to which the blood will come.

Pentheus

> Show me off through the heart of Thebes.
> I want them all to see: I'm the man
> who will brave anything.

Dionysos

> > > > > > Indeed you will.
> The suffering of Thebes
> is on your shoulders now. Yours alone.
> Something violent lies ahead
> and you won't miss it.
> > > > > Come with me,
> I will see you through it.
> Someone else will bring you home.

Pentheus

> Mother!

Dionysos

> > > Yes! As a great symbol to mankind

Pentheus

> That's my wish.

Dionysos

> you will be carried here

Pentheus

> What luxury!

Dionysos

> hugged in your mother's arms.

Pentheus

> You'll make me go
> all to pieces!

Dionysos

> I'd have it no other way.

Pentheus
>Then I'll have what I deserve!

Dionysos
>You are amazing! — but no more amazing
>than the fate you go out to meet. Its glory
>will lift you like a god into heaven!
>Reach out and take him, mother Agave,
>and all you daughters of Kadmos.
>I lead this boy to his supreme ordeal
>which I — and the God Who Cries Out — will win.
>What happens next will explain itself.

[*Exist* DIONYSOS *leading* PENTHEUS *toward Cithaeron.*]

Chorus
>Chase him into the hills, you mad hounds
>>from Lyssa's pack!
>>Catch Kadmos' daughters
>in the fury of their dance
>>and train it
>on this boy in woman's clothes,
>>this crazed spy
>>hunting maenads.
>Agave, looking out from her high spike of rock,
>will catch sight of him first:
>>"Maenads!" she'll say, "who is
>that Theban scout who comes up here
>>to spy on mountain dancers?
>Don't tell me his mother's a woman —
>>she's a lion —
>>or a Gorgon
>from the African desert."

>Vengeance! bring it out
>>into the open
>where every one of us may see:
>with your righteous sword
>>cut this godhater's
>>>throat —
>his pride is savage, unscrupulous,

he's Echion's son, snakeborn
　　from the muck of the earth.

That rebel tries to shout down
　　your mysteries, Bakkhos;
　　your mother's cult
drives him wild.
As first he tries to outwit them
　　but his boldness
　　carries him away —
　　　　he flails
at Invulnerable Power.
But death will soon set him straight.
The gods give no one
　　a second chance.

Never question the gods,
　　do what they ask.
　　Live quietly,
within mortal limits.
　　Obedience,
alone, frees human life from pain.

　　I don't envy
those who struggle to be wise —
though I might join that hunt
　　my heart's not in it — it's in
hunting what I see
clearly — those great obvious things
which make our lives graceful,
　　worth living —
　　day and night
to love the gods we hold in awe,
to defend every age-old truth,
　　and forget all the rest.

Vengeance! bring it out
　　into the open
where every one of us may see:

with your righteous sword
cut this godhater's
throat —
his pride is savage, unscrupulous,
he's Echion's son, snakeborn
from the muck of the earth.

O God
Who Cries Out — show us *now*
what wild great
beast you are!
Be a
BULL
a
SNAKE WITH A HUNDRED HEADS!
a
LION IN FLAMES!

Go out to your maenads
where they're dancing
out of the maenad-hunter's grasp —
ready at last
to strike back.
Smile at him
when your noose wrenches his throat
as he stumbles
under the murdering hands of
your maenad pack.

[*Enter* MESSENGER *from Cithaeron.*]

Messenger
This house was once the luckiest in Greece.
Its tough old founder came here from Sidon,
seeded the earth with teeth from the great snake
and harvested fighting troops one summer.
But now this house and its people are finished.

Leader
What do you have — fresh news of the Bakkhai?

Messenger
Echion's boy Pentheus has been killed.

Leader

O Bakkhos, what a god!
There's your power in plain sight!

Messenger

Do I hear you right, women?
Why this elation at my lord's murder?

Leader

We love his death. We're Asians! Barbarians!
And now we have a barbarous song to sing —
now that your prison can't scare us.

Messenger

Thebes isn't so emasculated that it can't . . .

Leader

Can't what? Bakkhos tells us what to do.
Not Thebes. Bakkhos!

Messenger

Look, I can ignore your barbaric speech —
but why such pleasure when a man dies?

Leader

Your master was an evil man.
Tell us who killed him.

Messenger

That stranger — who promised to show Pentheus
these mysteries — guided us out. I went with my master.
We left behind the last valleys farmed by Thebans,
we forded the swollen Asopus, then climbed the rocky
switchbacks well up the mountainside.
We paused in a wooded hollow
sensing we were near, mouths shut and moving quiet
on the forest grass, to a safe lookout.
No one saw us — but we could see —
down a deep gorge with sheer cliff on both sides.
Streams cut through it, and large firs kept it dark.
There sat the maenads, working at pleasant chores —
some stripped the withered ivy from their wands
and spliced in fresh vines. Others frisking
here and there like colts whose painted bridles

had just been lifted, sang
Bakkhic hymns back and forth.
Pentheus ached — that unlucky man —
for a long unobstructed look at the women.
"Stranger," he said, "from this spot I can't see
those supposed maenads. If I were up
that tall fir tree on the cliffs, I could look down
on the lewd games of those wild females."
The stranger replied with a miracle.
He reached into the sky and seized the fir
by its crown, bending it gently, gently down
full circle, until it touched earth.
He made it perfect, like a powerfully
drawn bow, or a wagonwheel rim
cleanly bent from steamed wood.
With ease the stranger curved
the mountain fir into a circle —
no mortal man could have done it.
He set Pentheus astride a top limb
letting it rise, his hands braking
the returning pull of the trunk, which straightened
to its full height without a creak,
the stranger careful not to throw Pentheus off,
as he rode high into the airy sky.
But Pentheus, even from that height,
couldn't see maenads. They say him, though,
just risen into view — thereupon the stranger
disappeared and a voice sounded from the heavens —
it must have been Dionysos the god —
commanding,
            "O my women, I have delivered to you
the man who mocks you, mocked me,
mocked our sacred lives! REVENGE!"
While he spoke a holy light
      flared upon us,
binding heaven and earth.
      The world hushed;

the air above, the whole forest
   stilled its leaves —
no living sound broke the quiet.
Straining to revive that great voice
the maenads sprang alert, eyes flashed wide
searching the woods.
             God roared again,
the same horrible command. But now
the maenads heard him clearly, and obeyed.
They flew off like woodcocks
all over the watery glade,
clawing up the cliff face so high
god must have blown mad power through them.
They looked up, saw my master, grabbed rocks
and stoned him cruelly, scrambling
from foothold to foothold
up and down the rock wall.
They slashed at him with spiny pine boughs
and shot their hard wands across the gap.
But the barrage fell short —
Pentheus clung too high beyond their frenzied
clawing, but he was treed, cut off.
The maenads splintered an oak trunk,
fists cracking down like lightning,
and with the jagged staves dug at the roots,
hoping to fell the big fir — but they couldn't.
Agave yelled, "Maenads! surround that trunk!
Pull down that climbing beast! If we
let him escape, he'll tell all he knows
of our secret dances."
               One hand
made of thousands tore the tree from the earth —
screaming and moaning as he fell
Pentheus smashed into the hard black ground.
His life was over and he knew it.
His mother, like a priestess,
began to slaughter him. Pentheus ripped

his false hair away, to show his mother
who he was, to stop her from killing him.
He touched her crazed face: "STOP! Mother,
I am Pentheus, your son! Born to Echion!
Let me live!
I've failed you — but don't kill me for that!"
Saliva poured from her mouth,
her eyes were empty, she was senseless,
totally possessed by Bakkhos.
And she denied her son. Grabbing his elbow
and digging her foot into his rib cage
she pulled until his shoulder parted, not
because her strength was brute,
but the god in her muscles
made the appalling work easy.
Ino worked at the other side, ripping flesh away.
Autonoë and the whole pack of blood sisters
came screaming from their dance to swarm over him.
Pentheus threw all the breath he had left
into his own death-scream
which the women drowned out, yelping for joy.
They laid his ribs bare, their bloody hands
playing catch with his flesh
like children lost in their game.
His body's scattered over the mountain,
parts strewn on the rocks, the rest in the forest.
We'll never find it all.
His mother is walking unconscious, she's spiked
her son's dumb-screaming head on her green wand.
She holds a mountain lion, she thinks,
and shows it off
down the ravines of Cithaeron —
her maenad friends are still celebrating.
She's yelling — coming right through
the gates into Thebes with her trophy,
naming Bakkhos her partner in the hunt
and her partner in victory.

> She's won nothing but tears.
> I'll go before she comes,
> I won't stay here, waiting for this horror.
> The best wisdom is knowing what the gods want,
> and then humbling yourself before them.
> Mankind should hand on to that
> if it needs something to live by.

[*Exit* MESSENGER.]

Chorus

> Now we will dance, now we can sing it out!
> Bakkhos wins, Pentheus dies!
> That doomed spawn of the great snake
> put on a woman's gown,
> took the green wand of miracle,
> the wand of joy which kills,
> always kills, and went down
> to Hades, led by a bull.
>
> That wild roar from the maenads in triumph
> turns over as it carries to us,
> turning to suffering and tears for those women
> who fought their hard war, and have won
> a son's lifeblood smeared on their hands.

Leader

> Here comes Agave running home.
> Look at her eyes: she's mad. Expect
> the whole maenad pack to arrive next
> screaming their love for Bakkhos.

[*Enter* AGAVE, *breathless, exhilarated. She carries the severed head of* PENTHEUS *on her thrysos; later she will cradle it in her arms.*]

Agave

> Bakkhai from Asia —

Leader

> What do you want from us?

Agave

> Do you see this ivy frond
> I picked on the mountain,

this blessed kill to adorn our palace?
Leader
I see it. Now you're one of us,
a reveler. Welcome.
Agave
I took this yearling lion
without ropes. Look at him!
Leader
You took him where?
Agave
Cithaeron . . .
Leader
Cithaeron?
Agave
. . . slaughtered him.
Leader
Who struck him first?
Agave
I did. He's mine.
Leader
Should we call you "Blessed" Agave?
Agave
The maenads did.
Leader
Who helped you kill?
Agave
It was Kadmos' . . .
Leader
Kadmos!
Agave
                Kadmos' daughters helped —
they were all in on the kill.
Our hunt was lucky, now let's feast! And share!
Leader
Share *what* with you, woman?
Agave
This bull! He's young. Blooming!

Feel his thick wavy mane.
It crowns him and blends
with the soft down under his jaw.
Leader
He is a beast, to judge by that hair.
Agave
That priest of Bakkhos
tracked him for us — O he was wise! —
then signaled our attack.
Leader
Our leader knows how to hunt.
Agave
Are you still praising me?
Leader
You can take it for that.
Agave
Soon the people . . .
Leader
Start with Pentheus, your son . . .
Agave

                                  will praise
his mother, for killing this young lion.
Leader
Stunning game!
Agave
And killed in a stunning way.
Leader
Are you proud?
Agave
Aching with pride.
I have done something great for Thebes.
Killing this beast still makes me tremble.
Leader
Show us your prize, poor woman.
Show Thebes what you have killed.
[AGAVE *lifts* PENTHEUS' *head high while she speaks.*]
Agave
People of Thebes, citizens of our lovely towers,

I want you to see this quarry which your women
have just surprised and killed.
No javelins you throw
from a safe distance, no iron nets,
only our delicate fingers, our white feminine arms
did this. Men, all your clanging weapons
are for cowards. From now on, who will take pride
if he lets steel do his killing?
I caught this one, and my bare hands
tore his limbs off.
                    Where's Father?
He should see this. And my son!
Someone go look for Pentheus. Tell him
to raise a ladder to our palace roof
so he may hang a trophy on the front beams —
this lion's head I've just brought home.

[KADMOS *enters leading several servants who carry a heavy tar-
    paulin holding* PENTHEUS' *body.*]

Kadmos

Bring him this way, men. Lay Pentheus'
dead wretched weight down, by the palace.
I found him piece by piece,
I looked in a hundred places.
His body was dismembered and hidden
in rock clefts and thickets
all over Cithaeron, no two pieces
together.
                    We had just reached our walls,
Tiresias and I, walking home
from those mountain dances of the Bakkhai.
A man told me what my daughters had done —
their hideous bravery.
I climbed straight back up the mountain
to find what I could of my grandson's body
insanely butchered by those women, and bring it home.
I saw Actaeon's mother Autonoë up there —
Ino beside her, both trotting deranged

and wretched through the oak forest.
                              I'm told Agave
came running here at a maenad's pace —
It's true. There she is.
I can see her misery with my own eyes.

Agave

Father, now you can boast that you've fathered
the bravest daughters a man could!
I say "daughters" but the daughter I mean is me.
I quit my loom and found more serious work —
now I hunt wild animals barehanded. Here's one
still warm, cradled here in my arms.
You must be fearless to kill this animal.
He's something to hang up over our doors.
You hold him, Father. Don't you love him?
Don't you want to call our clan together?
We'll celebrate! You'll all share
the glory of my success.

Kadmos

There is no way to comprehend this pain.
What you have
         in your deluded, murderer's hands
is too much to look at. Yes,
this is the noblest sacrifice
you could ever give this god! *This*
is the feast you want to feed to your city!
Pain crushes me.
And will crush you.
What the God Who Cries Out
does to us is justice, barbaric justice.
This god was our blood-kin, born
in our house, yet, without one qualm
he destroys us all.

Agave

Old age dries men up. They're bitter
all the time, spiteful and scolding.
Let my *son* be a good hunter, let him

inherit my genius for killing. Let it show
when he hunts next time with the young Theban men.
His only talent now is for fighting god.
Discipline him, Father. That's your job.

Call him here,

let him see me
in my glory!

Kadmos

Hopeless
madness.
When you find out what you have done
you will suffer all the pain
this life can hold.
But if, somehow, you dream out your life
in this insane euphoria
you'll seem happy,
you'll seem blessed!

But you won't be.

Agave

I won't? What could hurt me now?

Kadmos

Stop! —

look up at the sky.

Agave

I'm looking.

Why must I do this?

Kadmos

Is it the same sky? Or has the sky
changed?

Agave

Much brighter now. *Much* clearer.

Kadmos

Is something in you still soaring?

Agave

Did you say *soaring?* No, I'm changing,
I feel peaceful. My mind's clearing.
I'm not flying anymore.

Kadmos
> Now. Try hard to hear me.
> Can you answer a question?

Agave
> Ask it, Father.
> I have lost track of what we said.

Kadmos
> Who was the man you married? From what great clan?

Agave
> You married me to Echion. He was snakeborn.

Kadmos
> And the son born to you and Echion?
> Name him.

Agave
>   Pentheus.
> We made love and Pentheus was born.

Kadmos
> Look down at what you're holding.
> Whose head is that?

Agave
>   A lion's head,
> my fellow killers said a lion.

Kadmos
> Now look directly at its face.
> Will it hurt you just to look?

Agave
> Ohhh. What is this?
> What *am* I holding?

Kadmos
>   Look harder.
> Force your whole mind to know
> what it is.

Agave
>   All the grief there is,
>   I see it!

Kadmos
> Does it still look like a lion?

Agave

No. It's Pentheus.
His head
in my hands.

Kadmos

My eyes were in tears
before yours saw the truth.

Agave

Who killed him?
Why am *I* holding him?

Kadmos

TRUTH, you are savage . . .

Agave

Say it! Say it!
My heart's terrified. It knows.

Kadmos

And she's defenseless.
You killed your son. You
and your sisters.

Agave

Where? In this house? Where?

Kadmos

Out where his own hounds tore Actaeon apart.

Agave

Why did Pentheus go to Cithaeron?

Kadmos

To sneer at you maenads. And at god.

Agave

What were we women doing there?

Kadmos

You were insane.
The fury of Bakkhos had crazed Thebes.

Agave

Dionysos destroys us, all.
I see that. Now.

Kadmos

You denied he was god, you blasphemed him.

Agave
   Why was Pentheus punished for *my* crime?
Kadmos
   Like you, he mocked and enraged the god.
   He's crushed us all — our whole
   bloodline, with one murderous blow.
   He hurts me worst, because I have no son.
   I see this boy, born from your body,
   you suffering woman, I see him killed
   in the most heartless brutal way,
   this boy who brightened us.
   He was our future.
[*He turns to address the corpse of* PENTHEUS.]
   My son, my daughter's child, it was you
   who held us together. How this town
   shrank from your rage!
   I am one old man nobody dared harm
   because your warning glare protected me.
   If they abused me, you'd punish them, justly,
   and they knew it.
                  Now I'm thrown out of my home,
   stripped of my rights. I was Kadmos, the great man
   who gave Thebes an army by growing one.
   I sowed murderous seeds. And harvested power.
   You I loved most, my son. And though you are gone
   I love you still, you blessed boy,
   though you won't tug my beard ever again,
   saying "Grandfather," hugging me,
   "Who's giving you a hard time?
   Name that bully bothering you. I'll stop him."

   All I have left of you is barren grief,
   and you have nothing left.
   I see your mother devastated,
   I see her sisters weak from their tears.
   Does your mind still resist the gods?
   Study how this man died. You will believe, all right.

Chorus
Kadmos, I grieve for you. Your grandchild
suffered what he deserved. But the pain
you feel because of him is too harsh.
Agave
Father, where is my son's body?
Let me see it.
Kadmos
Over there.
Agave
Have his limbs been decently set together?
Kadmos
No.
Open the canvas
Show her Pentheus. Her son.
Agave
What is this dead flesh I'm holding?
Don't say it's a man!
Kadmos
It's Pentheus.
I found him on the rocks, in broken shreds.
Agave
Father, you see my life
changed. There is no way back.
How can I mourn my son? Or hold him in my arms?
His blood pollutes my hands, my mind.
How may I in this wretchedness
touch him
in the pure reverent way?
I killed him. Now, how do *I*
honor and love him?
Kadmos
Mourn him child, compose his body.
No one here will stop you.
Agave
Father, help me find again his handsome shape.
From these horrible pieces

make him perfect!
I made him once in my womb.
I make him now, again.
How can I do it — embrace his whole body
    and kiss him
as when he was a child?
Father, bring me his head.
Set it where it belongs.
I loved his face, his gentle chin.
I loved every part of him.
On his journey to Hades
now, we must leave him
exactly as he was when he was king.

Kadmos
Child, that cannot be done. Look at him.
[*She looks intently for some moments.*]

Agave
With this veil I cover him
    forever
from all our eyes.

[DIONYSOS *appears as the god he is, on the roof of the palace.*]

Dionysos
I am the god Dionysos, son of Zeus,
the son of Semelê the Theban,
come back to Thebes, where I was born,
to make you face what madness blinds you to:
the power I hold as your god.

Because he fought me, jailed me, denied me,
I unleashed appetites in Pentheus
only ecstatic death could end.
                        To please me
he was murdered by those who loved him most.
What Pentheus suffered was justice —
he was blind to my nature
and to his own.

Hear, now, what you Thebans must endure.

Kadmos, I will change you to a serpent.
Your wife, Harmonia, the daughter of a god,
I name a venomous female snake.
As snakes, you both shall drive an oxcart
commanding a vast barbarian army
whose killer hordes burn many cities.
The oracle of god proclaims it.

But the moment your army
crushes Apollo's shrine
at Delphi, you must disperse
in shame to your homelands.

You, Kadmos, Ares will spare —
he will spirit you and Harmonia
to the Islands of the Blest.
These are not human words I speak
but words of Dionysos, son of god.
During all this crisis
if you had known what true sanity is,
you would have found
me, Dionysos, fighting
on your side forever.
And you would be happy now, at peace.

Kadmos
We beg your mercy, Dionysos. We admit guilt.

Dionysos
                                        Too late.
When the time came, you did not know me.

Kadmos
I know you now. *You are*
Vengeance — without feeling or limit.

Dionysos
Kadmos, you dishonored me. And I am god.

Kadmos
Gods should improve on blind human wrath.

Dionysos
We *do* improve on it. The agony

you now feel Zeus sharpened and shaped
from the first in his cosmic mind.

Agave

Father, nothing can touch the gods.
Or change their minds. We're banished.

Dionysos

If your Fate says, *Leave!* why
do you stand there stunned?

Kadmos

Child, we have come to the final evil
which breaks us all.
I am sent to barbarians
despised and old — a hated stranger.
Over me hangs that oracle, telling me
I will lead a confused barbarian swarm
against my homeland Greece.
By then, we'll both be snakes,
strangling our own holy shrines!
My life will be an open wound,
for I shall never die, never be blown
down through the black peace of Acheron.

Agave

Father, in our exile
we shall not meet.

Kadmos

Why hold me, child,
like a swan whose white wings
shelter its useless father?

Agave

Because I don't know who
can help me now, or where I should go,
I hold on to you.

Kadmos

Nor can I tell you, child,
where exile must take you.
Your father is too weak to help.

Agave

My evil luck will go with me. Never

will it let me come home
to you, my own loved country,
or to you, house where I came
as a bride: farewell.

Kadmos

Hide in the mountains, child.

Agave

I pity, you, Father.

Kadmos

    Mourn
for each other, and for our dead.

Agave

Lord Dionysos dooms us in his terrible way.

Dionysos [*From on high.*]

And in what way did Thebes honor me?
Disdain of fools was what you gave me.

Agave

Father, farewell. Find safety and peace.

Kadmos

Daughter, I can barely breathe an answer —
no one is safe.

Agave

Let me go out to my miserable sisters,
my sisters in exile.
Lead me away from Cithaeron.
I hate to look at that mountain,
I don't want it to see me!
Let its rocks and its screaming dances
bring grief to other Bakkhai.

Chorus

The gods can do anything.
They can frustrate
whatever seems certain,
and make what no one wants
all at once come true!
Today, this god has shown it all.

[*Exit.*]

The Bacchae: A City Sacrificed to a Jealous God
by Richard Schechner

At the heart of Euripides' masterpiece, *The Bacchae*, is a communal sacrifice. The city of Thebes is sacrificed to Dionysus to satisfy his capricious ego. In supporting this thesis I will contest several widely held theories about the play: (1) that Dionysus represents Fate or any of its equivalents; (2) that the god is a life force or some other pantheistic "god of ecstasy in religion"; or (3) that the play gathers its primary force from the encounter between Dionysus and Pentheus.

My reading of *The Bacchae* is an internal one: I want to see what the play will yield on only its own terms. I realize, of course, that political and social ideas both press in on the play and, if we seek them, emanate from it. These ideas are, I believe, extra-dramatic: they radiate from the script, enriching it and partially explaining its genesis, but they are not present as a dramatic immediacy. Other critics have dealt quite successfully with these extra-dramatic ideas; I shall turn my full attention to the play as we might see it on stage.

The Bacchae does not end, as so many classical tragedies do, with the restoration of order under the aegis of a new ruler. The egocentric, vengeance-ridden, and capricious Dionysus obliterates all of Thebes by destroying its ruling family and exiling in slavery all its people. The terror which the play engenders rises out of this divine caprice of Dionysus. It is awesome, dreadful, and terribly absurd to see a god improvise the destruction of a people.

The key to Dionysus' divine caprice is revealed, of course, in the god's character. To understand this personality we must first examine the motives which impel it. The situation at the beginning of the play is clear. In the first fifty-four lines Dionysus tells us that he has returned to Thebes, the city of his spawning, to avenge the slander repeated by his aunts that Zeus was not his father; secondly, he intends to introduce the Dionysian rites into the community, by force if necessary. These motives are interdependent. For it is only by making the people worship him that he can conclusively prove his godhead and, conversely, it is only by demonstrating his godhead that he can demand worship. The important thing, in terms of the play, is the means which Dionysus chooses to achieve his goals. He decides to put on the skin of a man; and, as the play develops, the awesome brutality and totality of his vengeance becomes the means by which he proves himself a god-revealed, true son of Zeus.

In fact, the performance of his rites is from the very beginning a minor issue, since the Theban women have already been driven from the city to pursue the Dionysian ecstasy on the hillside. We learn soon enough, too, that the acceptance of Dionysus' godhead is another *fait accompli*, since the entire population of Thebes, Pentheus excepted, admits that Dionysus is a Zeus-begotten god. True enough, Cadmus accepts the new god for political and familial reasons, and Tiresias may be a religious quack, but Dionysus does not quibble about the motives of his devotees.

We are, therefore, presented with an unusual situation at the outset. The twin goals of Dionysus — worship and godhead — have already been won before the play get under way. Yet he chooses to remain in Thebes to finish the job. What job? The job of vengeance. The city which bred him must pay for denying him. Even though that denial has been retracted by all but one member, the entire city must suffer obliteration. The ultimate ironic comment on Dionysus' apparent goals of worship and godhead is given to us at the very end of the play when Agave throws down her holy thrysus and says:

> Lead me, guides, where my sisters wait,
> poor sisters of my exile. Let me go
> where I shall never see Cithaeron more,
> where that accursed hill may not see me,
> where I shall find no trace of thrysus!
>   That I leave to other Bacchae.

Dionysus does not strike her down, nor does he make her repent once more and worship. He does not care. As the play works itself out on the stage, worship and godhead are not true motives.

If that is so, and Dionysus' actual motive is vengeance, we may be sure, then, that the Dionysus of *The Bacchae* is no pantheistic life force. To feel that he is, is to confuse the Dionysus of the Chorus' imagination (believed, too, by Agave and, to a lesser degree, Tiresias and Cadmus) with the Dionysus we see on stage. The god of life force — the "force that through the green fuse drives the flower" — is a thing *felt* by the Chorus and not the god *enacting* his character before us. Euripides is confronting us with two Dionysiae. But only one of them is bodily represented on stage. The other — the god of ecstasy, life force, even madness — functions within the mind of the Chorus and, at a crucial moment, in the mind of Agave. He is no real Dionysus, but an idea — or true daemon — which, when he inhabits Agave, murders and dismembers Pentheus. The Dionysus-of-the-stage turns Pentheus over to those who are infected by the Dionysus-of-the-mind.

The Dionysus we see, then, uses what the Chorus and Agave feel him to be as the tool with which he achieves his revenge.

In dramatic terms this dichotomy is very important. Much of the power of the play vibrates from the tension between Dionysus as we see him and Dionysus as the Chorus believes him to be. We are torn between what we see and the infectious madness we feel. The Dionysus-of-the-stage is cool, ironic, sarcastic, and totally self-controlled. The Dionysus-of-the-mind is the antithesis of all that. He is hot, direct, devoid of wit, and without inhibition. The stage Dionysus calmly — even gloatingly — hands Pentheus over to his wild engine of destruction. It is an act which inspires deep awe and terror. But to confuse the engine with its manufacturer clouds the sharp and effective dramatic outline of the play, draining away much of its dread.

What kind of god is Dionysus as we see him on stage? He is no amoral being, though it is true that he cares nothing about what we or Pentheus would call sexual morality. He does not, as Tiresias has it, "compel a woman to be chaste." The chief value of Dionysus' morality is vanity. He is a personal, capricious, and egocentric god. His final words in the play, like his first, refer to the sins committed against his vanity: "I was terribly blasphemed,/and my name dishonored in Thebes." Lest we underestimate the sophistication and power of such a god, I should like to compare Dionysus to the God of the Old Testament. Both deities are cut from the same pattern. Let us recall the first Three Commandments of the Mosaic Decalogue:

1. I am the Lord thy God. . . .
2. Thou shalt have no other gods before me . . . for I the Lord they God am a jealous God, visiting the iniquity of the fathers upon the children, and upon the third and fourth generation of them that hate Me. . . .
3. Thou shalt not take the name of the Lord thy God in vain. . . .

Dionysus wholeheartedly adheres to this moral scheme. But, unlike the God of the Old Testament, Dionysus does not have seven other commandments of a more worldly nature following the first three.

Clearly it is because members of the Theban ruling family (who are no less Dionysus' own family) have denied his godhead, put other gods before him, and taken his name in vain — even worse, slandered that name — that Dionysus has returned to Thebes. The Mosaic God is the only true god; Dionysus recognizes other divinities, but because he is a jealous god he must be first in the Pantheon — not even Zeus deserves more reverence. And like the Mosaic God, Dionysus visits the guilt of a few upon many: all of Thebes is sacrificed because of what Semele's sisters said and what Pentheus does. If we remember the anger of the Mosaic God when the Israelites cast the golden calf and worshipped it, then we may understand the wrath of Dionysus. The Israelites were saved from the hot fire of total destruction only by the intercession of Moses; Thebes was not so fortunate, owning no intercessor.

But if Dionysus shares a great deal with his fellow-god, in one respect they are utterly different: Dionysus is a capricious god. And in this caprice his morality takes on a wild aspect. The Mosaic God expresses himself in an abundance of law and, although he is strict, he is coherent. Dionysus has only the laws of his own vanity and, furthermore, he does not foresee the ramifications of his actions — he improvises and improves on his rage. When he first comes to Thebes he envisions violence only in terms of leading the Maenads against the armed might of the city. As the situation progresses he devises the murder of Pentheus by Agave so that the king may be humiliated and sacrificed. At this point a "normal" classical tragedy would end. But Dionysus goes on and as the play closes the god decides that the whole family (i.e., the city itself) must be utterly rooted out to assuage his vanity.

Now that we have come so far and established the *being* of Dionysus, let us look at this *being-in-action*. As William Arrowsmith correctly notes, Dionysus changes under dramatic pressure. In other words, he is not the agent of some impersonal Fate which works itself out inexorably — as it does, for instance, in *Oedipus Rex*. A god who can change his mind and thereby change the action of the play is not some force following the preordained patterns of heaven.

After the prologue, Dionysus leaves the stage to the Chorus. He goes off in high spirits, foreseeing a quick and total victory. He will teach naughty Thebes a lesson. Indeed, he has already driven the women mad. He knows nothing about Pentheus except that the young king has added new insult to old by refusing to recognize the divinity of the beautiful god. Dionysus' rage is clearly personal:

> . . . [Pentheus] now revolts against the divinity in *me*;
> thrusts *me* from his offerings; forgets *my* name
> in prayers. . . .

As the Mosaic God was enraged by the golden calf, so Dionysus is enraged by Pentheus. However, he does not expect to have a hard time of it. He plans to leave Thebes shortly, when "all is well," and continue upon his proselytizing mission.

So Dionysus exits and the Chorus takes over, imprinting on us the image of Dionysus-of-the-mind. The long choral ode establishes this daemonic force, the engine of the god on earth: the god's ultimate weapon. The entrance of Tiresias and then of Cadmus further establishes the nature of Dionysus-of-the-mind. With the dexterity of a Pirandello, Euripides builds both the god and the god's machine at once.

To reinforce this dichotomy, when next we see Dionysus, far from being the spirit of ecstasy, prophesy, or war (these are the qualities Tiresias ascribes to the god), he is the willing and effeminate prisoner of Pentheus' attendant. The *agon* between the god and Pentheus which follows reveals Dionysus as a clever person, owning great self-control: two characteristics not usually linked with the Dionysian frenzy. The god does not balk when his thrysus is seized or when his curls are cut. Neither does he use any superhuman tricks at this time to humiliate Pentheus. Rather, he gives the king every license to enlarge upon his blasphemy and sacrilege. These insults, the more grave because they affront Dionysus' person and vanity, are stored up by the god to be used as fuel to feed the intensifying fire of his vengeance. The boy-king is stubborn, irresolute, and not very bright. The dialogue is loaded with dramatic irony and sarcasm — all of it to Dionysus' advantage. Finally, Pentheus catches on and shouts: "Seize him. He is mocking me and Thebes." The god goes willingly, accepting the chains as he had tolerated the seizure of his thrysus and the scissors. But as he is led away, he warns Pentheus:

I go, though not to suffer, since that cannot be.
But Dionysus whom you outrage by your acts,
who you deny is god, will call you to account.

Dionysus is smug in his encounter with Pentheus because the king is so easy to beat and the god realizes that he has found in Pentheus the means by which to avenge himself. However, the full scope of that vengeance is not yet clear in Dionysus' mind.

Thus the dramatic pressure — what happens to him — has already eliminated the revelation of godhead as an effective motive of Dionysus. For if he wished to convince Pentheus of his divinity he had ample opportunity to show the king. Pentheus asks, "What form do they take, these mysteries of yours?" Dionysus puts him off by telling him that the uninitiated cannot know. (We may ask, parenthetically, what then are the Theban women, Cadmus, and Tiresias learning in the hills? And how does Dionysus spread his rites if not by revealing them?) Then Pentheus asks, "Tell me the benefits that those who know your mysteries enjoy?" Dionysus answers, "I am forbidden to say, but they are worth knowing." The Chorus, we remember, outlined the benefits of the Dionysian mysteries in great detail during the first ode. Even Tiresias, not yet initiated, spoke of the good things Dionysus gives to all men. Therefore, it is clear that Dionysus is merely playing a game with Pentheus. He wants to infuriate the king so that Pentheus will heap blasphemy on blasphemy, sacrilege on sacrilege and thereby further stimulate the god to vengeance. As Dionysus later puts it: "Our prey now thrashes in the net we threw." The net is not cast out suddenly; even in this first meeting the strong snare settles on Pentheus.

Let us note here that the direct encounters between Pentheus and Dionysus are never even matches. There is not true dramatic conflict between them as there is, for example, between Oedipus and Tiresias in *Oedipus Rex*. Euripides, we may hope, was no fool, and he could have made the dialogue more evenly balanced and theatrically interesting. We, as audience, are excited by it — but only because of the dramatic irony. We know who the pretty, blonde fellow really is; Pentheus, the blustering hothead, does not know and we anticipate the terrible consequences of the king's irreverence. We may further note that although Dionysus is disguised as his own prophet, the other people in the play give this "prophet" much reverence and show him great respect. Man's skin is very thin and divinity glows through. Dionysus himself continually emphasizes that he is speaking for the god. And, of course, we in the audience know from the first moment of the play that the prophet is the god. I suggest that Euripides omitted the king versus god conflict on any effective theatrical level because he did not want the theme of his play occluded by a false conflict. While the outrages Oedipus heaps on Tiresias are central to the theme of that play: the king represents the individual fleeing from fate and the seer represents fate pursuing the individual, the dialogue between Pentheus and Dionysus is not central to any theme in *The Bacchae*. Pentheus is led on into sacrilege by the god; he is prodded and pushed toward his own disaster, as Oedipus flees toward his. But Pentheus himself is only the means by which Dionysus partially avenges himself. He is merely the catalyst for the communal sacrifice, entering into this larger scheme only insofar as he is a member of the ruling family. And, as we shall see, it is against Agave and Cadmus (and through them the city) that Dionysus directs his full force. Euripides makes Pentheus a small man, and removes him from the play when it is barely two-thirds over, in order to make the communal sacrifice that much more effective.

After Dionysus is led away the Chorus is at once confused, frightened, and enraged. They cry out to their god for deliverance, sensing that what threatens their "prophet" endangers them. They do not have to wait long. The palace is shaken, fire leaps up about Semele's tomb, and the Chorus — in describing the destructive miracle — cries out again, this time prophetically: "He has brought the high house low!" Dionysus reappears and gleefully relates how Pentheus has been shamed in the barn, trussing up cattle. The speech is laced with sarcasm and the obvious personal pleasure the god has had in humiliating the king. Toward the end of the speech there is this crucial line: "For Pentheus I care nothing." The god is no longer interested in the man — that victory is too easy and unimportant. Hereafter, Dionysus will treat the king impersonally, with detached, sardonic interest. Just as Pentheus enters, Dionysus slyly confides to the Chorus:

> What, I wonder, will he have to say? But let him
> bluster. I shall not be touched to rage.

The man can no longer goad the god, for the goading in the first place was by invitation only. The relationship between the two characters now enters its final, bizarre form. We hold back our laughter only because we suspect that the butt of the joke, poor Pentheus, will come to no pleasant end.

After the release of Dionysus from the barn, the play's action accelerates towards the death of Pentheus. Euripides knows that the king is no longer a strong character on stage — he can be acted on, but he can no longer effect action. Since Pentheus has no means of any direct conflict-contact with Dionysus, he is quickly disposed of. The lines he speaks show him up as the tool of Dionysus and we witness the god stripping the last vestiges of self-will from the king. The Messenger enters and describes what has happened to the Maenads on the hillside: their progression from gentle unity-with-nature love to mad orgiastic-destructive love. Pentheus prepares to take his troops out to disperse the women. This is the situation Dionysus had foreseen at the very beginning of the play:

> But if the men of Thebes attempt to force
> my Bacchae from the mountainside by threat of arms,
> I shall marshal my Maenads and take the field.

But the god — improvising as the situation develops — does not follow through with his announced plan. He changes his mind simply because another idea seems better to him at this later moment. As Pentheus is about to leave, Dionysus stops him and offers to lead the king to the mountainside to observe the revels of the Maenads which were, but a few lines ago, "forbidden rites." Pentheus, as interested in seeing an orgy as in stopping one, seizes this opportunity. He then balks temporarily when Dionysus tells him he must disguise himself as a woman. But his prurient imagination is too fired up for him to turn back for any reason — he is too much wrapped in the god's net — and he goes into the palace to don the female clothes he will die in. Dionysus is overjoyed. The king will be humiliated again — this time in public — and then he will be butchered. The god will have his revenge; and it will be: O, so sweet!

> I want him made the laughingstock of Thebes,
> paraded through the streets, a woman. Now
> I shall go and costume Pentheus in the clothes
> which he must wear to Hades when he dies, butchered
> by the hands of his mother.

Dionysus has come so far from his originally stated motives of godhead and worship that what Cadmus had called "the costume of the god" is now, by Dionysus' own wish, the ridiculous garb which will make Pentheus a "laughingstock." It is in this speech, too, that Dionysus first mentions that Agave will kill her son. This is, as I have noted, a different plan than that outlined in the prologue. It is another indication that Pentheus is not going out to meet his "Fate," but is rather fulfilling the constantly changing plans of Dionysus, who is working out the means of his vengeance pragmatically. The murder of Pentheus is a particular kind of death dreamed up on the spot by Dionysus and designed specifically for the king. Cadmus and Tiresias have gone previously to the hillside, uninitiated, dressed as Bacchantes, and they have suffered no hardship or harm, although Cadmus openly declared to Pentheus that the god may very well be false but that it is expedient politics and good for the family to worship him. No, Pentheus goes to meet a "Fate" cut peculiarly and absurdly to his own pattern.

It may be, even, that Dionysus is not yet certain when he sends Pentheus out to die that his murder will serve as the catalyst for the communal sacrifice. For Dionysus says to Pentheus: "You and you alone will suffer for your city." That things do not work themselves out this way emphasizes the pragmatic nature of Dionysus' vengeance. It is only when Agave returns to Thebes with Pentheus' head impaled on her thrysus that the full horror of Dionysus' revenge takes its mature shape.

The great length of the scene in which Agave recognizes that the quarry she has killed is Pentheus (it takes nearly 135 lines) may indicate, as some have said, the gradual understanding of what Dionysian worship means. But it seems rather to be the *actual form* of Dionysus' penultimate revenge. First, Pentheus is humiliated; next he is killed; thirdly, Agave, with the anguished help of Cadmus, realizes what she has done. Finally, Dionysus discloses the future misfortunes of the family and the city. It is, however, the penultimate vengeance — Agave's recognition of Pentheus — which is most graphic and horrible. First the Chorus and then Cadmus confront Agave. The long, agonized trail of her recognition stings to the roots:

Look, look at the prize I bring. . . .

I stuck him first.
The Maenads call me "Agave the blest.". . .

I have won the trophy of the chase. . . .

Why do you reproach me? Is there
something wrong? . . .

What is it? What am I holding in my hands? . . .

No! O gods, I see the greatest grief there is. . . .

But who killed him? . . . .

Now, now I see:
Dionysus has destroyed us all.

The tremendous drop from ecstatic joy to recognition and finally
to bottomless grief is the full savor of Dionysus' revenge. Both
Cadmus and Agave realize what Dionysus has done. They do not
need the epiphany.

Cadmus
Justly — too justly — has lord Bromius
this god of our own blood, destroyed us all,
every one.

Agave
Dionysus has destroyed us all.

Cadmus sees early, Agave late — but when both have seen it, and
said it, savoring the profound bitterness of it all, the action of the
play is completed. The realization that "Dionysus has destroyed
us all, every one" is the essence of the play. The frenzy of the Dionysus-of-the-mind is the machine, Pentheus the catalyst, and
Thebes the victim.

After this recognition, Dionysus appears again, this time as
god, to explain in detail how the final destruction of Thebes will
be carried out and why he was moved to such terrible vengeance:

I am Dionysus
the son of Zeus, returned to Thebes, revealed,
a god to man. But the men of Thebes blasphemed me.
they slandered me; they said I came of mortal man,
and not content with blasphemies,
they dared to threaten my person with violence.

These crimes this people whom I cherished well
did from malice to their benefactor. Therefore,
I now disclose the sufferings in store for them.
Like enemies they shall be driven from this city
to other lands; there, submitting to the yoke
of slavery, they shall wear out wretched lives,
captives of war, enduring much indignity.

Once again, it is not Dionysus' godhead which is revealed, but his egotism. He assumes that everyone knew (or should have known) who the "prophet" was; for it was against the god disguised as man that the indignities were heaped. But Dionysus does not make this distinction between god and prophet now. Furthermore, if we compare this speech with what actually happened on stage we find that no one but Pentheus blasphemed the god (unless we take Cadmus' expediency as blasphemy); that whatever slander was uttered, was spoken before the play began; that everyone in Thebes, with the exception of Pentheus, gave reverence to the god. Cadmus, Tiresias, the Chorus, the Attendant, the Messenger — from highest to lowest, urged the king to recognize and honor the god. As for threatening Dionysus' person with violence, again only Pentheus is guilty: of attempting to harm not the god explicitly revealed, but the god's "prophet." However, Dionysus is not interested in facts, but rather in rationalizing what has happened. Since the city has been destroyed — "too justly" — he must give divine reasons for that obliteration.

We are left, then, with one serious problem unresolved. Did Dionysus always mean to sacrifice the entire city, or did this idea develop only after the murder of Pentheus? If the first is true then the line — "You and you alone will suffer for your city" — was a bald lie. If the second is true, Dionysus is, indeed, a capricious god who fits the consequences of his actions into the framework of his desires.

The text leaves us no alternative. Dionysus comes to Thebes to avenge himself. Pentheus is the perfect catalyst for this vengeance and the murder of the king gives Dionysus the opportunity to exercise fully his wrath and indignation. But we may be certain that the unrestricted scope of this vengeance was not apparent to Dionysus at the outset. Wanting his vanity appeased, he continues to scourge the people until he is satiated. His means of satisfying his urge for vengeance shifts and expands recklessly as the play proceeds. Like a glutton at a feast, he neither knows nor cares what the next course will bring: he gorges himself until he is appeased. "So it has happened; I am satisfied; so be it" — this is the rationale of the god.

The city itself becomes the sacrifice because, finally, Pentheus is too weak and too unpopular with his own family and people to be an adequate scapegoat. Pentheus is no savior and father to Thebes as Oedipus is. Pentheus *qua* Pentheus is no great loss to Thebes. But Pentheus, king of Thebes, son of Agave, grandson of Cadmus, murdered by his own mother — that is enough to bring down the royal house and with it the city. And the city — that is a full and acceptable sacrifice.

It is in this communal sacrifice, and the capricious manner by which it is accomplished, that the heart of the terror and the power of the play rests. In this regard, *The Bacchae* stands in fierce contrast to that other great play of sacrifice, *Oedipus Rex.* In *Oedipus* one man is sacrificed in harmony with inexorable Fate so that the city may be cleansed and reborn. The relationship between Oedipus' unknowing sin and the plague sweeping the city is unmistakably clear. But in *The Bacchae* an entire city is sacrificed to assuage the offended vanity of a god and Fate, as such, is extraneous. As the play closes there is no hope for man or the city, no cleansing, no new harmony: no future.

There are too many alternative actions open to the characters of *The Bacchae* for Fate to play a role. In particular, too many courses are open to Dionysus; he changes his mind too often; he is always improvising. With such a fickle god in control of the action, we may dismiss Fate entirely from the scheme of the play. If this is so, there is no "meaning" to the play. There is nothing man can "learn" from the experience of the play. We may be awed, terrified, destroyed; but we cannot map out any way of acting in the future so that the gods will not once again swoop down in anger and jealousy and obliterate us. A great gap opens between man and the universe, when the universe acts out of human emotion, as Dionysus does. For if we expect nothing more of heaven, we expect it to be impersonally rational and just. The great and overwhelming paradox of *The Bacchae* — and perhaps the reason why it fascinates us today — is that Dionysus, acting out of human pride, represents a cosmic scheme that man can never be sure of, prepare for, or satisfy. In *The Bacchae* we have a capricious god enjoying jealous vengeance, which is the absurd right of divinity.

Seneca
OEDIPUS

Translated by
David Anthony Turner

Characters
    Oedipus

    Iocasta

    Chorus of Theban Elders

    Creon

    Manto

    Tiresias

    Messenger

    Elder

    Slaves

    Phorbas

TRANSLATOR'S NOTE: Seneca's play is modeled on Greek tragedies written four hundred years before his time. His idea of theatre would be about as far from the Greek originals as a modern off-Broadway staging of *Othello* from Shakespeare's first London production. Greek tragedy was a cross between a Broadway musical and a church service. The nearest modern equivalent might be an Olympic Games opening ceremony.

Drama probably began from a tribal singing-dance which gradually got more complex. One relic of this is the *Chorus*. By Seneca's time it is simply a vehicle for powerful reflective verse about the woes of human life, or a lyrical poem about the gods and heroes of Greek and Roman legend. *Oedipus* is written to be performed, or declaimed, without interruption. It has been produced like this in modern times, although I must admit at the National's first night I saw a member of the audience faint. If the play is to be done without interruption it is important to give the audience good warning. If breaks are required I have suggested a division into three Acts or Movements. The best thing is for each production to discover its own preferred structure during the process of rehearsal.

Choral speaking is an art in itself. So in most modern productions the Chorus is divided up among individual members, each taking a few lines in turn.

ACT ONE

[*The steps of the Palace. Thebes.* OEDIPUS *is alone.*]

Oedipus

Night has lost . . . Now the sun limps back, glints through a tawdry cloud . . . Woebegone . . . Spread out below it, houses . . . ours . . . Fodder for the hungry plague.

Day coming will show us how many died last night . . . Can any man enjoy being a King? A blessing? What a cheat! Behind the smile, the smooth front, — agony!

High peaks always catch the wind. Great dynasties are like that, exposed to Fate. . . . How good it all was! Running away from my father's domain. A prince. A refugee. But free from the fear . . . Wandering, it was brave, and stumbling (Gods in heaven be my witness), I *stumbled on*, a kingdom. The Fear. . . .

I cannot word it — Polybus, my father. Delphi. The oracle, warning. I would kill him someday. And the other . . . The indictment . . . the worse one. Supposing. . . . I — murder my father . . . can anything be greater sacrilege? . . . family feeling? Cry for it. Apollo threatens me, the son, with — even think the destiny into words and I blush — with the room, the *bed* of his father, made monstrous, by illicit lust made — the tool of incest! It drove me from my father's kingdom, this, aghast.

I didn't leave home as a renegade, no. Only — I didn't trust myself. The Law of Nature — I determined to keep it safe from assault. When you are afraid, really afraid, you go in fear of — even the impossible. . . . I live in terror. I choose not to trust — myself. . . .

Yet even now, events plot against me . . . Why? Try and think. This plague, killing so indiscriminately, spares only me. I am being saved for. . . . what disaster? The ruins of our state, tears over and over again for fresh deaths all round me, a nation dying, yet I stand untouched, the man Apollo has impeached. Could you have hoped, Oedipus? Bad blood like yours, presented with an uninfected kingdom? Ugh, I've made heaven hellish!

Our lungs are on fire, gasping, but there's no breath of wind, cool, soft, caressing. . . . Instead the sun stokes up the dog day heat. The rivers have no water, the grass no green. Dirce is parched; Ismenos, a shrunken river hardly damping the bare sand-banks with his poor trickle. Moon sidles across the sky, dim. Pale, gloomy earth, cloudy skies, no bright stars twinkling through the night. Instead a black mist weighs on the land like lead. The corn is ripe, tall spikes quivering golden, but there's no grain, the crop withers, sterile, shrivelled, straw. There's no escape from death for anyone, no distinction of age or sex. The sickness treats young men and old alike, as fatal for fathers as their sons. Bed-mates share the same pyre at funerals without tears, for no-one is left to mourn. A scourge, but the very nature of it has dried up our tears. The bitter end, only to be expected: with too much tragedy *crying* dies. I saw a man; his father, sick himself, carried him to the last fires. I have seen a frenzied mother bring her child and hurry back for another — the same pyre will do for both. Death breeds death, and another man's funeral ends as the mourner's own. They burn their own families on other people's pyres, even stealing the fire. Damned men feel no shame. They say: "They've caught light? That's enough. No time to let them burn." There's a shortage of plots for graves now. The woods have no more pyres to give. No prayers can relieve the infected, no healing art. Those who would nurse grow sick; and disease traps every helping hand.

On my knees to the altars of the Gods, I stretch my hands in prayer! Please. Fate, now. Let me be gone, before my tottering country. I do not want to be last to fall, the final death in my kingdom to be mine. Gods, you are too cruel. Was I born to be racked? Death is prescribed for the nation: am I the only one to be left out? Oh Oedipus, turn away from the place your fatal touch has infected. Leave the tears and the burying, and the cancer-curse on daylight you drag with you, deadly visitor. Run! — and the quicker for having waited too long, back, even to — your father!

Iocasta [*Approaching.*]
Oedipus, my husband. What use is complaining? It only makes bad things worse. To my mind the essence of being a king is to take on challenges. The more your throne trembles, the faster your power and majesty slip into decline, then all the more fearlessly you should take your stand, controlled, unwavering. Running away is no behavior for a man.

Oedipus
Cowardice? Disgrace! Far be it from me! Or any suspicion of it. Courage such as mine doesn't know how to be abject, to cringe. If drawn swords faced me, if the savage rush of War charged down on me, I would turn my hand to fight and not give it a thought. Not even the Sphinx, plaiting words into hidden riddles, that sybil defying description, I did not run away from her. I faced her — bloody jaws and all. The earth round about grew white with scattered bones. There she crouched on a high rock, cowing her victim from the start, ruffling out her wings, that tail, backwards and forwards, switching like a lion's. I demanded to know the question. She gnashed her fangs — a noise above my head, blood-curdling. She dug at the rocks with her talons, all ready for my bowels, impatient at any delay. I took what she gave me, words in knots, a tangle of tricks, the wild Bird-Woman's riddle of death — and solved it.

Why the frenzy now, praying for death? It's too late. You could have died *then*. This glorious sceptre . . . This is your return for destroying the Sphinx. Your prize. . . . But the subtle monster, see her rising rebellious from her grave . . . The scourge of Thebes. I killed her once. . . . Thebes. Now she wrecks it! There is only one chance left now. Will Apollo give an Oracle, and save us?

Chorus of Theban Elders
Down you crash, noble nation of Cadmus and all your city too.

Poor Thebes, see around you fields without farmers. Bacchus, our patron, death harvests your soldiers, comrades to farthest India even, who dared to gallop the plains of the East and plant your flag at the ends of the earth. We sons of the unbeaten race are dying, we fall, and harsh destiny snaps us up. On and on, burials, over and over. Sad ranks of corpses jostle for graves.

The first blow fell on our sheep, ambling through their rich pastures, grazing. Then the charger in mid-gallop totters, tumbles to the ground, throwing its rider in the fall. Stags forget fear of ravening wolves. Angry lions' roaring stops. The lurking snake has lost its sting, and burning with fever, venom dried up, it dies.

No dark shadows pour over the mountains from woods dressed out in their leaves. The vine has no branches bending with wine-grapes. The curse on us has its way with everything.

The furies with their torch from Tartarus have shattered the gates of Erebos far below. Phlegethon changes course. In our Theban rivers run the waters of Styx. And word spreads that the Hound of Hell, his steel chains burst, strays through our fields. Among the trees phantoms wander, taller than men. Twice the river Dirce has seethed with blood, and in the silence of the night, the dogs of Amphion have howled.

This new way of dying, worse than death. A numbing paralysis grips weak arms, the face, flushed, sickly and dotted with ulcers. The cheeks puff, strange fire eats up the limbs, the ears ring, black blood trickles from the twitching nose. A crowd lies prostrate at the altars, prays to die. The only present that the Gods give readily.

Oedipus
But who is this, hurrying to the Palace? Is it Creon? Creon, noble in birth and deeds, is it he? Or is my mind sick and confusing false and true?

Chorus
Our constant prayer has been for Creon, now he is here!

Oedipus
A shudder. Fate . . . where is it leading? My heart is pounding.
I am afraid. . . . Whenever happiness or agony are equally pos-
sible, the soul sweats, longing to find out, but frightened to. . . .

Dear brother of my queen, we are exhausted. Do you bring us
help? The news, quickly, tell us.

Creon
The chances are — it is confusing. The answers of the oracle
— it's hard to say . . .

Oedipus
When a man is in torment, help he cannot trust is no help at
all.

Creon
The God of Delphi is not straightforward. Shrouded secrets,
complexity, that is his way.

Oedipus
Very well, very well. It is ambiguous but tell us; only one
man has the gift for riddles — Oedipus.

Creon
Here is the God's command:
Exile as penance for the murder of our king — vengeance for
the death of Laius.

Then the bright sun will skip across the sky, give pure air,
safe to breathe. But not before.

Oedipus
Laius the glorious?

Creon
Our king before you came.

Oedipus
Murdered? By whom? Who is it Apollo indicts? Tell us. He
will pay the penalty.

Creon
Tell you what I saw and heard? But the awe of it. . . . Please
God it's safe to speak. I set foot in Apollo's holy shrine, a suppliant, and dutifully raised my hands in prayer to the God, following the rite. As I did, the twin peaks of Parnassus, white

with snow, rumbled threateningly. Apollo's laurel tree —
there overhead — rustled, shook. Suddenly, the sacred water,
the spring of Castalia, stood still. . . . Apollo's medium, the
priestess, began to undo her tumbled hair, writhed about, felt
stabs of pain. This was the God. She had not yet reached the
cave when there was a flash that, that was — louder than any
man could imagine, that was — speaking. . . .

> "Kind stars will come again to Cadmus' Thebes
> If the runaway guest, the guilty regicide
> Known to Apollo now and from infancy,
> Shall leave Ismenian Dirce, river fair.
> Brief joy is thine for that damn'd murdering.
> War with thee bring, bequeath war to thy sons.
> Who went with filth back to a mother's womb."

Oedipus
The Gods give us a command, and a warning. And shouldn't
the dead king's ashes have been honored, to discourage plots
against the sanctity of thrones? Royal security is a king's concern. We have it in hand. Someone who in his lifetime is a
man to fear, dies, and then no-one gives him a thought.

Creon
We meant to do honor to the king, though he died far away,
but fear drove it out of our minds —

Oedipus
However great the fear, can it stop duty, loyalty?

Creon
She could. The Sphinx, with her blood-curdling threats, her
damn'd riddle!

Oedipus
Well, the Gods demand it. Now someone will pay for that
atrocity. All you gods who look kindly on the work of kings,
be near me. May no house be a haven, no home secure, may
no country welcome in his banishment the man whose hand
struck down King Laius. May shame torment his bed, may his
seed mock heaven. With that same hand may he kill even his
own father, and may he — can any curse be more deadly? —
may he do all the things I have escaped. There shall be no for-

giveness anywhere. Apollo who moves the lips of the priestess to speak the future, come yourself as witness to my words. By the kingdom here of which I am guest, and master, by the gods of that home I left behind — I make this oath. My father, and a quiet old age for him, peaceful possession of a high majesty till death; for Merope my mother — marriage to Polybus only, never to — someone else. . . . On all this may mercy for the guilty man depend. May I not spare him. . . .

But the scene of that foul murder — where did it take place? Tell me again. Was it a fair fight or an ambush?

Creon

King Laius was on his way to Delphi. At that point the highway is narrow, thick bushes on either side, and the road divides in three. One goes through Phocis where the soft line of Parnassus sweeps up from the deep valley fields to its twin peaks and the sky. One leads to the Isthmus. The third, a steep pass, winds on into the farm lands of Olenia to the meandering Eleis. There it makes a ford. The water is icy. Laius was expecting a peaceful journey, but here, at the crossroads, he was suddenly set upon by robbers and fell in the fight, a sword wound, no-one saw it. But here is Tiresias! He comes at the right moment. He is excited, it's the oracle. His haste is slowed by old, unsteady limbs. And his sight is gone; so Manto leads him.

Manto

No, father, this way, King Oedipus is here . . .

Oedipus

Next to Apollo himself! Tiresias! Explain the oracle to us. Someone is marked out for Justice. Who?

Tiresias

You are a great man. So it is beneath you to show surprise at this. I ask for time. A blind man misses a great deal, I dare not be in a rush to speak. But I will follow the call, of my country and of Apollo. Destiny? Let us look. Now, if my blood were young and warm, my own heart would be sufficient medium for the God. As it is. . . . Bring a white bull to the altars, and a heifer whose neck has never felt the yoke.

Manto

They are here father, waiting.

Tiresias

You look after your blind father, don't you, child? Describe
for me any clear signs of augury from the sacrifice.

Manto

There are victims at the holy altars now.

Tiresias [*To* OEDIPUS.]

The sacrifice will tell me the future.

Manto [*Examining.*]

Yes. . . . They are without blemish.

Tiresias

Ask the Gods to hear us. Use the ritual prayer. And cover the
altars with incense.

Manto

I have put incense on the God's holy hearth — there!

Tiresias

What is the flame like? We have fed the fire, and well. Does it
eat?

Manto

It flared up with a sudden blaze, and just as suddenly went
down again.

Tiresias

Did it rise? Did it shine clear?

Manto

It changed. Like Iris who comes with the rain, paints half the
sky with an arch of color, that was the flame. It flickered, a
tinge of blue, patches of yellow, then blood-red, and at the end
it grew dim and died. — But look!

Tiresias

What?

Manto

The wine we poured in libation — turns to blood. Thick
smoke curls around the king's head; it is seething all about
him now; his face . . . It is a cloud blotting out the daylight.
Father, tell us what does this signify?

Tiresias

Tell what? How can I? My mind lurches and reels, I am

speechless. Well? What shall I say? The curse is terrible, but obscure. Usually, wrath of the Gods is shown to us by clear signs. What can this be that they want it brought to light, yet do not want? Such anger spells death, and they are hiding. . . . It is — I don't know. But the Gods blush at it.

[*With decision.*]

Quickly. Bring the victims here. Sprinkle the salted meal on their necks.

[*Additional sounds, realistic, musical, or electronic, might be used in the following sequence.*]

Tiresias

Do they allow hands to touch them? Do they take the sacred ritual calmly?

Manto

The bull, he is tossing his head! He has shied back from the light. He is trembling.

Tiresias

Is one blow enough to fell them?

Manto

The heifer . . . abandons herself to the sword. It barely touched her, one stab and she fell. But the bull has been struck twice. He heaves blindly back and forward. . . . He is spent. There is no struggle now, hardly. He coughs out his life.

Tiresias

The blood, does it spurt out? Was it a clean blow?

Manto

The heifer's blood comes pumping from her breast right where the cut is. But the bull's, they were sore wounds but they are only marked by a thin ooze. Everything is the wrong way round. The blood pours through its mouth and out of its eyes.

Tiresias

My flesh creeps, this is a black scarifice. Now into the entrails. Describe any clear omens.

Manto

The organs are. . . . nothing is in its right place. They . . . it is all upside down. The lungs are on the right . . . so full of blood they could never take air. The heart is not where it should be, on the left. There's no sheath of soft tissue enfolding the entrails. And the womb — I cannot understand. It's firm and hard — why? Can it be — Ugh! Obscene! — in the heifer, she was never mated, but — an unborn calf! And its position in the mother's belly is strange. It moans! Its legs — they are moving, twitching, weakly, in spasms, trembling. But all bloody the victims are straining to rise up! A gutted carcass stands on its legs and lunges at the holy priests with its horns! The intestines slide through their hands! The very stones of the altar bellow! There, it is over.

[*Pause.*]

Oedipus

These miracles, this fearful sacrifice, what does it mean? Tell me plainly, my ears are ready, yes greedy for your words. I am not afraid. At breaking point, a man finds peace.

Tiresias

The pangs you flee now, you will live to long for.

Oedipus

The gods want me to know just one thing, tell me it. Who bloodied his hand with the murder of the King?

Tiresias

Birds flying high across the sky, organs cut from still-warm victims cannot spell out the name. We must risk another way. Laius himself must be summoned back from below, from everlasting night. We must unlock the earth and pray to the unprayable. To whom will you entrust the rite? Speak. It cannot be you, the eyes of a king may not look on ghosts.

Oedipus

You, Creon. You are the next in line, this is work for you.

Tiresias   [*Going off.*]

While *we* undo the bolts of Styx and Hell, let the men chant a hymn. Praise Bacchus our patron god.

ACT TWO
Chorus

Weave, weave, the ivy in your hair and toss your head, gently take up the magic wand, of Bacchus! Pride of heaven, Bright God, hear the prayers of the Thebans, your own noble race raise their hands in entreaty. Turn your face here to us, beautiful, kindly. Bright as the stars you look, scatter these clouds, doom stalking us, black threat of Hell.

All the East has seen you enthroned in your chariot of gold, your lions caparisoned in flowing robes. Old Silenus on his moth-eaten donkey shambles after you, tousled-head tied with a garland of ivy, with your lusty followers sporting in mystic orgies.

When young, you were stolen by Tyrrhian pirates. But Nereus stopped the waves and the tide, and turned the turquoise sea into meadow. Then comes a budding of spring-leaves on plane-trees, a copse of laurels, Apollo's favorite, and twittering birds fill the green with noise.

The oars are covered with rioting ivy, tendrils of vine entwine the tops'l. Suddenly on the prow there's a lion roaring, and crouched on the poop a tiger from the Ganges. The pirates are in the water swimming, terrified. But now as they sink they take on new shape. Tiny fins spring from their side, they dive through the waves with curving backs, crescent-moon tails slicing out of the water. They follow swift ships as arch-back dolphins.

Naxos, which the Aegean encircles, gave you Ariadne to marry. That day from dry rocks wine ran bubbling, rivers of wine criss-crossed through the meadows. Sweet juice with pure streams of snow-white milk and wine of Lesbos and a scent of thyme. The earth drank deep. The new bride is led home to the vastness of heaven. Apollo, hair tumbling round his shoulders, sings a rhapsody. Two Cupids beat out the rhythm with their torches. Jupiter puts down his fiery bolts and lays aside his thunder when Bacchus comes.

While bright stars speed across the Universe, while it grows old. While Ocean hems the world around, while full moon takes back light it gave away, as long as morning star says dawn is near. We shall adore thy clear face, Bacchus, Bacchus. Bacchus!

Oedipus

I see from your face you bring bad news. Still we will placate the gods with a life. Whose is it to be?

Creon

'Speak!' you say, ordering me, but fear warns me not to.

Oedipus

Thebes is at the point of collapse. If that does not move you surely the downfall of your own royal family will?

Creon

You are eager to know, too eager. For when you do you will pray not to have known.

Oedipus

Will you conceal information vital to the state? When something is wrong, not knowing is no cure.

Creon

Sour medicine makes sore treatment.

Oedipus

Tell me what you've heard, or it will go hard with you. You'll find what swords can do when a king is angry.

Creon

Kings may hate words they ordered to be spoken.

Oedipus

You will pay for this with your worthless life, unless. . . . The secrets from the sacrifice, you have a tongue. Speak.

Creon

No. Allow me silence, surely the smallest favor one can beg a king?

Oedipus

For a king, for a state, freedom of silence is often more of a threat than freedom of speech.

Creon

What freedom is left when a man is not free even to hold his peace?

Oedipus
If he is commanded to speak yet stays silent, it is sedition. . . .
Creon [*Pause.*]
Very well. You've forced me. I will tell you. But I beg of you
hear it calmly.
Oedipus
Did any man ever suffer for what he spoke under orders?
Creon
Very well. . . . Some way from the city is a clump of black ilex
trees, round the glen Dirce and the stream. In the middle a
huge lone tree holds the smaller ones vassals to its deep shad-
ow, spreading its branches, a vast canopy, it stands guardian
of the wood. Underneath, the overflow of a small pool, so cold
for so long — ice forms on it. Around it marsh, and slime.

Once the old priest had reached the spot, there was no need to
wait. The place itself provided night enough. . . .

They dug into the ground and threw over the hole fire
snatched from funeral pyres. The seer himself makes movements with his wand, then dresses in a black cloak, a flowing
funeral-robe reaching his feet. In these forbidding vestments,
a wreath of poison yew in his silver hair, the old man steps
forward, face downcast. Black-fleeced sheep and bulls, black
too, are dragged in, backwards. The flames gulp in their rich
food, while the beasts, still alive, thresh in the fire as it over-
comes them. Now he calls to the ghosts, to Dis their king, repeating over and over a magic incantation, and in a passion
chants a spell to the shimmering phantoms, now coaxing,
now compelling. He pours drink-offerings on the fire-pit,
blood. The beasts burn in holocaust. Then more blood, till the
hole is drenched. Other libations are poured, snow-white
milk, and wine — he pours this with his left hand — and
chants again, his voice deeper, and awe-struck. He conjures
the departed spirits. He stares at the ground.

And then — there rose the yelping of — the Hounds of Hell.
Three times the deep valleys rang with that howl of death. . . .
The earth throbbed, the ground under our feet was being

pounded, from below. "They have heard me" said Tiresias. "Dark chaos is cracking, making a passage for the troop of Hell to rise up to Earth." All the trees cringed. A shudder woke the leaves. Oaks split. Earth groaned. Suddenly it gaped, yawning in a bottomless abyss. With my own eyes I glimpsed through the shadows darkness without end, pale spirits, stagnant water. A wild army leaped out, snaked up, stood armed, the whole tribe, the horde of earth brothers sown from dragon-teeth. Then the ogre Erinys screamed, blind fury, horror, and every ghastly creature eternal Night breeds, and hides. Grief tearing its hair, sickness, old-age, fear, and the curse of our people, the wolf of Thebes, Plague. My breath wouldn't come. Manto even, familiar with the old man's spells and powers, stood petrified. Now Tiresias conjures the Death-God's bloodless army, without fear, boldly even. *He* could not see. . . .

And now, flitting light as cloud, free, relishing the air, the breeze, . . . they come. Eryx forest has not so many leaves falling from its branches. Waves in the sea, birds changing Arctic snow for the warm Nile are nothing to the host the wizard's chant brought here. The shimmering ghosts jostle feverishly for the darkest places in that glen of shadows.

At last he came, skulking, hanging his head in shame, keeping his distance from the crowd, trying to hide his face. With secret charms, more and more, the priest followed him till he showed it. He. Laius. . . . The telling makes me shudder. He stood before us; his body was covered in blood, hair foul, matted, filthy with mud. His mouth jerked, he was speaking

"Mad family of Cadmus, stomachs for the blood of your own kin, tear your sons apart with frenzied hands, it would be better, for the vilest sin of Thebes is mother-love. My country rots, yet not by anger of the gods. No, *guilt*. You blame the fierce-blowing death-wind from the South, the rainless sky, the panting earth, the drought! — It is not them. It is that bloody king, a son to hate, who has his father's throne — usurped by savage murder — and, damn the act, his *bed*. But worse still is the mother, the diabolical womb again with child . . .

He shoved his way back to where he began, to bring his dam a gift, forbidden fruit. Beasts even, hardly behave like him, he fathers brothers to himself. You, yes, you with that guilty sceptre in your hand, I am a father unavenged. I will hound you and all your city too. I'll bring a bridesmaid to the wedding, a fury with a whistling lash. I will set sons at each other's throats. I will upturn this house of incest, and crush it, utterly. So, quickly, whip this king out of your land, drive him to turn his fatal steps somewhere, anywhere. Make him leave Thebes; and flowers of spring, green grass will come to it again. His own desire will be to scuttle away from this land of mine as quick as his legs will take him. But I will break his heart, slow him, hold back his feet. People of Thebes, take from him the ground he stands on, his father will make sure he sees no sky . . . "

Oedipus

My bones freeze. A palsy invades my whole body. Have I done what I lived in fear of doing? I am accused of it. But Merope is still the wife of Polybus, so there can be no question of incest by me. Polybus is still alive, not murdered, so my hands are clean. My parents are there, both of them, that makes murder or incest impossible — where else can I go wrong? And Laius. Thebes was in mourning for him long before I stepped on Boeotian soil. Perhaps the old man is lying? Or has one of the powers of heaven a grudge against Thebes? I see it now, yes. Conspiracy, a plot. Clever. . . . But it's a lie. The prophet's making it up, it's a trick, using the gods as a pretext. He's playing kingmaker. It's for Creon. You!

Creon

Me? Would I want to see my own sister deposed? Even if duty to my family was not enough to keep me content with the rank I have, a king's life would terrify me — such responsibilities, they are too much. If I were you, I would give it all up, shrug off the burden. You will have no more trouble. Go away. Choose some state less exalted, it is safer.

Oedipus

So, you urge me, do you, to lay aside the burden of being king?

Creon

For myself, I would give this advice to anyone who was free to choose his own position in life. But for you, now — it is your fate, you cannot do anything else.

Oedipus

Yes. The surest way is ... to glorify the humble life, to talk about peace of mind and a decent sleep. The surest way. . . .

[*Rounds on* CREON.]

for someone who aches to be king himself! Soothing words often hide rebellious thoughts.

Creon

Do all my years of loyalty mean nothing?

Oedipus

For a traitor loyalty is a means to an end.

Creon

But the benefits of being a king — I have them already, with none of the responsibilities. My house is crowded with suitors. Not a day passes but there's some present to my family from their royal cousins. *I* have a horde of dependents who owe their security, their sumptuous food, even the clothes they wear, to my patronage. I am well blessed; what else do you think I need?

Oedipus

The one thing that is missing. The crown itself. No-one ever had enough good fortune.

Creon

I shall be damned like a felon then? No defense?

Oedipus

Was I defended when the ghost of Laius accused me? Who pleaded my case before Tiresias? Yet I stand convicted. You two have shown me how it is done. I simply follow.

Creon

And if I am innocent?

Oedipus

Kings live with fear. For them, suspicion is as good as proof.

Creon

A man who trembles at groundless fears deserves to find them come true.

Oedipus

Turn a guilty man free and he'll hate you. The fate of weakness is defeat.

Creon

Talk like that breeds hate; it must.

Oedipus

Anyone who is afraid of being hated does not know how to rule. Nothing keeps monarchy secure like fear.

Creon

A king who rules tyrannically fears the people he terrorizes. Men who use fear become its slaves.

Oedipus

I am going back to the palace. As for him, he's guilty. Look after him. The prison in the rock, lock him in there and watch him . . .

[*Exits.*]

Chorus

Thebes stands in mortal danger, yet it is not his fault nor does doom haunt it for some act of his. No, we are hounded by ancient hatred from the gods. A stranger came from Sidon and the grove of Castalia gave him shade, the stream Dirce washed the settlers from Tyre.

And ever since, our country has been a breeding ground for new monsters. This was the land that brought to hellish birth a race of — armed men. A call to battle rang from their curving horn, and the bronze bugle sang its strident song, the tongues in their heads had never moved before, their voices never spoke, now their first utterance was a battle-cry.

Brothers in regiments fill all the plain, true children of that seed of dragon's teeth, living their lives out in a single day. Born since the Day-star crossed the sky, they die before the Evening star appears. Cadmus, for he was the stranger, stood aghast seeing such monsters and watched, trembling, the war of the new-born men, till all those savage youths fell; and Mother Earth saw all the children, so lately born, return to her. No more. Let this be the last of killing in this city. No more fighting between brothers in Thebes.

And there was the tragedy that overcame the grandson of Cadmus, when the branching horns of a full grown stag suddenly were on his brow and his hounds hunted their own master. He galloped headlong from the forests, from the hills. Actaeon could run, but now with hooves faster; through trees and outcrops, running from snares that he himself had set. Until he was in the still water of a pool, horns, and on his own face, a wild animal's! Pool that had caressed the virgin body of a goddess too jealous of her modesty.

ACT THREE
Oedipus

The anxiety. . . . turning it over and over inside myself. The death of Laius my doing? Heaven and Hell agree in that. And yet . . . My conscience is clear. It says no. I know myself better than the gods can. That memory again . . . a faint trace. Someone in the way, I hit him with my staff, he fell, he died. An old man, using his chariot to crowd the younger man off the road. . . . But that was far from Thebes, in Phocian country, that place where the road — divides in three. . . .

Iocasta

Oedipus? Oedipus. . . .

Oedipus

Ah dear wife! Half of my soul! I have questions without answers, and I beg your help. How old was Laius when he met his death? In his prime would you say, or overcome with age?

Iocasta

My lord was in his middle years, but old rather than young.

Oedipus

Were there many retainers with him?

Iocasta

The road is difficult, many had lost their way. Only a faithful few kept up with the chariot. It was not easy.

Oedipus
Did any of his companions share the king's fate?

Iocasta
There was one man who loyally and bravely died with him.

Oedipus
I know the culprit now. The numbers fit, the place. One more thing. How long ago was this?

Iocasta
Ten years ago this summer.

[OEDIPUS *catches breath.*]

Messenger
My lord, an embassy. From Corinth.

Oedipus
Corinth? From my father! Let them approach.

Elder   [*Entering.*]
Great Oedipus! The people of Corinth call you back to your ancestral throne. Polybus is gone to his eternal rest.

Oedipus
Oh cruel, cruel. Fate attacks from every side. . . . But have you some word of how my father died?

Elder   [*Coming near.*]
The old man's soul went gently, in his sleep.

Oedipus
So my father is dead, and in his grave.

There was no murder! God be my witness, I can raise my hands to heaven, a good son. No sin to fear there now. But in my destiny there is still something to dread, something more.

Elder
Your father's kingdom — that will banish all your fears.

Oedipus
My father's kingdom . . . Corinth. I will go back there. But my mother — the thought is terrifying!

Elder
Terrifying? Your mother? When she waits there, longing for your return.

Oedipus
Being her son is what drives me away.

Elder

She is a widow. Would you leave her alone?

Oedipus   [*Shudders.*]

You touch on the very thing I fear.

Elder

Tell me the hidden fear that is torturing you. Go on, I am used to being trusted by kings. I can hold my tongue.

Oedipus

It is the oracle from Delphi, a warning. I am terrified that I will marry my mother.

Elder   [*Bursts out in a laugh.*]

No. Stop.

Oedipus

How can you laugh?

Elder

There's nothing in these worries, no. That's what you're afraid of, is it? It's nothing.

Oedipus

But Merope. . . .

Elder

Merope? She wasn't your real mother!

Oedipus

Not —

Elder

No.

Oedipus

But what could she gain from a son who was not hers?

Elder

A king with heirs has a much greater hold on his people's loyalty and ambition.

Oedipus

But how did you come by these secrets between a man and his wife?

Elder

These very hands, mine, gave you to your mother when you were an infant.

Oedipus

You gave me to my mother? But who gave me to *you*?

Elder

A shepherd at the foot of snow-capped Mount Cithaeron.

Oedipus

But you? How did you come to be there?

Elder

I was on the mountain with my flocks.

Oedipus

Tell me something else. There is an unmistakable mark on my body. Can you describe it?

Elder

Your feet were injured, by an iron nail. That's where your name comes from — Oedipus, swollen foot, because of your inflamed feet. You were crippled.

Oedipus

A child, wrapped in a bundle. . . . Who gave it to you? I must know.

Elder

He was pasturing the king's flocks. He had a company of shepherds, working beside him.

Oedipus

His name. Tell me.

Elder

For old men early memories fade. Things that have been there so long get buried.

Oedipus

Could you recognize your man by his face, if you saw him?

Elder

I might, perhaps. A tiny clue sometimes brings back a memory that time has dimmed.

Oedipus

Have every herd driven to the altar, to sacrifice — have their shepherds come too. On your way, slaves.

Slaves

Sire!

Oedipus

Quickly, summon all the chief herdsmen.

Elder

This is all a secret, whether by chance or design it doesn't

matter. But it has lain long enough already, surely. Let it lie
for ever. Men often go ferreting out the truth, only to find it,
and then wish they hadn't.

Oedipus

Can anything be worse than having a fear like mine?

Elder

This must be something serious, if such pains are needed to
discover it. There is a conflict here — on the one side you
have the common good, on the other your own as king. Both
mean as much. Don't stir things up. Fate will reveal itself of
its own accord.

Oedipus

When things are going well it's unwise to disturb them. But
when they're desperate, a change can do no harm.

Elder

Being a king's heir is not enough for you?
You want something grander still? Take care. You may regret
finding out who your real parents are.

Oedipus

I want to know whose I am by blood. Even if I regret it afterwards, I want something definite.

[*Enter* PHORBAS.]

Ah, look. This old man is called Phorbas. At one time he was
in charge of the king's flock. Now, do you remember this old
fellow's name? Or his face?

Elder

He looks familiar to me. I'm not quite sure, but somehow I
feel he's no stranger to me.

[*To* PHORBAS.]

My good man ... were you a slave when Laius was lord of
this kingdom? Did you ever, at any time drive his fat sheep on
the grasslands at the foot of Cithaeron?

Phorbas

Oh, a lovely place, Cithaeron. Fresh grass, yes. . . . Fine summer feeding-grounds for our sheep, always.

Elder [*Raising voice.*]

Do you recognize me?

Phorbas
Well, I'm not sure. . . . I can't say. It's my memory. . . .
Oedipus
Was there once a little boy, given by you to this man here?
Speak.
Phorbas
Well, I couldn't rightly. . . .
Oedipus
You hesitate. Your face — why do you change color?
Phorbas
My lord, I —
Oedipus
You're fumbling for words. Why?
Phorbas
I — I —
Oedipus
Truth doesn't need time to think.
Phorbas
You're trying to turn up something that was buried long ago.
Oh, it's been an age. . . .
Oedipus
Speak! Or will torture force the truth out of you.
Phorbas
I did make this man a present of — of a baby. But it was no
use, it couldn't have lived to see the light of day.
Elder [*Aside.*]
No don't say that. Far from it. He is alive and, please God,
will live on.
Oedipus
Why are you so sure that this baby you handed over did not
survive, eh?
Phorbas
Through both his feet, fixing his legs together, there had been
driven a thin iron nail. Gangrene caused by the wound in-
flamed the child's whole body, it was diseased, it stank.
Oedipus [*Aside.*]
What more do I need? Fate is poised to spring.
Who was the child? Out with it.

Phorbas

Honor forbids me —

Oedipus

Bring fire, one of you!

Phorbas

No!

Oedipus

Now we'll have that honor out of him, burn it out.

Phorbas

The truth, you'd find it out? And by such bloody means.

Slave

A torch, great King.

Phorbas

Forgive me, I beg of you!

Oedipus

Do I seem savage? Was the body swollen? Then revenge lies to your hand: stab me with the truth. . . . Who was it? Who was his father? Who was the mother that bore him?

Phorbas

His mother was — your wife.

[*Pause.*]

Oedipus

Earth! Gape open! And you, emperor of darkness, snatch this monstrous soiler of birth and bed down to the farthest pit of Tartarus! Countrymen, together now. Pile stones on my head — bury me! Take weapons — butcher me! Fathers, sons, make me the target for your swords. Wives, brothers, take up arms, sick people, drag brands from your funeral fires, hurl them at me . . . ! My life infects the air like a pox fouling the universe, scourging the hallowed laws of marriage, tainting even the gods. The day I drew my first struggling breath, *then* I should have died.

Hold back. Hold. Choose the right course. Some deed worthy of your outrage. Something . . . Do you dare to do it? What are you waiting for? Go now. Walking. No hurry. To the palace. My mother's family has grown . . . another child. I go to offer my congratulations.

Chorus

> Let me weave destiny to my own plan, and a breath of wind would be enough. I would reef in for fear that a gale might rock the rigging.
>
> Waft the wind gently, not swelling the sails, no veering off course, a breeze merely. Drift on your journey, my ship, with no troubles. Only let life ease me through safely without extremes.
>
> Fearing the King of Knossos, Icarus reached for the stars, madly trusted the strange invention, rivalled real birds, tried to do better. . . .
>
> But wise old Daedalus chose the middle course. He hovered by a cloud half-way, waiting for his winged son. Until. . . . his child threshed in the sea, hands caught up in the harness of his bold attempt. Whatever exceeds moderation hangs where it may fall. . . .
>
> But what's this? The doors creak. Look! One of the King's slaves, he is beating his head with his fist.

Slave [*Approaching.*]

> Oedipus. . . .

Chorus

> You have some news? Tell us.

Slave

> After Oedipus saw the meaning of his promised destiny and the curse on his birth, he passed sentence on himself — guilty of this enormity.
>
> He made for the Palace and went in, under the roof he hated now, and Death walked behind him . . . In Lybia a mad lion will go roaming the fields, tossing his yellow mane; a spine-chilling sight. Oedipus was like that. Face contorted with emotion, eyes wild, he groaned and muttered darkly. His body was running with cold sweat, he foamed at the mouth, cursed. The agony deep down in him spilled out. In a rage with himself he worked on some act of vengeance, something, anything, that would fit what he had done. He said:

"Why put off punishment? Someone should thrust at me with a sword, and snuff me out. Crush me with rocks, devour me with a blazing fire. Find me a tiger or a vulture to fasten on my body. Cithaeron you've had your share of violence, send out your wild beasts after me, mad dogs, or Agave, who butchered her own child: Yes, send back an Agave. What, my soul? Afraid to die? Death is the only thing that saves the innocent man from Fate."

When he'd said this his hand went to his sword. Yes, suicide. . . . He unsheathed it, then said:

"Is it to be like this then? Such a quick punishment for those *years* of sin? Redress the whole balance with just one stroke. Suppose you die — that will do for your father; but what about your mother? What about the children you have so vilely brought into the world. What of your country? Cry for *that* — doing penance for *your* sin by its own destruction. And you, poor bankrupt, cannot meet the bill. . . . Nature plays havoc with normal ways of life, with laws, with Oedipus. For him alone, a new way of siring children. . . . for him let's likewise have new punishment. . . . I will be condemned to live: To live to die over and over again. Continually to be born, to face . . . more of my sentence. Use your imagination, dog! If it cannot happen often, at least let it last a long time. Choose a slow death. Look for a means. To wander. . . . not in the congress of the dead, no, but as an outcast from the living. Die, oh yes. But do not join your father. Oedipus? Why do you delay?" Suddenly his face melted in a flood of weeping. You should have seen it, his cheeks ran with tears. He said:

"Weeping? Is that enough? Shall nothing else fall from my eyes? *They* shall go with their tears, I'll gouge them from their sockets. Will that do, you gods who guard marriage? These eyes — they must come out!"

That's what he said. He was beside himself with rage. His cheeks burned ominous, insane. His eyes stood out from his head. His face was all violence, desperation, rage like an animal's, or a lunatic's. He groaned, he screamed horribly. His hands were at his face, they were all crooked. His eyes were rolling, staring, bulging to meet his groping fingers, offering themselves to be hacked. He clawed at them, slobbering. He tears them from their roots, wrenches out the eyeballs, but his fingers still can't leave the gaping holes, they jab into them, digging inside, nails tearing the empty hollow. He raged impotently, and his fury was not human.

He need not fear to see ever again. He lifts his head. Two rings of emptiness look round for where the sky should be. He had not torn them out cleanly — some threads still dangled. He broke them off. Then he let out a scream of triumph, addressed to all the gods.

"See . . . ! Have mercy on my country, I beseech you. I've done it. Justice has been done, I have taken the punishment. I am in darkness — the right darkness for my dark kind of love."

Something drips. . . . from his face . . . it is ghastly. The vessels in the torn flesh inside his head burst. The blood from them spews out over him.

Chorus
We are the creatures of Destiny, give way to it. The wheel turns, the thread is spun, and scheming and worry can do nothing. Whatever the human race suffers, whatever it achieves, comes from above. Lachesis spins, and stands by her decisions; no hand can turn them back. There is a clear cut path, and everything must follow it: from the first day of our lives, the last day is determined. Some effects are bound up with what causes them; those even God may not change. The pattern of a man's life is beyond the power of prayer to alter; it must go on. For many the very fact of being afraid is their undoing, and many men have met their fate avoiding fate.

A creak from the gates! It is he. . . . he fumbles his own way here, with no guide, and no eyes. . . .
Oedipus
Good. . . . It is finished; I have paid what I owe my father. . . . I

like this darkness. . . . At last one of the gods — which one I wonder — is pleased with me. . . . He has shed over me, over my head, this black cloud. . . . He has forgiven my sins. . . . Day knew my secret; but I have escaped it. Daylight has left you . . . run away. . . . Do you like your new face, Oedipus? . . . It suits you . . .

Chorus
Look, bursting from the palace, Iocasta! She comes in furious haste, running. Distracted and amazed like Agave after she had ripped her son's head from his body.

She wants to speak to Oedipus.
Look at him, grief-stricken.

Iocasta   [*A sound.*]
Chorus
She hesitates.
But his tragedy matters more to her than shame.

Iocasta
My —
[*Incoherent noises.*]
Chorus
She starts to speak but the words stick in her throat.

Iocasta
What should I call you . . . ? My son . . . ? Is that the right word? You *are* my son. Does it make you feel ashamed: "son"? Nevertheless, speak. You turn your head away! Your face is blank. What is it?

Oedipus
Who is that? I was enjoying my darkness, who is stopping me? Who forces sight onto me again? My mother? . . . yes, my mother's voice! My effort is wasted then. . . . It is not right that we should meet any more. We are cursed. There should be an ocean between us, and then a barrier of lost deserts. Is there some world perhaps on the other side of this; facing other stars, with a different sun wandering overhead. One of us should be there.

Iocasta
It is the fault of destiny. When a thing is fated to happen, no-one is to blame.

Oedipus

Spare yourself! Say no more! I beg you by this mutilated body,
by the children of my blood — damned from their birth — by
all *we* stand for, holy and unholy. . . . spare me.

Iocasta

My soul is dead. Why . . . ? You shared the sins, woman, why
do you refuse to take the punishment? Incest. . . . yes, you. . . .
The pride of the laws of men, because of you, has been per-
verted and destroyed. Yes. . . . No more breathing, Iocasta, it
is under a curse; exorcise it, with a sword. Even the hand of
Jupiter himself throwing thunderbolts, blazing destruction to
shake the universe — even that would not settle my account
with punishment equal to what I have done. Devil-mother.
. . . Death. . . . I like the sound of that. . . . But how to die? I
must answer that question.

[*To* OEDIPUS.]

You! You killed your father, didn't you?
Why not your mother — with the same hand?
It's all that's needed to finish off your work! Quick! let's have
that sword of his!

[*She seizes his sword.*]

My husband lies dead, and this is the sword that did it. . . .
(Husband? No, there's another word, a truer word — my father-in-law,) Now for the sword. . . . My breast? Is that the
place to stab? Or a deep gash in my naked throat? . . . At least
I can choose where to strike. Here — be steady, my hand — in
this womb, which bore sons . . . and a husband — up here!

[*Pause.*]

Chorus

That is the end. That is a corpse now lying there. Death loos-
ens her hand, it drops from where she stabbed herself. The
rush of blood is squeezing the sword to withdraw.

Oedipus

Apollo, spokesman of destiny, fate only demanded my father;
but I have brought death to my mother too. The havoc I've
caused is worse even than I feared; *two* parents murdered. My
sin meant her death. I indict you, Apollo. I have exceeded

even my black destiny. Patron and god of truth? *Liar!*

Follow with faltering feet your road of shadows. Hesitate, feel out your steps. With groping hand be king of this blind night. Start. Hurry. Take a step — will I fall? Leave here. Run away, go on. . . . Stop! Take care — don't trip — it's your mother's body.

My people, your bodies are worn out. You are broken by the plague; your hearts ache on, only half alive. I am going away, look. . . .

Lift up your heads again. Once you've seen my back, there'll be a change of weather; it'll be better. . . . Is anyone lying at death's door, who feels he still has life in him? Breathe, gulp in the air, it will be fresh now. Go, take help to those who had abandoned hope. The mortal infection of this land, I'm taking it away . . . with me. . . . A stick, someone!

Chorus
Here, Oedipus.

Oedipus
Ah. . . . Blood-thirsty fate — and you ravaging diseases, consumption and black plague — and you, wild agony, my friend — come with me. . . .

[*Moving off.*]
with me. . . . You can show me the way. . . . Yes, that's good. . . .

Seneca's *Oedipus*
by Charles Marowitz

As you enter the theater, for Peter Brook's *Oedipus*, you find actors in roll-neck sweaters and slacks perched all over the auditorium. They cling to the pillars like birds awaiting migration-orders. They are remote and preoccupied. They are droning out one note, varying its volume in relation to signals being passed from one to the other.

On a cue, the actors turn over the cubes on which they have been sitting, and begin to beat out a tattoo which steadily increases. When it reaches its highest point, the drumming cuts out sharply and the play begins. Or, one might say the oratorio begins, for what Brook has done is to treat the Senecan text like a richly-textured piece of music, with syncopation, parallel harmonies and counterpoints. The sound components of the words have been carefully organized to create a maximum degree of tonal variety. Actors hiss, throb, vibrate and intone throughout the evening. Individual speeches are constantly invaded by group-sounds, frequently mickey-mousing narrative descriptions, occasionally providing a subtle counterpoint to speech.

There is a certain physical excitement in the sounds themselves and the incessant drumming and droning makes frontal assaults on an audience who traditionally expect the auditorium to be a sanctuary from the drama. On the second night, several people filed out wincingly. They were disturbed. Brook set out to disturb them. The whole production is, in one sense, a calculated affront to conventional audience sensibilities. But they were disturbed on a social rather than an artistic plane. There was too much grating noise and too many jarring auditorium effects.

There is a lot to be said for disturbing the equilibrium of the spectator. Especially when he comes to be reassured, but is there really much to be said for provoking physical responses by physical means when no dramatic purpose is being served?

What Brook has created in this newly-adapted version of Seneca's *Oedipus* is an extremely clever and extremely different production. In the *Marat/Sade*, the ingenious externals with which Brook swamped the play were more fetching than the play itself. One didn't complain. Also, in the Weiss, there was a theatrical context (inmates performing a play) which justified the most extravagant theatricalist happenings. In *US*, he once again grafted a production onto a theme. In that case, the disparity between production-style and actual content was painfully evident and the film *Tell Me Lies*, based on that production, revealed its ideological paucity even further. Now again, Brook has devised an ingenious theatrical overlay, the principles of which belong to his own aesthetic rather than the need or purposes of his text.

In one sense, Brook always gives us the same production. Violent imagery couched in the boldest theatrical language, drawing on the full potential of the physical powers of the theater. Actors operating as spatial components in a formalist design, relying on dynamics rather than characterization. It is often a fascinating experiment in pure formalism; it is rarely the outward expression of the play's inner meaning. It is almost always the eclectic result of Brook's current theatrical philosophy, the present one having germinated during the Theatre of Cruelty season, and recently spiced up with happening-experiments in America, and vocal innovations in Poland.

Brook has gradually become the purveyor of avant-garde clichés to the mass audience. *Oedipus* is thinly disguised Open Theater techniques, Grotowsky-tactics and lifts from The Living Theater. Plagiarism doesn't enter into it. All theatre-workers borrow from each other all the time. The new anti-traditional theater is a gradually-evolving language being shared and simultaneously discovered in exactly the same why in which Renaissance English came into being. But what in Grotowsky or the Becks appears to be an inevitable expression of personally-arrived-at discoveries looks, in Brook, like elaborately-camouflaged second-hand goods. The National Theater Company wears Brook's production like an extravagant Carnaby Street outfit bought off the peg. It's splendid but doesn't quite fit.

The daily reviewers, who are almost totally oblivious of experimental techniques unless they "transfer to the West End," tend to be bowled over by effects which, to the initiated, are known to be current theatrical vernacular. In this way, Brook is like the liaison between the true avant-garde and the bourgeois public and critics. It is interesting that the people who most railed against *US*, a re-jigged Living Newspaper experiment, were all knowledgeable pros; Tynan, Esslin, Pinter, etc.

It may sound contradictory to go on to say that this production despite (or perhaps because of) its outsize dimensions has some powerful moments. Oedipus blinded is John Gielgud being fitted with two black eye-patches. In the last moments of the play, after blind Oedipus and his dead mother are led off, a glittering veiled carriage is brought on, the coverings slowly removed to reveal an enormous golden phallus. Women in the front rows bowed their heads, whether out of respect or embarrassment one couldn't say. A moment later, the cast, now caparisoned in glittering gold costumes, dance on accompanied by a dixieland band playing "Yes, We Have No Bananas." (Musical phallic symbolism, no doubt.) The audience caught up with the driving rhythms of the jazz join in the festivities and the tragedy of Oedipus is banished in a bout of contemporary jollity. It is an effective finish and, in typical Brook tradition, prevents any chance of catharsis setting in. But in his last two choices, the phallus and the jazz, his strategy stands revealed. It is the overplaying of the hand that puts everything else into perspective.

During the course of the evening, he has applied every sound-gimmick he could muster to keep the verse-heavy Senecan tragedy bristling and alive. And in this, he has certainly succeeded. The moments of blinding and suicide take care of themselves. (Death in the theater always earns its passing respect no matter what the context.) Now, just in case his other devices haven't worked, it is necessary to have some trumps up one's sleeve; the final *coups-de-theatre*, the self-applauding maniacs of *Marat/Sade*, the immolated butterfly of *US*, and so out comes the shocking phallus and the all-demolishing jazz. No doubt there are sound rationalizations for each of these moments. The phallus is a stock Roman prop and connects, supposedly, with the fertility-myth ingrained in the play. The jazz, one imagines, is intended to induce that sense of ritual celebration which also was indigenous to the Roman theater. The fact remains that both choices have been hauled in as safety devices and although they create a *frisson*, being unexpected and incongruous, one is more conscious of the motivation which produced them than the rationalization needed to justify their existence.

As with *US*, one eye has been cocked on public reaction and, along with the legitimate motives of production, there was the conscious or unconscious bid for controversy. On a superficial plane, the production dazzles and seduces us with novelty, but a lingering dissatisfaction quickly banishes these virtues. One clings to the idea that a production must be the expression of a play's integrity, and not a demonstration of vivid or fashionable techniques, even when those techniques are superior to the material on which they are being imposed. However effective theater may be, some part of ourselves demands to know we are being overwhelmed for some reason greater than a director's desire to overwhelm us.

A Lost Art
by Peter Brook

Seneca's play, *Oedipus*, has no external action whatsoever. It may never have been acted during the author's lifetime, but possibly it was read aloud in the bath house to friends. Anyway, it takes place nowhere, the people are not people, and the vivid action, as it moves through the verbal images, leaps forward and back with the technique of the cinema and with a freedom beyond film.

So this is theatre liberated from scenery, liberated from costume, liberated from stage moves, gestures and business. We may not wish to observe this, but at least we know where to begin. All the play demands is the ear of an exceptional musician with theatre in his veins—in this case my inseparable collaborator, Richard Peaslee, and a group of actors, standing stock-still. However, these motionless actors must speak. They must set their voices in motion. To do so, many other motions must invisibly be activated: the still exterior must cover an extraordinary inner dynamism. Today, a body-conscious theatre has liberated a generation of actors who can express a powerful emotional charge through intense physical activity. This text demands not less than that, but more: it asks physically developed actors not to go backward but to push forward in the most difficult direction to the discovery of how leaps, rolls and somersaults can turn into acrobatics of larynx and lung, while standing still. Above all, this text demands a lost art — the art of impersonal acting.

How can acting be impersonal? I can see at once what would happen if a trusting actor hearing this word and trying to be faithful to its suggestions tried to depersonalize himself: his face a set of taut muscles, his voice a foghorn, he could produce unnatural rhythms. Perhaps he might believe that he was taking his place in ritual theatre — but while seeming hieratic to himself he would just seem phoney to us. And yet if he simply allows free rein to his personality, if he sees acting as a form of personal expression, another phoneyness can easily appear, which swamps the text in a morass of groans and cries, all stemming from a ready exposure of his own phobias and fears. The worst features of the experimental theatre come from a sincerity that is essentially insincere. Such a state is at once revealed when words appear, for a false emotion clogs clarity.

Of course, all acting is made by people and so is personal. Yet it is very important to try to distinguish between the form of personal expression that is useless and self-indulgent and the sort of expression in which being impersonal and being truly individual are one and the same thing. This confusion is a central problem of contemporary acting, and the attempt to stage this text of *Oedipus* brings it into focus.

How can the actor approach this text? One common method would be to identify himself with the character of the play. The actor looks for psychological similarities between Oedipus and himself. If I were Oedipus, he would say, I would do X, Y or Z because I remember that when my father... He tries to analyze Oedipus and Jocasta as "real people" and is bound to discover the total failure of this approach. Jocasta and Oedipus may be concentrations of human meaning — but they are not personalities.

There is another approach to acting which throws psychology aside, and seeks only to release the irrational in the actors's nature. He tries to cultivate a form of trance to awaken his subconscious and it is easy for him to think that he is getting closer to the level of universal myth. He can easily imagine that out of these he can draw valid dramatic material. But he must beware of being taken for a ride by a dream — the trip into the subconscious can be an illusion that feeds an illusion, and his acting remains where it was.

It is not enough for the actor to find his truth — it is not enough for him to be open blindly to impulses from sources inside himself that he cannot understand. He needs an understanding that must in turn ally itself to a wider mystery. He can only find this link through a tremendous awe and respect for what we call form. This form is the movement of the text, this form is his own individual way of capturing that movement.

It is not for nothing that the greatest of poets always have needed to work on existing material. *Oedipus* was never "invented": before the Greek dramatists there were the legends — the Roman writer reworked the same material — Shakespeare often reworked Seneca — and now Ted Hughes reworks Seneca and through him reaches the myth. And an interesting question arises: Why in great drama is there a wish amongst creative and inventive men not to invent? Why do they put so little store on personal invention? Is there a secret here? In serving a pre-existing pattern, it is not himself and his own meaning that the dramatist is trying to impose — it is something he is seeking to transmit. Yet to transmit properly he realizes that all of him — from his skills, his associations, to the deepest secrets of his subconscious — has to be potentially ready to leap into play, into rhythmic order, to act as carrier. The poet is a carrier, the words are carriers. So a meaning is caught in a net. Words drawn on paper are the mesh of the net. . . .

So we return to the actor. Can he be a carrier too — in the same way? It involves his understanding of two very difficult concepts: distance and presence. Distance as Brecht has described it means keeping his personality at arm's length. It means the individual voluntarily subduing many subjective impulses, because he wishes something to appear that for him is more objective. What can help to do this? Not a moral nor an artistic decision. Willful dehumanizing is mechanical, and many Brecht productions have shown how easy it is to fall into the trap — using the willpower of the intellect as a sort of Pentagon holding rebel elements at bay.

The only help is understanding; the more the actor understands his exact function on all levels, the more he finds the right performance pitch. To take a very simple example, a radio newsreader is intuitively impersonal and distant because he understands his function — he is a voice put at the disposal of making a news sheet clear — he needs clarity and tempo — his intonations must be neither too warm nor too dry — and yet for him to bring his personal emotions to bear on the information, coloring it according to whether the news makes him bright or sad, would be silly.

The actor's task is infinitely more complex than that of the newsreader. The way opens when he sees that presence is not opposed to distance. Distance is a commitment to total meaning: presence is a total commitment to the living moment; the two go together. For this reason, the most eclectic use of rehearsal exercises — to develop rhythm, listening, tempo, pitch, ensemble thinking or critical awareness — is most valuable provided none of them is considered a method. What they can do is to increase the actor's concern — in body and in spirit — for what the play is asking. If the actor truly feels this question to be his own he is unavoidably caught in a need to share it: in a need for the audience. Out of this need for a link with an audience comes an equally strong need for absolute clarity.

This is the need that eventually brings forth the means. It forges the living link with the poet's matrix, which in turn is the link with the original theme.

Seneca

by David Anthony Turner

Lucius Annaeus Seneca was a gifted, prolific, sickly, tormented, noble and powerful philosopher. And filthy rich. He killed himself in AD 65. By then he had helped to rule the known world, suffered a purgatory of diseases in soul and body, and written his way into a central heritage of European literature. He was the son of an imperial bureaucrat. He had two brothers — Mela, the father of the poet Lucan, and Gallio, who appears in the pages of the New Testament:

> "But when Gallio was pro-consul of Achaia, the Jews with one accord rose up against Paul and brought him to the judgment seat, saying: This man persuadeth men to worship God contrary to the law. And when Paul was beginning to open his mouth, Gallio said to the Jews: 'If it were some matter of injustice or an heinous deed, O Jews, I should with reason bear with you. But if they be questions of words and names and of your law, look you to it. I will not be the judge of such things.' And he drove them from the judgment seat."

Seneca was born in Cordoba around 4 BC. We do not know whether his parents were native Spaniards or Roman importations. He was educated in Rome. By then the Roman Empire was widely though not yet fully extended — Britain was in the geographer's book but not the tax-collector's. The monarchy of Augustus Caesar was thirty years established, grafted onto the stock of the old Roman Republic and maintaining its titles and honors. Advancement worked by a series of junior ministries through Quaestor and Praetor to Consul, but the only person who mattered was the Emperor. In AD 33, when Seneca's brilliance won him a Quaestorship, it was Tiberius.

After Tiberius came Caligula. He seems to have hated Seneca

but did not persecute him, because he did not give him long to live. Next, under Claudius, the Empress Messalina had Seneca driven into exile on the island of Corsica in AD 41. The charge was adultery with the Princess Julia — a most unlikely tale. He rotted and wrote for eight years: then Claudius divorced Messalina and married Agrippina. At her insistence Seneca was brought back to Rome, lavishly honored and put in charge of the education of her son, now heir to the Empire. The boy was talented and good-looking, but history does not remember him for these qualities. When he became Emperor, Seneca — in association with Burrus, prefect of the Praetorian Guard — for five years practically conducted a regency of the Roman Empire. Burrus died in AD 62 and Seneca's power was eclipsed. He escaped from the seesaw of state affairs to write books on physics and philosophy. Retirement was not enough. In the purge following the conspiracy of Piso in AD 65 he was proscribed, along with his brothers. Bowing to the imperial displeasure he died laboriously — cutting his wrists, taking hemlock, then finally suffocating in a steam bath. So the tutor fell victim to his own former pupil. A treatise of Seneca's, entitled — ironically enough — "On Mercy," had been specially written for the young prince. It begins: "Dear Nero. . . ."

If the physical context of Seneca's life and writing was a circus in the Roman sense — all beasts and bloodshed — his spiritual ambience was a maze. All the contradictions of Greek myth were compounded with the ancient Roman pantheon to produce a muddle of Hellenistic accretion and rationalization. Emperor-worship was used as a tool of political manipulation. Official religion controlled public life but had lost any hold on private thought. So intelligent men worked out their own salvation from a mixture of mysticism and quasi-scientific humanism. Two ideologies were dominant — that of Epicurus, and that of Zeno the Stoic. For Epicurus the gods were not dead, simply detached. His cosmos left man with only one guide — sense-experience — and only one criterion — pleasure. The Stoics, on the other hand, taught belief in providence. The gods intimately controlled all human affairs, though they were not so much the manufacturers of crisis — which still rested with fate — as its retail outlets. The Stoic doctrine was: ascetic preparation of the will to nullify the painful reversals of fortune by disregarding them. Romans always cared more for ethics than metaphysics, and found this a flexible and inviting philosophy.

Seneca's Letters are a source-book of Stoicism. They are addressed to Lucilius, a young meritocrat employed in the colonial service in Sicily. Some reckon they are too polished to be genuine letters. I find them too repetitive to be anything else. They must be our best clue to what Seneca was like, as a thinker and as a man. "Philosophy is the only thing that will stir us, wake us up from our leaden sleep. Dedicate yourself to it totally." Through a hundred and fifty letters the message is the same. Only in Stoic philosophy can we find the strength to meet life with human dignity. Events pounce. We must not scream. Fate does not matter, or rather we must make it cease to matter. The same goes for what other men think of us:

> "Only believe you are doing well when you can live your life in the public eye — when you need walls for shelter, not for concealment. Most of us surround ourselves with walls not to keep our lives safe, but to keep our sins secret."

And Rome knew all about sins, private and public. In addition to the casual murders of imperial politics there were the abiding monstrosities — human blood-sports and inhuman slavery. Against them Seneca raised a lone and noble voice. No Roman but this one could have held up for approval a gladiator who resented the brutalizing treadmill of slaughter-for-fun and made the ultimate protest:

> "Recently a slave was being taken in a cart under guard. He was due to appear in the morning show. He started nodding as if he felt sleepy. He got his head so far down that he could push it between the spokes, then stayed there until the wheel came round and broke his neck. . . . It is a great man who can not only take the decision to die, but invent the way."

Apart from his letters, Seneca wrote essays — on Providence, on Anger, on Favors, etc. And there are his plays — nine tragedies in all.

Seneca's importance in European literature varies with time. The early Christians were attracted by his spirituality, the Middle Ages by his philosophy. Above all, he was the mediator between Greek tragedy and the Elizabethan theatre. But the transmission was not merely mechanical. Every time the ghost walks in *Hamlet* (or *Macbeth*, or *Julius Caesar*, or *The White Devil*, or the *Spanish Tragedy*) the controlling aesthetic comes not from Sophocles but from Seneca. Medea speaks the prologue to Seneca's play about her, and sets a tone of mystery and supernatural hazard. Compare it with the witches in the first act of *Macbeth*. The Greeks kept violent action off stage and used messengers. Seneca brought violence on stage and showed death. Shakespeare only mentions him as a playwright once ("Seneca cannot be too heavy, nor Plautus too light," *Hamlet*, II, 2) but he flatters him sincerely by imitation a hundred times. Through the Newton translations of 1581, Seneca was accessible to the founding fathers of modern drama, while the Greeks were not. Perhaps it was an accident of history, but Seneca was the writer it happened to; bereft of the axioms of religion, he propagated the sanction of human emotion. Seneca's alarmingly modern aesthetic took drama out of the temple and put it into the theatre.

Seneca can sound so modern. He was bald, skinny and asthmatic, and admitted it. He made such a study of teeth-gritting in the face of fortune that his jaw seems locked in a permanent wince. I think he must have been brave, not because he seems so fearless but because he seems so frightened. Exposed to a society quite as overwhelming as ours, threatened by all the wounds men suffer in the tempest of the world or the volcano of their souls, he went on and on. He tried to save something and — perhaps even braver — tried to tell other people about it. All his beautiful words — those lovely short sharp sentences — are now dismissed to post-graduate research, but even two thousand years is not long enough for a soul like that to die.

Seneca
MEDEA

**Translated by
Frederick Ahl**

Characters   *Medea, daughter of king Aeetes of Colchis;*
rejected wife of Jason

Nurse, servant, compatriot, and confidante of
Medea

Creon, king of Corinth who granted Jason and
Medea asylum, and who is about to marry his
daughter to Jason

Jason, husband of Medea and nephew of Pelias,
king of Thessaly recently killed with Medea's
help; leader of the naval expedition on the
Argo which captured the Golden Fleece.

Messenger

Medea's Two Sons (nonspeaking)

Chorus, Corinthian people

Various Attendants (nonspeaking)

ACT ONE

[*The curtain rises to reveal* MEDEA, *alone in the courtyard of her house in Corinth, praying before a shrine of the gods. In the background music can be heard: singing, in celebration of* JASON's *wedding to Creusa.*]

Medea

Gods who couple men and women, hear me!
Lucina, listen, bright guardian of birth,
midwiving children from the womb.
                                    Pallas,
you taught Tiphys how to guide Argo,
the first ship, to master a straight course,
making itself at home upon the seas,
now straits themselves.
                         Hear me.
                                 Neptune, vicious
enough to master Ocean's heaving threats,
I pray to you.
             And you, Titanic god,
marking and making day with blazing eye
of light.
        You too, perceptive Hecate,
governor of heaven, hell, and earth,
illuminating rituals that are,
and should be, secret,
                      I appeal to you.

I call those gods upon whose names Jason
swore his oaths, names Medea might
more rightly spell in prayer.
                             Hollow oneness
of eternal night, realms faced away
from life above, ghosts in chains, dripping
loathsome murder.
                 Ominous master
of those realms of horror, hear my prayer,

my hideous prayer.
                    You too, Proserpina,
ominous mistress, carried off like me
but not abandoned, treacherously left.

Powers of feuding vengeance, snakes writhing
repulsively upon a single head,
come to me now. Grasp the black fires of death
in ghastly hands dripping blood, and stand
menacing, as when I married him.
Kill his new partner, kill his new father,
snap all the royal family's living shoots.

For the groom, may something worse remain.
I want him to live: to wander through
cities as yet unknown, his confidence,
his livelihood destroyed; refugee,
frightened and with nowhere to call home,
looked on, if he's looked upon at all,
with hatred; a notorious would-be guest,
seeking shelter in someone else's house.
I pray he'll wish we were together still.

I now request the worst prayer of them all
that the children show the qualities
of their father and their mother combined.
My final vengeance is already born:
and I have given it birth.
                         But I'm sowing
seeds of verbiage, complaints that have
no harvest. I will tear wedding torches
out of their hands, I'll tear the very light
out of the sky. Sol, the Sun himself,
sowed my family's seed, yet watches now
impassively, and lets himself be watched,
firmly keeping to his usual,
solitary course through open space
and the pure fire of heaven. He does not
return to his own rosy birth, unmake

this day.
　　　　　Shining father, give me control,
let me drive the coupled power of fire.
Then Corinth's Isthmus, double boundaries
of land dividing seas, delaying ships,
could be consumed with flames, the seas joined.

One thing remains. I long to bear the torch
blazing before them to the bridal suite,
to make the sacrificial prayers, butcher
the beasts on consecrated altar-stones.
If, my soul, you have some force of life,
if traces of your fabled energy
still linger on, seek out an opening
so you can penalize them, ruthlessly
slicing through their guts as if through wax.
You must banish from yourself all fears
a woman has. Take on your native mind,
your Cossack mind, that hates all foreigners.
Whatever criminal acts the Crimea,
Rioni River, and Black Sea have seen
the Isthmus soon will see. Evil actions
of brutality unknown — enough
to send shivers through heaven and earth alike.
That's what the mind within me urges me
to bring upon them: slashing butchery,
roving death, approaching limb by limb.

I am wasting time. I did all this
in virgin innocence. Some fuller pain
should rise within me now I've given birth.
People expect it. Medea, bare your rage
for fighting, and prepare yourself to kill,
work to a frenzy. When tales of your life
are told, men will, I hope, pair your divorce
with your wedding in well-matched rivalry.

When you leave him, your trail will be the same
as once it was when you pursued him here.

Delays damp fire. So break them off. This home
was quickened and born in crime. Quickly
and criminally must I leave it now.
[*The* CHORUS *enters, chanting for* JASON *and Creusa's wedding,*
and moving toward MEDEA's *house.*]
Chorus
This is a wedding of kings   and so we hope
gods, kings of sky above   or bounded sea,
will come, responding to   the people's prayers.

A white-skinned, radiant bull,   neck carried high,
should honor the powerful gods,   the Thunderers.

A body, female and virgin,   snowy white,
pleases the goddess who brings   life to light.

Love, busying War's hands   bloodstained and rough,
giving the nations truce   from death and strife,
you store inside your horn   fertile riches.
Your prize for gentleness: sacrifice tender.

At legal weddings you,   Hymen, scatter
shadows of night with fire: a good omen.
Step lurching this way,   merry with wine,
crowning your temples with   wreaths of roses.
Light of temporal twinning,   evening star,
always too late for lovers,   twilight hour:
greedily mothers and brides   yearn for you,
and the moment you prick the sky   with brightness.

Her virgin luster conquers,   when compared
to Athenian brides, or Spartans   limber and lithe,
mountain-exercised   like boys
in a wall-less stronghold.   Lovelier she
than girls bathed in crystal   Alpheus,
washed in waters of   Aonia.

If Aeson's sons, Jason,   let judges' eyes
assess his looks, gods would   concede first place.
Bacchus in tiger chariot,   lightning-born,
and great prophetic Phoebus   brother of

heaven's taut huntress-virgin   would give way.
Pollux, with castigating fists   concedes;
Castor as well, his match,   except with gloves.

Gods of heaven, I pray   I pray you: let
this woman conquer,   surpass other wives;
let this man rise far   above other men.

When she stands among women at the dance
her face alone outshines all others there.
So stars fade and die before the sun,
so flocking Pleiades coyly hide
when Moon's arched horns, with mirrored brightness,
complete a whole and sunlike circle.
So whiteness drenched in Punic crimson
blushes red; so shepherd, rosily
glistening in the new days light, sees
the gleaming crest of sunrise surging up.

Bridegroom, raped from a Tartar's bed,
afraid, yoked to a wife unbridled,
unsolaced by unwilling daily
contact, reap virgin fruit, the daughter
of the wind. This is your first time too —
first time with full parental consent.

Come, lads. Your songs can be a little lewd:
Bounce your lyrics anyway you want.
Rare's the chance for free speech against kings.

Bacchus' child, white-robed Hymen who carries the thyrsus!
Time to inflame the piny torch's myriad fibers!
Whip up that solemn fire with fingers no matter how listless!
Let us speak out our jest in style ribald and Italian.
Leave the crowd free for farce.
                                We consign to silence
       and darkness
any woman who runs from home, wedding-veiled for
       an alien husband.

[*Exit* CHORUS, *laughing and mocking* MEDEA.]

ACT II
Medea

My twilight before night; my urge to kill.
The wedding hymn pounds at my ears; and still
I find it hard to grasp that this evil
is really happening.
                    How did Jason
find the power to do it? First he took
my father and the country that we ruled
away from me. Now he casts aside
the seeds of my existence — ruthlessly
left in solitude on foreign soil
to wither. I have earned better than this.
He's seen me mastering the energy
of fire and water, yet he despises me.
Can he suppose my power to inflict
evil has been totally burned out?

I'm sick at heart; I can't see what to do.
My mind is ravaged by insanity,
I'm torn to pieces, scattered everywhere.
What source can I tap for vengeance now?
He doesn't have a brother, I regret;
but he does have a wife. So into her
my knife will go. Yet this is not enough
for what I've suffered. There must be some crime
that cities, Greek or savage, do not know,
something your hands have never tried before.
You must devise it, your past crime must spur
you on, it must come back to you, it must.

The Golden Fleece, symbol of royal power:
recall how it was torn away, recall
the tiny boy who followed his sister,
sheared from himself, limb by limb, butchered
as an act of war against father,
his body scattered upon open sea.

Recall the limbs of Pelias, himself
an old man and a father, boiled in bronze.
So often when I've been the cause of death,
the blood that's spurted has been kindred blood.
Yet I have never killed in anger. Love
makes me destroy.
            But Jason had no power,
and surely did not plot this by himself;
he too was foreign under Corinth's laws.

He owed it you to steel himself for death,
not steal away.
            Don't say that, please, oh please,
raging voice of my pain. Jason must live,
be mine, just as he was, if he has strength;
even if not, I still want him to live,
and to remember me. I don't want him
to hurt the gift of life I gave him once.

Creon's to blame. He uses royal power,
his only potency, to cast off ties
that bind together marriage partnerships,
to separate a mother from her sons.
He tears up pledges that should be intact.
It's solely his responsibility,
and he alone should pay due penalty.
Go after him! I will bury his home
in ash and cinders; Malea will see
this citadel in black against the flames,
Malea, whose arching promontory
holds fast ships of war with long delays.

Nurse
Silence, I beg you. Hide your grievances.
Mute them to fury held within yourself.
Endure without a sound wounds that cut deep,
and bide your time. Maintain a level head;
then you will have the power to repay.
Your anger hurts when it is camouflaged;

> if you proclaim your hatred, it will lose
> the space it needs for vengeance, and the time.

Medea

> Your pain has little bite if it retains
> the power to reason and conceal itself.
> Great sufferings do not lurk in disguise.
> It is a pleasure to retaliate.

Nurse

> Stop it, my child. Aggressiveness is mad
> when even stillness of body and tongue
> scarcely protects you.

Medea

> Pluck up courage; then
> Luck fears you. But she crushes all cowards.

Nurse

> Test her when there's a place for manliness.

Medea

> Place can't deny itself to manliness.

Nurse

> There is no hope to light your pathway there.

Medea

> If one is strong enough never to hope,
> there is no reason to abandon hope.

Nurse

> The Colchians have gone. Your partner's oaths
> are valueless. You once had everything,
> but nothing now survives to stand by you.

Medea

> Medea still stands. In me you see
> the energy of earth and water, fire,
> steel, the gods, and heaven's vengeance.

Nurse

> Beware the king.

Medea

> My father too was king . . .

Nurse

> Don't armies frighten you?

Medea
> I do not care
> if they sprout up like harvests from the earth.

Nurse
> You'll die.

Medea
> I wish I would.

Nurse
> Run!

Medea
> I have run
> enough, and I'm ashamed.

Nurse
> Medea . . .

Medea
> Yes,
> I shall become Medea.

Nurse
> But you are
> a mother . . .

Medea
> And you see the kind of man
> who made me one.

Nurse
> Yet still you hesitate
> to run away?

Medea
> Oh, I will leave. But first:
> revenge.

Nurse
> Then vengeance will follow you.

Medea
> I'll find a good excuse to slow it down.

Nurse
> Hold your wicked tongue! You've lost your mind!
> Less insolence now, less talk of teaching
> lessons. Honor allows us to adjust
> to what a situation demands.

Medea

> Fortune has power to ferret out my goods
> but not my spirit.
> Somebody's pounding
> the palace door. I hear it opening:
> Creon is here, in person, swaggering
> with blue-blooded Hellenic arrogance.

[*Enter* CREON, *with* ATTENDANTS. *As he comes in,* MEDEA *holds her ground in center stage.*]

Creon [*Stopping with displeasure and fear when he observes that* MEDEA *has not yet left.*]

> Medea! That lethal child of Aeetes,
> King of Colchis! Has she not yet removed
> herself from my domains? Mill-like, her mind
> works on inexorably, grinds and refines.
> Her treachery leaves its mark; so does her hand.
> Will she leave anyone alive or safe
> from fear of butchery?
> Swift action,
> to wipe out the disease her presence brings:
> this I was planning. But my son-in-law
> conquered my better judgment with his prayers.
> She was allowed to live. Now she may go
> in safety. Let her free my land from fear.

[MEDEA *approaches* CREON *slowly and steadily with eyes fixed.*]

> Beastlike, aggressive, threatening, she stalks
> towards me to converse now face to face.
> Keep her away! Don't let her touch me, men,
> don't let her near me. Tell her not to speak
> a word. Sooner or later she must learn
> to tolerate imperial commands.

[CREON'S MEN *retreat before* MEDEA'S *advance, leaving* CREON *to confront her himself.*]

> Go away! Yes, run away, take flight,
> take your hideous viciousness away,
> so I don't have to look on it again!

Medea

> What crime, what act of immorality,

brings sentence of exile as punishment?
Creon
That's for an innocent woman to ask.
Medea
If you're the judge, then hear my cause and case;
if you're the king, just tell me your commands.
Creon
You will obey the king's commands, however
just or unjust their balance may be.
Medea
Justify power's balance, or it falls.
Creon
Complain in Colchis. Go!
Medea
                                   I'm going back.
But let the man who brought me take me there.
Creon
Your appeal's too late. Sentence is passed.
Medea
The man who passes sentence without hearing
the defense: his ruling may be just —
agreed. But he has not himself been just.
Creon
Did you give Pelias a hearing when
you put him to death? Still, here's your court.
State your peculiar case. Regale us now.
Medea
When I lived regally in my own right,
I learned how hard it is to redirect
one's energy of mind from anger once
anger is aroused. I also learned
that those who so ambitiously reach out
for power's regalia think that to pursue
unswervingly the policies that took
their fancy at the outset is the heart
of all true government.
                                   True, I am now

a pitiable sight, annihilated
by total disaster. I asked mercy;
I was thrown out. Sole and friendless,
I was deserted. Waves of misfortune
have washed me down. Yet, on my father's side,
I was illustrious. Like lightning,
I gleamed. For I derive the brightness of
my origin from my grandfather, Sol,
the Sun itself. Those fields gently winding
Rioni stiffens to harvest, all
the Black Sea looks upon towards the east,
this, with the glitter of regal power,
my father rules. There the bitter sea
is sweetened by fresh water, there women
are only kept inside the natural bounds
made by the Thermodon. They need no men.
And when they band together for a fight,
they need no armor to protect themselves
and rout their enemies out of their land.
Nobly born, I promisingly flowered;
I gleamed in the regalia of power.
Princes then begged to marry me; now
I must beg them. For fickle Luck has wrenched
all this away. She swooped down, tore me from
my throne, and dropped me into banishment.
Trust in your royal power, when fickle Chance
tosses great riches to and fro!
                              Yet kings
do have a huge and marvelous resource
which time cannot destroy: the power to help
the suffering, the power to protect,
not punish, those who beg mercy.
                              The sole
resource and treasure I salvaged from days
of power in Colchis was precisely this.
I saved the glory of your race of Greeks.
The wondrous flowering beauty, sprung of gods

without me would have been by now erased.
Orpheus softens granite with magic
of song and makes the forests walk. He lives,
thanks to me. Castor and Pollux
are my gift, a double offering.
So too the twin sons, seed of the North Wind;
then Lynceus, whose penetrating sight
sees lands that lie beyond the Black Sea's shores.
I saved the lives of all the *Argo's* crew.
Their king of kings I now omit. For him
you owe me nothing. I set no price on him.
The others I brought back for all of you;
this one alone I brought back for myself.
Come on, pile high against me in the scale
every moral outrage I have done;
I will confess to each. But the sole crime
I surely can be charged with is just this:
that I restored the *Argo*.
                            A good girl's
pleasure should be in her virginity
and in her father's love. But let us see
what happens to The Past if I am good.
Your pure Hellenic land will go to ruin.
Why? All its leaders, don't you see, will die!
And first to fall will be your son-in-law,
seared by the flames from a raging bull's mouth.

Fortune may crush my case in any way
she likes. Yet having saved so many scores
of kings causes me no regret. I think
it glory. If my immorality
has brought me a reward, you are the one
with power to lay me down the terms for it.
If it takes your fancy, then condemn
the accused. But give me back the thing
I am accused of taking. I admit,
Creon, to guilt; for I create danger.
You well knew what I was when first I asked

for mercy at your knees, begged you to give
your hand as a guarantee of your good faith.
Now I request some corner of a room
within your land, some squalid lair to hide
in misery. However, if you'd rather
drive me out of town, give me some place
that is remote, yet under your control.

Creon

No. I am not a man who brutally
and heavy-handedly wields royal power.
When I see misery, I am not proud;
I do not grind it underneath my heel.
I call as witness to this claim the fact
I married my child to a refugee,
a banished man, a beaten man, a man
quaking with abject terror. Acastus,
king of Thessaly, now wants him seized
and sent back for punishment and death.
This is his complaint. His own father,
he says, was killed — a man advanced in years,
almost senile, weak and prone to spasms.
He was butchered and his limbs were diced.
Acastus admits it was his sisters
who dared to carry out this ghastly act
of family murder. But he also claims
they did it as an act of family love,
deluded by your trickery.

                        A case
can be made for Jason if we keep
you clear of it. He took no part in this.
No drop of blood touched him. His hands were clean.
For they came nowhere near the instrument
of butchery. He kept his distance then,
unstained by an intercourse with them
or you. But you, the criminal mastermind,
combine a woman's boundless, brazen schemes
with a man's stamina. And your good name

is so long lost it lies beyond the power
of memory to recall.
                    Get out. Drain
this kingdom of its filth, and, as you go,
take all your poisons and your lethal herbs.
Liberate my citizens from fear.
Set up your house in someone else's land
and sunder there the peace of heaven above.

Medea

You force me to get out. Then give me back
my boat so I can leave, and give me back
my fellow traveler. Must my exile
be solitary? Why? My journey here
was not a solo venture. You're best off,
if you fear war, to drive out both of us.
Why draw the line between two criminals?
Pelias died for Jason's benefit,
not mine. Jason is why I went from home
and stole the fleece. For him I left father,
murdered my brother, mutilated him.
You can't blame me for what he taught and still
teaches his new wives to do. I've harmed
the many I have harmed not for myself
but because I have been made to harm.

Creon

You should have gone by now. You have waited
too long to sow delaying verbiage.

Medea

A final plea for mercy as I go:
my sons have done no harm. Don't let the sins
their mother has committed drag them down.

Creon

So go. I'll raise them with a father's love,
as if I had begotten them myself.

Medea

Good omens for the royal wedding day

and for its consummation. That is what
you want. For you have hopes to be fulfilled,
you want your royal powers to hold firm
in spite of shifting Fortune's fickleness
which harasses them.
                    Here is my plea:
be generous. Just grant me a short delay
in the enforcement of my banishment
so I may be a mother to my sons,
pay them the last, perhaps the dying, dues
of love.

Creon
                    You mean you want time for a plot.

Medea
How can you fear a plot? Time is too short.

Creon
The evil hardly require time to harm.

Medea
A little time for tears. Can you deny
this much to me in all my suffering?

Creon
Fear grafted deep inside me fights against
you and your request; but nonetheless,
a delay is granted so you can
prepare for banishment — but just one day.

Medea
That is too much. Cut it back, if you wish.
I'm in a hurry too.

Creon
                    You will be killed.
No pleas for mercy will be heard unless
you are gone from the Isthmus well before
the Sun brings back the light of day. But now,
the wedding sacrifices summon me.
I must participate. This day is marked
for Hymen and it summons me to prayer.

[*Exit* CREON *towards his palace and the wedding.* MEDEA *watches*

him go, then retires into her house. The CHORUS, *moving on
quietly, watching her as she withdraws into the building, begins to meditate somberly.*]

Chorus
Far too audacious
was the man who first broke
through narrow waters
promising and faithless.
Though his raft was fragile,
he trusted life and
breath to shifting breezes'
gossip as he cut
over level waters,
out from his homeland.
Not knowing where his
voyaging would take him,
he dared to trust a
slender shell of kindling,
a much too thin line
laid down between the
passages of living
and those of dying.

No one yet knew stars
or used the constellations
painted upon the
sky's eternal brightness.
Shipping could not yet
survive by just avoiding
Hyades' rainstorms.
Then the stormy She-goat,
and Northern Wain, which
Boötes slowly
follows like a herdsman,
were nameless, as were
north wind and west wind.

Yet Tiphys dared spread
canvas on the vast sea,

and write new laws for
winds to mock and follow:
how to run full sail,
how to catch the crosswinds —
haul in the for'ard sheet —
how to make the yards safe —
drop them down to midmast —
how to lash them topmast
when impatient sailors
pray for winds to rise,
when red streamers
flutter on the topsail.

Our fathers saw an
age of purest brilliance
when treachery was
far removed from mankind.
Men lazily kept
to their own shores, aged well
in the poor fields their
fathers tilled before them.
Still they were rich, though
knowing only that wealth
yielded by soil which
they themselves were born on.

Rightly the laws of
nature fenced the world off.
But *Argo* tore down
fences, made the world one.
She bade the seas be
lashed by sweeping oarstroke.
Seas: a dimension
once, and more, a boundary
of human fear, now
well within fear's limits.

Yet *Argo's* pines from
Thessaly paid dearly

for acts of trespass,
steered through long-drawn terror.
Two mountains, great dams
sealing off the water's
surge from the deep sea,
rose from below, groaned loud
as heaven's thunder,
drenching the peaks and clouds
and then, in firm grip,
trapping the ocean.

Bold Tiphys blanched; he
loosed the hawsers he held;
silenced was Orpheus,
torpid grew his harpstrings.
Argo lost voice too.

Then there was Scylla,
virginal Sicilian,
madness' hounds en-
circling her womb; she
opened their great mouths
all at once. What sailor's
limbs did not stiffen,
totally in terror
at this one evil
mass of jaws all howling?

Then came destructive
sounds of singing softening
Italy's seas; yet
on his lyre Olympian
Orpheus from Thrace re-
sponded and resounded.
Usually a Siren's
song holds ships in her spell.
But now his music
prevailed, and almost forced her
to come in his wake.

What did this voyage
gain? A fleece of gold and
a fruit of evil
worse than the harsh sea brine:
it won Medea,
merchandise fit for
this, the world's first vessel.

By now the sea has
given up the struggle,
puts up with our laws:
we don't look for *Argos*,
famous and seamed by
skilled hands of Minerva,
oars manned by monarchs.
Coracles and skiffs rove
at will on deep sea.
Boundaries have all moved;
cities now build walls
in lands just discovered.

Nothing is left where
once it was; the world is
open to travel.
Indians quench their
thirst in cold Araxes,
Persians now drink from
Elbe and Rhine routinely.
There will come an age,
a distant Chinese year when
Ocean will lose its
power to limit knowledge,
and the gigantic
earth will open to us.
Tethys, sea goddess,
will disclose whole new worlds;
no more will Iceland
be our far horizon.

ACT III

[*Enter* MEDEA *hurriedly from her house, followed by her* NURSE.]

Nurse

My child, you leave the house so hurriedly.
Where are you going? Stay where you are! Put down
your anger and control your violent urge
to go on the attack.

[MEDEA *motions her to keep her distance and moves on down-
stage, seething with anger.*]

Nurse [*Inwardly.*]

Like a woman
who has taken god into herself
upon the whitecapped mountain pinnacle
and the paired peaks of Nysa, she cannot
dam the madness, dashing to and fro,
a wild beast in her movements, and wearing
searing trademarks of insanity
upon her face. The sharpness of her glance,
blazing, startles the very soul in her,
shouts her secrets aloud, moistens and shines
her eyes with welling tears, mirroring every
twist of feeling.
Now she is standing still —
threatening and heaving, howling, groaning.
Where will the crushing force of her intent
strike? When will it moderate its threats?
Like the sea her madness swells. When will
its moaning breaker crash upon itself?
What she turns over in her mind will be
no ordinary deed; she will surpass
her median of crime; she will conquer
herself. The moment I saw them, I knew
the ancient hallmarks of her angry rage.
Some enormity looms over us,
some bestial act of inhumanity.
I read upon her face the savage wish

to have revenge. I hope to god I'm wrong.
Medea [*Inwardly.*]
  Poor woman, if you ask what bounds to set
  upon your hatred, imitate the cruel
  limits that you placed upon your love.
  Am I to tolerate this royal event,
  endure the blaze of wedding torches, yet
  not respond with vengeance? Shall I let
  this day go by without my usual fire,
  this day so intricately politicked
  and engineered by both contracting sides?
  While earth mediates the sky's balance,
  while gleaming universal order rolls
  in radiant waves of predetermined change,
  while grains of sand are numberless, and Day
  follows the Sun and Stars the Night, and while
  the Great Bear never dips into the sea,
  my passion for exacting punishment
  will never cease but ever grow greater.
  No monster of the land, no bitch Scylla,
  no maelstrom of Charybdis sucking in
  the seas of Italy and Sicily,
  no volcanic Aetna which crushes
  the gasping forces of the earth boils
  with anger as destructive as my own.
  Rivers in flood, the ocean churned by storms,
  the Black Sea whipped to fury by the winds,
  the violence of fire fanned by blast
  from bellow have no power to stop the rush.
  Did Jason fear Creon and the wars
  threatened by the king of Thessaly?
  True love has power enough to fear no one.
  But, granting him the benefit of doubt:
  suppose that he was overwhelmed, gave in
  and gave his hand. It certainly was still
  within his power to come to his partner
  if only for a final word or two.

Our lionheart was too frightened even
for this. As son-in-law, he certainly
did have the chance to ease the time limits
harshly imposed upon my banishment.
We have two children; I am given one day.
I'm no complaining that the time is short.
I can extend it farther. For this day
will brand its face of fire upon the world
so man will never lose its memory.
I shall attack the gods, and I shall shake
the very elements.

Nurse
                    Your woes, madame,
make thought run riot. So, control yourself,
calm your mind.

Medea
                    My solitary chance
of calm comes when I see the elements
shattered with me as I fall. I want
the world to die with me. When you pass on,
there's joy in taking everything with you.

Nurse
If you maintain this course, how many forms
of retribution you must fear. No one
is powerful enough to make attacks
upon the powerful and still survive.

[*Exit* NURSE; MEDEA *withdraws backstage as she sees* JASON *enter.*]

Jason
Fate is always hard, Luck hopelessly
rough and — whether she devours us whole
or lets us go — impartially evil.
The remedies god finds are much too often
worse than the dangers that they save us from.
If I had wanted to make good the pledge
I gave my partner — and she's earned it, too —
my life would have been forfeit in exchange.
And, if I did not want to die, poor man,

my pledge to her had to be forfeited.
It was not fear that triumphed over pledge,
but an uneasy sense of what was due
my family. Once their parents were dead,
our children clearly would have followed us
on to the grave.
                          If sacred Justice lives
above us in the skies, I call on it
to give approval and bear out my words:
my children forced their father to give in.
Although she has the heart of a wild beast,
and finds it hard to work in partnership,
under constraint, she will herself, I think,
prefer to act on her children's behalf
than to maintain her standing as my wife.
My mind's resolved to go appeal to her,
angry as she may be.

[*Noticing* MEDEA.]
                          And she is here.
She's seen me and she's leaped out of the house,
burning with anger. Hate and every pain
that she has ever suffered are inscribed,
willful and vengeful, now upon her face.

Medea

We're on the run, Jason, we're on the run.
Not that moving home is new. Rather,
the reason we are moving home is new.
I'm used to being on the run solely
for you.
                          I'm on my way. I *am* leaving.
You are compelling me to run away
from what is now your homestead in the sun.
You send me back.
                          Where to?
                                        Should I head for
Phasis and Colchis, for my father's realm,
the soil I watered with my brother's blood?

Do you tell me to head for somewhere else?
Where? What monstrous seas do you point out?
The Black Sea's jaws? Through them I brought back home.
a fistful of kings, when I cut back
between the Clashing Rocks as I pursued
a roving lover.
        Iolcus, perhaps:
a little place — or, if in Thessaly,
should I head on to Tempe?
        Everywhere
I've opened up a road for you, I've closed
one for myself.
        You send me back? Where to?
You order an exile into exile,
and don't provide her anywhere to go.
Well, let that pass. A king's new son-in-law
has ordered it. It therefore must be right.
Inflict upon me any penalty,
grim as it may be. I'll not resist.
My services must match what I am paid.
Your king can penalize his new son's whore
with all the blood and anger that he likes.
He may put her down and lock her hands
in chains, then he may seal her in with rocks,
and crush her in a never-ending night.
What I shall experience will be
far less than all the payments I have earned.

Thankless mind without a body: think.
Wind your thoughts back to your encounter with
the scorching breath of the flame-breathing bull,
the terror tripping you among people
never tamed. Think of Aeetes' herd,
their fire, in a field whose harvest was
steel-clad fighting men. Think of a foe
which sprouted without warning from the earth.
I bade them slaughter one another. They
sank back to death without a human word.

Throw on the fleece, plundered from Phrixus' ram,
and the nightmarish, vigilant monster.
I ordered him to shut his shining eyes
in sleep he'd never known. Think of my brother:
I put him to death: one child cut down,
but with how many cuts.
                        My schemes took in
an old man's daughters. With deluded hopes
that he would be reborn, they carved his joints.

You have hopes for your children, for a place
to call your home.
                        Remember horrors seen
and overcome, these hands which showed no pity
when employed for you.
                        Remember too
the sea and sky that witnessed our mating,
and
      pity me.
                        Return the debt you owe me:
give me life. In seeking power for others,
I threw my own away.
                        My Scythians brought
plunder from distant lands as far away
as India with her burned and harried tribes.
Our house could hardly hold its great treasures,
it was so full. So we made living trees
bow with loads of gold. From all this wealth,
I brought only my brother's limbs; and these
I spent for you. I gave up brother, father,
fatherland, and my virginity.
This was my dowry when I married you.
I want it back now that you run me out.

Jason
Creon wanted you dead; he hated you.
My tears crushed him. I won exile instead.

Medea
I see it now. Exile is a reward.

I'd thought it was a form of punishment.
Jason
    Run while there's chance. Go, tear yourself away.
    There's always harshness in a ruler's wrath.
Medea
    You take Creusa's part with this advice.
    She hates your mistress. So you move me out.
Jason
    Medea judges morals and amours?
Medea
    Premeditated murder . . . treason too.
Jason
    Cite one specific charge against me now.
Medea
    Whatever crime I did.
Jason
                    This is too much.
    To be held guilty of your crimes as well.
Medea
    They are your crimes, they're yours! You gained by them
    so you committed them. I don't care if
    the whole world holds your partner to account:
    be her sole counsel for defense, sole voice
    calling her innocent. If she's guilty
    for your sake, for you she's innocent.
Jason
    I owe you my life. But when one is
    ashamed to stand in someone else's debt,
    it's hard to take that gift with gratitude.
Medea
    Ashamed? Don't take the gift then, give it back!
Jason
    Why don't you master your emotions,
    and, for the children's sake, calm yourself down?
Medea
    I renounce them. I deny they're mine,
    I swear them away. Why should I let

Creusa supply brothers to my sons?

Jason

As queen, she has the power needed to help
the suffering children of us refugees.

Medea

That will be an evil day for them,
poor creatures, mingling shining families
with base and low. So may it never come.
May sons of Phoebus never mix with sons
of Sisyphus.

Jason

Poor woman, do you want
to drag the two of us to banishment?
Please go away.

Medea

Creon heard my appeal.

Jason

Tell me. What could I do?

Medea

For me? Perhaps
a crime.

Jason

But how, with kings on either side?

Medea

There's also something you should fear much more:
Medea. So set me against the rest,
let us fight it out; let Jason be
the prize.

Jason

I'm tired of evil. I withdraw.
You too should be afraid; by now you've had
enough experience of life's pitfalls.

Medea

Never has Luck with all its twists and turns
challenged as yet my primacy in power.

Jason

Acastus does so now.

Medea
And Creon is

a closer enemy. So run away
from both. Medea is not forcing you
to play at civil war, to take up arms
against your in-laws or bloody your hands
by slaughtering your relatives. You need
harm nobody. Just run away with me.

Jason
And who will stand against them if they pose
a threat of war upon two fronts? What if
Acastus joins his forces with Creon's?

Medea
Throw in the Colchians and Aeetes.
Add Scythians to Greeks. I'll sink them all.

Jason
I fear great power.

Medea
Mind you don't lust for it.

Jason
We've talked too long. Let's cut this short right now.
People will start to get suspicious.

Medea
Almighty Jupiter, thunder across
the skies, stretch out your arm, ready your fires
of vengeance, burst the veil of clouds, and shake
this tidy world to its foundations.
As you take aim, don't worry which you hit.
If either of us falls, the guilty die.
Your thunderbolt cannot go wrong.

Jason
Get a grip

on sanity, on calm and rational speech.
If there is something from my in-laws' house,
to solace loneliness, ease banishment
for you, just ask.

Medea
You know my will is strong

and that my sole response to all the wealth
of kings is pure contempt. I simply want
my children to be free to come with me
while I am on the run. So, when engulfed
in tears, in deep despair, I'll have soothing
kisses. As for you —
                              Aye, new children,
a steady flow, remain to haunt your steps.

Jason

I admit I wish I could obey,
and grant what you apparently desire.
But I *am* their father, and I *must*
refuse. Even my father-in-law, the king,
could not coerce me to comply with this.
It's more than I could stand. My children are
the reason I live on, the thing that makes
me able to endure the pain of all
my ravaged feelings and emotions.
I would more quickly sacrifice my soul,
my body, life itself.

Medea [*Aside.*]

                              Is this how much
he loves his sons? That's good. Then he is caught.
Apparently his armor has a chink.

[*To* JASON.]

I'm sure you will allow me to tell them,
as I go away, a few last things
I'd like to have them do, and to give them
a final, warm embrace. Even this much
would give me pleasure. Now my last request,
my parting word.
                              I know that, in my pain,
unsure which way to turn, I blurted out
some cruel words. Don't let them haunt your mind.
I want to leave you with a more profound
memorial of me in my better days.
Let every word uttered in anger be
erased to its last letter.

Jason

                    I untie
the thread of hatred and I banish it
utterly from my mind.
                    Now I myself
have a request: that you please get control
and guide the passionate seething of your mind
into still waters. Calm soothes misery.

(*Exit* JASON. MEDEA *watches him in disbelief. The* NURSE *enters
quietly and comes to her side.* MEDEA *at first ignores her; she
turns and holds an inner dialogue with herself, alternating
between her "first" and "second" persons.*)

Medea

He's gone. Is *that* it? You just stroll away,
erase me, erase everything I've done?
Have I just died inside your memory?
Am I cut out? No, I shall never be
cut out.
                    Come on then, summon all your strength,
and all your skills. The blessing of a life
lived criminally is that you don't think
of anything as crime.
                    I hardly have
the latitude to spring a trap because
they're all afraid of me.
                    You must attack
along a path no one can think could be
a path from which to fear attack. Be bold!
Undertake whatever lies within
Medea's power, whatever lies beyond.

[*To* NURSE.]

You've stayed staunch by me through my ups and downs of
          feelings and of fortunes, my dear nurse.
So help me now with my pathetic plans.
I own a robe, a present from the Skies,
the bright possession of my house and realm,

a fiery mark of love the Sun once gave
to Aeetes, his child. I also have
a necklace, flashing bright with woven gold.
And there's a crown whose radiance of gems
dulls even the bright flame of gold itself,
comets the wearer's hair to sunlike glow.
I want my sons to carry these as gifts
to the veiled bride. But my infernal skills
must first contaminate them.
                                        Let us pray
to Hecate. Prepare the formulae
for death. Erect altars, then kindle fires.
Let flames scream up within the palace walls.

[MEDEA *and the* NURSE *retire into the palace. The* CHORUS *emerges
     and chants.*]

Chorus
No force of flame, no gust
of swelling windstorm,
no torqued javelin
threatens greater danger
than a wife deprived of
her husband's affection:
seething and hating.

Not when the south wind
brings the rains of winter;
not when the Danube
floods in raging torrents,
forbidding bridges
to couple its waters,
wandering unbridled.

Not when the Rhone's flow
drives into the salt sea;
not when, dissolving
under solar brightness,
snowcaps become streams,
ice in strong spring sunlight

melts in the Haemus.

Fire has no eyes; and
bellowed up with anger
wants no controls, nor
tolerates containment,
never fears death, but
yearns to rush and meet with
swordpoints advancing.

Spare him, o gods, we
beg you to forgive him,
he who has tamed the
seas, let him live safely.
But the lord of ocean,
second just to heaven,
seethes now he is third.

Phaethon, who dared drive
Sun's eternal horses,
forgot the pathway
marked out by his father
until the flames he'd
strewn about the heavens
brought ruin on him.

No one has lost much
following the known road.
Go by the path proved
safe to those before us.
Nature is holy;
do not breach her sacred
order with violence.

Each man who roamed in
that daring ship, the *Argo*,
and, to make oars, robbed
Pelion of its timber,
stripping the shade of
its forbidden forests;

each man who passed through
sea's great drifting mountains,
then measured out the
ocean with his bold strokes
and reached his goal, hawsers
tied on foreign coastline,
hot to steal foreign
gold and then return home,
each earned cold justice
from the ocean's hardships —
extermination.

Tiphys was first; the
Breaker of the Ocean
waived his control of
the ship to a raw helmsman.
Far from his homeland,
on a foreign seashore,
his star of life set.
Buried like a pauper,
forlorn he lies with
ghosts dank and uncremated.
Aulis, from then on,
recalling him, her lost king,
holds vessels. They stand
in the windless harbor
motionless, grieving.

Orpheus, born of
Italian Muse of singing,
plucking his strings in
skillful modulation,
once charmed to standstill
rivers in their rushing,
silenced the winds — each
songbird ceased her trilling,
came to his side, with
the very trees they'd sung in.

Scattered, dismembered
his poor body rotted
on Thracian farmland;
but his head kept swimming
down the grim Hebrus
to the Styx and Hell's pit:
no return this time.

Hercules cut down
the twin sons of North wind,
slew the sea's child whose
shape was ever shifting,
exposed to light death's
cruel realm of darkness,
thus bringing peace on
land and upon water.
Then still alive, he
lay on blazing Oeta,
and gave his limbs to
the vicious fire's cremation —
a last resort to
escape his hideous torment
of the twin poisons
of watersnake and centaur,
gift of his dear bride.

The bristling boar cut
Ancaeus down with its blow;
you, Meleager,
impiously slaughter
your mother's brother,
then, when she is angry,
you die at her hands.
All of them deserved death
like that of Hylas,
great Hercules' young friend,
a tender boy who
paid the price for trespass,
dragged to his death in

springs that nymphs were guarding.
Go, plow the salt seas
safely, all you brave men.
But fear fresh fountains.

Idmon, who knew what
was to be beforehand,
dies of a snakebite
in Libyan Sahara;
Mopsus, unerring
in prophecies for others,
failed in his own case —
precious loss for his Thebes.
Yet if he truly
sang about the future,
Thetis' husband
aimlessly will wander,
a refugee, and
Nauplius will plunge in
waters that drown him,
after he's tried to
wreck the Argive convoy.
Ajax, the son of
Oileus, when sailing,
will pay, struck by lightning,
the sins of his father.
Admetus' wife will
buy back with her own death
her husband's life; and
Pelias who ordered
the Golden Fleece brought
back in this, the first boat,
was seared with skill in-
side a heated cauldron:
a steward wandering
on narrow straits of torment.
Enough, gods, the sea

is avenged now; so spare Jason,
for he had no choice.
[*Exit* CHORUS.]

ACT IV
[*Enter* NURSE.]
Nurse
My soul quivers in terror; a hideous act
of savagery impends. Some monstrous thought
has taken root and grows, her anguish fuels
itself and gathers its spent violence.
I've often seen her rage, claw down the sky,
attack its deities; yet now Medea
readies for us some huger spectacle,
huger than these. As if lightning-struck,
reeling, she came out, then plunged into
her inner sanctum where she compounds death,
opening every vial and cabinet,
taking ingredients that even she
had always feared. She set out her evil
potions in chaotic rows: arcane
secrets of her own experiments.
Raising her left hand in prayer before
her darkly sacred fire, she calls upon
lethal energy Saharan sand
unleashes and creates with seething heat,
and energy the northern mountains hold
motionless, frozen in Arctic ice —
everything that stuns the eye comes forth.
Lured by the enchantment of her voice,
scaly creatures in chaotic mass
snake from their nests: a savage serpent worms
its monstrous body, poises, flickering
its pitchfork tongue, and wonders who to kill.
As it hears her song, it stiffens, twines
its swollen length, forced into heaps of coils.
But Medea says: "The evils earth

creates below, within its deepest shafts
make shafts too paltry for my use. I'll seek
poisons from the skies; for it is time
to conjure something loftier, beyond
mere common magic tricks and sleight of hand.

I want the Dragon from the sky, whose coils
are so immense that heaven's two stellar Bears
feel its effect. Phoenicians guide their ships
by the Lesser of these Bears; the Greeks
sail by the Greater.
                Then, let Hercules
relax his grip upon the snake he holds
so that its viral venom spurts.
                   Then let
the Python respond to my song, a snake
who dared attack Diana and her twin.

I want the Hydra back. Its every head,
cut off by Hercules, must be restored.
For it renews its life by being cut.

Guardian dragon of Colchis, you come too,
lulled to your first sleep by these songs of mine."

Everything snakelike now evoked, she then
prepares her fruits of evil, heaping them
into a pile: all that the wilderness
near Eryx grows; produce of Caucasus,
those ridges smothered in endless winter,
splattered with Prometheus' blood.
The fighting Mede, the flighty Parthian,
the wealthy Arab: she employs toxins
into which they dip their arrowheads.
She uses juices Suebian ladies seek
amid the dankness of their black forests
under an ice-cold sky.
                Her hand harvests
whatever earth creates in nesting spring

or when brittle frost balds trees' beauty,
forcing life inside itself with cold:
grasses virulent with deadly flowers,
harmful juices squeezed from twisted roots.

Mount Athos brought her those particular herbs.
These came from massive Pindus. That she cut
on a high ridge of Pangaeus; when it lost
its tender, hairlike crown, it left traces
of blood upon the sickle blade.
                              Now these
grew by the Tigris at low-water time;
those by the Danube, these, by Hydaspes
whose warm streams bear rubies through arid
plains; these by Baetis — hence the name
Baetica — which languidly lashes
the western ocean at its estuary.

These felt the steel while Phoebus readied day.
That shoot? Cut down at dead of night. And this?
Snipped by her consecrated fingernail.

She harvests deadly grasses, milks the snakes'
venom, mixes in birds that bode death:
heart of the mournful horned owl, and the guts
of raucous screech-owl cut out while the bird
was still alive.
                    My mistress of black arts
keeps some ingredients separate. In them
there is the tearing violence of fire.
In others, the icy chill of cramping cold.
Then to her venoms she adds words equal
in terror. Hear the sounds made by her mad
steps and songs at whose first utterance
the ordered universe shudders. Look!

Medea

Silent hordes and gods of death, I call upon you all in prayer:
Chaos — unseeing and unseen abyss — dark home of ghostly
    Dis,

caverns of decomposing Death, dungeoned by Tartarus' steep
    slopes,
tormented souls, take respite, run and see this novel wedding
    night.
The limb-wrenching wheel must stop, and Ixion must touch
    the ground;
Tantalus must slake his thirst at Corinth, fearing no deceit;
one exception: Sisyphus, forebear of Jason's new in-laws —
increase his torment, let the slipping stone roll him across the
    crags.
You Danaids whose leaking urns mock your attempts to fill
    them up,
come, be fulfilled together. This day needs your husband-
    killing hands.

Hecate, star of night, I call you to my ritual. Come now,
you have three faces you can threaten vengeance with; put on
    your worst.

For you my hair falls down, unribboned, free,
as is traditional among my race.
With bare feet I have crossed the hidden grove,
enacting lasting rites, drawn water forth
from dry veils of cloud and forced the sea
down to its depths, I have outdone the tides;
Ocean has sucked his massive waters deep
into himself. Laws of astrology
break down: the universe sees sun and stars
together, and the Great and Lesser Bears
dip in forbidden moisture of the sea.
I have bent the laws that govern time:
my spells make spring flowers bloom in summer heat;
I force the goddess of the grain to watch
turf turned to fruit and crops in winter's cold.
Back to its springs raging Rioni turns;
the Danube idles all its many mouths,
squeezes its surging flood within its banks.
Waves roar, the mad sea swells although the winds

are muted. Rooflike shade provided by
a sacred, ancient wood is gone: sunlight,
at my command, has been brought back again.
Bright Phoebus halts at his zenith. Down slip
the rainy Hyades, moved by my spells.
Time now, dark Phoebe, for your sacred rites.

For you: these wreaths I wove with bloodstained hand with
nine snakes intertwined.

For you: these limbs from rebel Typhoeus who shook Jupiter's
control.

This, treacherous Nessus' dying blood. He swore safe passage
over streams.

These, ashes from Oeta's dying fire, which drank Hercules'
poisoned manhood.

Here, Althaea's brand of vengeance: holy sister but unholy
mother.

These plumes the Harpy left in pathless lair when fleeing
North wind's son.

Add feathers of Stymphalian bird, shot down by Hydra-
poisoned arrows.

Altars, you cry aloud: I see my cauldrons stirred by god's consent.

I see the witching moon moving in swift arc
yet not driving with her full face shining
night long. Like torchlight, lurid in a graveyard,
she glows as when magicians' spells torment her.
Reins taut, she holds course, hugging the horizon.
Moon, now your fire has hues of deathly pallor,
pour waves of grim light on the winds to frighten
mankind. Give people something new to awe them.
Corinthians can pound upon their precious bronzes
to ward off spells.
                    On grass red with bloodstains,
I offer to you beasts ritually butchered.
For you a fire-torch snatched from a cremation
burns in the night; for you I arch and toss back

my head, I sing, I loose my hair, then bind it
with sacred headband, as they do at funerals.
For you I grip this bough shriveled with death's dew.
For you I bare my breast, slice into my arms
with holy knife, shed my sanity and blood.

Let blood on handsome altars; let hands alter
habits, steel themselves, turn caring to carnage.
[MEDEA *slashes her arms with a sacrificial knife, and lets her
blood drip on the altar.*]
I strike. The stream flows. I have given it.

Do you complain, Hecate, child of Perses,
that in my prayers I summon you too often?
However often I summon you the cause is
ever one and the same: his name is Jason.
[*She takes out the robes which are to be her present to Creusa
and sprinkles them with poisonous liquid.*]
Tincture the robes I present to Creusa.
Flame, snake, and sear your way into her bones
the very instant that she puts them on.
[*She packs the robes in a box made of gold.*]
Locked in this yellow womb of gold lurks fire.
She'll never fear its presence. Prometheus,
who concealed stolen celestial flames,
gave it to me. He taught me to conceal
its power with art. He paid the penalty:
the life that grew in him.
                              Vulcan gave me
fire hidden in powdery sulphur.
Phaethon, like me, kindled from fire, supplied
bolts of living flame. And I have gifts
from medial parts of dragon Chimaera,
flames ripped from seared throat of fire-breathing bull,
mixed with Medusa's gall. These I control;
they work my evil will in total silence.

Hecate, stiffen my poison's potency,
and keep its seminal fire deep buried in

my gifts. They must deceive the eye and trick
the touch. The heat must surge into her breast,
come into veins, her limbs must melt,
her bones must smoke, the new bride's hair must burn
outshining the torches of her wedding night.

My prayer is granted. Hecate boldly
bays approval, proclaims it with
gleaming torch of blessed fire.

My energy has done what it must do.
Summon my sons to bear these priceless gifts
to the veiled bride.
[*Enter* MEDEA'S SONS, *who take the gifts.*]
                    Go, go my sons,
brood of a cursed mother, and appease
your stepmother, mistress of your fate,
with this offering and many a prayer.
Be off! But hurry home so I can have
the pleasure of a farewell kiss from you.
[*Exeunt* MEDEA *and her* SONS; *enter* CHORUS.]
Chorus
Already she is bloodied;
savage love ravishes
sanity, sends her reeling.
But does her rage have power
to shape itself to action?
Vengeance burns in her face,
quickened, then set with anger.
Proudly tossing her head,
beastlike, this mere exile,
make threats on a king.
It is beyond believing.

Her cheeks flare red. Then cloaking
fear routs red with whiteness —
wild shifts of shape and color.
So, when her children perish,
a tigress roams through Ganges'

jungle: mad, obsessed with
ritual, futile searching.

Medea does not know how to
rein in love or anger.
Now love and anger couple
in common cause. What follows?
Will this heathen Colchian
never take her madness
from Greek lands, dissolving,
as she sails, fear's grip on
realms and reigning monarchs?
Phoebus, run your course now
with no reins to hold you.
Let kind night bury sunlight,
and evening star that brings night
drown daytime deep in Ocean.

ACT V

[*Enter* MESSENGER, *approaching* MEDEA's *house*.]

Messenger

  Death is everywhere. Whatever stood
  within this royal house has fallen now:
  father and daughter dead, their ashes mixed.

Chorus

  How were they trapped?

Messenger

                              The way all kings are trapped
  by gifts.

Chorus

          What treachery could have been there?

Messenger

  I am amazed, hardly believe myself
  the evil that is done could have been done.

Chorus

  Is there no limit to catastrophe?

Messenger

  Fire rages greedily through every part

of the king's residence. It's now destroyed,
completely. The city'll go next we fear.
Chorus
Use water on the flames to put them out.
Messenger
That's what is so unnerving in this blaze:
water fuels the flames. Uncannily,
the fire burns fiercer when we damp it down.
It overwhelms our one line of defense.
[MEDEA *and the* NURSE *enter during this interchange, just before
the* MESSENGER'*s last words. Exit* MESSENGER *at the end of this
last speech.*]
Nurse
Quick, leave this land where kings kill sons.
Hurry, Medea, to any land you want.
Medea
I withdraw? Even if I'd run away
before, this I'd return to see: marriage
in a new style.
              And yet you *do* withdraw,
my soul. Why? Your attack has just paid off.
Follow it up! You take delight in such
a tiny fraction of your vengeance.
If it's enough for you, demented mind,
that Jason not remarry, then you still
love him. Try to find some novel way
to penalize him, and prepare yourself.
Your sense of sin, of shame must be expelled;
it is what must get out, withdraw, not you.
If the hand that punishes is clean,
its vengeance is impugned. So put your back
into your anger, wake up from your sleep.
Aggression, which has penetrated deep,
lurks at the bottom of your heart. Suction
it out, be violent, let everything
you've done till now be called an act of love.
Move, and make them learn how trivial

and like a petty criminal's have been
the past crimes I devised. With them my pain
just flexed it strength. What power have untrained arms
to dare great deeds? The bloodlust of a girl!
Now I'm indeed Medea. My genius
has grown with all these evils I have done.
I'm pleased I killed my brother, took his head,
and sliced his limbs. I'm glad I tore away
my father's secret source of potency,
I'm glad I armed old Pelias' daughters,
had him killed.
           You feel the pain, so find
something to exorcise it on. Your hand
is trained for any deed that you must do.
Anger, you must find a way. Our foe
has broken his agreement. So what shafts
do you have poised to hurl?
                My mind within
increasingly decrees atrocity
of some sort; but as yet it lacks courage
to describe it to itself.
            Fool!
I've moved too soon. I should have waited till
my foe had fathered children on his whore.

But anything that's yours and came from him
Creusa brought to birth.
            In fancy, then,
it pleases me to penalize him thus
as he deserves. It pleases me. My mind
must be readied for the ultimate crime,
I recognize this now. Children, once mine,
you pay the penalty for father's crimes.

My heart has missed a beat, my limbs are cold.
I feel a shiver in my breast. Anger
has gone, the wife in me has been expelled,
the mother has returned. How can I shed

the blood of my children, my own flesh?
Anger and madness must not come to this!
This is a hideous and unnatural act.
I do not understand it. Far be it
from me! What crime would they be paying for,
poor lads? That Jason is their father — or
worse, that I, Medea, am their mother?

They must die, they are not mine. They're mine,
so they are doomed.
                    But they are innocent.
They've done no crime, they're guilty of no sin.
That troubles me — and yet my brother, he
was harmless too.
                    Mind, you vacillate
so much. Why do tears dampen your face,
why does anger tear you one way now
and love another? Passion's fierce swell
controls me but cannot decide which way
to toss me. It is as if I were the sea:
violent winds wage war, waves full of grief
that rends the heart attack from either side,
the waters seethe in indecision. That
is how my heart wavers. Anger routs love
then love routs anger.
                    Pain, yield to love.

Flesh of my flesh, come here. For only you
have shared my loneliness, my ruined home.
Bring yourselves here and drape your limbs round me;
snuggle you little couple. Your father
can have you safe and sound provided your
mother can have you too.
                    But exile looms,
and I'll be on the run. They'll soon, too soon,
be torn from my embrace, weeping, groaning
as they kiss me. To their mother they are
forever gone and lost, so they must be
gone and lost to their father as well.

My pain grows once again, my hatred boils,
the old avenging fury reaches out
for my unwilling yet so lethal hand.
Anger, I follow your lead. I wish my womb,
like proud Niobe's, had produced a riot
of children, oh, I wish I'd given life
to twice her seven sons. I am as good
as childless now it comes to penalizing
him. I bore only two; but they're enough
to avenge my brother and father.

A riot of furies, overpowering,
is moving in. Where? Who are they hunting?
Who will they strike with brandished, searing lash?
This army from the pit of hell waves torches
blazing with blood. At whom? A huge snake snaps
loudly like a whip. Who is Megaera
pursuing with firebrand of doom?
                                    A ghost
appears, I can't see whose, all dismembered:
It is my brother, come to punish me.

We'll pay the penalty, all of us will pay!
Fix blazing torches where my eyes now shine,
then rip and sear my breast; see now, my heart
lies open for the Furies to enter.

Brother, go from me now and tell the dead
and the avenging goddesses they can
cut back beneath the earth without a care.
Leave me to myself, I'll handle this.
See, brother, I have drawn my sword for you.
[*Drawing out a knife and pulling back one* SON's *head.*]
My hand's deed placates my brother dead.
[MEDEA *kills the* CHILD *but is then distracted by a sudden noise of
people approaching from offstage.*]
A sudden sound. What does it mean? Weapons!
They're taking up arms to kill me.
                                    Then I'll climb

onto the very rooftop of my house.
The slaughter's just half done.
[*To her living* CHILD.]

You, come with me,
and keep me company.
[*To her dead* CHILD.]

I'll also take
your body with me as I leave.

Mind,
concentrate and face things like a man.
Don't hide your deed. The people will applaud.
[MEDEA *climbs up to the rooftop as* JASON, *accompanied by a crowd of* CORINTHIANS, *enters and speaks.*]

Jason

If you are loyal and feel sorrow and pain
at the calamity that strikes your kings,
then join me quickly, and we will arrest
the perpetrator of this hideous crime.
This way, men-at-arms, and bring your spears.
Turn this house over from top to bottom.

Medea

Now I have you back again: my power,
my brother, and my father. Now Colchis
has regained its stolen fleece of gold.
My kingdom has come back to me again;
now my rape, my motherhood, are gone
and my virginity returns. At last,
powers of nature, you have been appeased.
This is a real wedding-day of joy.
The crime is now complete, so go. But no:
I am not yet avenged.

Then finish it
while your hands can act. Don't fail me now,
dear mind, don't delay, you have the power.
Your anger has already dropped. You now
regret what you have done. You are ashamed.

Pathetic woman, what have you done —
what have *I* done? Pathetic? Sorry I am,

but I have done it. And against my will
a sense of pleasure subtly penetrates
my being, and it grows, constantly grows.
It lacked only one thing to be perfect.
He should have seen it. So I have achieved
nothing as yet. For any criminal act
is just a waste without him here to see.

Jason

Look! There she stands. See, where the roof slopes down,
threatening. Bring torches, one of you,
then let her fall, scorched by her own fires.

Medea

Gather wood to build your sons a fire,
build them a tomb, Jason. Your new father
and wife have all the rites the dead should have.
I saw to their interment. This one son
has met his doom. Now you are here to watch,
the other will be given a matching death.

Jason

By every power of nature, by ordeals
we suffered through together on the run,
by me sexual fidelity
to you, which I never betrayed, I beg you,
spare our son. If there is any crime,
it's mine; I yield! The guilt is on my head!
So kill me, and make me your sacrifice!

Medea

Here, where you beg me not to, I shall drive
the steel; here, where it gives you pain. So go,
proud hero, hunt down virgins in their rooms,
leave them when they are mothers.

Jason

                                          One is enough

to penalize me.

Medea

                        If the slaughtering
of only one could satisfy my hand,

I would have killed no one at all. And two
are trivial repayment for my pain,
If, even now, there is, unknown to me,
some fetus spawned by you inside my womb,
I'll use this sword and tear it out with steel.

Jason

You've started your great deed. So finish it.
That was my final prayer for mercy. This
is now the favor that I ask: do not
delay my punishment.

Medea

Enjoy your crime,
my aching heart, enjoy it to the full.
The day is mine; I urge you not to hurry.
We are using the time that we were given.

Jason

Damned woman, kill me.

Medea

Pity is your demand.
I pity you. It's done.

[MEDEA *kills the other* CHILD.]

I had no more
to offer, aching heart, in recompense.
Jason, lift up your swollen eyes to me.
Ungrateful Jason, do you now know your wife?
This is my sole, inevitable way
of going into exile. A pathway
into the hidden sky that my paternal
ancestry reveals has opened up.
Twin serpents offer me their scaly necks
to bridge me to the stars. Obey, dear parent,
take your children back, and I shall ride
in winged course upon the breath of winds.

Jason

Wade through the deep expanses of boundless,
shining sky. Wherever you may go,
you will be proof that gods do not exist.

Seneca in Elizabethan Translation (excerpts)
by T.S. Eliot

No author exercised a wider or deeper influence upon the
Elizabethan mind or upon the Elizabethan form of tragedy than
did Seneca. To present the Elizabethan translations of the tragedies in their proper setting, it is necessary to deal with three
problems which at first may appear to be but slightly connected:
(1) the character, virtues and vices of the Latin tragedies themselves; (2) the directions in which these tragedies influenced our
Elizabethan drama; (3) the history of these translations, the part
they played in extending the influence of Seneca, and their actual
merit as translation and as poetry. There are here several questions which, with the greater number of important Tudor translations, do not arise. Most of the better known translations are of
authors whose intrinsic merit is unquestioned, and the translations derive some of their prestige from the merit and fame of
the author translated; and most of the better-known prose translations have an easy beauty of style which arrests even the least
prepared reader. But with the Elizabethan translations of the
Tenne Tragedies (for they are by several hands) we are concerned
first of all with a Latin poet whose reputation would deter any
reader but the most curious; with translations of unequal merit,
because by different scholars; and with translation into a meter—
the "fourteener"—which is superficially a mere archaism, and
which repels readers who have not the patience to accustom their
ears and nerves to its beat. The translations have, as I hope to
show, considerable poetic charm and quite adequate accuracy,
with occasional flashes of real beauty; their literary value remains
greater than that of any later translations of Seneca's tragedies
that I have examined, either in English or French. But the appreciation of the literary value of these translations is inseparably
engaged with the appreciation of the original and of its historical
importance; so that although at first sight a consideration of the
historical problems may appear irrelevant, it should in the end en-

hance our enjoyment of the translations as literature.

In the Renaissance, no Latin author was more highly esteemed than Seneca; in modern times, few Latin authors have been more consistently damned. The prose Seneca, the "Seneca morale" of Dante, still enjoys a measure of tepid praise, though he has no influence; but the poet and tragedian receives from the historians and critics of Latin literature the most universal reprobation. Latin literature provides poets for several tastes, but there is no taste for Seneca. Mackail, for instance, whose taste in Latin literature is almost catholic, dismisses Seneca with half a page of his *Short History of Latin Literature*, and a few of the usual adjectives such as rhetorical. Professor Mackail is inclined by his training to enjoy the purer and more classical authors, and is inclined by his temperament to enjoy the most romantic: like Shenstone or some other eighteenth-century poets, Seneca falls between. Nisard, in his *Poètes Latins de la décadence*, devotes many pages and much patience to the difference of conditions which produced great tragedy in Athens, and only rhetorical declamation in Rome. Butler, after a more detailed and more tolerant examination from a more literary point of view (*Post-Augustan Poetry*), commits himself to the damaging statement that "to Seneca more than to any other man is due the excessive predominance of declamatory rhetoric, which has characterized the drama throughout Western Europe from the Renaissance down to the latter half of the nineteenth century." The most recent critic, Mr. F. L. Lucas (*Seneca and Elizabethan Tragedy*), admits "the exasperatingly false rhetoric of the Senecan stage, with its farfetched and frigid epigrams." Yet this is a dramatist whom Scaliger preferred to Euripides, and whom the whole of Europe in the Renaissance delighted to honor. It is obviously a task of some difficulty to disentangle him from his reputation.

We must admit, first, that the tragedies of Seneca deserve the censure that has been directed upon them. On the other hand, it may be true — I think it is true — that the critics, especially the English critics, have been often biased by Seneca's real and supposed bad influence upon the Renaissance, that they have included the demerits of his admirers in his own faults. But before we proceed to what redemption of his fame is possible, it is expedient to resume those universally admitted strictures and limitations which have become commonplaces of Senecan criticism. First, it is pretty generally agreed that the plays of Seneca were composed, not for stage performance, but for private declamation.[1] This theory attenuates the supposed "horrors" of the tragedies, many of which could hardly have been represented on a stage, even with the most ingenious machinery, without being merely ridiculous; the Renaissance assumption to the contrary gave license to a taste which would probably have been indulged even without Seneca's authority. And if the plays were written to be declaimed, probably by a single speaker ("elocutionist" is really the word), we can account for other singularities. I say "account for," I do not say without qualification that this peculiar form was the "cause"; for the ultimate cause was probably the same Latin temper which made such an unacted drama possible. The cause lies in the Latin sensibility which is expressed by the Latin language. But if we imagine this unacted drama, we see at once that it is at one remove from reality, compared with the Greek. Behind the dialogue of Greek drama we are always conscious of a concrete visual actuality, and behind that of a specific emotional actuality. Behind the drama of words is the drama of action, the timbre of voice and voice, the uplifted hand or tense muscle, and the particular emotion. The spoken play, the words which we read, are symbols, a shorthand, and often, as in the best of Shakespeare, a very abbreviated shorthand indeed, for the acted and felt play, which is always the real thing. The phrase, beautiful as it may be, stands for a greater beauty still. This is merely a particular case of the amazing unity of Greek, the unity of concrete and abstract in philosophy, the unity of thought and feeling, action and speculation, in life. In the plays of Seneca, the drama is all in the word, and the word has no further reality behind it. His characters all seem to speak with the same voice, and at the top of it; they recite in turn.

I do not mean to suggest that the method of delivery of a play of Seneca was essentially different from that of Greek tragedy. It was probably nearer to the declamation of Greek tragedy than was the delivery of Latin comedy. The latter was acted by professional actors. I imagine that Seneca's plays were declaimed by himself and other amateurs, and it is likely that the Athenian tragedies were performed by amateurs. I mean that the beauty of phrase in Greek tragedy is the shadow of a greater beauty—the beauty of thought and emotion. In the tragedies of Seneca the center of value is shifted from what the personage says to the way in which he says it. Very often the value comes near to being mere smartness. Nevertheless, we must remember that "verbal" beauty is still a kind of beauty.

The plays are admirably adapted for declamation before an imperial highbrow audience of crude sensibility but considerable sophistication in the ingenuities of language. They would have been as unactable on the Greek stage as they are on the English. Superficially neat and trim, they are, for the stage, models of formlessness. The Athenians were accustomed to long speeches from Messengers, speeches which embarrass both the modern actor and the modern audience; this was a convention with practical advantages; their other long speeches usually have some dramatic point, some place in the whole scheme of the play. But the characters in a play of Seneca behave more like members of a minstrel troupe sitting in a semicircle, rising in turn each to do his "number," or varying their recitations by a song or a little back-chat. I do not suppose that a Greek audience would have sat through the first three hundred lines of the *Hercules Furens*. Only at the 523rd line does Amphitryon detect the sound of Hercules' tread, ascending from Hell, at which inopportune moment the chorus interrupt for two or three pages. When Hercules finally appears, he seems to be leading Cerberus, who presently evaporates, for he is not on the stage a few minutes later. After Amphitryon has in a rather roundabout way, but more briefly than might have been expected, explained to Hercules the pressing danger to his family and country, Hercules makes off to kill Lycus. While Hercules is thus engaged in a duel on the result of which everybody's life depends, the family sit down calmly and listen to a long description by Theseus of the Tartarean regions. This account is not straight monologue, as Amphitryon from time to time puts leading questions about the fauna, and the administration and system of justice, of the world below. Meanwhile, Hercules has (contrary to the usual belief that Seneca murders all his victims in full view of the audience) despatched Lycus off-stage. At the end of the play, when Juno has stricken Hercules with madness, it is not at all clear whether he destroys his family on-stage or off. The slaughter is accompanied by a running commentary by Amphitryon, whose business it is to tell the audience what is going forward. If the children are slain in sight of the audience, this commentary is superfluous. Amphitryon also reports the collapse of Hercules; but presently Hercules comes to, certainly on-stage, and spies his dead wife and children. The whole situation is inconceivable unless we assume the play to have been composed solely for recitation; like other of Seneca's plays, it is full of statements useful only to an audience which sees nothing. Seneca's plays might, in fact, be practical models for the modern "broadcasted drama."

We need not look too closely into the conditions of the age which produced no genuine drama, but which allowed this curious freak of non-theatrical drama. The theatre is a gift which has not been vouchsafed to every race, even of the highest culture. It has been given to the Hindus, the Japanese, the Greeks; the English, the French, and the Spanish, at moments; in less measure to the Teutons and Scandinavians. It was not given to the Romans, or generously to their successors the Italians. The Romans had some success in low comedy, itself an adaptation of Greek models, but their instinct turned to shows and circuses, as does that of the later race which created the Commedia dell' Arte, which still provides the best puppet shows, and which gives a home to Mr. Gordon Craig. No cause can be assigned, for every cause demands a further cause. It is handy to speak of "the genius of the language," and we shall continue to do so, but why did the language adopt that particular genius? At any rate, we should discourage any criticism which, in accounting for the defects and faults of the plays of Seneca, made much of the "decadence" of the age of Nero. In the verse, yes, Seneca is unquestionably "silver age," or more exactly he is not a poet of the *first* rank in Latin, he is far inferior to Virgil; but for tragic drama, it would be a gross error to suppose that an earlier and more heroic age of Rome could have produced anything better. Many of the faults of Seneca which appear "decadent" are, after all, merely Roman and (in the narrower sense) Latin.

It is so with the characterization. The characters of Seneca's plays have no subtlety and no "private life." But it would be an error to imagine that they are merely cruder and coarser versions of the Greek originals. They belong to a different race. Their crudity is that which was of the Roman, as compared with the Greek, in real life. The Roman was much the simpler creature. At best, his training was that of devotion to the State, his virtues were public virtues. The Greek knew well enough the idea of the State, but he had also a strong traditional morality which constituted, so to speak, a direct relation between him and the gods, without the mediation of the State, and he had furthermore a skeptical and heterodox intelligence. Hence the greater efficiency of the Roman, and the greater interest of the Greek. Hence the difference between Greek Stoicism and Roman Stoicism—the latter being the form through which Stoicism influenced later Europe. We must think of the characters of Seneca as offspring of Rome, more than we think of them as offspring of their age.

The drama of Antigone — which Seneca did not attempt — could hardly have been transposed for Roman sentiment. In the drama of Seneca there are no conflicts, except the conflict of passion, temper, or appetite with the external duties. The literary consequence, therefore, is the tendency which persists in modern Italy; the tendency to "rhetoric"; and which, on such a large scale, may be attributed to a development of language exceeding the development of sensibility of the people. If you compare Catullus with Sappho, or Cicero with Demosthenes, or Thucydides with a Latin historian, you find that the genius is the genius of a different language, and what is lost is a gift of sensibility. So with Seneca and the Greek dramatists. Hence we should think of the long ranting speeches of Seneca, the beautiful but irrelevant descriptions, the smart stichomythia, rather as peculiarities of Latin than as the bad taste of the dramatist.

The congeniality of Stoicism to the Roman mind is no part of my duty to analyze; and it would be futile to attempt to decide what, in the dialogue and characterization of Seneca's plays, is due to Stoicism, what due to the Roman mind, and what due to the peculiar form which Seneca elected. What is certain is the existence of a large element of Stoicism in the plays, enough to justify the belief that the plays and the prose are by the hand of the same Seneca. In the plays, indeed, the Stoicism is present in a form more quickly to catch the fancy of the Renaissance than in the prose epistles and essays. Half of the commonplaces of the Elizabethans — and the more commonplace half — are of Senecan origin. This ethic of sententious maxims was, as we shall see, much more sympathetic to the temper of the Renaissance than would have been the morals of the elder Greek dramatists; the Renaissance itself was much more Latin than Greek. In the Greek tragedy, as Nisard and others have pointed out, the moralizing is not the expression of a conscious "system" of philosophy; the Greek dramatists moralize only because morals are woven through and through the texture of their tragic idea. Their morals are a matter of feeling trained for generations, they are hereditary and religious, just as their dramatic forms themselves are the development of their early liturgies. Their ethics of thought are one with their ethics of behavior. As the dramatic form of Seneca is no growth, but a construction, so is his moral philosophy and that of Roman Stoicism in general. Whether the Roman skepticism was, as Nisard suggests, the result of a too rapid and great expansion and mixture of races cancelling each other's beliefs, rather than the product of a lively inquiring intelligence, the "beliefs" of Stoicism are a consequence of skepticism; and the ethic of Seneca's plays is that of an age which supplied the lack of moral habits by a system of moral attitudes and poses. To this the natural public temper of Rome contributed. The ethic of Seneca is a matter of postures. The posture which gives the greatest opportunity for effect, hence for the Senecan morality, is the posture of dying: death gives his characters the opportunity for their most sententious aphorisms — a hint which Elizabethan dramatists were only too ready to follow.

When all reserves have been made, there is still much to be

said for Seneca as a dramatist. And I am convinced that the proper approach to his appreciation and enjoyment is not by comparison and contrast — to which, in his case, criticism is violently tempted — but by isolation. I made a careful comparison of the *Medea* and the *Hippolytus* of Seneca — perhaps his two best plays — with the *Medea* of Euripides and the *Phèdre* of Racine respectively; but I do not think that any advantage would be gained by reporting the results of this inquiry, by contrasting either the dramatic structure or the treatment of the title figures. Such comparisons have already been made; they magnify the defects and obscure the merits of the Senecan tragedy. If Seneca is to be compared, he should rather be compared for versification, descriptive and narrative power, and taste, with the earlier Roman poets. The comparison is fair, though Seneca comes off rather ill. His prosody is monotonous; in spite of a mastery of several meters, his choruses fall heavily on the ear. Sometimes his chorus rhythms seem to hover between the more flexible measures of his predecessors and the stiffer but more impressive beat of the mediaeval hymn.[2] But within the limits of his declamatory purpose, Seneca obtains, time after time, magnificent effects. In the verbal *coup de théâtre* no one has ever excelled him. The final cry of Jason to Medea departing in her car is unique; I can think of no other play which reserves such a shock for the last word:

Per alta vada spatia sublimi aethere;
testare nullos esse, qua veheris, deos.[3]

Again and again the epigrammatic observation on life or death is put in the most telling way at the most telling moment. It is not only in his brief ejaculations that Seneca triumphs. The sixteen lines addressed by the chorus to the dead sons of Hercules (*Hercules Furens*, I. 1135 ff.), which are exquisitely rendered by the Elizabethan translator, seem to me highly pathetic. The descriptive passages are often of great charm, with phrases which haunt us more than we should expect. The lines of Hercules,

ubi sum? sub ortu solis, an sub cardine
glacialis ursae?

must have lain long in the memory of Chapman before they came out in *Bussy d'Ambois* as

> fly where men feel
> The cunning axle-tree, or those that suffer
> Under the chariot of the snowy Bear.

Though Seneca is long-winded, he is not diffuse; he is capable of great concision; there is even a monotony of forcefulness; but many of his short phrases have for us as much oratorical impressiveness as they had for the Elizabethans. As (to take an unworn example) the bitter words of Hecuba as the Greeks depart:

> concidit virgo ac puer;
> bellum peractum est.

1. I must admit, however, that this view has recently been contested with great force by Léon Herrmann: *Le Théâtre de Sénèque* (Paris, 1924). See p. 195 of that book.
2. O mors amoris una sedamen mali,
    O mors pudoris maximum laesi decus. (*Hippolytus*, 1188-89.)
3. Here the translator seems to me to have hit on the sense:

    > Bear witnesse, grace of God is none in place of thy repayre.

    A modern translator (Professor Miller, editing the Loeb Translation text) gives "bear witness, where thou ridest, that there are no gods." It seems to me more effective if we take the meaning to be that there are no gods *where* (*ever*) *Medea is*, instead of mere outburst of atheism. But the old Farnaby edition observes "testimonium contra deorum justitiam, vel argumento nullos esse in caelo deos."

An Ecstasy of Madness
by Robert W. Corrigan

Whenever something intended to have great dramatic significance takes place in one of Seneca's plays, it is sure to be either preceded or followed by the stage direction, "In an ecstasy of madness." Scholars usually explain this direction by going on at great length about Seneca's belief in the supernatural and its role as the motivating force in his plays. While such an interpretation may well be correct, it is not the whole story. The long history of tragic drama shows us that, when the most important events in a play do not spring from the characters themselves, it is a sure sign that the playwright has not presented a dramatic action, but only a recounting of dramatic deeds. Such is the case with Seneca. For all of his concern with dramatic motivation — both natural and supernatural, the characters in a play like *Medea* have little or no life of their own. They are flat and two-dimensional; and, like pawns in a grandiose stage chess game, they have no choice but to move forward. Psychological explanations are not enough to make a play, as many of our contemporary playwrights have discovered, especially if, in its crucial moments, we do not believe the characters are responsible for what they do.

T. S. Eliot, in his important essay, "The Three Voices of Poetry," reminds us that the fact that lines in a play are spoken by many characters does not necessarily make them dramatic. To be dramatic, characters must speak for themselves; and it is the playwright's job to extract the language out of the characters rather than impose it on them. Nor is complexity of character essential, so long as we believe that communication between the characters is taking place. In the end, drama is concerned only with human relationships, with what men do to each other. Aeschylus' characters in the *Oresteia*, for instance, are not very well developed psychologically; in fact, they are so simple they could be described as monolithic. But we always believe them as characters, because they are individuated parts of an action. They have an existence — independent of the playwright — within the action. We do not experience Seneca's characters in this way; rather, we feel that he — much like Browning — was always speaking for himself through the characters.

This failure to achieve a dramatic idiom is in large measure due to the fact that, as far as we know, Seneca composed his plays for private readings rather than public performances on the stage. But it can also be explained in terms of the entrenched Roman oratorical tradition, which we know had a strong influence not only on Seneca's style, but on his whole approach to the dramatic event. The most revealing evidence of this influence is to be found in Seneca's continued use of *sententiae* (wise sayings) in his dialogue. These pat verbal solutions and moral clichés first appeared in the plays of Euripides, but there is some justification for the Greek tragedian's use of them. There were some problems and dramatic issues which Euripides could not resolve, nor did he believe they ever could be resolved; the meaning of several of his plays resides in this very lack of a resolution. However, since the play as a theatre piece had to come to an end, Euripides resorted to the use of the *deus ex machina* (a plot device) and the *sententiae* (a device of language) as means of resolution. There is no doubt that this is a shortcoming in Euripides' work, but it is an understandable, and even justifiable, one. But in the Roman drama the use of *sententiae* was not a strategy of despair. Because of the state-oriented nature of Roman life, virtue, and artistic expression, its writers were not given to private utterance. And the *sententiae* were an essential part of Rome's long and well-established oratorical tradition. Every great speaker from Demosthenes and Cicero to Kennedy and Stevenson is considered effective because of his ability to express complex issues in a meaningful but brief statement. (Loftiness of tone is another essential characteristic of great oratory, and it is interesting to note that the early investigations on the sublime were seldom concerned with the drama.) But the substitution of statement, no matter how apt or lofty, for dramatic process inevitably reduces the range of the theatre. Nowhere in the history of drama can this reduction be more clearly observed than in the plays of Seneca. He consistently aborted his dramatic situations with the persistent maxim. Note for example:

Medea
> [My crimes] are yours, they are yours, indeed!
> The one who profits by a crime is guilty of it.

and in Act V:

Messenger
> Ruin, total ruin! Our royalty is annihilated.
> Daughter and father are one low heap of ashes.

Chorus
> How are they trapped?

Messenger
> As kings regularly are, by gifts.

A similar debilitating tendency can be found in the bloody images Seneca uses to describe death. For all the gore, these passages are purely ornamental. They are a substitute for both dramatic and moral significance, and while they may be horrifying they are never horrible. They lack the sharp bite of a conscience which is involved in human suffering. The passion of these rolling speeches is only a *declared* passion; it does not involve developed feelings. It is merely a pose, a passion of attitude.

Again, the public nature of Roman life at the time of the Caesars may account for this tendency in Seneca's drama (Eliot, for one, argues that "the ethic of Seneca's plays is that of an age which supplied the lack of moral habits by a system of moral attitudes and poses"), but it must finally be attributed to Seneca's failure to understand the demands of the theatre. In the plays of Seneca everything is in the word, but his words are not supported by any other concrete reality. They neither require nor imply an actor, a stage, or a specific emotional actuality. His plays, as Eliot observed, are, in effect, radio plays "full of statements useful only to an audience which sees nothing." Such plays are not without qualities, but they are qualities which find the stage an inhospitable medium.

Thus, in reading Seneca today, we cannot help but feel his significance is only of an historical nature. This does not mean his plays do not have value. They do, for instance, embody — probably better than anything else in Roman literature — the qualities of Roman Stoicism. Also, there is no doubt that the rhythms of his language especially as they were translated into English in the sixteenth century, had a profound influence on the development of the blank verse which reached its fullest flower in Elizabethan drama. No one should deny the importance of these facts; but, finally, Seneca has been kept alive by the scholars and not by the theatre. And one cannot help but wonder if this is not one of the reasons that classical literature has declined as a meaningful force in the imaginative lives of modern men.

CLASSICAL COMEDY
GREEK AND ROMAN: Six Plays
Edited by Robert W. Corrigan

The only book of its kind: for the first time Greek and Roman masters of comedy meet in this extraordinary new forum devised and edited by a master scholar of comedy himself, Robert Corrigan. Corrigan has enlisted six superb translations to create an unmatched Olympiad of classical comedy.

ARISTOPHANES **LYSISTRATA**
translated by Donald Sutherland
THE BIRDS
translated by Walter Kerr

MENANDER **THE GROUCH**
translated by Sheila D'Atri

PLAUTUS **THE MENAECHMI**
translated by Palmer Bovie
THE HAUNTED HOUSE
translated by Palmer Bovie

TERENCE **THE SELF-TORMENTOR**
translated by Palmer Bovie

paper • ISBN: 0-936839-85-6

❦APPLAUSE❦

THE MISANTHROPE
AND OTHER FRENCH CLASSICS

THE MISANTHROPE • Molière
PHAEDRA • Racine
THE CID • Corneille
FIGARO'S MARRIAGE • Beaumarchais
paper • ISBN: 0-936839-19-8

LIFE IS A DREAM
AND OTHER SPANISH CLASSICS

LIFE IS A DREAM • Calderon de la Barca
FUENTE OVEJUNA • Lope de Vega
THE TRICKSTER OF SEVILLE • Tirso de Molina
THE SIEGE OF NUMANTIA • Miguel de Cervantes

paper • ISBN: 1-55783-006-1   cloth • ISBN 1-55783-005-3

THE SERVANT OF TWO MASTERS
AND OTHER ITALIAN CLASSICS

THE SERVANT OF TWO MASTERS • Goldoni
THE KING STAG • Gozzi
THE MANDRAKE • Machiavelli
RUZZANTE RETURNS FROM THE WARS • Beolco
paper • ISBN: 0-936839-20-1

❀APPLAUSE❀

ERIC BENTLEY'S

D R A M A T I C   R E P E R T O I R E

INSPECTOR
AND OTHER PLAYS

Eric Bentley brings to the attention of Gogol's still growing American public not only a new version of *Inspector* but three other dramatic works: *The Marriage, Gamblers* and *From A Madman's Diary*, the last-named being Bentley's dramatization of a famous Gogol story

paper • ISBN: 0-936839-12-0

BEFORE BRECHT
FOUR GERMAN PLAYS

LEONCE AND LENA • Georg Büchner
LA RONDE • Arthur Schnitzler
SPRING'S AWAKENING • Frank Wedekind
THE UNDERPANTS • Carl Sternheim

paper • ISBN: 1-55783-010-X   cloth • ISBN 1-55783-009-6

THE BRUTE
AND OTHER FARCES BY ANTON CHEKHOV

THE HARMFULNESS OF TOBACCO
SWAN SONG • **A MARRIAGE PROPOSAL**
THE CELEBRATION • **A WEDDING**
SUMMER IN THE COUNTRY • **THE BRUTE**

paper • ISBN: 1-55783-004-5   cloth • ISBN: 1-55783-003-7

❦**APPLAUSE**❦

THE THREE CUCKOLDS
by Leon Katz

"They loved him in Venice and Rome, and Verona, and Padua. That was 400 years ago, but they also love him NOW! Arlecchino, chief clown and scapegoat of commedia dell'arte commedy makes a triumphal comeback in *The Three Cuckolds*!" —LOS ANGELES TIMES

paper • ISBN: 0-936839-06-6

THE SON OF ARLECCHINO
by Leon Katz

Watch out! CAUTION! Arlecchino and his band of madcaps are leaping out of centuries of retirement. They're fed up with being shoved around like second-rate citizens of the stage. Their revolt is led by none other than the champion of present day commedia, Leon Katz, who incites the troupe to perform all their most famous zany routines.

paper • ISBN: 0-936839-07-4

CELESTINA
by Fernando de Rojas
Adapted by Eric Bentley • Translated by James Mabbe

The central situation is a simple one: a dirty old woman is helping a courtly young gentleman to seduce a girl. The wonder of the thing lies in the art with which de Rojas derives a towering tragedy — or rather tragi-comedy.

paper • ISBN: 0-936839-01-5

APPLAUSE

SOLILOQUY!
The Shakespeare Monologues
Edited by Michael Earley and Philippa Keil

At last, over 175 of Shakespeare's finest and most performable monologues taken from all 37 plays are here in two easy-to-use volumes (MEN and WOMEN). Selections travel the entire spectrum of the great dramatist's vision, from comedies and romances to tragedies, pathos and histories.

"SOLILOQUY is an excellent and comprehensive collection of Shakespeare's speeches. Not only are the monologues wide-ranging and varied, but they are superbly annotated. Each volume is prefaced by an informative and reassuring introduction, which explains the signals and signposts by which Shakespeare helps the actor on his journey through the text. It includes a very good explanation of blank verse, with excellent examples of irregularities which are specifically related to character and acting intentions. These two books are a must for any actor in search of a 'classical' audition piece."

ELIZABETH SMITH
Head of Voice & Speech
The Juilliard School

paper • MEN: ISBN 0-936839-78-3 • WOMEN: ISBN 0-936839-79-1

❧APPLAUSE❧

SHAKESCENES
SHAKESPEARE FOR TWO
Edited with an Introduction
by John Russell Brown

Shakespeare's plays are not the preserve of "Shakespearean Actors" who specialize in a remote species of dramatic life. John Russell Brown offers guidance for those who have little or no experience with the formidable Bard in both the Introduction and Advice to Actors, and in the notes to each of the thirty-five scenes.

The scenes are presented in newly-edited texts, with notes which clarify meanings, topical references, puns, ambiguities, etc. Each scene has been chosen for its independent life requiring only the simplest of stage properties and the barest of spaces. A brief description of characters and situation prefaces each scene, and is followed by a commentary which discusses its major acting challenges and opportunities.

Shakescenes are for small classes and large workshops, and for individual study whenever two actors have the opportunity to work together.

From the Introduction:

"Of course, a way of speaking a character's lines meaningfully and clearly must be found, but that alone will not bring any play to life. Shakespeare did not write for talking heads ... Actors need to be acutely present all the time; ... they are like boxers in a ring, who dare not lose concentration or the ability to perform at full power for fear of losing consciousness altogether."

paper • ISBN: 1-55783-049-5

❦APPLAUSE❦

THE MISER and GEORGE DANDIN
by Molière
Translated by Albert Bermel

Harpagon, the most desperate, scheming miser in literature, starves his servants, declines to pay them, cheats his own children if he can save (or make) a few coins, and when his hoard of gold disappears, insanely accuses himself of being the thief.

Dandin, in this rousing classic, not previously available in English for sixty years, is a man in a plight that everybody but him will find entertaining.

paper • ISBN: 0-936839-75-9

THE DOCTOR IN SPITE OF HIMSELF and THE BOURGEOIS GENTLEMAN
by Molière
Translated by Albert Bermel

In *The Doctor in Spite of Himself*, Molière's scalpel-sharp satire of the medical profession, Sganarelle's wife spreads the word that he is secretly a brilliant doctor who won't reveal his skills unless he is unmercifully punished.

Bourgeois Gentleman, Molière's classic treatment of snobbery, presents Monsieur Jourdain's obsessive desire to move up out of the ranks of the middle class and associate with the gentry.

paper • ISBN: 0-936839-77-5

❦APPLAUSE❦

NINETEENTH-CENTURY AMERICAN PLAYS
Edited by Myron Matlaw

From Broadway to Topeka these four smash hits were the staples of the American dramatic repertoire. Their revival in this landmark collection will once again bring America to its feet!

MARGARET FLEMING
James A. Herne

THE OCTOROON
Dion Boucicault

FASHION
Anna Cora Mowatt

RIP van WINKLE
Joseph Jefferson

Myron Matlaw's comprehensive Introduction provides a splendid survey of the development of American drama from its inception through the 19th Century. Individual prefaces focus each work in the perspective of its historical context.

paper • ISBN: 1-55783-018-5   cloth • 1-55783-017-7

❦**APPLAUSE**❦

3 GREAT JEWISH PLAYS

Edited and in Modern Translations
by Joseph C. Landis

"All the plays in this volume have intrinsic merit. These are 'classics' reflecting the essential Jewish view of life . . . Yet if the book contained nothing else, the introduction by Joseph Landis would make it worth preserving. Landis gives us what is virtually a summation of the Jewish world view."

—**Harold Clurman**

THE GOLEM by H. Leivick
A masterpiece of poetic drama.

THE DYBBUK by S. Anski
The most famous of all Yiddish plays.

GOD OF VENGEANCE by Sholem Asch
Bold, theatrical triumph around the world.

paper • ISBN: 0-936839-04-X

❦APPLAUSE❦

MEDIEVAL AND TUDOR DRAMA
TWENTY-FOUR PLAYS
Edited and with Introductions
by John Gassner

The rich tapestry of medieval belief, morality and manners shines through this comprehensive anthology of the twenty-four major plays that bridge the dramatic worlds of medieval and Tudor England. Here are the plays that paved the way to the Renaissance and Shakespeare. In John Gassner's extensively annotated collection, the plays regain their timeless appeal and display their truly international character and influence.

Medieval and Tudor Drama remains the indispensable chronicle of a dramatic heritage — the classical plays of Hrotsvitha, folk and ritual drama, the passion play, the great morality play *Everyman*, the Interlude, Tudor comedies *Ralph Roister Doister* and *Gammer Gurton's Needle*, and the most famous of Tudor tragedies, *Gorboduc*. The texts have been modernized for today's readers and those composed in Latin have been translated into English.

paper • ISBN: 0-936839-84-8

❦APPLAUSE❦

ELIZABETHAN DRAMA
Eight Plays
Edited and with Introductions by
John Gassner and William Green

Boisterous and unrestrained like the age itself, the Elizabethan theatre has long defended its place at the apex of English dramatic history. Shakespeare was but the brightest star in this extraordinary galaxy of playwrights. Led by a group of young playwrights dubbed "the university wits," the Elizabethan popular stage was imbued with a dynamic force never since equalled. The stage boasted a rich and varied repertoire from courtly and romantic comedy to domestic and high tragedy, melodrama, farce, and histories. The Gassner-Green anthology revives the whole range of this universal stage, offering us the unbounded theatrical inventiveness of the age.

Arden of Feversham, **Anonymous**

The Spanish Tragedy, by **Thomas Kyd**

Friar Bacon and Friar Bungay, by **Robert Greene**

Doctor Faustus, by **Christopher Marlowe**

Edward II, by **Christopher Marlowe**

Everyman in His Humour, by **Ben Jonson**

The Shoemaker's Holiday, by **Thomas Dekker**

A Woman Killed with Kindness, by **Thomas Heywood**

paper • ISBN: 1-55783-028-2

✿APPLAUSE✿